Thomas Schneider

Language Contact in Ancient Egypt

Einführungen und Quellentexte zur Ägyptologie

herausgegeben von

Louise Gestermann und Christian Leitz

Band 16

LIT

Thomas Schneider

LANGUAGE CONTACT IN ANCIENT EGYPT

LIT

This book is printed on acid-free paper.

Bibliographic information published by the Deutsche Nationalbibliothek
The Deutsche Nationalbibliothek lists this publication in the Deutsche Nationalbibliografie; detailed bibliographic data are available on the Internet at http://dnb.dnb.de.

ISBN 978-3-643-91507-8 (pb)
ISBN 978-3-643-96507-3 (PDF)

A catalogue record for this book is available from the British Library.

Contact:
Fresnostr. 2 D-48159 Münster
Tel. +49 (0) 2 51-62 03 20 Fax +49 (0) 2 51-23 19 72
e-Mail: lit@lit-verlag.de https://www.lit-verlag.de

Distribution:

In the UK: Global Book Marketing, e-mail: mo@centralbooks.com

For Ela, Manuel and Juliana

TABLE OF CONTENTS

Berber speakers on Egypt's Western periphery...54
2.2.2.3.4.3 Proto-Berber linguistic evidence in Egyptian sources of the Graeco-Roman Period..............55
2.2.2.3.4.4 Proto-Berber linguistic evidence from the Third Intermediate and Late Period...................56
2.2.2.3.4.5 Proto-Berber linguistic evidence from the New Kingdom...58
2.2.2.3.4.6 Proto-Berber linguistic evidence from the First Intermediate to Second Intermediate Period.......61
2.2.2.3.4.7 Proto-Berber linguistic evidence from the Predynastic Period to the Old Kingdom............67
2.2.2.3.4.8 Concluding assessment..68
2.2.2.3.5 Chadic languages..68
2.2.2.4 Language convergence through a *sprachbund* situation.......69

3. LANGUAGE CONTACT WITH THE NEAR EAST..................................71

3.1 **From corpus languages to undocumented languages**................................71

3.2 **A historical survey of language contact with Near Eastern languages**............72

3.2.1 Prehistory..72
3.2.2 Early Bronze Age..73
3.2.3 Middle Bronze Age...76
3.2.3.1 A Case Study: The languages at Avaris..........................81
3.2.4 Late Bronze Age...85
3.2.4.1 Lexical transfer..85
3.2.4.1.1 Semitic languages..89
3.2.4.1.2 Anatolian languages..96
3.2.4.1.3 Hurrian..97
3.2.4.1.4 Other Near Eastern languages of the LBA......................98
3.2.4.2 Bilingualism and Interpreting...................................98
3.2.4.3 Interference in texts: Interlanguages and translation..........100
3.2.4.3.1 A presumed interlanguage: 'Akkadian by Egyptians'......100
3.2.4.3.2 Translation and the adaptation of texts.....................101
3.2.5 Iron Age...103
3.2.5.1 Hebrew, Aramaic, Phoenician, Ancient North and South Arabian, Akkadian...104
3.2.5.2 Carian...106
3.2.5.3 Old Persian and Median...107

4. LANGUAGE CONTACT WITH ANCIENT MEDITERRANEAN LANGUAGES...109

4.1 **Non-Indo-European paleo-languages of the Mediterranean**.......................109

4.2 The Indo-Europeanization of Europe and the Mediterranean……………109

4.2.1 Indo-Europeanization hypotheses……………110
4.2.2 A Proto-Indo-European adstrate in early Egyptian?……………113

4.3 Contact with individual languages and language groups since the 3rd millennium BCE……………116

4.3.1 Unknown Mediterranean substrate languages……………116
4.3.2 Languages of ancient Crete……………117
4.3.3 Languages of ancient Cyprus……………117
4.3.4 Mycenean Greek and later Greek……………119
4.3.5 The languages of the Sea Peoples and "Tyrsenian"……………122
4.3.6 Italic languages……………124

5. PHENOMENA OF LANGUAGE CONTACT – AN ANALYTICAL OVERVIEW..125

5.1 Loanwords……………125

5.1.1 Loanwords prior to the New Kingdom……………125
5.1.2 Loanwords in the New Kingdom……………127
5.1.3 Loanwords between the New Kingdom and the Ptolemaic period……………130

5.2 Calques……………131

5.3 Non-Egyptian texts in Egyptian script……………132

5.4 Bilingualism, multilingualism, interpreting, translation……………133

5.5 Language education and re-education……………135

5.6 Interlanguages, mixed languages, pidgins……………136

5.7 Language convergence through a *sprachbund* situation……………137

6. CONFLICT AND COMMUNICATION: FOREIGN LANGUAGE COMMUNITIES IN THE MILITARY……………139

6.1 The military and the "mercenary" terminology……………140

6.2 Case studies of military foreign language communities……………143

6.2.1 Language preservation:
Cushitic-speaking troops of the First Intermediate Period……………143
6.2.2 Language attrition:
The language of the Sherden troops in Ramesside Egypt……………145

6.2.3 Multilingualism at war and peace:
Greeks, Carians and other linguistic units in the Saïte army……..……………148

7. CONCLUSION:
MULTILINGUALISM, INDEXICALITY, AND LINGUISTIC IDENTITY……..…153

8. BIBLIOGRAPHY……………………………..……………………………….157

9. INDEX…………………………………………………………………........205

9.1 Afroasiatic languages...……………………………………………………..205

9.1.1 Words, names and phrases attested in ancient Egyptian sources................…205
9.1.1.1 Words, names and phrases in regular Egyptian orthography……..205
9.1.1.2 Loanwords, names and phrases in Egyptian transcription............…209
9.1.1.3 Words and phrases attested in Napatan Egyptian…….............……216
9.1.1.4 Words and names attested in Demotic……............………………...216
9.1.1.5 Words and names attested in Coptic……...........…………………..217
9.1.2 Semitic languages................……………………………………………..218
9.1.2.1 Words and roots attested across different Semitic languages……...218
9.1.2.2 East Semitic: Akkadian and Eblaite…............…………………...220
9.1.2.3 West Semitic…….............………………………………………...221
9.1.2.3.1 Ethio-Semitic……........……………………………………221
9.1.2.3.2 Modern South Arabian..............……………………………221
9.1.2.4 Central Semitic….........……………………………………………221
9.1.2.4.1 North Arabian (including Classical Arabic).......………221
9.1.2.4.2 Northwest Semitic….........…………………………………222
9.1.2.4.2.1 Ugaritic….......…………………………………..222
9.1.2.4.2.2 Aramaeo-Canaanite…….......……………………..223
9.1.2.4.2.2.1 Phoenician and Amarna Canaanite......223
9.1.2.4.2.2.2 Hebrew.......………………………………223
9.1.2.4.2.2.3 Aramaic.......……………………………224
9.1.3 Berber languages (including ancient Libyan)................……….……….225
9.1.3.1 Ancient Libyan………………........………………………………..225
9.1.3.2 Modern Berber…....……........……………………………………226
9.1.4 Cushitic languages…............……………………………………………227
9.1.4.1 North Cushitic (Beja/Tu-beḏawiye and Blemmyan)...............……227
9.1.4.2 Other Cushitic languages….........……………………………..……228
9.1.5 Omotic languages……...........……………………………………………228
9.1.6 Chadic languages…...............……………………………..…………….228

9.2 Nilo-Saharan languages.................…………………………………………228

9.2.1 Northern East Sudanic…............………………………………..………….228
9.2.1.1 Meroïtic...….......................……228
9.2.1.2 Old Nubian…...........…………………………………………………229

9.2.2 Saharan languages......229
9.2.3.1 Western Saharan......229
9.2.3.1.1 Kanuri......229
9.2.3.1.2 Teda/Daza......229
9.2.3.2 Eastern Saharan......229
9.2.3.2.1 Beria [Zaghawa]......229
9.2.4 Other Nilo-Saharan languages......230
9.2.4.1 Maba......230

9.3 Indo-European languages......230

9.3.1 Proto-Indo-European......230
9.3.2 Anatolian languages......230
9.3.2.1 Hittite......230
9.3.2.2 Luwian (also Hieroglyphic Luwian)......231
9.3.2.3 Other Anatolian languages......231
9.3.3 Indo-Iranian languages......231
9.3.3.1 Indo-Aryan languages......231
9.3.3.2 Iranian languages......231
9.3.3.2.1 Ancient Iranian languages......231
9.3.3.2.1.1 Old Persian......231
9.3.3.2.1.2 Median......232
9.3.4 Greek......232
9.3.4.1 Mycenean Greek......232
9.3.4.2 Words and names attested in Classical Greek......232
9.3.5 Italic languages: Words and names attested in Latin......233
9.3.6 Armenian......234

9.4 Isolated and paleo-languages of the Near East and the Mediterranean...... 234

9.4.1 Sumerian (and sumerograms)......234
9.4.2 Hurrian and Urartian......234
9.4.3 Tyrsenian (including Lemnian)......234

9.5 Subject index......235

APPENDIX: MAPS......244

Acknowledgments

The work on the manuscript of this book began in 2020, when I was working at the Southern University of Science and Technology (SUSTech) in Shenzhen, China, in a context of different languages and writing systems: a Mandarin-speaking metropolis within a traditionally Cantonese-speaking province (using simplified Chinese writing vs. the traditional Chinese script in neighboring Hong Kong). Inhabited by large numbers of speakers of other Chinese languages, it attracted talents from across the globe that would increase the use of English as a language of business and technology, in addition to the languages of the expatriates. This book is a token of admiration and appreciation for my multilingual friends from SUSTech's Global Engagement Office, in particular my magnificent Global Education team (*aka* "Pink Group"): 刘洁 Liú Jié (Olivia), Christopher Clarke, 韩宇 Hán Yǔ, 纪雨汝 Jì Yǔrǔ (Sarah), 焦婕 Jiāo Jié (Emma), 赖温妮 Lài Wēnnī (Winnie), 李飞亮 Lǐ Fēiliàng, 孙梦蝶 Sūn Mèngdié, 王芳 Wáng Fāng, 于智 Yú Zhì (Isaac), and our group's ranking specialists, 许海玲 Xǔ Hǎilíng and 杨松楠 Yáng Sōngnán.

This study includes several building blocks initially written for other venues: chapter 3 is an expanded and revised version of the contribution, "Language Contact of Ancient Egyptian with Semitic and other Near Eastern Languages" (Schneider 2020). The chapter on Proto-Berber (= 2.2.2.3.4) was originally conceived as the contribution, "Was Proto-Berber Spoken on Ancient Egypt's Western Periphery? A Review of the Linguistic and Contextual Evidence" for a *Festschrift* project. Chapter 5 is a modified version of the UEE article, "Language contact" (Schneider 2022).

I am grateful to many colleagues who have sent me relevant literature and information: Manfred Bietak, Francis A. Breyer, Julien Cooper, Franco De Angelis, Frank Förster, Orly Goldwasser, Hermann Jungraithmayr, Ido Koch, Christian Langer, Kate Liszka, Barbara Lüscher, Elena Mahlich, Matthew McCarty, Juan Carlos Moreno García, Elena Panaite, Carsten Peust, Joachim F.

Quack, Peter Raulwing, Thomas Richter, Helmut Satzinger, Anthony Spalinger, Brad Sparks, Andréas Stauder, Christoffer Theis, Susanne Töpfer, Willeke Wendrich, Katharina Zinn, as well as my father, Hans Schneider. Parts of this book have also benefited from the remarks of the anonymous reviewers of my 2022 UEE article on Language Contact (Schneider 2022).

I acknowledge gratefully the support this project has received in the form of an *Explore Grant Arts Research* of the *Social Sciences and Humanities Research Council of Canada*, a contribution of the *UBC Scholarly Publication Fund* as well as a travel grant of the *Austrian Academy of Sciences* – for the facilitation of this latter grant I am much indebted to Manfred Bietak.

I would like to express my gratitude to Louise Gestermann and Christian Leitz for having accepted this volume for the *Einführungen und Quellentexte zur Ägyptologie* series, and for the support received from Martin W. Richter of the LIT Verlag. In the final stage of the manuscript preparation, Caroline Barnes has provided invaluable help with proofreading and formatting. As a matter of course, all remaining mistakes and oversights are mine.

I dedicate this book with gratitude to my wife, Ela, who has provided unwavering support to me throughout the several decades of my life and career, and to our wonderful children, Manuel and Juliana, whose unceasing love and encouragement have enabled us, through happy and sad days, to persevere.

Vancouver, October 2022 Thomas Schneider

1. Introduction: Language contact in ancient Egypt

Language contact is a universal phenomenon of human interaction that has received considerable attention in recent years (Grant 2020; Hickey 2010; 2020; Adamou and Matras 2020). Ancient Egypt was at all times in direct or indirect contact with neighboring and more distant linguistic areas (cf. Grossmann and Richter 2015, 80-1), received significant numbers of immigrants, and during certain periods of its history, controlled regions outside its traditional borders or was itself subject to foreign rule. The cohabitation of speakers of different languages in Egypt, the migration and transfer of people, the trade of objects and the exchange of ideas were accompanied by language contact and linguistic interference – reflected by a wide variety of linguistic phenomena.

Despite the fact that there is clear evidence of multilingualism in pre-Ptolemaic Egypt, ancient Egypt has never been described as a multilingual society. In her introduction to the 2010 volume *The Multilingual Experience in Egypt, from the Ptolemies to the Abbasids*, Arietta Papaconstantinou emphasizes rightly the increased recent interest by historians in the study of multilingualism in historical societies (see also Hasselbach-Andee 2020; Jonker, Berlejung and Cornelius 2021). Still, she restricts this phenomenon to Egypt's Hellenistic and post-Hellenistic societies – "from Alexander the Great onwards, the ancient and medieval kingdoms and empires all encompassed such multilingual societies" (Papaconstantinou 2010, 1; for multilingualism in Greco-Roman Egypt, see also von Lieven 2018). There is no reason to believe that the situation in earlier Egypt was much different from Mesopotamia where, as Piotr Michałowski has stated, "[m]ultilingualism was often the norm" (Michałowski 2017, 19). One of the very few recent voices speaking up for an earlier "multilingualism along the Nile" is Luigi Prada (Prada 2018; Zinn's 1998 thesis on Egypt's engagement with foreign languages remained unpublished). Three factors have contributed to the fact that the pervasiveness of multilingualism in ancient Egypt has never been fully acknowledged and explored:

- The overwhelming self-presentation that ancient Egypt has left us, as a culturally monolithic civilization, has helped to nurture an Egyptological narrative that subscribed to this imagination for much of the discipline's history. As recently as 2008, Frandsen claimed that "ancient Egypt was a geopolitical and cultural unity and is therefore to be regarded as an early, as well as a good, example of a nation-state" (Frandsen 2008, 47).
- Ancient Egypt also created the enduring impression of an all-encompassing *hieroglyphic culture*, eminently visible in its 'monumental discourse' (Assmann 1994) and impactful in the later reception history of ancient Egypt. In this hieroglyphic space, no place was reserved for the presence of other languages, different writing systems and non-Egyptian linguistic communities.
- Thirdly, the academic training and institutional history of the field has for a long time not encouraged the pursuit of a linguistically more complex Egyptian culture.

It is also important to point to the difficulties of the evidence. Despite the likely omnipresence of language contact and linguistic interference, only a small fraction of it is actually visible to us and can be studied – a consequence of the limitations of the preserved written sources and our inability to study spoken languages and communication. Despite these limitations, the topic is of utmost significance for the linguistics of the ancient languages of Northeast Africa, the Near East and the Mediterranean. For many of these linguistics, the Egyptian documentation represents the oldest available historical evidence even if the material is not readily available and is often poorly processed. Thus, the study of language contact is a field of significant interdisciplinary promise between Egyptian linguistics, other linguistics of neighboring languages and general linguistics. It is the goal of this volume to provide an introduction to the field of language contact from the late 4th millennium BCE to the Late Period, to present a comprehensive survey of the available material during that time period and to encourage interdisciplinary dialogue.

This book is organized in way to present the material systematically, including a diachronic survey of the individual language areas, an analysis of the phenomena of language contact and a sociolinguistic case study.

- Chapter 2 discusses evidence for language contact in Egypt's African context. Given the lack of contemporary sources from outside Egypt about the historical populations and languages that coexisted with ancient Egypt, an initial section outlines the current archaeological evidence about ancient population shifts as well as the Egyptian textual and pictorial sources. The contact with African languages will then be organized according to language groups – starting from Egyptian in the Sudan (the Napatan language and script) and proceeding to the Nilo-Saharan languages (Meroïtic and Old Nubian as members of the Northern East Sudanic branch), Saharan languages, and the largest sub-section, Afro-Asiatic languages in Africa – particularly Cushitic languages, Ethio-Semitic, hypotheses about the languages of other groups identified in the material record (Kerma, A-Group, C-Group, Pangrave, Punt) and Proto-Berber. One section will also present ideas on language convergence in an African context through a *sprachbund* situation.
- Chapter 3 of the book focuses on language contact between Egyptian and Near Eastern languages, including the Semitic languages of the Near East. Given the comparatively rich contemporary sources from the Near East, this section will be organized as a historical survey, moving from prehistory through the Early, Middle and Late Bronze Age, and subsequently, the Iron Age. In the best-documented Late Bronze Age (LBA), different topics will be treated in more detail: the lexical transfer with Semitic languages, Anatolian languages, Hurrian, as well as other Near Eastern languages of the LBA; bilingualism, interpreting and translation; interlanguages. For the Iron Age, separate sub-chapters will treat the evidence for contact with Hebrew, Aramaic, Phoenician and Ancient North as well as South Arabian; with Carian; with Old Persian and Median.
- Chapter 4 attempts to capture key problems of linguistic contact between Egyptian and ancient Mediterranean languages, starting from the historical situation of the paleolanguages of the Mediterranean basin and hypotheses about the Indo-Europeanization of Europe and the Mediterranean, and moving to a discussion of contact with individual languages and language groups since the 3rd millennium BCE.
- Chapter 5 of the book will analyze and summarize the material according to

linguistic phenomena (loan words, calques, etc.).

- Chapter 6 of the book presents a case study of a sociolinguistic area where language contact is attested – foreign language communities in the Egyptian military – and attempts to sketch different scenarios of their language status.
- The concluding chapter 7 will raise one question – where was the communicative space of foreign languages within and alongside the Egyptian space of languages and scripts? Egyptian linguistics has traditionally focused on the study of aspects of inner-Egyptian linguistic diversity (such as dialects, diglossia) but has not surveyed systematically, and analyzed the presence and use of, Egyptian *vis-à-vis* other languages.
- This book concludes with the bibliography and a detailed index which makes easily accessible hundreds of lexical terms from Egyptian and dozens of other languages quoted throughout the book, including many new etymologies. Maps showing the distribution of major languages and language groups dealt with in this study are added as an appendix.

It is to be hoped that this volume marks the beginning of a more conscious reflection within Egyptology on pre-Hellenistic Egypt as a multilingual society. May it spur an effort within the field to engage in a systematic conversation with the linguistics of Africa, the Near East and the Mediterranean.

Note: The transcription used for Egyptian in the present volume

A major obstacle for the study of language contact is the continued use by most scholars of an ahistorical Egyptological transcription system that dates back to the late 19th century (Kammerzell 1998, 24) for all phases of the Egyptian language prior to Demotic. Throughout this book, I use instead the transcription symbols of the Tübingen School for their greater phonological accuracy in the context of a comparative linguistic study (for the reasons, see Schenkel 2005, 32). I therefore use <i̓> instead of <j>, <ś> instead of <s>, <s> instead of <z>, <č> instead of <ṯ>, <č̣> instead of <ḏ>. I retain <q> instead of <ḳ>. In several instances (e.g., the reassessment of Semitic loanwords, below pp. 91-5), I indicate the Egyptian classifiers used by the Egyptian scribes, applying the system developed in Schneider 1992, pp.12-3 (e.g., *m-k-m-rw-ti̓*^{STRING}).

2. Language contact within the African Continent

2.1 The Problem of Historical Populations

The Egyptian categorization of humanity into four stereotypical ethnicities – Egyptians, Asiatics, Libyans and Nubians – obscures a historical ethnic and linguistic complexity of the highest order. Whereas the ancient Near East to the Northeast of Egypt – the Levant, Anatolia, Mesopotamia – has left us with sources often contemporaneous to the Egyptian evidence, permitting us to sketch the historical shifts of populations and polities and to estimate the extent of language contact with a certain degree of accuracy (see part 3), this is not the case for the African context of Egypt – regions to Egypt's west, southwest and southeast. The vague terminology for populations often used in scholarship ("Libyans", "Nubians") equally obfuscates the diversity that existed in these areas synchronically and diachronically in terms of populations, cultures and languages. Since sources contemporaneous to the Egyptian ones do not exist – for some areas, such sources appear in Classical times, for most of them only in the modern period –, trying to reconstruct an ancient linguistic geography for those regions and to determine the degrees and types of language contact with Egypt is extremely precarious.

The purpose of this chapter is to present an overview of modern hypotheses that exist regarding the ethnic and population history of these areas over time (for an overview of Egyptian-African relations, see Manzo 2022). In the subsequent chapter (2.2), I will discuss the linguistic evidence for particular language families (for an overview of which, see Cooper 2020b).

2.1.1 Populations and mobility from the Neolithic to the 3rd millennium

Recent scholarship has emphasized the existence of a 'pastoral crescent' stretching from the Western desert of Egypt across the Egyptian Nile delta and into the Levant (Moreno García 2014; 2018). During the climate optimum (6900-5550 cal BCE), population groups to the west of Egypt were herders of livestock, but also foragers, gathering wild cereals such as sorghum (Gallinaro 2018). The intensified desiccation of the areas west of the Nile valley and the retreat of the monsoon regime to the south led in the 5th millennium BCE to the move of population groups into 'refuge zones', including the Sudan and the oases, as well as the Nile delta and valley (see Clarke et al. 2016, 115-6; Riemer 2011, 260-88). Mediterranean winter or spring rainfall also created subsistence niches, e.g., at the Gilf Kebir plateau between 5700-5000 BP and sporadically until 3700 BP (Butzer 1999, 197; Gatto 2019, 263). The same situation can be confirmed for the Eastern desert of Nubia with pastoral mobility, and the transition from foraging to food production and animal husbandry (Gatto 2011, 24; Gatto 2012, 51; Gatto 2019, 263). Sheep and goat were introduced from the Near East from c. 6000 BCE on, as were cereals (Haaland and Haaland 2013, 541; Linseele 2021), but they constituted a significant component of human subsistence only since c. 5000 BCE (Riemer and Kindermann 2019, 210-1); a domestic tradition of cattle breeding inferred from sites such as Nabta Playa or Bir Kiseiba continues to be questionable (see Honegger 2014, 26-7). It is apparent that culturally different groups shared similar forms of subsistence; research should therefore focus less on "peoples" – with alleged fixed "ethnic" attributes – than on lifestyles (Moreno García 2018, 147-9). Recently, Philipps, Holdaway and Wendrich (2017, 10-12) have reviewed the history of scholarship that situated the origins of the Egyptian Neolithic within postulated movements of "populations" or "cultures" induced by climatic change, often supplementing the dearth of evidence by explanatory large-scale models. In particular, they critiqued how select specimens of portable material culture were used to create "culture histories" without taking into account the entire record at the individual sites and the importance of variability within groups (Philipps, Holdaway and Wendrich 2017, 13-16).

In the context of this study, it is obvious that any insight into the historical languages of the populations of the Neolithic is even less accessible. Even in cases that reach from the late Neolithic into historical times and pertain to sites close to Egypt, it is impossible to have an informed view of the ethnic or linguistic reality behind certain groups that can be identified archaeologically. I single out here three examples:

(1) In the oasis of Dakhlah, the so-called Sheikh Muftah culture (3800–2200 BCE; see now Jeuthe 2021) displayed less wealth and social complexity than the previous culture of Bashendi B. It consisted of small groups of herders of cattle and goats who also entertained 'base camps' at a distance of 20-30 km from Dakhla and trade contacts from the Gilf Kebir in the southwest to the Nile Valley in the east (Riemer 2011, 284-8). In the Old Kingdom, Egyptian settlers co-existed in Dakhlah with Sheikh Muftah people (Riemer 2011, 288; Ricketts 2020). The linguistic reality behind the Bashendi and Sheikh Muftah people is unknown; place names and words attributed to an "Oasian" language cannot be identified linguistically (Cooper 2017a, 83 with reference to pertinent entries in El-Sayed 2011).

(2) The Western Nile delta seems to have provided 'Libyan' tribes that bred cattle and livestock with access to water and grazing grounds (Moreno García 2014; 2018). The Egyptian center of the cattle industry here was Kom el-Hisn which also provisioned the Egyptian state and may have overseen the trade with the 'Libyan' breeders from the West (Moreno García 2014, 7-9). However, there is no positive archaeological evidence for 'Libyans' at Kom el-Hisn (Wenke, Redding and Cagle 2016, 24-5); even extended exchange between Libyan pastoralists and the Egyptian administration may not have left material evidence, and the administrative records are lost to us. Linguistic evidence for early 'Libyans' hardly exists (see below, p. 66-7).

(3) To the south, the Nubian "A-group" is attested for a millennium from c. 3800–2800 BCE, from Kubanniyeh north of Aswan to the 2nd cataract of the Nile in Lower Nubia, providing trade between the Upper Egyptian Naqada culture and the first two Egyptian dynasties with sub-Saharan Africa (Liszka 2012; Török 2009, 23-53; Gatto 2006; Somaglino and Tallet 2014, 26-7). This indigenous Nubian archaeological tradition was probably semi-nomadic with some sedentary centers, based on animal husbandry and, secondarily, on agriculture. In its final phase, there may have existed a proto-state centered at Qustul (with elite tombs). Much scholarly debate focused on whether just the last 500 years of this archaeological tradition represent the "real" A-group (Gatto 2006, 73), as well the connections of the early A-group with the Terminal Abkan culture of the 2nd cataract, the final phase of the Upper Egyptian Badari culture (Gatto 2006, 65-7) and the Pre-Kerma culture of the Sudan (Honegger 2019, 222). While a Cushitic language has been suggested as the "most economical solution" for the linguistic affiliation of the A-group (Rilly 2019, 134; see below p. 48 for El-Sayed's suggestion of East Cushitic), the origin of Lower Nubian toponyms in this presumed language of the A-group is uncertain.

2.1.2 Egyptian pictorial and textual evidence I: the 'Libyans'

Egypt's statehood found itself in an inherent conflict with the pastoral and nomadic groups encroaching on its territory and competing for its resources (Moreno García 2014; 2018; Ritner 2009a). The Egyptian pictorial and textual evidence from state artefacts and monuments is characterized by this systemic opposition.

2.1.2.1 Evidence until the end of the Middle Bronze Age (1600 BCE)

The term Tjehenu (*čḥnw*) 'Libya' is a toponym used almost exclusively with reference to the northern Western desert (cf. Manassa 2003, 83 who, however, takes it as an ethnonym). Its first attestation occurs towards the end of the 4th millennium on the preserved lower part of the 'Libyan palette' (or 'town palette') which shows cattle, donkeys, rams and olive trees, and next to them, the label 'Libya' to one side. The other side features seven town enclosures on which the Upper Egyptian ruler sits in different animal forms, holding a hoe and destroying (or alternatively, establishing) the cities (Gundlach 1994, 19-33). Moreno García has suggested that the settlements point to Libyan sedentarism (Moreno García 2014, 3-4; 2018, 159), but the town enclosures may be entirely unrelated to the mention of Libya on the opposite side. From the reign of Narmer (c. 3000 BCE), a seal depicts the king as a catfish smiting seven (bearded and long-haired) prisoners identified as Tjehenu (*čḥnw*) 'Libya' (Gundlach 1994, 41-4; Wilkinson 1999, 137; Brovarski 2016, 83 and fig. 2). It has been suggested that the "Battlefield Palette" equally shows the defeat of Tjehenu (Brovarski 2016, 85-8). Less convincing is the proposed identity of these 'Libyans' with the enemies of 'papyrus land', maybe the people of the Lower Egyptian Buto-Maadi culture, depicted on the Narmer palette and an ivory tag (Brovarski 2016, 88-9). We could equally be dealing with entirely different ethnicities and population groups in the Nile delta, people from Tjehenu in the West and groups labelled 'Nu (or, An)' and 'Waᶜsh' on the Narmer palette, an ivory tag and a decorated box from Narmer's tomb (Dreyer 2014-5, 96-7, where 'Waᶜsh' is clearly a place name, not a personal name). The large numbers provided as booty or a census figure of 'Northerners' on Narmer's mace head (120,000 captives), in addition to cattle and livestock (400,000 cattle; 1,422,000 sheep and goats), and similarly on the statues of Khasekhemui in the 2nd dynasty (47,209 captives), point in a general way to a fertile region that sustained vast herds and populations (Moreno García 2014, 3-4). What ethnicities or languages they may have represented is impossible to establish.

For the reign of Snofru at the beginning of the 4th dynasty (c. 2600 BCE), the Cairo annals fragment mentions "bringing back from the land of Tjehenu (*čḥnw*) 1100 prisoners and 13,100 cattle and livestock". A famous scene from the funerary temple of Sahure (c. 2400 BCE), reports the smiting of the "Chieftains of the Tjehenu" (*ḥꜣti.w-ʿ n čḥnw*, rather a designation of their tribal leaders than of Libyans more generally), depicts the (main) chieftain with his family (Stockfisch 1996; Bestock 2017, 93-6) and provides their names and two toponyms as their places of origin. Remarkably, the depictions of the "Chieftains of the Tjehenu" resemble closely the appearance and vestments of the Egyptian king: men and women, with their skins rendered red and yellow like Egyptians, are shown with long, wavy hair; a hair lock on the forehead is turned upright (where Egyptian kings would wear the uraeus snake). Men have a pointed chin beard (where the Egyptian king would carry an artificial ritual beard). Among details specific to the Tjehenu (e.g., belt with a penis sheath; pearl collar, two bands crossed over the chest; necklace), the men also wear an animal tail attached to the belt, similarly to the Egyptian king's ritual tail (Hölscher 1937, 14-6; Trost 2012). If the Sahure scene refers to a historical event is uncertain; the depiction itself was often copied until the reign of Taharqa in the 7th c. BCE (Stockfisch 1996; Ritner 2009a, 44-5). The similarity of the Libyan dress to that of the Egyptian king has often been regarded as proof that the "Chieftains of the Tjehenu" were related to the Egyptians, and more precisely, to the Naqade II culture of the later 4th millennium BCE. This would require us to assume that the Sahure depictions can be seen as authentic renderings of a situation 800 years earlier. In turn, Ritner has pointed to the parallels in the depictions of Libyans in Egyptian art with carved or painted depictions in Libyan rock art from the Fezzan (Ritner 2009a, 48-9).

One "Chieftain of Tjehenu" (*ḥꜣti-ꜥ n čḥnw*) with his personal name is prominently depicted under Mentuhotep II (see p. 62); the Execration Texts mention again the "Chieftains of Tjehenu" (*ḥꜣti.w-ꜥ n čḥnw*) but without any details characteristic of the Asiatic and Nubian sections (Ritner 2009a, 46-7).

While the term Tjehenu (*čḥnw*) remains in use in official texts as a generic term for Libya, it becomes conflated with a different expression for Libyans, Tjemehu *(čmḥw),* that appears in the sources first around 2300 BCE (see below pp. 67-8 for hypothetical etymologies of the two terms). An example of this conflation can be found in the Tale of Sinuhe (R 11-16; c. 1900 BCE):

> "Meanwhile, His Majesty had sent off to the land of the Tjemehu an army whose leader was his elder son, the good god Sesostris. Now, he had been sent in order to smite the foreign countries and to punish those of Tjehenu and now he was returning, having brought prisoners of the Tjehenu and all kinds of cattle beyond number." (Loprieno 1995, 188).

Another example is from as late as the 10th year of Psammetikhos I. (654 BCE), when a stele of the pharaoh from the Dahshur Road speaks about Tjemehu *(čmḥw)* as a population from the "desert land of Tjehenu" and then refers back to them as "those of Tjehenu" (*čḥnw.iw*) (Ritner 2009b, 586-7).

The new term Tjemehu *(čmḥw)* appears from the 6th dynasty (c. 2300 BCE) on in the new genre of biographies of expedition leaders and expedition inscriptions. The oldest mention of the Tjemehu is in the expedition report of Weni from Abydos (latest treatment in Stauder-Porchet 2017) when Weni specifies that he drafted mercenaries from Nubia and "the land of the Tjemehu" for his campaign against "the Asiatics who are on the sand" (ʿꜣm.w ḥrỉ.w šʿ), probably nomads of the Sinai frontier (Cooper 2020b, 74; for the term, Gundacker 2017, 349-52). In the slightly later biography of Harkhuf from Elephantine, the expedition leader is sent to Yam where he learns that the ruler of Yam "had gone off to the land of the Tjemehu, to smite the Tjemehu to the western corner of heaven. I went up after him to the land of the Tjemehu and satisfied him, so that he praised all the gods for the sovereign".

The Tjemehu-Libyans are therefore located to the west of Upper Egypt where the recently documented Abu Ballas caravan trail (Förster 2015) led from the oasis of Dakhla to the high plateau of the Gilf Kebir and the Jebel Uweinat and maybe further into the Chad basin of Central Africa (Schneider 2010). A recently found Egyptian inscription from Jebel Uweinat refers to "Yam bringing incense" (Cooper 2012, 12-5). While Yam has often been identified with the site of Kerma and the culture of *Kerma ancien* (Raue 2019, 300), according to Cooper's recent reassessment (Cooper 2012), Yam as the node of a trans-Saharan trade network may have been located in the Western Nubian desert, between Jebel Uweinat in the north and Darfur in the south, east of the Ennedi mountains. Here the desiccating climate still allowed for surface water, and in the area of the former West Nubian Palaeolake, left a landscape of marshland and small lakes until 2200 BCE. The Wadi Howar, the place of the extinct Yellow Nile tributary (9500-4500 BP), would also have been a main east-west conduit in Northern Sudan, between the Nile Valley and the basin of the Chad.

The Harkhuf passage led scholars to identify the presumed incursion of Tjemehu-Libyans with the influx of C-group Nubians in Lower Nubia (for the C-group, see p. 17). Edel (1967, 155-6) assumed that "Tjemehu" *(čmḥw)* served as an umbrella term for people of different origin to the west of the Nile who, after their 'Nubianization' as C-group people, could also be labelled "Nubians" *(nhśi.w)* by the Egyptians. While several scholars regarded the language of the Tjemehu and C-group as Proto-Berber (cf. the discussion in El-Sayed 2011, 9-20), other hypotheses have connected the spread of the C-group instead with the expansion of Nilo-Saharan and assigned their language to Northern East Sudanic (see Rilly 2019, 130-1), or identified the C-group language as Cushitic (El-Sayed 2011, 45-6, 144; Cooper 2017b, 206). Much later (and not necessarily with the same ethnic or linguistic reference), Tjemehu-Libyans are said to have been captured in the Nubian oasis of Dunqul or Kurkur during year 44 of Ramesses II and put to work in an Egyptian temple at Wadi es-Sebua (Moreno García 2018, 166). In depictions, the Tjemehu-Libyans have a light skin colour; body and extremities carry tattooages, their hair can also be reddish-brown (Trost 2012, 199). Given the fuzzy situation with the presence of groups of similar lifestyle but different ethnic, cultural and linguistic affiliation to the west of the Nubian Nile, Darnell speaks about the individuals engaged in the ritual worship of the goddess Hathor at Hierakonpolis and Wadi el-Hol as "Libo-Nubians" (Darnell 2002, 126-7; also Manassa 2003, 84; cf. Moreno García 2018, 165-6).

It is important to notice that Egyptian evidence about 'Libyans' is concentrated in certain time periods and virtually absent in others. After the evidence presented above from 3200/2900 BCE, and 2300/2200 BCE, the Middle Kingdom and Second Intermediate Period are virtually silent about Libyans. Scenes in provincial governors' tombs at Beni Hasan and el-Bersheh show the involvement of Libyans in the trade with cattle and labour (Moreno García 2018, 163). The fact of a cursory reference to Libyans in the Execration Texts (Moreno García 2014, 8; 2018, 164) was presumed to show "the Egyptian court's ignorance of Libyan social components, territories, or rulers" (Ritner 2009a, 46-7). It is only in the Ramesside era, from 1300 BCE, that 'Libyans' become a focus of Egyptian textual and pictorial documentation. There may be different reasons for the Egyptian silence on historical 'Libyans' for almost a millennium: the coincidence of the preserved evidence, changes in the interests of the Egyptian documentation, or actual changes affecting Libyan populations and the migration patterns of the "absentee Libyans" (Ritner 2009a, 47).

2.1.2.2 Evidence from the Late Bronze Age to the 1st millennium BCE

'Libyans' become an important and persistent topic of Egyptian state narratives of the New Kingdom, and especially the Ramesside era (c. 1300-1070 BCE). It should be noted that these narratives that have shaped the modern historiographical discourse hail from the ritual context of royal stelae (erected in temples) and temple reliefs; their purpose was not to provide historically or culturally authentic reports. Recently, Moreno García has challenged the traditional view of Libyans as "backward herders". On the basis of textual evidence (the list of booty captured from defeated Libyans) and archaeological finds from the Ramesside fort of Zawiyet Umm el-Rakham (according to Moreno García, possibly a trading post) and Bates' Island (trade, metallurgy), Moreno García instead suggests that Libyans were "active partners in exchange networks extending from inner Africa to the Levant and the Aegean", and potentially, had established a (proto-)kingdom in the late second millennium BCE (Moreno García 2014, 3; Moreno García 2018, 171).

In the 19th and 20th dynasty, Egypt suffered massive invasions by Libyans (Spalinger 2005, 202-4) in alliance with groups of "Sea Peoples" (for which, see below, pp. 122-4), particularly under Merenptah (Manassa 2003; Spalinger 2005, 235-41) and Ramesses III (Redford 2018). While these invasions are mostly presented as real military events (Spalinger 2005, 235-7, 249-60), Moreno García has recently suggested that this was how the official political discourse framed a conflict "about land use and cattle management, a process whereby autonomous herders were forcibly integrated within the fiscal structure of the pharaonic kingdom" (Moreno García 2014, 10). The 'invasion routes' would correspond to the two main trade routes to Egypt (Moreno García 2018, 171). At any rate, the Ramesside texts document the discontinuation of mobile life style and enforced settlement (cf. Victory Stele of Merenptah [Israel Stele], 271-K*RI* IV 15, 9-12). The biography of Nebre, the Egyptian commander of the Ramesside fortess at Zawiyet Umm el-Rakham· 320 km west of Alexandria emphasizes that the Egyptian king "made [the Libyans] owners of settlements, so that they would plant trees; so that they would work many vineyards and [...] in the countryside" and says about the 'Town of Ramesses II' that he built it "for these Libyan people, who had been living in the desert like jackals" (Moreno García 2018, 172). In the 20th dynasty, Libyans were widely attested in settlements in Egypt (Spalinger 2005, 271-2) and rose to positions of military and political power, a transition that led to their assumption of rule in Egypt in the Third Intermediate Period (O'Connor 1990).

2.1.3 Egyptian pictorial and textual evidence II: the 'Nubians'

2.1.3.1 Methodological remarks

While Egypt's southern political border was located at the 1st cataract of the Nile at Aswan, the term *Ta-Seti,* "Nubian land" (on the term, see p. 22) comprised both Lower Nubia south of the border and the territory north of it – the 1st Upper Egyptian nome, which adopted the same designation, testifying to its inhabitation by 'Nubians' (for a reassessment of the Nubian presence, see Raue 2018). This cultural reality persisted until the modern day, when, after the building of the Aswan dam and the flooding of the Nubian territory between the 1st and 2nd cataracts (Lower Nubia) in 1964, the affected population (consisting of Fadetchi, Kenuzi and Arabs) was resettled to areas north of Aswan (Rouchdy 1991). The political and cultural interface of Egypt and the Nubian Nile valley created a contact situation very different from the other border zones. Up to the 4th cataract, Nubia was colonized by ancient Egypt in the Middle and New

Kingdom; conversely, a Sudanese kingdom centered at Napata on the 4th cataract conquered Egypt c. 725 BCE, initiating the Kushite 25th dynasty. In the following paragraphs, I provide a brief overview of populations and archaeological traditions identified for Nubia and the Sudan from the 4th millennium onward, as well as suggested hypotheses to identify material evidence with ethnic groups mentioned in the Egyptian textual record (for suggestions regarding their linguistic affiliation, see pp. 48-50).

Current scholarship continues to use conventional labels for archaeological traditions that were coined in the early 20th century, and has tried to identify those traditions with textual data, ethnonyms and depictions from ancient Egypt. As late as 2006, Hafsaas held for the Middle Nubian cultures of the later 3rd and early 2nd millennium, in alignment with earlier research, that she "will thus argue that the archaeological units of the C-Group, the Pan-Grave, and the Kerma peoples should be identified as separate ethnic groups, which were recognized by both the Nubians and the Egyptians" (Hafsaas 2006, 4). By contrast, Dietrich Raue, editor of the 2019 *Handbook of Ancient Nubia*, pointed to the existence of an "international style" from Egypt to Kerma and the earlier Gash culture (in Eritrea), the shared life forms of different population groups, and the problem of cultural or ethnic discrimination:

> "At first it might be a bit surprising that a number of classical topics like 'C-Group', 'Pan-Grave' or Kerma-Culture are not treated as separate chapters [in the handbook]. These terms were coined 100 years ago by archaeologists with a different cultural imprint, limited access to data and a rather coincidental section of a cultural landscape that they were just starting to investigate. Nowadays these terms create more problems than they solve. Even though they will (for the sake of unambiguity) have to be used in the future, the division into isolated groups is, at least in the present writer's view, part of the problem of current interpretations: Obsolete terminology is applied to excellent new archaeological data." (Raue 2019, 293)

Similarly, Kate Liszka, after reviewing differences and similarities among the C-group, the Pan-Grave and the Kerma culture, concludes:

> "The similarities among these three material cultures and the differences evident within them beg the question: How much are we beholden to our established typologies? The real problem with the division among Pan-Grave, C-group and Kerma may not be how archaeologists diagnose differences in their individual archaeological cultures, but rather how they have felt compelled to classify their finds (often awkwardly) into one of these three categories. The more generic classification of Middle Nubian does help relieve some of these problematic categorizations. Yet Middle Nubian does not explain why there is so much variation within each of these material cultures." (Liszka 2015, 43; cf. also Näser 2013, 116 who keeps C-group, Pan-grave culture and Kerma culture apart but observes a convergence of their funerary practices in the later Second Intermediate Period).

In particular, Liszka points to the fact that the presumed differences in the physical constitution – with the presumably larger and more robust Pan-Grave people as opposed to those of the C-group people (so still Spalinger 2013, 459 following Manfred Bietak's Sayala excavations) – are based on an extremely small, statistically not significant sample size; the strong local variability of the skeletons may also have been caused by other factors such as gene flow or diet (Liszka 2015, 49).

2.1.3.2 Middle Nubian Cultural Groups

The Nubian "A-group" (conventionally labelled with a term coined by George A. Reisner in the early 20th century who distinguished archaeological remains of the A, B [since dismissed], C and X [= Ballana] groups) is attested from c. 3800–2800 BCE, from Kubaniyeh north of Aswan to the 2nd cataract of the Nile in Lower Nubia (Liszka 2012; Török 2009, 23-53; Gatto 2006). An indigenous Nubian archaeological tradition based on animal husbandry and secondarily, on agriculture, it was probably semi-nomadic with some sedentary centers and in its final phase, may have developed a proto-state with elite tombs centered at Qustul. There has been much debate on the question if just the last 500 years of this archaeological tradition represent the "real" A-group (Gatto 2006, 73), as well the connections of the early A-group with the Terminal Abkan culture of the 2nd cataract, the final phase of the Upper Egyptian Badari culture (Gatto 2006, 65-7) and the Pre-Kerma culture of the Sudan (Honegger 2019, 222).

After a hiatus of several centuries, the C-group (Hafsaas 2006) is attested in approximately the same area as the A-group – the northernmost C-group cemetery is known from Hierakonpolis (Friedman 2004, Hafsaas 2006, 64) – and based on the same subsistence model (cattle breeding and agriculture). There has been much debate about the C-group's origin, and their possible immigration from the Western desert and/or the Southern Nile Valley; now it appears likely that they are local successors to the earlier A-group (Shinnie 1996, 55; Raue 2019, 298). Large cemeteries at Qurta, Dakka, Aniba and Faras (Raue 2019, 300-1) are contemporary to the first half of the 6th dynasty (c. 23rd century BCE). They may be evidence of the elite of Lower Nubian chiefdoms mentioned in contemporary Egyptian texts (Wawat, Irtjet, Setju; Hafsaas 2006, 71-2). While the evidence from the later Old Kingdom and First Intermediate Period shows an emulation of Egyptian practices by the C-group, it is conspicuous that during the Egyptian colonial rule over Lower Nubia in the 12th dynasty, the material cultures of Egypt and the C-group show hardly any interference. This may be explained by both the Egyptian refusal to allow for cultural engagement with the occupied and the C-groups attempt to protect their traditional identity (Morris 2018a, 84-6). After the end of the Middle Kingdom, the C-group flourished again throughout the Second Intermediate Period (c. 1750-1550 BCE). This time evinces substantial cultural entanglement between Egyptian culture and the C-group (Morris 2018a, 90-101) and overall a "remarkable hybridity between C-group, Kerman, Egyptian and pan-grave cultures in Lower Nubia" (Morris 2018a, 94).

The Nubian Pan-grave culture is attested for a limited time only, between c. 1800 and 1550 BCE, through isolated small cemeteries on the edge of the desert with the typical 'pan'-shaped graves after which the archaeological tradition was named, while permanent settlements are almost completely absent.

Stretching from the 2nd cataract northward, the cemeteries are attested throughout the core territory of Egypt from Elephantine up to Dahshur in the area of Memphis, a fact explained traditionally by an attempt of the Pan-grave population to resettle in Egypt. Recent scholarship on the Pan-grave material culture, new surveys and the critical review of past research (Liszka 2015; Liszka and De Souza 2021) has put into doubt many of the conventional assumptions about the Pan-grave people, including their presumed place of origin in the Eastern desert and 'racial' physiognomy. Liszka has more specifically invalidated the long-held claim according to which the Pan-grave people were identical with the *Medjay (mč̣ꜣy.w)* of the Egyptian textual records who, owing to their presumed robust physique, were deployed as mercenaries by the Egyptians (cf. still Hafsaas 2006, 129-30; Morris 2018, 98). The term later took on the professional meaning of 'policemen', 'desert rangers' (Schneider 2003, 92-3; a similar development may be visible in the term *mgꜣ*: Danilova and Valerio 2019). By contrast, the C-group Nubians would have been subsumed under the designation *nḥśỉ.w* (Barnard 2009, 18-9 has emphasized that a clear equation is not possible). Liszka advances the hypothesis that, as opposed to migration, the appearance of the Pan-grave culture can be explained by the cultural change of populations already living in the Nile Valley (Liszka 2015, 51).

Further to the south, the Kerma culture is attested in different phases – *Kerma ancien* or Early Kerma (2500-2050 BCE), *Kerma Moyen* or Middle Kerma (2050-1750 BCE), *Kerma Classique* or Classic Kerma (1750-1500 BCE), *Kerma Récent* or Late Kerma (1500-1100 BCE; Edwards 2004, 80-1; Raue 2019). There was clearly intense economic, cultural and political interaction between Egypt and Kerma. As the 'Kingdom of Kush', Middle Kerma presented a significant threat to Egypt's imperial and economic interests in Nubia. Towards the end of the Second Intermediate Period (c. 1600 BCE), the empire of Kush was allied with the Hyksos dynasty in the Eastern Nile delta; an inscription in Elkab reports the raid into Upper Egypt around 1550 BCE by an army of the Kingdom of Kush (Judd and Irish 2009, 709-10). The presumed presence of Kerma people at Deir el-Ballas and Tell el-Dabʿa in the later Second Intermediate Period and under Ahmose may not stand up to scrutiny (see Matić 2014b; Walsh 2018; an overview of Nubian material evidence at Egyptian sites can be found in Raue 2018).

From the late 12th to the early 18th dynasty, Classic Kerma is also attested in individual tombs and groups of two to three tombs, from Gurob in the north of Egypt to Western Thebes, containing Classic Kerma pottery (Meurer 1996, 88). It is important to emphasize that material and cultural similarities also exist between these Middle Nubian groups and regional cultures in Eastern Sudan, the Butana Group (4th-3rd mill. BCE), the Gash Group (early 3rd-early 2nd mill. BCE) and the Jebel Mokram Group (early 2nd to early 1st mill. BCE) (see Monza 2019). These regions are today also inhabited by Beja tribes, and a similar overlap seems equally likely for antiquity.

2.1.3.3 Egyptian ethnonyms for 'Nubians' and their historical correlates

The presumed cultural, ethnic and linguistic complexity in ancient Sudan was not reflected adequately in ethnonyms attested in Egyptian texts. Much – inconclusive – scholarship has been devoted to that ancient terminology (the etymologies provided by Michaux-Colombot 2014 do not seem acceptable).

A generic Egyptian term for people from beyond its southern border was *nḥśỉ.w*, an ethnonym attested since the 2nd dynasty (El-Sayed 2011, 220-2). Conventionally translated as "Nubians", the term is also used for inhabitants of Punt and Black Africans; it thus seems to have had the wider connotation of "Southerners" (Drenkhahn 1967, 4-18; Zibelius 1972, 140-1).

The etymology of the term *nḥśỉ* is unknown; most likely it is a foreign designation of a Nubian population of the Middle or Upper Nile valley, according to El-Sayed of the Cushitic speaking A-group (El-Sayed 2011, 221-2). Alternatively, one might wonder if the term belongs to North Cushitic (Beja/Tubeɗawiye) *nehā́s* "clean, pure" ('the pure ones'; for the word, Reinisch 1895, 182; Hudson 2013, 123; cf. Rübekeil 1992, 206-8, 236-8 for the comparable original meaning of the ethnonyms *Germani, Suebi*).

It is instructive to demonstrate on the basis of *nḥśỉ.w* the fragility of the link established between ethnonyms, texts and historical hypotheses.

In 1958, Georges Posener posited that beyond its more generic use as "Southerners" (also Michaux-Colombot 2014, 508), *nḥśỉ.w* would denote more specifically the "Nile Valley Nubians" of the C-group (Posener 1958; Zibelius 1972, 141; Török 1997, 39 n. 194; Shinnie 1996, 54-77; Schneider 2003a, 82, 180; Cooper 2020b, 72), a view now generally abandoned. Prominent early examples of the term *nḥśỉ.w* appear in the reign of Pepi II: execration texts mention individually ca. 180 "Nubians", bearing preponderantly "Nubian" names and partly labelled as *nḥśỉ* "Nubian" (Espinel 2013 with the older literature).

> A developped transcription system for non-Egyptian terms and names is first attested here (Hoch 1994, 487-8; El-Sayed 2011, 73). This system allowed for a detailed grapho-phonemic and grapho-morphematic analysis (El-Sayed 2011, 59-119) that also shows Egyptian comprehension of foreign lexemes (e.g., by using the classifier hieroglyph for "dog" after foreign terms for dogs; El-Sayed 2011, 113-4).

On the assumption that the C-group immigrated into the Lower Nubian Nile Valley during the 6th dynasty and represented a threat to the Egyptian economic interests in Nubia, the appearance of execration figures was seen as a proof of this migration (Meurer 1996, 100; but see Raue 2019, 298 for the contrary view of a local population). The mention of *nḥśỉ.w ḥtp.w* "pacified/settled Nubians" in Pepi I's exemption decree for Snofru's funerary precincts at Dahshur may relate to (C-group?) Nubians who were successfully integrated in Egyptian society (see also below 145 n. 16).

If the evolution of the C-group was a local development, as mentioned above, these arguments lose their validity. From a terminological perspective, one may add that the ethnic identity of the Nubian mercenaries from the Gebelein stelae in the 1st Intermediary Period – some of whom are labeled *nḥśỉ* – is not certain (see p. 144); additionally, *nḥśỉ.w* can also be said to be originating "from the desert", as in the biography of an offical Mereri from Dendera (Moreno García 2018, 167). Thus, a straightforward identification of *nḥśỉ.w* with members of the C-group can no longer be upheld. This terminological problem is also valid for another term for 'Nubians', Medjay *(mč̣ꜣy.w)*, conventionally presumed to designate the "desert Nubians" and carriers of the Pan-grave culture. They would have immigrated to Egypt from the Eastern desert and been employed as mercenaries (Posener 1958; Zibelius 1972, 141; Török 1997, 39 n. 194; Shinnie 1996, 54-77; Schneider 2003a, 92-3, 179-80). The term derives from a toponym *mč̣ꜣ* designating, in the 6th dynasty, a territory in the Eastern desert of Lower Nubia (El-Sayed 2011, 215-6 with a doubtful Beḏawiye etymology as *m^{b}ič'-ʔare* = "Biḏa mountains"). Recently, Kate Liszka has deconstructed this scholarly consensus (Liszka 2015; see also Matić 2020, 27-8, 38-9). Liszka suggests as an alternative scenario to that of immigration the model of cultural change of a population living within the Nile Valley, bolstered by the need to display its different identity when the Egyptian state of the Middle Kingdom lost power. This *internal* explanation is thus a similar paradigm change as the one proposed recently for the C-group (see p. 20):

> "Although this theory has not been explored before, I would like to suggest as a possible scenario to explore that the Pan-Grave archaeological culture came from within populations already living in the Nile Valley. Based on their use of animals in their mortuary remains, some may have been pastoralists herding their animals along the Nile, like the C-Group. Egyptologists for the last 100 years have assumed that the Pan-Grave represented a completely separate *ethnicity* from the C-Group or Kerma cultures. However, the lack of internal phasing and the lack of closed vessel forms for the bearers of the Pan-Grave culture, as opposed to those of the C-Group or Kerma cultures, may instead point to a different type of shift in their identity, one that does not represent an isolated group. As opposed to an *ethnic* difference, perhaps the Pan-Grave archaeological remains represent <a> geographic, occupational, demographic, or even religious type of identity, distinct but related to the C-Group or Kerma culture." (Liszka 2015, 51)

Other vague terms for 'Nubians' are more likely connotated geographically or habitually, such as *sty.w* and *ỉwntỉ.w nw tꜣ stỉ* "bowmen of the Nubian Land", of which the latter may designate groups that were "more mobile and living in a desert environment and in the oases" (Moreno Garcia 2018, 169; for additional ethnonyms see Cooper 2020b with table 4, p. 80). The term *stỉ* (*tꜣ stỉ*, "Nubian land"; for the term, see Michaux-Colombot 2014, 507-8) is probably identical to a word used in Egyptian for "(red) ochre" which was extracted in Lower Nubia. El-Sayed holds that although an etymology is not evident, the term is likely a loanword (El-Sayed 2011, 254). A plausible etymology for both the ochre term and the toponym is the North Cushitic (Beja/Tu-beɗawiye) adjective *sōtay, sūtay* "dark-colored, dark green/brown/grey" (Reinisch 1895, 206). As a term for ochre, *stỉ* would be the "dark (brown) ochre". *tꜣ stỉ* would then be the "ochre land" (or if the adjectival meaning was still transparent, as much as *km.t* "Egypt", 'the dark brown, black land').

Depictions of Nubians in reliefs and sculpture display sometimes 'Nubian' ethnic markers but do not allow for a precise assignment to a specific cultural group. E.g., the famous Nubian mercenaries represented on a group of stylistically peculiar stelae from Gebelein (see p. 144) show archers, in some cases the ethnonym *nḥśỉ* and on one stela negroid features (Kubisch 2000, 247). They have often been classified mostly as C-group individuals (Näser 2013, 109-10; Meurer 2020, 292; see p. 144-5, however, for a potential Beja/Tu-beɗawiye proper name). Similarly, the wooden model of 40 Nubian archers from the tomb of Mesehti at Assiut is often regared as representing C-group people (Spalinger 2010, 429; Näser 2013, 109-10) or alternatively, either Kerma or C-group mercenaries (Meurer 1998, 94-5 and cf. p. 90).

2.2 Contact with African Languages

2.2.1 The modern situation

The extent of language contact between ancient Egyptian and languages spoken to the southwest, south and southeast of Egypt between the 3rd and the 1st millennia BCE is difficult to establish. The modern language situation in these areas is very complex and not sufficiently researched.

(1) The *Niger-Congo* language cluster contains languages mostly located in West Africa and thus not relevant here. However, it is conventionally believed to be represented in the Sudan by the Kordofanian languages, c. 20 languages spoken in the Nuba mountains. Their five subgroups are Heiban, Talodi, Rashad, Katla-Tima, Lafofa (Tegem-Amira). Both the affiliation of the Kordofanian languages with the Niger-Congo languages, their internal linguistic classification and the relationship to the Nilo-Saharan languages have been under scrutiny in recent years; Blench has argued that "there is no positive evidence for the genetic unity of Kordofanian" and that "the intensity of interaction with each other and with their Nilo-Saharan neighbours produced the perplexing mosaic of analogous number-marking systems testified in the present" (Blench 2013). The date of settlement of these populations in the Nuba mountains is not certain (Rilly 2019, 129 n. 1); interference with ancient Egyptian has so far not been signaled.

(2) Equally the subject of controversial debate is the linguistic coherence of the *Nilo-Saharan* language family (see map 1). We are on relatively safe ground for the two subgroups that are of relevance for the question of linguistic interference with ancient Egyptian. The genuine coherence of East Sudanic is now generally accepted. In the most recent analysis by Dimmendaal and Jakobi (2020), it splits into two major divisions, Northern East Sudanic (with a rich system of case markers) comprising the subgroups Taman, Meroïtic, Nubian, Nara, and Nyimang plus Afitti. Southern East Sudanic comprises one subgroup consisting of Berta and Jebel, and another one with Daju, Temeinian and the cluster of Surmic (Mursi, Didinga) and Nilotic (Dinka, Nuer, Luo, Maasai etc.)

languages. Particularly relevant for the ancient linguistic interference is the subgroup of the Northern East Sudanic languages, a group recently also corroborated in numerous studies by Rilly (see Rilly 2010, 157-350; 2019, 130). He places the original cradle of this language family along the banks of the Wadi Howar (the Yellow Nile) in Northwest Sudan and explains the historical split into different languages by migrations due to the increased desertification in the mid-3rd millennium. To this group belong Meroïtic (see pp. 31-7) and possibly also the earlier languages of the empires of Kerma/Kush and the C-group (Rilly 2019, 130-1; see pp. 48-9). A different branch of this family are the Nubian languages (Rilly 2019, 137), of which Kenuzi-Dongolawi and Nobiin (which are not mutually intelligible) were spoken along the Nile, between Aswan and Old Dongola. Ajang (Kordofian Nubian) was a language restricted to the north of the Nuba mountains; Midob and Birgid were spoken in North and South Darfur, respectively. The linguistic relationship of these languages is not entirely clear. Bechhaus-Gerst (1984/5) distinguished between Northern Nubian (Nobiin), Central Nubian (Kenuzi-Dongolawi, Kordofian Nubian, Birgid) and Western Nubian (Midob) and explained the current location and linguistic variety between these languages by migrations into and out of the Nile valley between the beginning of the Egyptian New Kingdom (1500 BCE) and early modern times. According to Rilly, Proto-Nubian split into Proto-Western and Proto-Nile Nubian not before the 1st millennium BCE; three varieties of the latter would have been spoken in the medieval Nubian kingdoms: Old Nubian (more precisely 'Old Nobiin') in Nobadia (with Nobiin as its modern successor); Old Dongolawi in Makuria (with Kenuzi-Dongolawi as its modern successors); Soba Nubian in Alodia. Proto-Western Nubian would have developed into the modern languages Birgid, Midob and Kordofian Nubian.

(3) The other subgroup of the Nilo-Saharan macrofamily that may be relevant to the question of linguistic interference is the *Saharan* one, consisting of the two subgroups of Western Saharan (with the two branches of Kanuri/Kanembu and Teda/Daza) and Eastern Saharan (with Beria [Zaghawa] and the extinct language of Berti) (Walters 2016, 1-3 with figures 1.1-1.2; Jakobi and Crass 2004). Close to Egypt and the Sudan are Teda – spoken in northeastern Niger, northern Chad, southern Libya, some speakers in the most southwestern corner of Egypt – and to the south of it, Daza – spoken in the southeastern Niger and west-central Chad. Beria is spoken in east-central Chad (in the Sahel) and northern Sudan (Darfur). Berti was equally spoken in northern Sudan (Darfur).

(4) Three, and maybe four, language families of *Afroasiatic* are relevant to this study: the Berber languages or dialect continuum; the Cushitic languages, particularly North Cushitic (Beja); the Ethio-Semitic languages; maybe the Chadic languages.

In the French tradition of *Berber* linguistics, the traditional position has been to see the different regional varieties of Berber as dialects of one language (Kossmann 1999, 15; one example is Chaker 2003), although a leading French scholar such as Lionel Galand has also spoken of "langues berbères" (Galand 1989). Maarten Kossmann considers the linguistic variety within Berber as comparable to Germanic or Romance languages (Kossmann 1999, 15; Kossmann 2020); his classification of Berber comprises these historically different blocks:

1. *Zenaga block* (Zenaga of Mauritania, Tetserrét in Niger);
2. *Tuareg block*;
3a. *Western Moroccan block* (SW Morocco, Central Morocco, i.e., Tashelhiyt and most of Tamazight);
3b. *possibly including NW Moroccan Berber* (Ghomara, Senhadja de Sraïr);
4. *Zenatic block* (Eastern Morocco, Western Algeria, Saharan oases, Tunisia, Zuara) extending towards the east with Sokna, Elfoqaha, Siwa;
5. *Kabyle* (N Algeria), possibly linked to the western Moroccan block;
6. *Ghadames* (Libya), probably to be linked to Djebel Nefusa (Libya);
7. *Awdjilah* (Libya).

(5) The *Cushitic languages* represent one of the macro-phylums of Afro-Asiatic, comprising c. 40 languages currently spoken mostly in the horn of Africa (Ethiopia, Eritrea, Djibouti, Somalia, Northeastern Kenya), with additional language areas in Tanzania as well as along the Red Sea in Southeastern Egypt and Eastern Sudan. There has been an extensive debate about the linguistic coherence of the group and its subgroups, as well as the genetic historical relationship to Afroasiatic vs. resemblances that are due to millennia of contact and convergence. Most classifications separate the Omotic languages ("West Cushitic") from the Cushitic languages as a separate Afroasiatic branch (differently Gragg 2001, 574-5: Beja, Agaw, East Cushitic, South Cushitic, Omotic).

The Cushitic languages would thus consist of 5-6 subgroups, according to Wolff 1998: (1) *North Cushitic* (Beja); (2) *Central Cushitic* (Agaw) (Bilin, Kemant, Kwara, Xamtage, and Awngi); (3) *South Cushitic* (Iraqw, Burunge, Gorowa, Ma'a/Mbugu, Dahalo); (4) *Highland East Cushitic* (Burji, Sidamo, Kambata, Hadiyya); (5) *Lowland East Cushitic* (Dasenech, Arbore, Saho-Afar, Oromo, Konso); (6) Omo-Tana (Somali, Rendille, Boni). Appleyard (2012, 200) proposes similarly a subdivision into (1) *Beja/North Cushitic*; (2) *Central Cushitic or Agaw*; (3) *East Cushitic* with the sub-branches Lowland East Cushitic (with Saho-Afar, Oromoid and Omo-Tana as sub-groups), Highland East Cushitic (with Sidaama and Hadiyya), Yaaku-Dullay, Dahalo; and (4) South Cushitic (including Iraqw).

(6) The third Afroasiatic language group to be mentioned here after Berber and Cushitic, are the *Ethio-Semitic languages*, attested and spoken in Ethiopia, Eritrea and the Sudan. They are classified by Hudson (2013, 289; cf. Meyer 2018; Weninger 2011, 1117) into the five groups:

(1) North Ethiopic (Tigre–Tigriñya – two national languages of Eritrea – and Ge'ez – the Classical language of Ethiopia);
(2) Gafat;
(3) Gunnän Gurage (Kistane, Mesqan, Muher, Chaha, Inor);
(4) Eastern Gurage (Silt'e, Zay) and Harari;
(5) Amharic – the *lingua franca* of Ethiopia – and Argobba.

(7) A possible candidate for another Afroasiatic language group in contact with Egyptian are the *Chadic languages* (for the following, see Caron 2020), comprising a total of c. 170 individual languages spoken today in Niger, Nigeria, Chad and Cameroon. According to the classification given by Newman (2013; see Caron 2020, table 26.1), Chadic splits into the four main branches:

(1) West Chadic
sub-branch A with sub-groups Hausa [lingua franca with 45 million speakers]; Bole-Tangale; Angas; Ron
sub-branch B with sub-groups Bade; Warji
sub-branch C with sub-group South-Bauchi (Barawa cluster)
(2) Central Chadic (Biu-Mandara)
sub-branch A with sub-groups Tera; Bura; Higi; Mandara; Matakam; Sukur; Daba; Bata
sub-branch B with sub-groups Kotoko; Musgu
sub-branch C with sub-group Gidar
(3) East Chadic
sub-branch A with sub-groups Somari; Lele; Kera
sub-branch B with sub-groups Dangla-Mubi; Mukulu/Mokilko; Somoro; Barain
(4) Masa

The evidence in favour of a classification of the Chadic languages as a constituent group of Afroasiatic is very limited and has been subject to recent scrutiny (see Caron 2020 for an extensive debate).

2.2.2 The ancient situation

The historical linguistic geography surrounding ancient Egypt on the African continent is very insufficiently known. The stereotypical categorization by the ancient Egyptian of its African neighbors as 'Libyans' and 'Nubians' clearly obfuscates a very complex reality (Moreno García 2014, 2; Moreno García 2018, 149; Michaux-Colombot 2014, 507). The Egyptological use of these terms has also been a reflection of the fact that North African sources contemporary with the Egyptian ones do not exist. Only very few of the ancient languages in these regions (Cushitic, Nilo-Saharan, Niger-Congo, Ethio-Semitic) are independently documented. Of these languages, only Meroïtic dates back into the time periods directly relevant here and is the only one that developed its own writing system, in use from the 3rd c. BCE to the 4th c. CE. Old Nubian is attested from the 8th-15th c. CE (translations from the Bible, hagiographic literature, inscriptions, administrative documents; Breyer 2014a, 186-91) and Old Beḍawiye (Blemmyan) in personal names and one single text from the 7th c. CE (Breyer 2014a, 192-97).

2.2.2.1 Egyptian in the Sudan – The Napatan language and script

Particularly interesting for the question of linguistic interference is the case of "Napatan" (Peust 1999b; Breyer 2021, 96-110). Napatan is a variety of the ancient Egyptian script and language attested in the Sudan in two long royal inscriptions from the 4th c. BCE, the Stelae of Harsiyotef (late 5th or early 4th c. BCE; Egyptian Museum Cairo JE 48864) and Nastasen (late 4th c. BCE; Egyptian Museum Berlin 2268) from the Kushite capital city of Napata. A third document, maybe from the 3rd c. BCE (for the discussion, Peust 1999b, 70-1; excluded by Quack 2002, 395 as being earlier and not representing the same language variety) is the stele of Ari from Kawa (Kopenhagen, Ny Carlsberg Glyptothek 1708). More controversially, the idiom is also attested on additional documents (see Peust 1999b, 21-3; "Nebenzeugen"; Breyer 2021, 99-101). The inscriptions are written in a special development of the hieroglyphic writing system and use different directions (sinistrograde in Harsiyotef and Nastasen; dextrograde in Ari). The script contains around 400 signs that are not part of the standard inventory of hieroglyphs and shows influence by (an unattested Nubian variety of) cursive sign forms (Peust 1999b). While the grammatical system of Napatan displays some peculiarities that may be owed to non-Egyptian substrate languages in the Sudan, its vocabulary is mostly related to that of younger Egyptian (Late Egyptian to Coptic). It is conspicuous that actual borrowings from local languages are very limited (so far only the Meroïtic priestly title *srḫs* and the word *tgr*, "ring" [Nubian *tigli*; "neck ring", Takács 2013, 576; "(ear) ring", Breyer 2016, 548, 564]) have been identified (for them and other words, particularly terms for containers, Peust 1999b, 137).

The linguistic character of Napatan has been assessed in very different ways. In his 1999 monographic study, Peust described Napatan as a Sudanese dialect of

Egyptian, based on Demotic (the contemporary stage of the Egyptian language). He contended that while Napatan Egyptian is attested only in monumental written form, it might also have been in wider use (Peust 1999b, 83). Peust emphasized that even though local substrate languages may have contributed to the development of this dialect, its grammatical morphology is entirely Egyptian in origin and African loanwords are very limited (Peust 1999b, 73): "The peculiarity of Napatan arises less from direct linguistic transfer from contact languages but rather a reorganization and refunctionalizing of the existing Egyptian language material". In his review of Peust, Joachim Quack (2002) sees the language as an example of "peripheral Demotic", a "non-standard use" of the contemporaneous Demotic language on the basis of a substrate language (394), used at the periphery of the Egyptian zone of influence and thus comparable to the "peripheral Akkadian" attested in the Levant (393-4). Napatan would therefore be an "interlanguage" (see pp. 100-1; 136-7) for limited usage and not a dialect actually spoken.

By contrast with these two assessments, Francis Breyer regards Napatan as a Creole language with a Meroïtic substrate although he admits that the degree of creolization is not particularly high (Breyer 2008, 326; Breyer 2021, 97-8). This assumption seems not very likely. While there is much debate about the linguistic and sociolinguistic features that characterize a Creole language (see Romaine 2017), key elements of a Creole are not visible in Napatan. There is a dominance of the higher norm (Egyptian) superstrate in the lexicon (= lexifier language), but there is no far-reaching reorganization and simplification of the grammar due to the substrate (the lower norm local language). Within a linguistic system whose lexicon, phonology, morphology and grammar are in overwhelming congruence with Demotic Egyptian, only three characteristics have been described as being due to a substrate language:

(1) Phonologically, the conflation of the sibilants /š/ and /s/ before palatal vowels, as in Meroïtic and Nubian, can be diagnosed as such an influence (Peust 1999b, 228). Other peculiarities that may originate from a substrate language are the existence of a palatal nasal /ɲ/ (written nn⟩) and a labiovelar /kʷ/ (Breyer 2008; 2014a, 184).

(2) The most distinctive feature of Napatan grammar is the loss of gender distinction for inanimate nouns; only animate nouns have preserved a grammaticalized natural gender. However, also in these cases the morphological indication of gender congruency of attributes (e.g., adjectives, definite article) has been abolished (e.g., *pꜣỉ-mw.t nfr* = **mon bon mère*). Peust sees this phenomenon as the accelerated development of a tendency visible in Later Egyptian but not attested to that degree in Egyptian (1999b, 232; the phenomenon also singled out but not explained by Quack 2002, 396). It seems more likely to regard this with Breyer (2008; 2014, 181) as another indicator of the existence of Meroïtic as a substrate language where the category 'gender' did not exist.

(3) A very distinctive feature of Napatan by comparison to Egyptian is a grammatically and morphologically new arrangement of the pronominal system used in verbal clauses (subject and object pronouns) whereas other areas (pronouns with nouns, prepositions, auxiliaries, articles) comply with later Egyptian (Peust 1999b, 255-266). Quack (2002, 395 with n. 17) lists this feature as the most visible proof of non-Egyptian linguistic interference but does not provide any correlation of the observed phenomena with the pronominal use of substrate languages. Breyer explains this phenomenon cursorily with the "agglutinative character of Meroïtic" (2008, 326), which is not sufficiently clear.

From a comparative perspective, I would like to point here to the parallels between Napatan and the (partially contemporary) Old Persian (for which, see De Vaan and Lubotsky 2009). Napatan is a small corpus language used for royal representation, written in an offshoot of the hieroglyphic script system, while the local substrate language was the unrelated Meroïtic. Old Persian cuneiform was invented by Darius I (550-486 BCE) for the same purpose of royal representation, to resemble the traditional cuneiform of Mesopotamia, while the local spoken language of the Persis was Elamite and the language of administration of the Persian Empire, Aramaic. It remained in use until Artaxerxes III

(358-338 BCE) and was also used in Egypt (see below p. 108 for the stelae erected at the Suez canal). Harsiyotef is a contemporary of the last years of Persian rule in Egypt or dates slightly later; Nastasen may just have overlapped with Artaxerxes III or may have ruled one generation later (for the different dates proposed, see Peust 1999b, 70).

Could it be feasible that Napatan was created as a language of representation on the model of Old Persian? Relations between the "Kushites" and the Persian Empire are well attested (for the following, Huyse 1998; Briant 2002, 172-180). An expedition against the "Ethiopians" by Cambyses, reported by Herodotus (Herodotus 7.17-22), ended in disaster. They are named among the populations of the Persian Empire in inscriptions of Darius I (Naqsh-I Rustam A 30; Susa E 30) and Xerxes (Persepolis H 28), and are included at the end of Herodotus's satrapy list (3.97, 2f.) although they do not seem to have been an actual part of the Persian Empire. Rather, they delivered tribute to the Persians – gold, ebony, boys, elephant tusks, exotic animals (a giraffe?). The Kushites also formed a war contingent in Xerxes' invasion of Greece in 480-79 BCE and are depicted on Greek vases; 150 years later, a delegation of Ethiopians was among those awaiting Alexander on his return to Babylon in the spring of 323 BCE. Finally, the *Aithiopiká* of Heliodorus of Emesa elaborate on a conflict between a Meroïtic king (Hydaspes) and the Persian satrap Orondates. In this respect, I would like to add to the discussion an obvious Akkadianism in Napatan, the phrase *nsw n pꜣ 4 qꜥ ḥ* "king of the four corners = the world" in the Nastasen stela (viewed by Peust 2004, 352 as an isogloss with Old Nubian). This is likely a calque from the Akkadian expression *šar kibrāti erbetti* "king of the four corners" (a phrase that remained in use until the Persian empire).

2.2.2.2 Nilo-Saharan languages

2.2.2.2.1 Northern East Sudanic

2.2.2.2.1.1 Meroïtic

Meroïtic was the language of the kingdom of Meroë in the Sudan from the 3rd c.

BCE to the 4th c. CE (for an overview, Rilly 2017, 330-373; Rilly 2019, 139-48; Breyer 2021, 110-7), written in both a monumental-hieroglyphic and cursive script with 23 phonograms each, derived from the Egyptian writing system (Rilly 2007, 71-229; for hypotheses about foreign templates for the creation of the Meroïtic script, Breyer 2021, 236-8). 1000 texts are inventoried in the *Répertoire d'épigraphie méroïtique*, the majority of which (450) are funerary and can be partially understood (for a new analytical dictionary of Meroïtic, Hallof 2022). The Meroïtic royal inscriptions – stretching from the late 2nd c. BCE (Taneyidamani-Stele from Napata/Gebel Barkal; Török 2002, 309-12) to the mid-5th c. CE (inscription of Kharamadoye from the Mandulis temple at Kalabsha; Török 2002, 479) still elude interpretation. The recent discovery of Meroïtic ostraca at Qasr Ibrim, between the 1st and 2nd cataract of the Nile, has increased the number of Meroïtic texts by 40% and also added a new source category – administrative documents (see Hallof 2011).

The breakthrough in the decipherment of Meroïtic is due to Francis Llewellyn Griffith (since 1909; for the history of research, Breyer 2014a, 213-228; Rilly 2007, 47-53) who determined the values of Meroïtic signs, recognized the correct reading direction (contrary to Egyptian in that animated signs look towards the writing direction, not the beginning of the text), established that the monumental and cursive script belonged to the same system and discovered the syllabic (Rilly 2010b: "alphasyllabary") principle of the writing system (for a discussion of different hypotheses about the Meroïtic writing system, see Breyer 2021, 258-60). Significant progress in our understanding of Meroïtic has been made in recent studies by Claude Rilly (Rilly 2007; Rilly 2010a; Rilly and de Voogt 2012). Building on an earlier proposal by Bruce G. Trigger, Rilly classifies Meroïtic as a Northern East Sudanic language (Rilly 2010, 351-411). This is now the majority opinion (El-Sayed 2011, 27; Dimmendaal and Jakobi 2020; see Breyer 2014b, 229-49 for an overview of past classifications), although the comparative basis for this categorization is still very limited. Typologically, Meroïtic is an agglutinative language with SOV word order; morphologically, it does not know grammatical gender. According to Rilly's latest analysis, the phonology of Meroïtic shows retroflex sounds (the dental stops and the single spirant) which would favor its proposed classification as Northern East Sudanic (Rilly 2007). However, it remains questionable if such assessments can be made for a language that is by and large incomprehensible (Hallof 2009, 146; Breyer 2012a, 118) – as to the lexical basis, only c. 45 Meroïtic lexemes are considered semantically certain (Rilly 2010, 114-47; cf. Breyer 2012a, 137-40). The kingdom of Meroë succeeded to the kingdom of Napata; and substrate features observed in Napatan (see p. 30) point to Meroïtic as the spoken substrate language. While most of the personal names of the kings of the Kushite 25th dynasty (c. 725-664 BCE) such as *Kꜣ-š-tꜣ, P(ʿnḫ)y, Šꜣ-bꜣ-tꜣ-kꜣ, Tꜣ-n-wꜣ-tỉ-ỉmn* cannot be explained fully (see Zibelius-Chen 2011, s.v.), their Meroïtic linguistic background seems established. E.g., Shabaqo *(Šꜣ-bꜣ-kꜣ)* may mean *šb-qo* "the noble prince" (Zibelius-Chen 2011, 217; Rilly's alternative interpretation is less likely from an onomastic viewpoint). This king's Egyptian titulary name *sḇꜣq-tꜣwỉ* (Horus, Nebti, Gold name; "the one who brightens the two lands") was likely chosen deliberately as a graphemo-phonological calque on the sound of the proper name. The invocations to the sage Imhotep of Pap. Brooklyn 47.218.47, probably composed during the 25th dynasty, contain foreign terms and divine names that might be Nubian or Meroïtic (Quack 2018b, 38-9 with a transliteration and translation; Quack 2018c). Numerous Meroïtic terms were later borrowed into Demotic (Breyer 2021, 228).

Evidence for the existence of earlier stages of the Meroïtic language ("Proto-Meroïtic") has been suggested to be reflected in foreign names and loanwords in Egyptian transcription of the 2nd millennium. Most interesting in this respect are foreign phrases and names from the 'supplementary chapters' (chapters 162-7[1]) of the Book of the Dead, attested since the 21st dynasty but presumed

---

[1] The invocations "of somewhat related nature in funerary papyri of the twenty-first dynasty" referred to by Quack 2010a, 319, are versions of chapter 166 (Wüthrich 2010, 98; Jansen-Winkeln 1994, A.1.1.74*).

to be composed as early as the late Ramesside period (Zibelius-Chen 2005; Wüthrich 2009, 2010, 2015).

According to a proposal by Wüthrich, these spells would be a kind of 'abracadabra' merely feigning Nubian. However, chapter 164 states (or pretends) that the language is that of the *nḥśi͗.w i͗wn.ti͗w n.w tꜣ-sti͗*, "Nubians and Nomads of 'Nubian Land' [the 1st Upper Egyptian nome]" (Quack 2018c, 481; Zibelius-Chen 2011, 201); chapter 163 mentions Napata as the location of the deity. Given our very limited knowledge of Meroïtic (and other ancient Nubian languages), it is currently not possible to determine the nature of these phrases with any certainty. From the expressions (discussed extensively by Zibelius-Chen 2005 and 2011), I single out one example. Chapter 166 invokes five gods for the protection of Osiris whose names are rendered in Egyptian syllabic writing, of which the initial one – *wꜣ-rw-bꜣ-gꜣ* – may be given here as an illustration. While there have been attempts of Egyptian interpretations of this name (Wüthrich 2010, 98: "celui au grand gémissement"; James P. Allen: "Lion (who) Parches the Lifeless One"), the unusual syllabic writing points to foreign origin. Zibelius-Chen regards a Meroïtic interpretation as possible but refrains from a suggestion (2005; 2011, 102). Hypothetical etymologies are possible, for example as Meroïtic *wle pke* /wal-pak/, "living dog" (*wle*, "dog"; *pke* "to live"). Similar foreign terms are also used in the isolated Book of the Dead spells of Paprus Berlin 3031 (for an individual discussion, see Zibelius-Chen 2011, e.g., 77-8).

The evidence for Proto-Meroïtic is more ambiguous in the New Kingdom. An indicator of intense religious contact is the fact that the names of Egyptian deities may have been borrowed into Proto-Meroïtic in the New Kingdom because Meroïtic has preserved them in a Paleo-Coptic vocalization.[2] Alternatively, they may reflect more recent borrowings from a dialect characterized by an archaizing vocalization or a transfer via Napatan Egyptian. Such borrowings of

---

[2] A term used since W.F. Edgerton (1947) for a (theoretical) stage of earlier Egyptian when the sound developments that led to the Coptic phonological systems had not yet taken place.

divine names are (Peust 1999a, 226; Breyer 2012a, 125-6; Rilly and Vogt 2012, 119, 124):

Horus	Meroïtic */ara/*	< Egyptian ḥā́rə < ḥāruw, but > Coptic ḥṓr
Isis	Meroïtic */usa/*	< Egyptian ȝū́sə, but > Coptic ēsə
Amun	Meroïtic */amani/*	< Egyptian amā́nə < 'amā́nuw, but > 1st millennium 'amū́n
Hathor	Meroïtic */atari/*	< Egyptian ḥw.t-ḥā́ruw, but > Coptic ḥatḥṓr
Khonsu	Meroïtic */ḫansa/*	< Egyptian ḫắnsaw (Schenkel 1983, 167), but > Greek χωνς
Harendotes	Meroïtic */arentate/*	< Egyptian ḥr-(ḥr)-nč̣-ỉt=f with final element ỉā́t˘f vs. kopt. yōt "father"
Mut	Meroïtic */mata/*	< Egyptian mắwt (? – with preservation of the –t) > Greek Μουθ

The (Proto-)Meroïtic term for "king", *qore* /q^wur/, is attested in Egyptian texts since the 20th dynasty (*k-ȝ-wȝ-rw/q-r*, Onomasticon of Amenemope, Gardiner 1947: no. 284, 285, 290); in the later historical inscription of Psammetichus II about his military campaign to the Sudan (592 BCE), it is used as the designation of the ruler of Napata (Zibelius-Chen 2011, 236-8). To judge by the cognates of the term in Cushitic languages (Burji, Sidamo, Maji), it appears to be an old loanword in Proto-Meroïtic from Cushitic (Zibelius-Chen 2011, 238; cf. also Beria (Zagawa) [see below p.41] *kire*, "great king" [Blench 2011, 23]). This is the only securely identified Proto-Meroïtic word in texts of the New Kingdom, although the many loanwords of uncertain Semitic etymology in Hoch's 1994 compendium have not been systematically checked for their possible Proto-Meroïtic (or Nubian, Cushitic etc.) etymologies; our very limited knowledge of the Meroïtic lexicon makes this also largely impossible.

The Egyptian hieroglyphic writing of the city name 'Napata' (since the 18th dynasty) as *n-p*^{WATER}*-t* with the water logogram before the final *t-* could be seen as associating the second part of the name with (Proto-)Meroïtic *ato* "water"

(Breyer 2014b, 123; for the writings of the toponym, Peust 2009b, 216). For a number of personal names of Nubians attested in documents of the New Kingdom, Proto-Meroïtic has been suggested as a source language. E.g., Zibelius-Chen considers the name of a Nubian (nḥśỉ) stone mason *tỉ-r-k-ꜣ-ỉ-ꜣ* from the time of Hatshepsut/Thutmose III as the historical proof of the existence of Proto-Meroïtic in the 15th c. BCE, identifying it with the Meroïtic name *trq-ye* (so also El-Sayed 2011, 30-1) or alternatively, suggesting a connection with the Meroïtic noun *tereki*, or else the verb *rike*, "to engender" (2011, 5-6, 270). The name of a Nubian rebel king *ꜣ-ꜣ-t-ꜣ* in the early 18th dynasty biography of Ahmose has similarly been compared to the Meroïtic name *Arereteli* (El-Sayed 2011, 31; for a discussion with alternative interpretations, Zibelius-Chen 2011, 9-11). Evidently, such comparisons are possibilities rather than linguistic proof; other languages spoken in the ancient Sudan may provide valid alternatives.

There is no certain evidence for the existence of Proto-Meroïtic in Egyptian sources prior to the 18th dynasty. Rilly has compared personal names of the 'Fayyum list' (Pap. Moscow 314 recto) with identical (but not comprehensible) consonant sequences in Meroïtic; his claim ("on tient assez vraisemblablement une première preuve que le royaume de Kerma, dont les rares témoignages écrits utilisent la langue et l'écriture égyptienne, était déjà d'expression méroïtique"; Rilly 2007, 11) cannot at present be confirmed (see below, pp. 63-6). He points to the observation that the Middle Kingdom execration texts of 'Nubian' princes do not attest the graphemes <p>, <f>, <h>, <ḫ> and <č> and contain only rare attestations of others (<ṭ>, <ḥ> and <q>), which would coincide with the phonology of Meroïtic (Rilly 2019, 139).

If the toponym "Kush", attested since the reign of Senwosret I in the early 12th dynasty (ca. 50 BCE) under the forms *kꜣs / kꜣś / kꜣš* and in the later 12th dynasty as *kwš*, is the predecessor of Meroïtic *Qes*, it would point to the language of the empire of Kerma. On this assumption, Rilly proposed to restitute the original form of the geographic name as *Kwuʂa* (with a Nubian retroflex sibilant) and also believes that this designation was already in use by the Nubian empire of *Kerma Ancien* around 2400 BC (Rilly 2001, 361 n. 51). The different Egyptian transcriptions can be seen as attempts to either render a foreign retroflex sibilant or else mirror a contemporaneous sound change in that language (El-Sayed 2011, 274-6). The older form would have rendered /ʂ/ by the sequence of an /r/ sound and a sibilant, the later with <š> would have opted for a different phoneme.[3]

2.2.2.2.1.2 Old Nubian and related dialects

Old Nubian is a historical language attested in inscriptions between the late 8th c. CE and the late 15th c. CE (Breyer 2014b, 186-91; Breyer 2021, 117-25). I outlined major hypotheses regarding the linguistic relationships above (p. 24). According to Rilly, Proto-Nubian split into Proto-Western and Proto-Nile Nubian not before the 1st millennium BCE. Proto-Western Nubian would have developed into the modern languages Birgid, Midob and Kordofian Nubian. Three varieties of Proto-Nile Nubian are assumed to have been spoken in the medieval Nubian kingdoms:

- OLD NUBIAN in Nobadia (1st to 3rd cataract; capital Faras; Old Nubian name *Migitn Gūl*; annexed by Makuria in the 7th c.). The modern successor of Old Nubian is Nobiin; in consequence, Old Nubian could also be called more precisely ‘Old Nobiin’.
- OLD DONGOLAWI in Makuria (south of the 3rd cataract to south of the 5th cataract; capital Dongola; Old Nubian name *Dotawo*) with Kenuzi-Dongolawi as its modern successors;
- SOBA NUBIAN in Alodia/Alwa (central and southern Sudan; capital Soba; cf. Breyer 2014b, 188-90)

The Old Nubian script is attested from 797 CE on; earlier Proto-Nile Nubian

---

[3] I have suggested that the Eblaite term of a foreign kingdom, *Du-gú-ra-su*^{ki}, may render Egyptian *tꜣ kꜣś* “*the land of Kꜣś* (later Kush)” (**Ta ’-kwuʂ(a)*, realized by the Egyptians as *Ta ’-k(w)urs(a)*), which would then pertain to *Kerma ancien* (Schneider 2015; for *Kerma ancien*, see now Bonnet 2019).

inscriptions used Meroïtic (Soba Nubian: Rilly 2011, 495-7; Rilly 2019, 138) or Greek (inscription by king Silko on the façade of the temple of Kalabsha on the occasion of his victory over the Blemmyes: Edwards 2004, 197-8; Dann 2009, 21; Rilly 2019, 138; for a discussion of multilingualism and multiscripturalism in medieval Nubia, see Ochała 2014). It uses the Coptic alphabet with additional characters derived from Meroïtic (ⳡ for /ŋ/, ⳟ for /ɲ/, ⳣ for /w/; Smagina 2017, 23-4). The relatively few preserved Old Nubian texts comprise literary (including Biblical), liturgical and documentary texts, the longest being an Old Nubian translation of Pseudo-Chrysostom's "Sermon on the Venerable Cross" *[In venerabilem crucem sermo],* from Serra East in Lower Nubia (see van Gerven Oei and Tsakos 2020, who also discuss the use of Old Nubian as a *literary koinē* and a possible diglossia situation with vernacular Old Nubian).
There is a consensus that the speakers of Old Nubian would have migrated into the Nile Valley only since the beginning of the Egyptian New Kingdom (c. 1500 BCE; Bechhaus-Gerst 1984, 81-4 and 103-6; El-Sayed 2011, 51-2). This view has been based on evidence of linguistic interference as well as the presumed first appearance of depictions of negroid individuals around the time of the archaeological disapperance of the C-group (El-Sayed 2011, 51-2 who admits, however [n. 267], that Black Africans are already present in the art of the Middle Kingdom; for the bioarchaeological problems of establishing a population history for Nubia, see Binder 2019).
The linguistic evidence for interference with Nubian during the Late Period and earlier times is scarce. Due to the very late written attestation of Old Nubian, some of that interference is only visible through the prism of Napatan and Meroïtic with the assumption of (Proto-)Old Nubian as a substrate language. E.g., *tgr*, "ring" is a loanword from Nubian in Napatan (see p. 28). Classifiers used after some Meroïtic words appear sometimes to associate a similar sound sequence in (Proto-)Old Nubian (Breyer 2014b, 199; 2012, 137-140). While Zibelius-Chen's 2011 monograph does not provide any single certain (Proto-) Old Nubian name or lexeme in Egyptian sources from the New Kingdom

through the Meroïtic period, Kerstin Weber and Petra Weschenfelder (2005) have pointed to a noun *mr/mol* "proximity" as part of a compound preposition in the Nastasen stele. Another example may be the term *Kalasiris* (on which see most recently, Vittmann 2019, nn. 3622-7 with literature; first attested in Pap. Lansing 2,3 as *kꜣ-r-iꜣ* *[foreign classifier]* *šri* "youngster" (> Demotic *glšr* "soldier, warrior" [CDD G, 61-2], Coptic ϭⲁⲗⲁϣⲓⲣⲉ "strong man, giant"). I now prefer to explain the initial element of this term as Old Nubian ⳟⲁⲗ/ŋal/ "boy" (as opposed to Schneider 1992, 284-5, where I suggested a Semitic etymology whose /r/ is difficult to account for).

An intriguing fact is that a number of Egyptian loan words in Old Nubian (Peust 1999a, 226; Breyer 2014b, 199) show a Paleo-Coptic vocalization, like in the case of Meroïtic (see above pp. 34-5, also for the term 'Paleo-Coptic'):

- ⳟⲁⲡ /ŋab/ „gold" (> Nobiin náb) < Egyptian *nā́bə (but > Coptic ⲛⲟⲩⲃ nṳ́β);
- ⲟⲣⲡ /orp/ "wine" < Egyptian *ỉṳ́rəp (but > Coptic ⲏⲣⲡ ērp);
- ⲥⲁⲓⲧⲉ /saite/ „olive" < Egyptian *č̣ait (but > Coptic ϫⲟⲉⲓⲧ tʸoit)

These names and words must therefore have been borrowed into a local form of Nubian during the New Kingdom, at the latest, and thus preserved the archaic vocalization pattern. Alternatively, they may reflect more recent borrowings from a dialect characterized by an archaizing vocalization or a transfer via early Meroïtic or Napatan Egyptian.

On account of an assumed migration of speakers of (Proto-)Old Nubian to the Middle Nile valley only after 1500 BCE, El-Sayed has rejected evidence for (Proto-)Old Nubian in earlier Egyptian sources (2011, 52-5). For a number of foreign personal names documented in sources of the Middle Kingdom, such a linguistic affiliation continues to be plausible, even though it cannot be proven. I mention, e.g., *wntt* and the Old Nubian personal name ⲟⲩⲉⲛⲧⲁ; *w-ỉ-t* and Old Nubian ⲟⲩⲉⲓⲧ *wit,* Nobiin *ūwitti* "second(-born)" (Schneider 2003a, 136; 137-8; these and additional onomastic suggestions in Breyer 2014b, 198).

2.2.2.2.2 Saharan languages

2.2.2.2.2.1 Western Saharan: Teda/Daza

Teda and the related Daza are a branch of the Saharanic languages, spoken to this day in Southern Libya, Eastern Niger, and Northern Chad. Egypt's connection to these regions has become obvious through the discovery and systematic exploration of the Abu Ballas trail which leads from the oasis of Kharga in a straight line towards the Gebel Uweinat and Gilf Kebir (now fully documented in the monograph by Förster [2017]). It is assumed that speakers of Proto-Saharan were present in this region since 7,000 BCE (Blench 2006, 95-108).

In a 2010 article, I suggested that Egyptian imaginations of the first three hours of the underworld (the access to which was located in Egypt's far West) were informed by the ancient paleo-ecology of Northern Chad (Schneider 2010 and 2011; see also Cooper 2017b, 383). I posited that two terms – the designation of the Egyptian chaos serpent Apophis (ʿꜣpp) and the name of the sweet water lake of the 2nd hour of the night (wrnś) – were borrowings from Teda/Daza. The relevant expressions from Teda/Daza belong to the excellent and good, respectively, Nilo-Saharan isoglosses established by Lionel M. Bender for the proto-language (Bender 1997, 81 [21.] and 78 [6.]).

- <ʿꜣpp> would have corresponded to a sound sequence /d-r-p-p/ in the First Intermediate Period (c. 2100 BCE) when the term is first attested; the proposed etymology is **dúro bu bu* "very big snake" (positively received by Hornung 2005, 78; Breyer 2014b, 203; Cooper 2017a, 82; Cooper 2020a, 110; more sceptical is Klotz 2007).
- The term *Wernes* (wr-n-s) may have been pronounced as *wūd ̆ì-ìensəu̯* (after Egyptian *wr-nś(w)* "The king is great"). Explained (or translated?) in the 2nd Hour of the Book Amduat (l. 307) as *n.t rʿ* "water expanse of the sun", it could be a transcription of the Teda phrase f^{w}*ódi–yezze–u* with the identical meaning, "water expanse of the sun" (also taken up by Cooper 2017a, 82).

As a possible example of a technological and linguistic transfer from Egypt, Julien Cooper has suggested that the Egyptian word for "lead, tin" *(čḥw.tỉ* >

ṯḥw.tỉ; Demotic *ṯḥṯḥ*, Coptic ^{S}ⲧⲁϩⲧ, ^{F}ⲧⲉϩⲧ, ^{S}ⲧⲁⲑ, ^{B}ⲧⲁⲧϩ) was borrowed into Teda *tuta*, Maba (a Nilo-Saharan language in Southeast Chad and neighboring Sudan) *tutu* "tin", *tuuta(i)k* "lead" (Cooper 2017a, 82).

2.2.2.2.2.2 Eastern Saharan: Beria

In the context of early contacts with Africa, it may be interesting to point to Eastern Saharan (Beria [Zaghawa]) ɟɔrbʊ "elephant" (Khidir 2001, 20; <jerbo> in Blench 2011) as an alternative etymology for Egyptian *ꜣbw* "elephant (also, place name "Elephantine"; /rbw/; mostly connected with East/Central Cushitic *'arb,* "elephant": Takács 1999, 103; differently Breyer 2003a). In this case, the initial /y/ of the word's later form (hieroglyphic *ỉꜣbw,* Demotic *yb,* Aramaic yēβ, Coptic ⲓⲏⲃ yēβ "Elephantine"; Locher 1999, 23-4) would not be a secondary development (Peust 1999a, 143-4, 303) but a reflection of the historical consonantic onset (proto-form *<ỉꜣbw> /yurb(u)w/ > /yu'b(u)/ > /yūβ/ > /yēβ/).

2.2.2.3 Afro-Asiatic languages in Africa

2.2.2.3.1 Cushitic languages and Omotic

2.2.2.3.1.1 Northern Cushitic: Old Beɖawiye (Blemmyan) and the language of the Medjay

Old Beɖawiye – the language of the Blemmyes – is now widely accepted as the historical predecessor of the modern Beja language (Kirwan 2002, 196; Browne 2004; El-Sayed 2004, 354; El-Sayed 2011, 34-6; Breyer 2021, 127-30). On the basis of comparisons of Blemmyan personal names with Beja words, Claude Rilly has recently claimed that "[t]he Blemmyan language is so close to modern Beja that it is probably nothing else than an early dialect of the same language" (Rilly 2019, 134). This is certainly a premature judgment in the absence of any corpus of Blemmyan texts – apart from personal names in late antique sources, Old Beɖawiye/Blemmyan is known only from a tiny rest (c. 15 words) of one single text: an ostracon in Old Nubian script from the 7th c. CE comprising parts of a translation of Psalm 30 (Browne 2003; 2004; Wedekind

2010; Breyer 2014b, 195-7; Breyer 2021, 267-8).

Beja *(Beɖawiye=t, Tu-beɖawiye)*, the only constitutent language of North Cushitic, is spoken by more than one million people, most of whom live in eastern Sudan, but also northern Eritrea, with a small number of speakers left in southeastern Egypt. There is little dialectal variation; the two main geographical varieties are a Northern one (*mi:m'h-i=t be'ɖawiye*) and a Southern one (*ga:'ʃ-i=t be'ɖawiye*), with a transitional variety around Sinkat (Vanhove 2014, 4; the Sinkat variety described by Vanhove 2017). The earlier scholarly subdivision along tribal groups (cf. Gragg 2001, 574) is mirrored, however, by a similar perception by modern Beja speakers (Vanhove 2006, 4-5).

In the context of our interest in the interference with ancient Egyptian, two questions are relevant, namely whether (Proto-)Old Beɖawiye can be identified with the language of the Medjay (Mč̣ꜣy.w) of the Egyptian evidence, and what the extent and antiquity was of the interference of (Proto-)Old Beɖawiye and Egyptian. While there is substantial consensus to the effect that (Proto-)Old Beɖawiye can be identified with the language of the Medjay (e.g., El-Sayed 2004; El-Sayed 2011, 36-41; Zibelius-Chen 2006; Rilly 2019, 132), this hypothesis is actually very fragile. A central argument comes from Papyrus Bulaq 18, an accountancy document of the mid-13th dynasty (c. 1750 BCE: Miniaci and Quirke 2009, 342; new edition Allam 2019). It also records the court visit of a delegation of Medjay to Thebes, listing the name of a "chieftain of the Medjay" of *ꜥwšq, K-w-y*. This (admittedly very brief) proper name has been equated by El-Sayed with Beɖawiye *kʷāya,* "friend, companion" (2004, 360-1; 2011, 279). A second argument is derived from a hieroglyphic inscription next to the depiction of a Pan-grave warrior on a bucranion from Mostagedda grave 3252, a grave containing a total of 40 bucrania. Here, *Q-s-kꜣ-n-t* is inscribed in a rectangle (Schneider 2003a, 187-8; Morris 2018a, 98-9; Cooper and Barnard 2017 propose to read *Q-s-mi-ꜣ-n-t* although the sequence *mi-ꜣ* would be highly unusual in group writing). This is the only linguistic sequence from an object of the Pan-grave culture; if the traditional assumption is correct which identifies the Medjay (Mč̣ꜣy.w) of the textual evidence with the archaeologically attested Pan-grave culture, and if the language of the Medjay can be seen as (Proto-)Old Beḏawiye, this sequence would also call for an interpretation from Beḏawiye. Accordingly, El-Sayed has suggested as a possible interpretation a Beḏawiye epithet *kōs-kuna* "lord of horns" (2011, 39 [*k'ās-kuna*], 264-5 [*kōs* > *k'os?-kuna*]; cf. 2004, 362 n. 69: *ko:sa-kuna*; *kōs* is the sg. form, *kōsa* the pl., Reinisch 1895, 148; the <t> would indicate here a vocalic *Auslaut*).

In order to signal that different interpretations from other languages might be equally viable, I mention that a cognate of the Beḏawiye 'horn' lexeme is also attested in (Lowland East Cushitic) Afar *gaysá* (Morin 2012, 440; Saho *gašša:* Vergari and Vergari 2007, 36) where there exists a collective noun *gōniytá* – a "nom de tribu (ancienne), synonyme de 'guerriers féroces'" (Morin 2012, 458). Therefore, **gaysággōniytá* (with <t> in *Q-s-k-ꜣ-n-t* as the rendering of an actual consonant; Afar's genitival –h would be assimilated to the second noun: Kamil 2015, 145, 172) might be postulated to mean "horn warriors". Such a hypothetical possibility would provide support to the recent critique of an identity of the Pan-grave people and the Medjay (Barnard 2009; Liszka 2015).

Recently, Cooper has suggested Cushitic etymologies for names of the Nubian wives of Mentuhotep II, most convincingly in the case of *Mkḥn.t*, which "perfectly matches the Cushitic lexical root *kḥn* (to love), known in Beja, Saho-Afar, and Somali, with a common Afroasiatic nominali-zing m-prefix appended to the root" (2020, 7; see also Cooper 2021).

From the New Kingdom and later, there is clear evidence for interference between Egyptian and (Proto-)Old Beḏawiye.[4] With the introduction of the horse to the south, the Egyptian word *ḥtr* > *ḥtỉ* "span of horses > horse" (> Coptic SϩΤΟ *hto* "horse") was borrowed into (Proto-)Old Beḏawiye as *hatāy* (pl. *hatay*) (Vycichl 1960, 260-1; El-Sayed 2011, 35; also for other possible loanwords

[4] Breyer (2018) proposes that the Egyptian suffix pronoun *=f* was borrowed as a genus marker from the adstrate language Tu-Beḏawiye. This would have had to occur in prehistoric times for which the areal linguistic situation is even less clear than in the 3rd-1st mill. BCE.

from Egyptian; Peust 1999a, 72, 255), a vocalization that reveals a possible transfer of the term in the Egyptian New Kingdom.

(Proto-)Old Beɖawiye may be present in proper names attested in Egyptian sources of the 1st millennium BCE and earlier. E.g., names of members of the Kushite 25th dynasty may contain a (Proto-)Old Beɖawiye word for "lord, god" (Blemmyan ⲭⲁⲣⲁ, Beɖawiye *hád'a*), to mention a son of king Piye/Piankhy, *Piye/Piankhy-ḥꜣ-rw,* "Piye/Piankhy is lord (?)" (Schütte and Schneider 2019, 79). A frequent element of Nubian toponyms in Egyptian transcription, *ꞽ-b /ab(a)-/,* can arguably be connected with Beɖawiye, *ˀaba*, "wadi" (El-Sayed 2004, 359-60). On one of the stelae of 'Nubian' soldiers from Gebelein from the First Intermediate Period (c. 2100 BCE), an individual carries the name *ꞽ-h-t-k,* which has been equated with the Blemmyan name ⲉⲓⲁϩⲁⲧⲉⲕ *yahatek* (El-Sayed 2004, 358-9; 2011, 156-7). Names of the formation *animal name+tak* "man" are regular in Blemmyan onomastics; in the present case I suggest to understand *ꞽ-h-t-k = (y)ihattak* with assimilation < *(y)ihā́m-tak "leopard man"* (ihā́m: Reinisch 1895, 11; yǐham: Hudson 2013, 159). El-Sayed uses this example to argue that the Medjay people spoke (Proto-)Old Beɖawiye. The Gebelein individual actually uses the other term for 'Nubian', *nḥśꞽ,* conventionally believed to be a designation of the C-group, and secondarily also presumed to be used in a generic way (El-Sayed 2011, 221-2, who thinks the donor language for the term *nḥśꞽ* was the A-group; see for an etymological suggestion p. 19). In turn, the Beɖawiye homonym *ihā́m/ yihā́m* "eagle" may be a late loanword from Egyptian *ᶜẖm*, Coptic S ⲁϩⲱⲙ , B ⲁϧⲱⲙ *aẖōm* "falcon" (Reinisch 1895, 242; Vycichl 1960, 261, 264; Tákacs 1999, 173).

It may be instructive to demonstrate the difficulty of identifying (Proto-)Old Beɖawiye in Egyptian sources on a text that has been posited to be in an early form of Beɖawiye, in a late 20th dynasty papyrus in the British Museum (Pap. BM EA 75025 rto). If confirmed, this text would predate the ostracon in Old Beɖawiye mentioned above (p. 41) by some 1800 years. Here, an Egyptian scribe on expedition in Nubia seems to have effaced an earlier letter and written down a text in syllabic writing with many 'foreign word' classifiers – since his letters refer to an illness, it is likely a magical spell (Demarée, Leach and Usick 2006, 27-8 with pl. 27; Zibelius-Chen 2011, 260). As the scribe was in Nubia and "so far, no certain connection with any Semitic language has been established" (Demarée, Leach and Usick 2006, 27), the spell was presumed to be in a contemporaneous language of Nubia. Most recently, Rilly argued that "[t]he passage in local language includes a sequence of three words *(kst rst nst)* ending with -t which could be a feminine marker, known in all the Afro-Asiatic languages. The presence of /f/ in the text points more precisely toward a Cushitic language. Finally, the spell begins with a first word *sq*, which is reminiscent of Beja *sigi* (masc.), *siga* (fem.) 'go away!' " (Rilly 2014, 1171; cf. 2019, 132). While the first argument may be valid, the second argument is not generally true. As a matter of fact, the spirant <f> shows up in the Egyptian transcriptions of Semitic words (e.g., of the root *rp'*, "to heal", both in the Middle and New Kingdom), and in the context of this spell, the beginning of line 2, *tỉ-r-f-ỉ*, could be a perfect rendering of Semitic *tirfə'i* (vocalization of the Hebrew Qal Impf.), "you (2. Sg. f.) heal/have healed". The third argument is unlikely; the place of the Egyptian classifier (word divider) shows that the initial word is actually *śꜣ-qꜣ-r*. The three consonants might then again point to a Semitic root. At any rate, (Proto-)Old Beḏawiye cannot be confirmed as the spell's language.

2.2.2.3.1.2 Other Cushitic languages and Omotic

The evidence for Egyptian interference with Cushitic languages other than Beja (North Cushitic) is problematic. Two 6th dynasty lexemes for "sorghum" formerly posited to be loanwords from Cushitic were **mś-w-q* (Bechhaus-Gerst 1989, 97-8; Schneider 2004, 14; Peust 2008, 399; Breyer 2012b, 206; Breyer 2014b, 202) and **śꜣt* (Breyer 2014b, 202). They both result from misreadings; the correct forms of the two words are *mśw.t* and *šśꜣt* (El-Sayed 2011, 42 n.192 and 241; Breyer 2012b, 207).

The etymology of the much-discussed Egyptian term for "dwarf, pygmy" – Old

Kingdom *ṯng / ṯ꜡g / ṯ꜡ng*, in New Kingdom syllabic orthography *ṯ-n-r-g-꜡* – is still not resolved conclusively. It is most often correlated with a Cushitic (Qemant *dink,* Awiya *dinki,* Oromo *dinkii,* Sidamo *dinke*, Hadiya pl. *dink'e*), Omotic (*dinkoo*), Ethio-Semitic (Amharic *dənk*, Tigriña *denkit*) and Berber (Nefusa *a-denžal*) 'Wanderwort' for dwarf, **dink-* (Takács 1999, 277 with the older literature; Breyer 2012b; Takács 2013, 575-6; Breyer 2016, 246-50). This correlation presents the difficulty of the Egyptian emphatic onset /*ṯ*/ and the consistent writing of a middle consonant /l/. By contrast, El-Sayed related it to Agaw *dereŋ* "short" (El-Sayed 2011, 305-6), although Appleyard posited Proto-Agaw **dədəŋ*/*dädäŋ* with /r/ as a secondary development. The etymology must remain open for the time being (see also Cooper 2020b, 102-3). I would not rule out that the term could instead originate in a different language group altogether (e.g., as the endonym of a pygmy population). In this regard, it should be noted that the African pygmy populations have all adopted the languages of the farming societies to which they adopted a client-relationship (equally those closest to Egypt, in the Ituri rainforest of Northeast Congo: the Mbuti, whose subgroups speak Central Sudanic and Bantu languages). Cf. here Bahuchet's assessment: "The question of 'the original Pygmy language' will probably stay unsolved for ever" (Bahuchet 2006, 19).

A Cushitic affiliation has been suggested by some scholars for the language of the empire of Kerma (see p. 48); for the possibility of the Pan-grave language being related to Lowland East Cushitic, see pp. 42-3.

Borrowings from Omotic languages (for the classification of which, see p. 26) are also a possibility A possible late loanword from Omotic, *dongor* "elephant" (see Orel and Stolbova 1995, 652; cf. also East Chadic *dogol*), is Demotic *tnhr* and Ptolemaic *ṯnhr*, "elephant" (CDD T, 249; Zibelius-Chen 2011, 297 with an incorrect reference 'Cushitic': Takács 2013, 576; see in detail Blažek 1994).

2.2.2.3.2 Ethio-Semitic languages

It is uncertain how old the Ethio-Semitic languages in Ethiopia, Eritrea and the

Sudan are (for their position within the Semitic languages, see p. 90). While conventional scholarship has held that Ethio-Semitic was introduced to the region from South Arabia (recently, Kitchen, Ehret, Assefa and Mulligan 2009 argue for a single introduction around 800 BCE), the linguistic evidence could favor the fact that Ethiopia is the place of origin of the Semitic language phylum. Weninger concludes his assessment of the evidence as follows:

> "E[thio-]S[emitic] was therefore an independent subgroup of Semitic already present in Ethiopia when the South Arabian colonists brought their language and culture to Ethiopia. Hence, either E[thio-]S[emitic] should be regarded as having arisen from a much earlier wave of immigration, or Hudson's suggestion (…), based on geo-linguistic arguments and on the principle of archaic heterogeneity that the Ethiopian region is the origin of Semitic, should be considered". (2011b, 1115; similarly Hudson 2013, 38)

The assessment of the antiquity of Ethio-Semitic is clearly paramount for the question of its interference with ancient Egyptian. In turn, the Egyptian lexicon may comprise evidence relevant to the problem. Further research is needed to determine if there are a number of Egyptian–Ethiosemitic isoglosses in Middle Egyptian that could be considered early Egyptian borrowings from Ethio-Semitic languages. If they can be confirmed, this would be a strong argument in support of the hypothesis by Hudson and Weninger. Cf. the following possible cases (Schneider 2003b, 195):

ꜥꜣg "hit, beat"	Ge'ez *ʿallaga*, "defeat, vanquish", Tigre *ʿalläga* "kill in close combat"
wꜥꜣ "to slander, defame"	Geez *waʿara*, "be rough, be coarse" (whereas arab. *waʿara* denotes "rough, uneven" only with regard to terrain!)
śčꜣ "weave, spin"	semit. *šzr*, "to twist (yarn)"
č̣bꜣ "to clog, bar"	semit. *ṣbr*, "to pile up; to tie up"
fnč̣ "nose" may also be of interest (not in Schneider 2003b)	Gurage *fənč̣ä, fīnč̣ä*, "forehead"

Several scholars (Breyer, Cooper, Tákacs) have recently reaffirmed the possibility that the language of Punt (or one of the languages spoken in the region of Punt) might have been related to Ethio-Semitic, which would be another piece of evidence in support of a genuine homeland of the Ethio-Semitic languages in Ethiopia (see the next paragraph 2.2.2.3.3 for further comments).

2.2.2.3.3 Hypotheses about other languages

(The languages of Kerma Ancien/Iam, Kerma Moyen, A-group, C-group, the Pan-grave Culture, Punt)

Different hypotheses have been advanced for languages spoken by the carriers of other prominent cultures attested archaeologically and/or textually. Many caveats are in place here: not only do we not have any approximate knowledge of the complex linguistic situation in the Sudan in the time periods under discussion here, it is also plausible that a material culture attested archaeologically could have been shared by different linguistic groups (see pp. 15-6). The following paragraph provides only a snapshot of a complex modern discussion.

El-Sayed has posited Cushitic for the language of 'Kerma ancien' (dynasties 6-12, c. 2300-1900 BCE), whereas with the ensuing 'Kerma Moyen' = Kush, Nilosaharan (Proto-Meroïtic) groups would have superseded the Cushitic ones in Upper Nubia (El-Sayed 2011, 41-46; following Bechhaus-Gerst). The linguistic evidence is limited to the toponym correlated with 'Kerma ancien', *ỉmꜣ*/ Yam, and two subunits, *ỉmꜣ-wtn.t* and *ỉmꜣ-nʿś*, as well as three personal names whose phonology looks Afroasiatic (El-Sayed 2011, 46, 144, relating *ỉmꜣ* to Central Cushitic [Agaw] *murí,* "village"; different Cooper [2012, 4]: Western Desert location of Yam near Gebel Uweinat/Ennedi, with a Teda etymology).

With the majority of researchers, El-Sayed distinguishes from these Cushitic speakers the C-group (2011, 19-20, 47-8). By contrast, Rilly has posited that the language of the C-group, like Meroïtic and the language of Kerma/Kush, belonged to Northern East Sudanic (Rilly 2019, 130-1) but this seems impossible on phonological grounds (Cooper 2017b, 205). Cooper finds possible etymologies of some Lower Nubian toponyms of the Middle and New Kingdom in North Cushitic (Cooper 2017b, 206, e.g., *Mỉ ʿm* = Beḏawiye *maiyyam,* "low lying land"). Similarly, El-Sayed postulates a Cushitic idiom for the language of the A-group (which settled Lower Nubia between 3800-2800 BCE), possibly preserved in the substrate of Lower Nubian toponyms and ethnonyms such as *stỉ, nḥś, wꜣwꜣ.t* etc. (El-Sayed 2011, 47, 178, connecting *wꜣwꜣ.t* with East Cushitic *walwal*, "pays découvert et aride"; cf. Cooper 2017b, 201). As mentioned above (p. 18), the presumed identity of the Pan-grave people with the Medjay, whose language would be a predecessor of Blemmyan and modern Beḏawiye, has been called into doubt. For the only certain Pan-grave word or phrase attested in our documentation, *Q-s-k-ꜣ-n-t*, a Lowland East Cushitic (Afar) interpretation – as *gaysággōniytá,* "horn warriors" – instead of a North Cushitic (Beḏawiye) one might equally be feasible (see p. 43).

Controversial is also the discussion about the presumptive language of the country of Punt, Egypt's provider with frankincense and other exotic products. There is a certain consensus about the location for Punt, for which I quote the summary by Breyer:

> "Much more convincing is the proposal of Fattovich, who connected P[unt] with the cultures of Eritrea, northern Ethiopia and south-eastern Sudan, especially with the culture of the Gaš delta. He brought into relief the steady contacts the cultures of Nubia (C Group), southern Sudan/northern Ethiopia (Atbara ceramics tradition: Butana, Gaš, Aqordat and Gabal Mokram groups), Eritrea (Ona culture A) and southern Arabia (Tihama culture) had among themselves and with Egypt. Evidence offered by rock art, ceramics and trade objects suggests a localization of P[unt] in the wider region around the rivers Gaš and Barka…The Puntite port should be therefore localized between Port Sudan and Asmära, with P[unt] stretching from the wider Gaš/ Barka lowlands to the Red Sea coast." (Breyer 2009, 241; also see Breyer 2016, 590-3; similar recent assessment by Cooper 2020b, 299-330).

Interestingly, recent scholarship has entertained the idea that the language of Punt could be Ethio-Semitic (Cooper 2020b, 411-3 with a list of etymologies for toponyms). The personal name of the ruler of Punt in the report about Hatshepsut's expedition in her funerary temple in Deir el-Bahari, *Pꜣ-r-h-w*, could by explained by Ethio-Semitic *frh* (<*prh) "to fear": Ge'ez *fəruh* "feared", *farāhi* "fearful, reverent" (Tákacs 2013, 573; Cooper 2020b, 100; differently Breyer 2014a, 6-7; Breyer 2016, 525-6 who compares the root *brh* and the Aksumite royal name *Abrəha*). The etymology of the toponym 'Punt' itself remains unknown (for the discussion, Breyer 2016, 12-4; Cooper 2020b, 277-9). One 'Puntite' sentence in hieroglyphic transcription is preserved in the texts of the festival of Min in the funerary temples of Ramesses II and III, the Ramesseum and Medinet Habu, as well as two late copies in the temple of Ptolemy XII at Athribis (synopsis by Carolina Teotino in Leitz 2017, 293). Here, a caption above the depiction of a (priest playing a) Puntite reads: "The spells of recitation – what the African (*nḥśi͗*) from Punt says". Embedded in an otherwise Egyptian text, we encounter the foreign sequence *b-ꜣ-wn-t-nw-y-ꜣ-wn-t-nw-y* (Gauthier 1931, 220-1; Medinet Habu IV, pl. 203, l. 20-1, 28-9; pl. 213, l. 46–48). While it is clearly entirely speculative to propose an interpretation across the time distance, Ethio-Semitic interpretations are possible (among others, cf. Amharic *bäwənu yawənna* "In actual fact, there he is!" – with <t> as vowel indicator; *bäwənu* "in actual fact, actually" (Kane 1990, 927), *yawənna* "behold, there is (m.), there he is!" (Kane 1990, 1688). This could be an exclamation during the festival (cf. Quack's view that the phrase was "fixed as liturgical formula", "for the Egyptians of the New Kingdom, it can hardly have been more than pure sound without intrinsic meaning" [2009, 318]).

2.2.2.3.4 Proto-Berber languages

With regard to the linguistic situation on Egypt's western border, a common assumption has been that earlier stages of the Berber languages of modern North Africa and its probably antique predecessor, Ancient Libyan, can be posited for some of the 'Libyan' populations attested in Egyptian sources. Most recently, Rafed El-Sayed's review has affirmed this assumption diachronically for the 'Libyans' until the 14th c. BCE, most likely also those of the 3rd and earlier 2nd millennium. He has also emphasized the likelihood that the Tjehenu-

Libyans and Tjemehu-Libyans were linguistically related (El-Sayed 2011, 17-27). By contrast, one of the leading current Berber scholars, Manfred Kossmann, holds that the Libyans of the western desert of Egypt who are mentioned in the Egyptian evidence were not speakers of (Proto-)Berber (Kossmann 2020) or at the very least, that there is no positive proof to that effect (Kossmann 1999, 16; Kossmann 2013, 56-7). In the following review of the evidence, I will dispute this assumption and reaffirm El-Sayed's assessment through a review of the linguistic and contextual evidence, while adding to the debate a number of new etymologies and interpretations.

2.2.2.3.4.1 Questions of terminology: "Berber", "Proto-Berber", "Ancient Libyan"

In the French tradition of Berber linguistics, the traditional position has been to see the different regional varieties of Berber as dialects of one language (Kossmann 1999, 15; one example is Chaker 2003), although a leading French scholar such as Lionel Galand has also spoken of "langues berbères" (Galand 1989; for the discussion, Breyer 2021, 31-3). Maarten Kossmann considers the linguistic variety within Berber as comparable to Germanic or Romance languages (Kossmann 1999, 15; Kossmann 2020). He classifies the Berber languages into these seven distinct groups:

1. *Zenaga block* (Zenaga of Mauritania, Tetserrét in Niger);
2. *Tuareg block*;
3a. *Western Moroccan block* (SW Morocco, Central Morocco, i.e., Tashelhiyt and most of Tamazight);
3b. *Possibly including NW Moroccan Berber* (Ghomara, Senhadja de Sraïr);
4. *Zenatic block* (Eastern Morocco, Western Algeria, Saharan oases, Tunisia, Zuara) extending towards the east with Sokna, Elfoqaha, Siwa;
5. *Kabyle* (N Algeria), possibly linked to the western Moroccan block;
6. *Ghadames* (Libya), probably to be linked to Djebel Nefusa (Libya) ;
7. *Awdjilah* (Libya).

In a diachronic perspective, the reconstructed language predating the differentiation into the individual dialects would be "Proto-Berber" (Kossmann 1999, 20; Galand 2002-3, 262; Breyer 2021, 35: "voraltlibysch"). Proposed dates for this proto-language vary between 4500 BCE, 2000 BCE, the first millennium BCE or later (Kossmann 2020). However, subsequent phases of "convergence, koineization, differentiation and mutual influence" over the past two thousand years have made it methodologically questionable whether a Proto-Berber language as such can be reconstructed (Kossmann 2020; cf. Galand 2010, 14; Múrcia Sànchez 2010, II, 905-1107 for an exhaustive discussion of "preamazic, protoamazic, paleoamazic"). With regard to the obvious linguistic similarities between Berber languages such as those of Siwa in Egypt, of the Rif in Morocco or of the Zenaga in Senegal, Werner Vycichl emphasized:

> "Hier handelt es sich meinem Dafürhalten nach zum großen Teil um Züge, die dem Berberischen nicht von Anfang eigen waren und sich erst in historischer Zeit wie ein Mantel über die zahlreichen örtlichen Verschiedenheiten breiteten und nun den trügerischen Eindruck einer ursprünglichen Gleichförmigkeit hervorrufen." (Vycichl 1961, 243).

In a recent discussion of the critique of the concept of Proto-Berber, Kossmann ponders the similarities as the result of a *koineization* process; however, the date of that process remains entirely unclear (Kossmann 2013, 51-6).

Particularly salient to the question of Proto-Berber is the assessment of ancient Libyan, the language of the Libyan inscriptions from Classical antiquity. Otto Rössler saw ancient Libyan as the historical precursor of the Berber languages and Libyan-Berber typologically as an early form of a Semitic language, with Akkadian as its closest correlate (Rössler 1952, 121; 1964, 199-200). In his vein, Burkart Kienast treated Libyan-Berber as one language continuum, to the extent that he labelled Medieval Berber "Middle Libyan" and the modern Berber languages, "Neo-Libyan" (Kienast 2001, 539-40). In his monumental doctoral thesis on ancient Libyan, Carles Múrcia Sànchez chose to adopt the modern designation for "Berber" (*Amazigh*, language: *Tamazight*) for ancient Libyan ('La llengua amaziga'; Múrcia Sànchez 2010). Also, Salem Chaker has advocated for Libyan to be a clear predessor of Berber (equally Pichler 1998,

17); in his view, in particular the personal names of the Libyan inscriptions are 'undeniably Berber' (Chaker 1984, 53).

Other scholars have been more cautious (Breyer 2021, 34-5). Kossmann (2020) recognizes in ancient Libyan "clear parallels with Berber", but emphasizes that it is difficult to define the relationship precisely. Similarly, Lionel Galand underlines the nexus between Libyan and "les parlers berbères actuels, qu'il faut bien considérer comme l'état présent de la même langue, puisque rien ne signale leur arrivée en Afrique à époque historique" (Galand 2002-3, 259). However, he criticizes the sometimes illusionary imposition of modern Berber morphology and vocabulary onto the ancient evidence, across two millennia (and with regard to Otto Rössler, also the imposition of Semitic linguistic features; Galand 2002-3, 263-5). Galand also emphasizes that there may have been other unknown autochthonous languages of North Africa that would have influenced Proto-Berber (Galand 2002-3, 260).

While the ancient Libyan and medieval Berber linguistic and onomastic evidence provides some help, it is impossible to gain a reliable reconstruction of the phonological or lexical situation of Proto-Berber at the time of the 3rd-1st millennia of Egyptian civilization. E.g., Kossmann's reconsruction of a Proto-Berber phonology from the modern consonantal situation does not account for the comparative Afroasiatic evidence; the assumed loss of Afroasiatic consonants of posterior articulation from Proto-Berber to modern Berber (Rössler 1952, 128-30; Galand 1988, 120; Chaker 1995, 237-9; Colin 1995-6, I, 179; Kienast 2001, 529) is thus not factored into his reconstruction.

For the purpose of the following remarks, I will use the term "Protoberber" to designate an early form of the modern Berber languages contemporary with the ancient Egyptian civilization, and "Proto-Berbers", for the speakers of that language. I will use the term "Libyan", in accordance with current Egyptological usage, with reference to various population groups mentioned in Egyptian texts as living to the West and Southwest of Egypt, irrespective of their ethnic or linguistic identity.

2.2.2.3.4.2 Evidence since antiquity for the presence of Berber speakers on Egypt's Western periphery

The only Berber-speaking region on the modern state territory of Egypt is the oasis of Siwa (for its modern Berber dialect, see Laoust 1932; Vycichl 2005; Souag 2013; Schiattarelli 2016; Serreli 2018). The antiquity of Siwa Berber is generally accepted, although there seems to be a consensus that the language has been impacted by substantial later migration, and that diachronically, multiple layers of Siwi have been superimposed (Múrcia Sànchez 2010, I, 75-88). The oldest explicit reference to the language is Herodotus (II 42) who speaks about "the Ammonians, who are colonists from Egypt and Ethiopia [t.i., Nubia, TS] and speak a language half-way between (the languages of) both" ('Αμμώνιοι, ἐόντες Αἰγυπτίων τε καὶ Αἰθιόπων ἄποικοι καὶ φωνὴν μεταξὺ ἀμφοτέρων νομίζοντες; Múrcia Sànchez 2010, I, 13, 76-7). Given that the Tjemehu-Libyans are inhabitants of the Nubian Western desert of Egypt (see pp. 11-2), "Ethiopian" could arguably be a term used here for a variety of Berber.

Not at Siwa, but at the near oasis of al-Arag, a number of potentially Libyan names are preserved (Múrcia Sànchez 2010, I, 77-8). A millennium later, the vita of Samuel of Qalamun from 633 CE mentions raids out of the oasis of Siwa of 'ⲙⲁⲥⲅⲝ who talk in their language", using a term that is most obviously the same as Greek Μάζικες and modern Berber *imaziġen,* "Berber (pl.)" (Múrcia Sànchez 2010, I, 79, 83-4). For the other oases – Kharga, Dakhla, Bahriya, Farafra – we do not have an ancient statement similar to the one by Herodotus on Siwa; the term "oasitai" may be identical in meaning to the "Libyes Aegyptii" mentioned in Greek and Latin sources (Múrcia Sànchez 2010, I, 88-9). With regard to the Western delta, Herodotus mentions that the inhabitants of the cities of Marea and Apis considered themselves Libyans (II, 18), which may also have meant the use of Proto-Berber (Múrcia Sànchez 2010, I, 97-8), and the likelihood of a Berber community exists also for the Fayyum, at least in late antiquity (Múrcia Sànchez 2010, I, 100-2).

Conspicuous is the epigraphic picture. The most recent comprehensive assessment by Y. and C. Gauthier of the more than 1200 chariot inscriptions and the more than 1000 sites with Libyan–Berber inscriptions in the Sahara (Gauthier and Gauthier 2011) shows that there is an almost total agreement in the distribution of chariot and alphabet attestations. While the youngest of the chariot depictions may overlap chronologically with the oldest alphabet inscriptions, in general, the chariot attestations predate the alphabetic ones. Importantly, there exist virtually no chariot depictions and no Libyan-Berber inscriptions between the Tenere and the Nile Valley (Gauthier and Gauthier 2011, 93-4, 106-8; Pichler 2007, 105-8; Múrcia Sànchez 2010, I, 56-60).[5]

2.2.2.3.4.3 Proto-Berber linguistic evidence in Egyptian sources of the Graeco-Roman Period

Texts of the Graeco-Roman period show some definitive evidence for Egyptian–Proto-Berber language contact (Múrcia Sànchez 2010, I, 65-6; Breyer 2014b, 200-1). The clearest example is *(tꜣ) mrt* "chin; beard" (demot. *mrṱ*, Coptic ^{SB}ⲙⲟⲣⲧ, ^{F}ⲙⲁⲗⲧ < berb. *(ta-)mart* "beard". The preserved ending *–t* in the Egyptian forms shows that this must be a late loan (Vycichl 1983, 120; Peust 1999a, 131; Takács 2008, 447-9; Knigge 2004, 55). Another example may be *ꜥmn* (Wb. I 185,6; written in syllabic writing as *ꜥ-m ꜣ-n-ỉ*) (Möller 1913, 32) in the Hieratic version of the Book of the Dead of Monthesuphis (Pap. Rhind I = National Museum of Scotland in Edinburgh, Inv. A 1956.313; about the text, Cole 2015, 32-4) from year 21 of Augustus, where the Demotic version has the Semitic loanword *brk.t*, "pond (with flowers)" (CDD B, 66). This could be a rendering of Berber *a-man* "water" (with the Berber masculine 'article' *a-* rendered with Egyptian ꜥAyin which by that time had lost its consonan-

---

[5] Three chariot depictions at Qasr el-Zabw north of Bahariya (Gauthier and Gauthier 2011, 102-3 with figs. 23-25); possible inscriptions at Qasr el-Zabw, at Khor Kilobersa and on a lintel at the entrance to the Great Pyramid at Giza (Gauthier and Gauthier 2011, 107-8; the map on fig. 31 has one more site of inscriptions (oasis of Selima) and two locations of chariot depictions (Kosha, Geddi-Sabu) in modern northern Sudan (see also Breyer 2021, 39-40).

tal value; Breyer 2014b, 200-1; Knigge 2004, 56; Takács 2008, 199). In turn, the words for "date" and "date palm" have been proposed to be Berber loans from Egyptian (not loans *from Berber to Egyptian*, as Breyer 2014b, 220-1, says), pointing to the introduction of date palm cultivation from Egypt: Berber *tiyni* (Ghadames: *aβēna,* pl. *βēnawen,* Haddadou 2006/7, *222*; Lanfry 1973, 14*)* "date" < Egyptian *bny(.t),* Coptic [S]ⲃⲛ̄ⲛⲉ (Vycichl 1983, 29; Kossmann 2013, 57; Blench 2021, 7-8 and table 21 on p. 9). Less likely seems Ghadames *azβān* "loose woody tissue around the palm tree stem" (< **a-sban*) < Egyptian *šny-bny(.t)*, Coptic ϣⲛ̄ⲃⲛ̄ⲛⲉ "palm fiber" (Kossmann 2002; Kossmann 2013, 57).

2.2.2.3.4.4 Proto-Berber linguistic evidence from the Third Intermediate and Late Period

Since the 20th dynasty, Libyans played an increasingly significant role in Egypt's society before they assumed political power after the end of the New Kingdom. Among the features often emphasized in the extensive debate about their degree of acculturation (Jansen-Winkeln 2000; 2012 with more literature), are their official adoption of the Egyptian language but adherence to 'Libyan' names, designations emphasizing their foreignness ("chieftains of the Libyans", *ḫꜣsti̓.w* "foreigners"), and ethnic markers (Libyan feather). Rather surprisingly, the foreign personal names of the Libyan rulers and other officials have never been explained comprehensively (cf. Sfaxi 2014, 569-70). To judge by the proper names of the Libyan kings of the 22nd dynasty alone, for which Proto-Berber interpretations can be proposed, it is plausible to assume that at least some of the groups these rulers represented were indeed speakers of Proto-Berber:

(1) For *Wsi̓rkn* (Greek Osorkon) (see Colin 1995-6, II 20-36 for the attestations of the name), the Neo-Assyrian sources give the form *Šilkannu*. Rössler compared the ancient Libyan (Numidian) name *Ślkn* (Rössler 1980, 271). Breyer (2014b, 200) interpreted the name as Proto-Berber *Wsr-kn* "Your eldest one", to be vocalized **Wessar–k(u)n* (adjektive sg. masc. *a-wessar* [Quitout 1997, 64; Haddadou 2006-7, 216]; poss. pronoun 2nd ps.pl. [Kienast 2001, 531, 547-8]),

which suits the Greek form well (Schütte and Schneider 2019, 75; differently Payraudeau 2020 who sees in *w-* a prefix).
(2) For *Takelot* (see Colin 1995-6, II 106-113 for the attestations), a possible ancient Libyan precursor *Tklṯ* has been cited (Vycichl 1961, 246). This appears like a Berber feminine noun (t-…-t) from a root *kl* (or similar), although a feminine noun without the later mandatory prefixe *t-* is also a possibility, in this case from a root *tkl.* A hypothetical etymology for the name is the noun *tekellawt,* "noon, midday" (Haddadou 2006-7, 94; root *klw*). Such a name would have been given to the child after the time when it was born (cf. the Tuareg personal name *takkest,* "afternoon": Aghali-Zakara 2003, 223).
(3) For the remaining name of the 22nd dynasty rulers, Šꜣ-šꜣ-n-q (Neo-Assyrian *^{m}šu-si-in-qu, ^{m}šu-sa-an-qu*; Hebrew *šîšaq*; Greek Σεσογχ-; Sagrillo 2015, 69; Colin 1995-6, II 61-88), so far no interpretation has been attempted. In order to demonstrate that a Proto-Berber explanation is in principle possible, I would like to advance one suggestion from the number of lexemes with genuine /š/ (Kossmann 1999, 221-225): *šišiw* (and similar, see Kossmann 1999, 220; Galand 2002, 401), "hatchling, chick", with the suffixed possessive pronoun of the 1st ps.pl., *-nneɣ*. *Šišiw–nneɣ* "our hatchling, chick" would have been a reference to the newborn child (and in an Egyptian context, may have been perceived as a reference to the young Horus as a falcon hatchling).

Several other proper names of Libyans in Egyptian sources have onomastic parallels in ancient Libyan names (see Colin 1995-6, I, 175-7; Rössler 1980, 271; for other Libyan personal names and ethnonyms attested since the New Kingdom, see pp. 59-61).
The Libyans may also have used a small number of 'Libyan' titles. For a long time, the most prominent has been the purported *ms,* "prince", equated since 1883 (Adolf Erman) with Berber (Tuareg) *məšš/mass*, but also ancient Libyan (Numidian) *ms* "lord" (Yoyotte 1961, 123). While both Berber scholars and Egyptologists often refuted this equation – the Tuareg word belongs to kinship terms which cannot be used by themselves but require a possessive pronoun

(Lionel Galand) and from an Egyptological perspective, the term could actually be *mś*, "child" (Pascal Vernus; for the discussion Colin 1995-6 I, 12-3) –, it has recently found followers in both disciplines (Kossmann 1999, 17; Breyer 2004, 28 and 2014, 200; Takács 2008, 549; Múrcia Sànchez 2010, I, 65; El-Sayed 2011, 20). Other Libyan titles of unknown meaning are *mk* (Yoyotte 1958) and *mtwhr* (Gardiner 1933, 27; Ritner 2009b, 173-178; Hubschmann 2010, 182).

2.2.2.3.4.5 Proto-Berber linguistic evidence from the New Kingdom

In a unique statement on a stele by Ramesses III from chapel C at Deir el-Medineh, the captivated Libyans (Libu and Meshwesh) are said to have been placed "into strongholds of the victorious king, that they might hear the speech of the (Egyptian) people while serving the king. He makes their speech disappear; he overturns their tongues" (Sagrillo 2009, 344, who speaks about 'military re-education centers'). The passage indicates not only the presence of a language (or languages) of the Libyan tribes, but also the importance of language for cultural and political identity. In the Libyan settlements, these languages may have continued to be spoken, despite the enforced acculturation. Unambiguous evidence for a Proto-Berber language and language contact with Proto-Berber also comes from texts of the Ramesside period. Examples are:

(1) A papyrus in the Egyptian Museum in Turin (CGT.54030) contains a Proto-Berber spell in Hieratic against snakes (Silvestri 2022). This papyrus had been known to exist since Ernesto Schiaparelli, who misinterpreted it as containing "Qeheq war chants" (Ritner 2009b, 79 n.1; Múrcia Sànchez 2010, I, 55 n. 219). The *Leitwort* of this text seems to be *a-zrem, a-ẓrem* "snake; tapeworm" (cf. Haddadou 2006-7, 242).

(2) Proto-Berber influence on Egyptian is visible through loanwords in specific lexical categories. The Magical Papyrus Harris from the late 13th century BCE, to give one example, in a spell to keep closed the mouth of predators (lions, jackals or hyenas), contains the term *bꜣ-gꜣ-ỉ-w* (vso. II, 5), clearly a rendering of a precursor of Tuareg *é-beggi, i-beggi*, "jackal" (Schneider 2004, 22). Other suggested loanwords are a Late Egyptian term *ỉ-ś-t-n-nw* "belt, strap", probably related to Berber (Central Morocco) *istawn* of the same meaning (Schneider 2004, 17), and Late Egyptian *swn* (Coptic ⲥⲟⲟⲩⲛ) "to know", from Proto-Berber *swn* (Peust 2013). The foreign term *gꜣ- wꜣ- nꜣ* (classifier V6, 'clothing'; also plural marker) appears as an item that Libyan soldiers leave behind when they flee. I had compared the term with Old Nubian ⲅⲟⲩⲉⲓ- "shield, armor", Nobiin *guñi* "shield" (Schneider 2004, 17); however, given the Libyan origin indicated for the troops and the fact that it seems to be a plural, Berber *a-giwen* (pl.; modern with the prefixed *a-*) "leather buckets" (Haddadou 2006-7, 82) is certainly preferable. Since the Libyans and the Sea Peoples entered into an alliance under Merenptah (who then integrated the male prisoners in his army), a foreign term *ỉwn-n:-m-k-t* used for the 'confederates' or 'confederation' of the Sea Peoples under Ramesses III might arguably be in origin a Libyan term of political organization (tuareg *anālkam* "liegeman; allied people", with metathesis 3-4: Schneider 2008a, 194; for the root Haddadou 2006-7, 121): "Their *ỉwn-n:-m-k-t* (classifier 'house') was the Peleset, Theker, Shekelesh, Denyen and Weshesh, lands united" (MH II pl. 46, 17 = Edgerton and Wilson 1936, 53).

In the official 'poem' about Ramesses III's second Libyan campaign, there is a speech of the Libyan chieftains (of Meshwesh and Tjemeh) reacting to their defeat. It contains a term in their native language: "It is its [Egypt's] *terror* that courses through our bodies" (MH II, pl. 80-83, 39; Redford 2018, 54). The word translated here as "terror", *ẖ-ỉ-m-čꜣ* (**ẖi/e-m-ẓi/e;* classifiers 'break', 'bad': Schneider 2004, 197) would seem to be from the native language of the chieftains. If that language was Proto-Berber, the term would be intriguing for providing the proof that another sound of posterior articulation (the velar fricative /ẖ/) still existed in the language at that time (Schneider 2004, 13; Hebrew *ḥāmās* "violence" fits semantically but has /*ḥ*/, not /*ẖ*/; cf. Arabic *ḥamisa*.).

(3) From the Ramesside and Third Intermediate Periods (c. 1300–700 BCE), a total of c. 80 personal names and ethnonyms identified by the Egyptian texts as 'Libyan' have been collected with all attestations by François Colin (1995-6).

While Colin has not analyzed the names linguistically (Breyer 2021, 37), he has established comparative tables of morphological elements common both to the Egyptian 'Libyan' material and the ancient Libyan onomastic material from North Africa as it is preserved in Libyan and Punic texts as well as Latin and Greek renderings ("rapprochement de séries", I 45-57). This methodology (applied by Otto Rössler in his study of the Numidian variety of ancient Libyan; Rössler 1958) has also been reiterated by Múrcia Sànchez (2010, I, 55-6) and Francis Breyer (2014, 200-1; cf. Galand 2002-3, 260). Some of the repetitive elements that might be analyzed as functionally identically morphemes are:

y-: verbal prefix 3rd ps. sg. masc. – *Ywpt, Ywrỉt, Ywksr, Ywtk, Ysbt, Yknwš.*
t-: verbal prefix 2nd pers. sg. masc. or 3rd ps. sg. fem. – *Twtwỉ, Twtmr, Twtnỉ, Try, Trpny.*
t-…-t: feminine circumfix – *Tnt, Tskrt, Tkrỉt.*
–t: feminine ending – *Wyhst, Wsỉrhrt, Wsšt, Wštht, Btt, Ptt, Mshrt, Msqhrt, Nmrt.*
y-…-n: could indicate a participle – *ywrn, ykn.*
w–: frequent initial element w-, as in Libyan epigraphic sources – *Wyhst, Wykshr, Wyd(y)n, Wsỉrhrt, Wsỉrkn, Wsšt, Wskws, Wstrknỉ, Wštht.*
m–: prefix for noun formation – *Mwsn, Mrly, Mrkwrs, Mshrt, Msqhrt, Mškn, Mksk, Mtwhrỉ, Mdnn.*
-kn: possessive pronoun 2nd ps. pl. – *Wsỉrkn, Wstrknỉ*

It is obvious that some of these cases are open to different interpretations. E.g., in a name like *Try*, the initial <t> can also be part of the root/lexeme. *Wsỉrhrt* and *Wsỉrkn* probably share the same element *Wsỉr*, *Wessar*, "the old/eldest one" (see above, p. 56). The element <hrt> occurs also in *Mshrt* and *Msqhrt* and allows for a segmentation of the latter ones into <ms>/<msq> and <hrt>.
In some cases, individuals characterized explicitly as foreigners in the Egyptian sources have personal names that can be explained as Proto-Berber, e.g., *m-ṭỉ-ṭỉ* (with the 'foreign' classifier; Ranke 1935, 167 [30]; Schneider 1992, 4) = *a-mdiddi* "the brave, courageous one" (attested as an element *mdd* in Libyan personal names; Toudji 93 [51]). Similarly, the name *kꜣ-pw-r* (once again with the

'foreign' classifier; Ranke 1935, 344 [14]) of a Libyan individual has been compared to the ancient Libyan personal name *kpr=sn* (Rössler 1980, 271).

2.2.2.3.4.6 Proto-Berber linguistic evidence from the First Intermediate to the Second Intermediate Period

From the Theban 11th dynasty, we have several documents potentially elucidating Egyptian-Libyan connections. The most famous of them is the "Dog Stele" of king Antef II, displaying the king with five dogs (Arnold 1976; Polz 2019; see also Polz 2014-5, 355 and fig. 6). All five dogs are accompanied by the notation of their foreign names; four of the names are also followed by the classifier 'dog'. In three of the five names, an Egyptian translation (*r č̣ṭ*, "this is to say") is added to the foreign designations. Ever since Gaston Maspero, in 1876, equated one of the untranslated names, *ꜣb-ꜣ-q-r*, with tuareg *abaykor*, "low race dog" (confirmed by Berberologist René Basset in 1896), most scholars assumed the language of the names to be Proto-Berber (for previous scholarship, Schneider 2006, 527-8). Maarten Kossmann recently refuted this and another dog name's etymology (*tqrw*, "basin", with berb. *tagra,* a kind of receptacle) (Kossmann 2011). He has rightly emphasized the fact that if the names cannot be proven to be Proto-Berber, they could also originate in "a language from the Eastern desert or from somewhere else" (2011, 84). His further conclusion to the effect that "there is no positive evidence whatsoever to place speakers of an ancestor language of proto-Berber in the neighbourhood of Ancient Egypt at this period", is not likely correct, given the evidence to the contrary provided in this chapter. A reassessment of the names suggests Proto-Berber interpretations for at least some of them (Schneider 2006; not seen by Kossmann 2011, nor by Múrcia Sànchez 2010, I, 64); it applies the older Egyptian transcription system that was in use in the late 3rd millennium. I single out two suggestions:

(1) "*tqrw*, which is to say 'basin, puffing belly' (*wḥꜣ.t h̠[.t] nfi̓.t*)" = berb. *tăġidda(u̯)*, "(natural) cauldron" (with a regular Middle Kingdom rendering of foreign /d/ by Egyptian <r>);

(2) "*phts*, which is to say 'black, dark one' (= *km*, colour of the Nile mud) "
= **p*^h^*ts* "red-brown" (tuar. *téfetest*, "dark, red-brown ochre").

This does not preclude alternative etymologies for some of the names; e.g., for *bḥkꜣỉ* (translated as 'gazelle'), Ge'ez *baḥakw* "male goat, sheep, antelope" (Takács 2013, 572; Cooper 2020a, 8) seems preferable at least for its initial element *bḥk.*

Relief fragments of the slightly later unifier of Egypt and first ruler of the Middle Kingdom, Mentuhotep II, are particularly noteworthy, as they depict a captured 'chieftain *[ḥꜣ.tỉ-ꜥ]* of Tjehenu' and indicate his foreign personal name, *Ḥč̣-wꜣ-w-š-ỉ* (El-Sayed 2011, 236-7; Cooney 2011, 61 with fig. 13; more cautious is Panaite [in press]). This fact would provide us with the opportunity to identify the language of the Tjehenu-Libyans around 2000 BCE. While a pharyngal such as /ḥ/ has mostly disappeared from Berber languages (reintroduced more widely through Arabic loan words), it is still extant in some genuine Berber words for 'dérivations expressives' (Kossmann 1999, 246-48). Although the actual meaning of the ruler's name may remain elusive, it is still interesting to point to the fact that the initial four consonants would be an exact rendering of */ḥzwr/* in Kabyle *ḥḥizwer* "to race, compete", a derivation from the common Berber root *zwr* "to be the first, precede, be senior" (Haddadou 2006-7, 245-6). A hypothetical equivalent for the entire name might be *iḥḥazwer-u=s* (aoriste) or – with a verbal adjectiv – *ḥḥezwar-u=s* with the meaning "His son is preeminent, competes" – which would be a suitable name for a newborn prince.[6]

Explicit evidence for the presence of a group of probably 'Libyan' or 'Nubian' speakers in Egypt towards the end of the Second Intermediate Period may come from a list of 58 names added on a free section at the end of Pap. Moscow 314 recto from the 17th dynasty (c. 1600 BCE; Quack 2018a, 152-55; photographic publication in Bommas 2013). The papyrus' main text contains hymns to the god Sobek of Shedet (Krokodilopolis) in the Fayyum. Attempts

[6] The proper names of two more Libyan princes are unfortunately lost in the Saqqara Execration texts (El-Sayed 2011, 24).

have been made to recognize in some of these names 'Nubian' language material (Vernus 1984, who compared two listings to names attested at Aniba; a Nubian element *sn–* was also highlighted by Römer 2014, 214 and adduced by Quack 2018a, 152 for a Nubian origin of the names). Claude Rilly sees in these names evidence of Proto-Meroïtic, both on the basis of the set of phonemes and possible lexical equations (Rilly 2007, 5-11; Rilly 2010a, 13; Rilly and de Voogt 2012, 5-6; this conclusion also accepted by Pope 2014, 8; skeptical is Zibelius-Chen 2007, 366-7). In his view, the listed individuals would be 'ambassadors on a mission' from the kingdom of Kerma in the Sudan, and "not a record of slaves since in such a case the names were not likely to be given in such phonetic detail". The latter argument is not valid; we have extensive records of the names of servants and foreigners from low social registers that are spelled very accurately (see Schneider 2003a, 112-76; Rilly accepts the slave option if the document dates to the early 18th dynasty). The most comprehensive recent treatment of these names is by El-Sayed (2011, 78–80, 87–90), according to whom a conclusive assessment of the list is not currently possible. He conducted a graphemic analysis of the writings, concluding that the names were most likely transcribed in the younger Egyptian transcription system for foreign terms. He presumes that the personal names are not likely to be linguistically homogeneous but may contain (Proto-)Meroïtic, Beja, East Cushitic and Berber-Libyan names, perhaps those of envoys of Nubian principalities allied under Egypt under the leadership of the empire of Kush. Such an alliance is attested in the description of a Kushite razzia to Upper Egypt in the 17th century tomb of Sobeknakht in El-Kab (Davies 2003). However, it should be emphasized that if the linguistic options for the list are open, there is no reason why some of the names could not be equally Semitic (e.g., (2) *y-k-ꜣ-r-ỉ*; (8) *q-r-m*; (18) *k-ꜣ-b* = *klb* "dog" [cf. Schneider 1992, 211 (444)]). The list shows Egyptian <ś> besides <š>, the full series of velar stops as well as <č̣> besides <č>, but interestingly no cases of <ʿ>, <h>, <ḥ>, <ḫ>.

Given the provenance of the papyrus from the Fayyum, an area suggested to have been inhabited by Proto-Berber speakers or to be located at the Egyptian/ Proto-Berber linguistic border zone (Múrcia Sànchez 2010, I, 100-2; see above p. 54), I would espouse the idea that the document may include servants drawn from a local Proto-Berber population of the Western desert and allocated to temple service at Krokodilopolis/Shedet. The temple administration would have added the names to the papyrus, a fact supported by their very diligent notation (cf. also Quack 2018a, 152 n. 9 against Martin Bommas' view of the name list as attesting to later secular reuse of the papyrus). The graphonemic interpretation of the notations is not entirely clear; some transcriptions correlate well with the older Egyptian transcription system (mostly one-consonant signs), while the successive use of *C+ꜣ* (e.g., *k-ꜣ-ś ꜣ-n-ꜣ-t,* 46) or the typical group *reed leaf + seated man* (/'a/) point to the younger transcription system of the New Kingdom (cf. El-Sayed 2011, 87-90). El-Sayed (2011, 87) states that the transcriptions display an intermediary stage between the two systems; alternatively, the names could also have been copied from different *Vorlagen* which used the older and the younger transcription system, respectively.

Analytically, identical segments (cf. p. 60) can be identified in several of the names (the numbering of the names after Schneider 2003a, 175-6). Cf.:

- <y-b> in *m-t-ꜣ-y-b* (5) and *y-b-ỉ* (9),
- <p-ꜣ-n> in p-ꜣ-n-ỉ (48) and p-ꜣ-n-y (17),
- <m-g> in ỉ-wꜣ-t-m-g (11), m-š-m-g-ś (29), m-g-ỉ (53, 54) etc.

On the assumption of a Proto-Berber hypothesis, a certain number of the 58 names can be explained to the extent that identical segments determined analytically can be correlated with specific grammatical forms of Proto-Berber. Cf. here the following four examples:

(1) *m-t-ꜣ-y-b* and *y-b-ỉ* may be parsed as a full theophoric sentence name and a hypocoristic form of a similar name, respectively, with either an aoriste or a perfective verb form 3. ps. sg. of the root *b,* "to bear": "Matila has borne/ bears" (with the verb in second position as often in Berber onomastics; for Matila as an ancient Libyan deity, Camps 1990, 142-3) vs. the short form "He (the deity) has borne/bears". A similar 3. ps. sg. verbal form might also be represented in the name *mꜣ-n-y-n-ỉ* (21; maybe from the root *n* "to speak") and the name *y-k-ꜣ-r-ỉ* (2).

(2) Several names in the list can be tentatively equated with ancient Libyan names attested in antique sources. E.g., (a) *M-ś-r-q-s* (19; with the older rendering of /d/ by Egyptian <r>) and *Mastigas* (in Latin transcription; king of the Mauro-Roman kingdom in the 6th c. CE); or (b) *M-š-m-g-ś* (29; for other Libyan names in Egyptian sources with the initial element *m-š-*, see Colin 1995-6, I 47) and *Masmacos* (Camps 2002, 239).

(3) *p-ꜣ-n-ỉ* and *p-ꜣ-n-y* may be derived from the root *prn* (> Berber *frn*), "to choose", well attested as *frn* in Berber names from antique and medieval sources. Toudji renders the simple personal name *frn* as "le choisi, élu" (Toudji 92 [11]; modern *U-frin*).

(4) For many other names, lexical and onomastic equations from Berber languages can be suggested although there is no way to ascertain such etymologies, e.g. *ỉ-ś-kꜣ-ỉ* (7) and berb. *a-skkur* "partridge" (cf. medieval female personal name *ta-skkur-t* "female partridge"; Greek personal name Πέρδιξ "partridge") or *t'-t-ꜣ-t* and berb. *ta-tri-t* (20) "little star" (a Berber personal name, Aghali-Zakara 2003, 223).

From the Middle Kingdom and 2nd Intermediate Period, hundreds of personal names of potentially North African origin are preserved in Egyptian documents, attesting to the presence of situations of language contact between different linguistic groups. Since, however, none of the name bearers is explicitly identified as 'Libyan', Proto-Berber etymologies are in all cases speculative (cf. as one example *M-ś-qṭ-nw* [CG 20559]: Schneider 2003a, 147).

2.2.2.3.4.7 Proto-Berber linguistic evidence from the Predynastic Period to the Old Kingdom

In the later Old Kingdom (dynasties 5 and 6; 25th–24th c. BCE), the evidence in Egyptian sources for the presence of Proto-Berber to the west of Egypt is scarce.[7] Explicit reference to the foreign language of Libya (*čḥnw*; see the

[7] The Libyan divine name ꜣš ("Ash"; attested since the early 3rd millennium; LGG I, 81) cannot be equated with the Berber word for "god", *yūš,* as claimed by Breyer (2021, 42):

comments about this term pp. 67-8), is made in *Pyramid Texts* Spell 301: "Acquire for yourself the crown from the elder and great gibberers/foreign speakers [*ꜣʿʿw*; on this term, see Schneider 2003a, 110-1], foremost of Libya, (as) Sobek, lord of Bakhu" (Woodcock 2014, 24; Spalinger 1979, 130; Allen 2005, 56). Only by inference from the Chief of the Tjehenu *Ḥč̣-wꜣ-w-š-ỉ* under Mentuhotep II (see p. 62), the hypothesis that his proper name is Proto-Berber, and the assumption that Tjehenu was home to speakers of one and the same language between 2400 and 2100 BCE, can we conclude that the language hinted at in PT Spell 301 is Proto-Berber.

Additionally, I mention from the Egyptian lexicon *wnš* "wolf" which is generally regarded as an Afroasiatic cognate of the generic Berber lexeme for "wolf", *uššen* (for which word, see Kossmann 1999, 223 {675}), with a metathesis II-III (Vycichl 1983, 20). However, as a cognate, the Egyptian word would have to be written **wnś*, since Egyptian /š/ (Old Kingdom) is the palatalized product of an earlier velar fricative (Peust 1999a, 115-7). *Wnš* is therefore most likely a very early loan from Proto-Berber.[8] From the same time, the name of the son of a Libyan chieftain on a relief of king Sahure of the 5th dynasty, *W–ś–ꜣ*, could be explained as (Proto–)Berber *Wessar*, "the old/eldest one" (Breyer 2014b, 200; cf. El-Sayed 2011, 182-3; for the depiction, Stockfisch 1996), an element that reoccurs (in later orthography) as *Wsỉr* in the name Osorkon (see in detail the discussion above, pp. 56-7).

Egyptian <ꜣ> represented at that time a liquid /r/, <š> a velar fricative. Yūš, in turn, also appears in the variants Akuš/Yakūš (Camps and Chaker 1986) and is commonly regarded as a noun derived from the root 'to give', *fk/kf* (Haddadou 2006/7, 54; Touareg, Chleuh, Kabyle) > *aš* (Central Morocco, Mzab, Ouargla; Chaker 1995, 222); *bwy* (Rössler 1964, 209-10).

[8] In an earlier contribution, I suggested that a term for dagger, mꜣ-g-św (Old Kingdom, Hannig 2003, 506) /bꜣ-g-św (Old Kingdom, Hannig 2003, 795-6; Middle Kingdom, Hannig 2006, 1018), might be a loan from Proto-Berber with a prefix *mr/br*, and a noun *gs* for a wooden or metal rod (Schneider 2008, 186, 191). However, the compound Berber term is not attested. Gundacker (2017, 73) has recently proposed to explain the term as an Egyptian *nomen agentis/instrumenti*, "the cutter".

Far from being solved is the question of the two Old Egyptian ethnonyms for 'Libya(n)', *čḥnw* and *čmḥ*. The term *čmḥ* 'Libyan' is attested for the first time in the 5th dynasty (Hannig 2003, 1447). While it has so far remained without any etymology, I hypothesize that it could be identical to the common Berber self-designation *a-maziġ* (plural *i-maziġen;* in Classical antiquity, without the later Berber 'article' a-, attested as Μάζικες, *Maxyes/Mazaces* etc., see above p. 54), although this would require a metathesis I-II (**zamiġ* for *maziġ*). After evaluating earlier inconclusive attempts to establish the etymology of *amaziġ*, Salem Chaker has suggested that this word might be a derivation of the Berber root *zġ*, "to put up a tent" (1987, with reference to Laoust 1935, 33-4).

Views about the etymology of the second term for "Libya", *čḥnw* (Hannig 2003, 1455), are divided. The term may be Egyptian (cf. Hölscher 1937, 17-8; Panaite [in press]). By contrast, El-Sayed considers to see in the term a genuinely Libyan expression, for which a phonological sequence /k-ħ-n/ would have to be posited for the time around 3000 BCE (El-Sayed 2011, 303). Possible is also a more complex relationship whereby the Egyptian term *čḥnw* is a reinterpretation of a foreign expression (Panaite [in press]).

In this respect, one hypothesis may be suggested. If *čḥnw* is not spelled out phonetically before the 4th dynasty and reflects a contemporary sequence <čḥn>,[9] could this term be in origin a participle plural **zaġen* (modern Berber, *i-zaġen*) derived from the same Berber root *zġ*, "those putting up tents, nomads" posited by Chaker for the term *amaziġ*, with the *nw*–hieroglyph as a sportive writing of the Proto-Berber plural ending /n/? Interesting in this regard is a passage from the early 12th dynasty Tale of Sinuhe where the two terms seem to be used indiscriminately. Amenemhet I is here reported to have led a campaign "to the land of the *čmḥw* ... in order to slay *those who are in čḥnw*". The unusual phrase *ỉmỉ.w-čḥnw*, "the ones in/from *čḥnw*" (Hölscher 1937, 22) might appear like an Egyptian scholarly etymology or interpretive rendering of

[9] The examples given by Kammerzell (2005, 191) in support of an earlier spelling **kḥnw* are not entirely certain. If we assume that the ideographic writing of the early dynastic time renders a phonological sequence whose later modernized form was *čḥn* (as the toponym *Kꜣš* is replaced by a later rendering *Kš*), his assumption is not valid.

the term *a-maziġ / i-maziġen:* ỉắm˘w-č˘ḥ˘n. If this assumption is correct, it would point to the existence of the Berber endonym as early as 2000 BCE, and to Egyptian awareness of it.

2.2.2.3.4.8 Concluding assessment

The assessment of the linguistic and contextual evidence conducted in the previous paragraphs reaffirms the existence of Proto-Berber in the first millennium BCE and the Ramesside period, as well as the likelihood that at least some of the Libyan tribes attested in these times, which were instrumental in the Libyan principalities of the Third Intermediate Period, were speakers of specific varieties of that posited early form of Berber. The evidence is scarcer and less explicit for the 3rd and most of the 2nd millennia, but that evidence still seems to point in the same direction. This being said, a cautious approach to the material is still advisable, in the words of Lioned Galand: "Mais revenons à la langue: il ne faut certes ni étouffer l'imagination créatrice des chercheurs, ni renoncer à jeter un pont entre le libyque et le berbère, mais une certaine méfiance devant les rapprochements qui impliquent des sauts de plusieurs siècles reste justifiée. Pour le plaisir d'être un peu provocateur, je dirai même que les ressemblances les plus parfaites sont aussi les plus suspectes" (Galand 2002, 264). At the same time, it also holds true that in the last twenty years, since the death of Werner Vycichl, *berbérisants* and linguists of ancient Egyptian have never collaborated to discuss, in a truly interdisciplinary way, the rich Egyptian *Nebenüberlieferung* of 'Libyan' material. This remains a desideratum of both fields.

2.2.2.3.5 Chadic languages

The Chadic languages are commonly seen as a constituent branch of Afro-Asiatic (e.g., Jungraithmayr 2021). Lexical correlations and linguistic parallels (such as the existence of Second Tenses) have mostly been treated as resulting from this cognate relationship. For the lexical comparison, cf. the Chadic materials provided by Takács (1999-2008) and Stolbova (2003); both authors use the phonological system of traditional Egyptian-Afroasiatic comparison. While scholars regarded direct Egyptian-Chadic language contact as unlikely (cf. Satzinger 2008, 280: "It is, however, not conceivable that the Egyptian of the 2nd to 1st millennia BC took over words from a Chadic language, as there do not seem to have been any contacts between speakers of Egyptian and historical Chadic idioms"), the increasing evidence for contact between the Nile valley and the Chadic language area in historical times, via the Abu Ballas trail and the Wadi Howar (see p.11), calls for a revision of this view (see Cooper 2017a). I single out here two examples adduced in the debate: The Chadic word for 'date palm' (Hausa *dàbínò*, Kanuri *dìbínò*) is probably a loan from Egyptian, most likely through the intermediary of Berber (Cooper 2017a, 81; for the term itself, see p. 56). Particular attention has also been devoted to the existence of Second Tenses in both Egyptian-Coptic and Chadic (Vycichl 1934; Jungraithmayr 1994; Satzinger 2001; Reintges and Green 2004) (see below 2.2.3).

2.2.3 Language convergence through a *sprachbund* situation

It is likely that languages in Northeast Africa developed parallel linguistic features due to convergence in areal proximity (for areal linguistics, see Matras, McMahon and Vincent 2006; Muysken 2008). Such phenomena would be a historical result of language contact and would extend beyond genetically related language groups. Scholars such as Helmut Satzinger (2000) and Carsten Peust (2004) have discussed dozens of features of Egyptian and other African languages that are typologically similar and would point to "Egyptian as an African language", as opposed to its appropriation for the Semitic languages (Rössler 1971). These features include *morphosyntactic characteristics* such as:

- the existence of morphologically distinct "second tenses" to express theme/rheme (Peust 2004, 382–90);
- similarities in nonverbal predicates (Peust 2004, 359-365) and relative forms (Peust 2004, 372-6);
- the fact that the main clause (rather than the subordinate clause) is marked (Peust 2004, 333-6);
- the use of an imperative followed by subordinate verb forms to express a

sequence of imperatives (Peust 2004, 338-40);

- the observation that interrogative pronouns cannot be used in a relative function (Peust 2004, 326-30);
- the use of certain verbal constructions for subordinate clauses (nominal forms as subordinate verbal forms, Peust 2004, 365-7; the use of the verb "to give" for periphrastic causatives, Peust 2004, 330-1);
- the expression of "before" by means of subordinate temporal clauses signifying "when not, until not, while not yet" (Peust 2004, 324-6);
- the use of auxiliary verbs instead of adverbs (Peust 2004, 336-7); etc.

The features also comprise many *lexical and phraseological similarities*, e.g.

- parallels to the Egyptian particle of address *m=k/č/čn* (Peust 2004, 323-4);
- the lexical differentiation between "concrete thing" and "abstract thing" (Peust 2004, 326; Eg. *ỉḫ.t* vs. *mṭ.t*);
- semantic and morphological parallels involving verbs of motion ("going to a person" expressed as "going to a person's place", Peust 2004, 331-3; "to exit" and "to go up" expressed by the same verb; for "to enter" and "to go down", two different verbs are used, Peust 2004, 337-8);
- suppletive imperative forms for the verb "to come" (Peust 2004, 341-3);
- the fact that negative pronouns and adverbs are expressed by the simple negation of the pronouns and adverbs (Peust 2004, 358);
- specifics regarding interrogative pronouns (no particle "when", Peust 2004, 390-1; the use of "who is your name" for "what is your name");
- the prominent use of body parts in certain expressions ("head" for "self", Peust 2004, 346-7; also for persons and as adpositions, Peust 2004, 347-50);
- the distinction between inalienable/alienable possession (Peust 2004, 340);
- many *lexical/phraseological parallels* (identical terms in Egyptian and select African languages for, e.g., *'mouth'/'door'; 'mouth'/'language'; 'sun'/ 'day'; 'skin'/ 'color'; 'tight'/ 'strength'; 'to put down'/'to last'; 'to hold'/ 'to begin'* (Peust 350-3); "to say" used as an auxiliary (Peust 2004, 376-8) and for "that" (Peust 2004, 378-9); pluralia tantum (Peust 2004, 368-9), etc.

These similarities require further, systematic research in the context of more generic hypotheses about the early relationship of languages in Northeast Africa (see below pp. 73, 113).

3. LANGUAGE CONTACT WITH THE NEAR EAST

3.1 From corpus languages to undocumented languages

From the different cases of linguistic interference discussed in this book, the study of language contact between ancient Egyptian and Near Eastern languages benefits from the fact that many of these languages have a vast written documentation of their own. This can be visualized conveniently on the basis of Peust (2000) who has estimated the size of the attested corpus languages of antiquity (until 300 CE). The following chart contains languages with >10,000 attested words (word forms), both from the Near East and the Mediterranean:

Size categories (decreasing)	**Number of attested words**	**Languages** ↗ = number of attested words expected to increase in the future through new texts
(1)	> 50 million	Greek
(2)	> 10 million	Akkadian ↗ Latin
(4)	> 6 million	Egyptian-Demotic ↗
(5)	> 1 million	Sumerian ↗
(6)	> 500,000	Hittite ↗
(7)	> 300,000	Eblaitic ↗ Hebrew
(9)	>> 100,000	Ancient South Arabic ↗
(10)	> 100,000 words	Elamite ↗ Ancient Iranian (OldPersian, Avestan)
(12)	100,000	Aramaic ↗
(13)	40,000	Ugaritic ↗
(14)	25,000	Etruscan ↗
(15)	> 10,000	Hurrian ↗ Middle Iranian (Pehlevi, Parthian) ↗
(17)	10,000	Linear A ↗ Meroïtic ↗ Phoenician-Punic ↗ Urartean ↗

This situation does not belie the fact that there existed an unknown number of additional Near Eastern languages that are little known or entirely unknown. Small corpus languages consisting of several hundred to several thousand attested words (Peust 2000, 255-6) comprise Hattian, Anatolian languages such as Luwian, Palaic, Lycian, Lydian, Phrygian, Carian (see below pp. 96-7, 106-7 and map IV). Other languages attested through less than 100 known words can be labeled *Trümmersprachen* ("debris languages"; cf. Untermann 1989), e.g., Kassite (Michałowski 2017, 24-7). No data for any comparative studies is offered by languages attested exclusively through personal names or mere references to them in texts (such as the languages of Marhashi, of the Guti and Lullubi); some languages may be rendered by undeciphered scripts like Proto-Elamite and Linear Elamite (Michałowski 2017, 32-7; for the latter see now Desset et al. 2022). One Semitic language of the late 3rd and early 2nd millennium BCE – Amurrite (Amorite) – has been reconstructed exclusively from personal names preserved in Cuneiform sources (Streck 2000; Streck 2012; there is an important Egyptian *Nebenüberlieferung* of potentially Amurrite names in Egyptian documents of the Middle Kingdom). Additionally, language varieties resulting from bilingual and multilingual contact situations – such as pidgin, mixed, and 'reduced languages' (Adams 2003, 93-105) – certainly existed but can only rarely be identified in our sources.

The following paragraphs survey the evidence for ancient Egyptian–Near Eastern language contact from the late 4th mill. BCE until the 4th c. BCE.

3.2 A historical survey of language contact with Near Eastern languages

3.2.1 Prehistory

In the 4th millennium BCE, the presence of immigrants from the Levant in Egypt has been ascertained at sites of the *Lower Egyptian Culture* (Buto, Maadi); vice-versa, Egyptian presence in the Southern Levant is attested at En Besor (Mączyńska 2013; Anfinset 2010, 70-2). While intense cultural innovation from Southern Mesopotamia in art, craftsmanship, architecture and maybe the domain of writing is visible in Egypt before 3000 BCE – although not necessarily mediated through the physical presence of individuals from the Uruk civilization in Egypt (Gimbel 2002; Wilde and Behnert 2002) –, cases of linguistic interference with the Near East have only rarely been discussed. One of the most intriguing ideas is to see the Egyptian royal title *nsw* (New Kingdom pronunciation *insi*) as a borrowing from Sumerian *ensi* "king" (Peust 2007). For the development of Archaic Egyptian (pre-Old Egyptian; Grossman and Richter 2015, 72-3), scholars have postulated the existence of different linguistic communities (Regulski 2016). Language contact has also been aduced since the 1970s for presumed lexical and grammatical (Egyptian stative vs. Indo-European medium-perfect) parallels between ancient Egyptian and Indo-European, through the intermediary either of a vanished substrate language or a *sprachbund* situation (see below pp. 113-6). More likely is extensive language contact between ancient Egyptian and African languages (see pp. 69-70).

3.2.2 Early Bronze Age

Egyptian contact with speakers of Near Eastern languages is attested throughout the 3rd millennium (Schneider 1998a, 10-30) – in Egypt, abroad and also in the East Delta border zone. It is important to account for the fact that the eastern Nile delta was likely populated by speakers of a Semitic language in the Early Bronze Age. The site of Tell Ibrahim Awad bears evidence of Levantine temples from late prehistory to the end of the Old Kingdom (Bietak 2009; understood by Bietak 2010b as a secondary settlement of a Levantine workforce). Sopdu, the patron god of the 20th Egyptian nome in the Southeastern Delta, continued to be portrayed as an Asiatic god even when that province had been incorporated in the Egyptian state. In the New Kingdom, the Ramesside capital city Piramesse on the Pelusiac branch of the Nile was still said to be "situated between Palestine and Egypt" (in the 'Praise of the Delta Residence', Pap. Anastasi II 1.2) and is addressed as the "outpost of every foreign country, hinterland of Egypt" (ostracon Ashmolean HO 1187 1942.64; Fischer-Elfert 2016).

Beyond the border zone, Egyptian-Semitic language contact in the Old Kingdom is implicitly plausible by Egypt's activity on the Sinai and its entertainment of a policy of political, military and commercial engagement in the Levant whose extent has only recently become more apparent (Sowada 2006; Forstner-Müller and Raue 2008; Schneider 2015). The Lebanese port city of Byblos served as Egypt's commercial gateway to Syria where the Egyptian administration cooperated closely with the city's chieftains, and where knowledge of Egyptian and religious exchange is attested, e.g., by Egyptian inscriptions and the identification of the local "lady of Byblos" (an Astarte-type goddess) with the Egyptian Hathor (Espinel 2002; Zernecke 2013). In the 5th and 6th dynasties, speakers of Semitic languages from Palestine were brought to Egypt as prisoners (biography of Kaemtjenenet; conquests of Palestinian towns depicted in tombs at Saqqara and Deshasheh). The Teaching for Merikare, set in the First Intermediate Period, speaks about incursions of Asiatics in the Eastern Nile Delta which can be supported by the mention of "Asiatics" in the Old Kingdom Execration texts and of nomadic "Asiatics who are on the sand" *(ʿꜣm.w ḥrỉ.w šʿỉ)*. Asiatic prisoners in Egypt are attested in the First Intermediate Period (Saretta 2016); warfare against Palestinian fortresses is depicted under Mentuhotep II (seen by Bietak 2010, 145-6 with fig. 5 as evidence for Palestinian settlements in Egypt).

Language contact is reflected in the transcription of foreign terms and names since earliest times (cf. the possible designation of a foreign chieftain defeated by king Dewen in the 1st dynasty; *ś-tm-n* = * *ṯu-taymani* "he of Tēman/Southland" or * *ʾiṯu-taymani* "the man of Tēman/Southland", Schneider 1998a, 10-1). A developped transcription system is first attested in the 6th dynasty (Hoch 1994, 487-8), on several series of Execration Texts preserved from the Memphite royal residences and directed against Nubian individuals, possibly from auxiliary troops (see above, p. 20). This system was probably also in use for the ren-dering of Semitic and other Near Eastern languages. A likely Semitic loanword attested first in the 6th dynasty is the term *ʿꜣm* "Asiatic (inhabitant of areas to the northeast of Egypt)" < *drmj* "inhabitant of the south (of Palestine)" (Schneider 1997, 194-195; with the older equivalency Egyptian <ʿ> = Semitic /d/; accepted by Gundacker 2017, 349). A possible associative transcription of the Semitic divine name ʿAṯtaru in the 6th dynasty makes use of the Egyptian phrase *ḫʿ-tꜣ.w* GOD that alludes in its meaning ("Who appears burning") to ʿAṯtaru's astral nature (Schneider 2000; more cautious Quack 2015, 261 n.29); one of the attestations is from a cylinder seal found in Byblos and inscribed in Egyptian hieroglyphs, thus pointing to Egyptian literacy at Byblos (see also Shalomi-Hen 2006, 93-4).

Depictions of sea-going ships from the funerary temple of Sahure and the Unas causeway depict translators that accompanied the Levantine and Egyptian crew members (Bietak 1988; Ćwiek 2003, 254-5). There is no reason to doubt that the court of the Old Kingdom was in intense diplomatic contact with political and trade centres in the Near East; the singular clay tablets found at the Egyptian western oasis residence of Balat/ʿAyn Aṣīl and inscribed in Hieratic, from the 6th dynasty, may actually be indirect evidence for the knowledge of Cuneiform tablets in Egypt (Breyer 2010a, 414 with fig. 55). Conversely, the similarity of signs of the undeciphered Byblos script with Egyptian Hieratic signs of the later Old Kingdom and First Intermediate Period indicates early influence of Egyptian writing on the development of a local script system (Hoch 1990). Recently, Richard Steiner suggested that a series of "serpent spells" in the Pyramid Texts from the later Old Kingdom (spells 232-238, 281-282, 286-287) are Egyptian transcriptions of Northwest Semitic incantations, made accessible to the Egyptians through Byblos (Steiner 2011). While the general context of linguistic interaction would make such transfers appear possible, the proposed reconstruction uses phonological values for the Egyptian sounds that are much later than the Old Kingdom, as well as Semitic lexemes attested only late, which renders the suggested interpretation of the texts unlikely (Breyer 2012b). Lexical transfer from Near Eastern languages is hardly attested during the Early Bronze Age. However, Egyptian *ssm.t* "horse" may be an example of an early loanword, borrowed around 2100 BCE from Akkadian *sīsû*. It displays Akkadian mimation (*sīsûm*) and uses a sibilant <s> (bolt-s) which in the Middle Kingdom, having lost its realization as an affricate /^{t}s/, could no longer be employed to render Semitic Samek (also an affricate /^{t}s/; Schneider 2008a, 189).

> To posit a dual (or plural), as Vernus (2005, 13-4) proposes, is unnecessary. Gee has made the suggestion to see in the Egyptian term a univerbation of Akkad. **sīsû māti* (Gee 2018); however, such a term is not attested in Akkadian and Gee admits himself that this hypothesis presupposes a misinterpretation of the term *ANŠE.KUR.RA*. It seems difficult to believe that a misinterpretation could be the source of a widely used horse term in Egyptian.

3.2.3 Middle Bronze Age

The Middle Kingdom and Second Intermediate Period (c. 2000-1550 BCE) appear less rich in evidence for language contact than the New Kingdom (1550-1070 BCE). However, this fact does not necessarily mean less intense actual contact, but also reflects a different preservation of documents and the absence vs. emergence of certain textual genres. This can be corroborated by other parameters such as deportations and immigration from abroad or evidence for cultural exchange, both of which were equally abundant throughout the entire 2nd millennium BCE. E.g., the ratio of the number of foreign personal names attested for individuals living in Middle Kingdom vs. New Kingdom Egypt is c. 1:3, not entirely dissimilar and pointing to a comparable degree of language contact. This contrasts with the different ratio of loanwords attested in Middle Kingdom vs. New Kingdom sources, which is c. 1:100. However, most terms of the New Kingdom are preserved on papyri and ostraca, which are key source types specifically of the New Kingdom, indicating a bias caused by evidence.

There is explicit evidence for direct Egyptian-Near Eastern language contact during the Middle Kingdom and Second Intermediate Period (c. 2000-1550 BCE), and such contact can also be deduced implicitly from the extent of political and cultural interaction. Within the last 25 years, increasing evidence has been published for wide-ranging Egyptian engagement with the Near East during the Middle Kingdom, such as fragments of Amenemhet II's annals from Mitrahine mentioning the Egyptian conquest of Cyprus and Ura in Southeastern Anatolia (see now Altenmüller 2015), the inscription of a vizier Khnumhotep at Dahshur depicting Egypt as a mediator in a conflict between Byblos and Ullaza (Allen 2008) and a Cuneiform tablet from Tell Siyannu refering to trade relations between Egypt and Cyprus (Ahrens 2006, 26 n. 66). Intense commercial and cultural contact can be inferred from Levantine commodities in Egypt and Egyptian products in Palestine and Syria (Forstner-Müller, Kopetzky and Doumet-Serhal 2006). The presence of Egyptian scarabs in the Levant and their emulation here and in Crete highlights the regional popularity of the amulet that was also a medium to disseminate Egyptian ideas (Bietak and Czerny 2004). In turn, Levantine, Mesopotamian and Aegean concepts and motifs were also transferred to Egypt. The tomb of Baqet III at Beni Hasan displays a scene of bull-leaping and the Mesopotamian tree of life, and fabulous creatures and griffons that reoccur in the Aegean (Morenz 2000).

Linguistic and scribal interaction is visible throughout the period. The early 12th dynasty Tale of Sinuhe portrays a fictional protagonist Sinuhe who rises in the Levant to the position of chieftain and controlls trade and diplomatic travel. It mentions explicitly that speakers of Egyptian were residents of the Levant, has the local sheikh, who adopts Sinuhe into his family, speak Egyptian (directly or through a translator), and implicitly credits Sinuhe with the acquisition of the local Semitic language when he establishes a family and builds his career. For Egyptian careers abroad, such as that of a priest of Sakhmet (Pap. Moskau Pushkin Museum 1695) or of a merchant to Byblos in Papyrus Lythgoe (Pap. New York MMA 09.180.535; Parkinson 2002), language contact was inevitable, and mutual Egyptian-Semitic language competency indispensable. The Khnumhotep inscription from Dahshur renders communication between an Egyptian expedition leader and the ruler of Byblos, and mentions also "speakers of Egyptian", by using the term "Egyptians" with the classifier sign of the speaking man (Allen 2008). Egypt's Asiatic forecourt, the Sinai peninsula, was the destination of mining expeditions throughout the Middle Kingdom, in which local personnel was employed and possibly bilingual Asiatic Egyptians were put in charge as expedition leaders (such as Ameni-Seshenu in Sinai Inscription 95). On his funerary stela (Cairo CG 20765), a dignitary Hepetrehu in the early 12th dynasty claims that he was able to "interpret the language of any foreign country" (Meyrat 2015, 322).

In turn, the Mitrahine annals of Amenemhet II report prisoners who were captured for the king's pyramid city and given as a tribute, but in addition provide the singular information that the Egyptian soldiers ate the Asiatic dishes of the prisoners. Large numbers of workers from the Levant, often with Semitic names, are attested at the major Middle Kingdom pyramid construction sites such as Illahun (Mourad 2015 passim; Di Teodoro 2018 passim); they are also documented in private households (e.g., 47 *ʿꜣm.w* 'Asiatics' [see pp. 74-5] in Pap. Brooklyn 35.1446: Schneider 2003a, 60-1; 11 'Asiatics' on stele Moscow, Pushkin Museum I.1.A.5349 (4161): Schneider 2003a, 59-61). The most prominent settlement of people from the Levant on Egyptian soil became, from the 12th dynasty on, Avaris/Tell el-Dabʿa, founded as a pioneer settlement east of the Pelusiac branch of the Nile and target of a repeated influx of population groups from Palestine. For this town alone, Manfred Bietak has estimated the number of Canaanite inhabitants during the 18th and 17th centuries at c. 30,000 people (Bietak 1988, 39 with n.34). It is thus obvious that Northwest Semitic must have represented an imported minority language in Middle Kingdom and Second Intermediate Period Egypt, creating within Egypt a situation of intense linguistic interference (see the case study on Avaris, pp. 81-4).

Middle Kingdom texts from official and private sources use a coherent subsystem of the hieroglyphic script to render foreign names and words, with matres lectionis after monoconsonantal signs for the rendering of the vowels /u/ and /i/ and the occasional use of CVC signs (Hoch 1994, 488-504). The most detailed use of this system is visible in the older and younger series of Middle Kingdom *Execration texts* from the 12th dynasty, which list the names of Levantine princes and their cities and territories (Wimmer 2010, 33-50). This onomasticon, together with c. 200 Semitic personal names preserved in other sources (Schneider 1998a, 35-46, 125-141; 2003a, 112-176), constitutes an important secondary tradition for Northwest Semitic. Written communication with the wider Near East in Egyptian or Cuneiform very certainly existed; a recently found fragment of a letter sent to the residence of the Hyksos (15th) dynasty at Avaris by one of the last kings of the First Dynasty of Babylon (Van Coppen and Radner 2009; Bietak 2010a) shows that Middle Bronze Age correspondence from Mesopotamia to Egypt has simply not been preserved.

Conversely, at Egypt's trade emporium Byblos on the Lebanese coast, the local rulers adopted the Egyptian title *ḥꜣtỉ-*ꜥ "mayor" (mayor of Byblos) and appear to be Egyptianized; they adopted the hieroglyphic script for their official stelae and reliefs in which their names appear in Egyptian transcription. We also see Egyptian Hieratic writing used at Byblos – the pseudo-hieroglyphic stela "L" –, although "it is…not clear whether this is an Egyptian hieratic tradition, a local Byblian adaptation of Egyptian forms, or a reflection of less than total competence with the language and standard Egyptian usage" (Hoch 1995, 65).

Egyptian inscriptions also appear as legends on some seals from the Middle Bronze Age Levant (Eder 1995, 51-57). Particularly interesting is one (Eder 1995, 241; Dok. 108; Tessier 1996, Dok. 73) that transcribes the Sumerogram ÌR ^{d}A(a) "servant of Aya" according to the conventions of the younger Egyptian transcription system as *ỉr* ꜥꜣ (Schneider 1998b, 186). On another seal (Eder 1995, 217 Dok. 48; Tessier 1996, Dok. 71) and an Egyptian royal scarab, we find the associative transcription of the Syrian god's name *Haddu* by Egyptian 'Horus' ≈ /Ḥāɾuw/ (or similar; Schneider 1998a, 128; 1998b, 186).

The Egyptian monumental and cursive writing systems seem to have prompted several, but unsuccessful, attempts by speakers of Northwest Semitic to design a script system for their indigenous language (Rollston 2010, 11-14): the Byblos script (Hoch 1995), the Proto-Sinaitic script (Goldwasser 2012a, 2012b and 2022; Colless 2014; Morenz 2014; Morenz 2016), and the Wadi el-Hol inscriptions (Darnell et al. 2005).

Despite this intense contact, and the assumed transfer of technological innovation to Egypt in the first half of the 2nd millennium BCE (cf. Shortland 2002; Bourriau and Philipps 2004), lexical interference is only rarely attested. Near Eastern loanwords appear, e.g., in the terminology of weaponry, such as *ỉśb.t* "quiver" (Papyrus Kahun 19.16 and 20.47) < Northwest Semitic *ʾaṯbāt* "quiver" (also attested in the New Kingdom; *ỉ-ś-p(ꜣ)-t(ỉ)*: Hoch 1994, 40-1; for the proposed etymology of Egyptian *wrry.t* "chariot" < Hittite *widuli*, see Schneider 1999; opposed Groddeck 2000). Another loan is a word for "chair" or "sedan" (Ugaritic *kḥṯ*, Amarna Canaanite *kaḫšu*, itself a loan with metathesis from Hurrian *kišḫu*, "chair"; Richter 2012, 216-7), attested as early as the Middle Kingdom as *kḥśy* (and maybe *kḥśś*, Meeks 1977, 86; Hoch 1994, 336-7).

Other old loanwords may not be attested but can be indirectly postulated (e.g., " the precursors of Coptic ⲗⲁⲕⲙ(ⲉ) "crumb" < Semitic [Arabic] *luqmat*; or ϭⲗⲟⲟϭⲉ, ⲧⲗⲟⲟϭⲉ (etc.) "ladder" < Semitic [Arabic] *darağat* "staircase"; Quack 2005, 312, 321). In turn, Northwest Semitic may have borrowed an earlier form of (Hebrew) *dəyō* "ink" from Egyptian *ry.t* (Rössler 1966, 227; with a regular Middle Kingdom sound correspondence when Egyptian <r> rendered Semitic /d/ and /l/), as well as other terms related to scribal and sealing practices such as the precursors of Hebrew *ṭabbaʿat*, "signet ring", and *ḥôtām* (< ḫtm), "seal". Evidence of the knowledge of royal titularies may also be the possible Luwian title *ḫntw-ỉ- ʿ-w-š* = *ḫantawattis* "ruler" (and two other titles) in the story of Sinuhe (Schneider 2002; accepted by De Vos 2004; Breyer 2010a, 101-104; Noegel 2018, 235; opposed Goedicke 2004; Simon 2011).

The first half of the 2nd millennium is marked by an enormous increase in the evidence about Near Easterners in Ancient Egypt who are attested throughout the whole socio-economic and professional spectrum, from prisoners of war and compulsory workers to cultic and priestly functions, high administrative offices, and royalty (for a comprehensive presentation and analysis of the material, Schneider 2003a). The most prominent urban site for the interrelationship of Egypt and the Levant in the Middle Bronze Age is Avaris/Tell el-Dab^{c}a, from the 17th–mid-16th century the capital of the Hyksos. Here the significant repeated settlement of immigrants from the Levant is visible between the 20th and the 16th centuries, featuring "cultural mixing" and a creolized culture (Bader 2013; Bader 2021); "born from Amorite practices within an Egyptian context" (Burke 2014, 368; see Mourad 2015 and 2021; Burke 2019; Burke 2020).

3.2.3.1 A Case Study: Languages at Avaris

In her new 2021 monograph, Bettina Bader has put the debate on hybrid ethnicities and cultures at Avaris on a new methodological foundation by pointing to the biases of the traditional culture-historical paradigm and its 'trait-list' approach to the populations and the diversity of culture visible here:

> "The concept of borderlands on the other hand may be applied whether a colonial situation can be proved or not, whether a frontier existed as a fortified line or not or whether it may be thought of as permeable or not. Thus, 'mutual appropriation' in a virtual or real 'space/place' is probably the best model in this situation because it saves us from having to decide beforehand if the individuals buried there were 'Asiatics' or 'Egyptians'." (Bader 2021, 101).

In the light of this debate and Avaris' complex population history as a borderland site – with immigration from both Egypt and the Levant, but also local population growth and intermarriages, and as a port city, the presence of temporary and permanent residents from other regions in the Mediterranean and the Near East –, it becomes problematic to clearly distinguish between ethnic and cultural segments of the population (Matić 2020, 29, 58; Bader 2021). The diverse demographics and culture of the city must also have entailed a complex sociolinguistic situation that so far has not been given consideration in scholarship (cf. the absence or limited significance accorded to language as an identity factor in Bietak 2018; Bader 2021). I will make some observations here on this situation, with a focus on the period when Avaris served as the capital of the kingdom of the Hyksos of the 15th dynasty (c. 1650-1540 BCE), rulers portrayed by Burke as representatives of the Amorite Koine (Burke 2021, 205-

212, 257-344). For that century of the city's history, there is direct or implicit evidence for multilingualism and multiscripturalism. I single out the following languages and repertoires – the actual situation of spoken and written languages, linguistic registers and norms will clearly have been much more complex:

- OFFICIAL MIDDLE EGYPTIAN: only very small rests of hieroglyphic monuments of the 15th dynasty have been preserved (documents listed in Helck 2002, 55-8; lintel of king Sikru-haddu, Bietak 1996, fig. 52), although longer inscriptions certainly existed, as is demonstrated by the fragment of the building inscription by king Apāpi from Bubastis. On the scribal palette presented by Apāpi to a scribe Atju, the king describes himself as instructed by the god of wisdom, Thoth, and the goddess of writing, Seshat, as the living image of the sun-god, a ruler who cares for mankind and abides by Maat (Goedicke 1988; Morenz 1996, 167-170). The other official document preserved is the dispatch sent by Apāpi to the ruler of Kush and intercepted by the Theban king Kamose, quoted verbatim in the Second Kamose stele, "in writing by the hand of the Ruler of Avaris". These two texts comprise a total of 10 lines of text – too little to establish the position of the variety of official Middle Egyptian used at Avaris within Second Intermediate Official Egyptian (for which, see Díaz Hernández 2016). Through the Mathematical Pap. Rhind, copied at Avaris, we are aware of the existence of hieratic scientific texts. Operating the temples of Avaris and administering both city and state must have produced a vast range of hieratic documents which are not preserved (for the patronage of science and religion under the Hyksos, see Morenz 1996, 159.163-5). However, titles of administrators of the kingdom of Avaris refer explicitly to scribal activity, such as "Personal scribe of the king's documents", " Great scribe of the overseer of the treasury", "Scribe of the document", and implicitly, many titles related to the Treasury (*ẖtmt*) and other administrative functions (Shirley 2013, 527-30 [Table 1]).
- VERNACULAR EGYPTIAN. For a city that became part of the Egyptian state in the 12th dynasty and in addition to its local population, attracted Egyptians

who came here to live and work, it is obvious that a vernacular East Lower Egyptian variety of Egyptian (maybe with a Semitic adstrate) was spoken, although no information on that variety is available.

- CUNEIFORM AKKADIAN: the fragment of a letter sent to the Hyksos residence at Avaris by one of the last two kings of the First Dynasty of Babylon (Van Coppen and Radner 2009; Bietak 2010a) demonstrates that the kingdom at Avaris corresponded with the kings of Mesopotamia in cuneiform and its *lingua franca*, Akkadian. While the archive as such is not preserved, it is *a priori* not impossible that some of the international correspondence was also conducted in other languages than Akkadian, such as Hittite (with the Old Hittite Kingdom) or Hurrian.
- AMURRITE (AMORITE): The personal names of dozens of rulers of the Second Intermediate Period, including those who ruled or are presumed to have ruled at Avaris, as well as dignitaries, are Northwest Semitic and may represent an important secondary tradition of Amurrite (Amorite) (Schneider 1998a; 2003a; for a reassessment of the linguistic position of the language, see Buck 2019; Golinets 2020). Within the Amurrite (Amorite) dynasties of Syria-Mesopotamia, Akkadian was used for official communication and presumably, Amurrite (Amorite) as a vernacular.
- CANAANITE AND NORTHWEST SEMITIC: as an original frontier city, there was an influx into Avaris of Canaanite speakers from the Egypt/Sinai border area and Palestine, and probably also of Levantine immigrants who spoke related Northwest Semitic dialects. Some of these individuals are attested exclusively through personal names that do not allow for any precise linguistic assessment of these communities.
- LITERARY NORTHWEST SEMITIC, HITTITE OR HURRIAN: the presence of a cult of the Syrian weather god at Avaris since c. 1700 BCE is attested both by later tradition (400-year stele of Tanis; cylinder seal from 1700 BCE featuring the Syrian storm god) and offering pits of the pertinent temple at Avaris (the Egyptians adopted the Syrian weather god as "Seth of Avaris" or simply

Seth). This fact of a cult practice for the Syrian weather god at Avaris makes it likely that we have to account for the use of mythical and ritual texts from Syria by the local priesthood, although neither the place of origin nor the language can be specified. In the late 18th and the 19th dynasty, Near Eastern texts adapted by the Egyptians for the cult of Seth-Baal came from Anatolia (the Hurrian-Hittite myth KBo XXVI 105 as a *Vorlage* for the Astarte myth, see pp. 102-3) and Ugarit (Schneider 2003b; 2008; 2011-12; see p. 103).

- "AVARITE": I coin this term as a label for a potential *bilingual mixed language* or a *pidgin language* that may have existed as a means of everyday communication among certain socio-economic sectors of Avaris as a hub of trade (for a useful discussion of the problem of 'mixed languages' in antiquity, see Mullen 2013; Anderson and Vita 2016), as much as Torallas Tovar has posited the use of a pidgin language within the Greek colony of Naukratis (Torallas Tovar 2010, 255). The existence and form of such a mixed language depends on the communicative status and the speakers' competency in the Egyptian and Semitic vernaculars spoken in the city (see above).
- OTHER LANGUAGES: While a Hurrian background of the Hyksos can be excluded and the presence of 'Nubians' (cf. Aston and Bietak 2017; Bietak 2018, 83-4; Matić 2014b and Matić 2020) and Minoans (date of the frescoes lowered to the time of Thutmose III: Bietak 2018, 85-7; a Hyksos date reaffirmed by Candelora 2012) is still being discussed, it is inherently likely that speakers of other Near Eastern, Anatolian, Mediterranean (also Cypriots, Bietak 2018, 81-3) and different African languages also lived in or temporarily visited Avaris.
- BILINGUALISM AND MULTILINGUALISM: the population of Avaris arguably comprised many bilingual or multilingual speakers. J.J. Shirley has summarized the evidence for state officials of the 15th dynasty with Amurrite (Amorite) personal names (Shirley 2013, 533-4), a fact that makes it plausible that those dignitaries had some degree of proficiency in (probably different registers and norms of) Egyptian and Semitic languages.

3.2.4 Late Bronze Age

The evidence for language contact between Egyptian and Near Eastern languages changes dramatically in the Late Bronze Age or New Kingdom (1550-1070 BCE) – in terms of the available quantity and diversity of sources, the multitude of attested phenomena of interference and the range of Near Eastern languages with which contact is attested. More richly documented is also the wider cultural context of language contact in the New Kingdom. Even so, biases of the evidence are prevalent and cause problems to any factual assessment: e.g., terms relating to warfare and military equipment account for the largest portion among the Semitic loanwords in New Kingdom documents (15%: Hoch 1994, 471) although war literature and documents of the military administration have hardly been preserved (Spalinger 2002, 347–365). At closer inspection (Schneider 2008a), most of them are attested only rarely, many just once. While they may not be examples of "nonce borrowing" (incidental borrowings practically equivalent with single-word code switches; Zenner and Kristiansen 2013, 4; Winand 2017 sees most of the terms indeed as examples of code-switching), they still illustrate the fact that all assessments are based on a very small and also coincidental set of data.

3.2.4.1 Lexical transfer

Lexical transfer in the Egyptian New Kingdom is the best-documented case for Egyptian-Near Eastern language contact. Loanwords are lexical units, but they are also cultural tokens, thus at the same time both an important linguistic and historical source of information. In the linguistics of borrowing (Hoffer 1996; for the following Schneider 2004, 11-31; see also Mahlich 2022, 565-8), loanwords are classified with respect to the geographic place of borrowing (diatopic) and the social place of borrowing (diastratic), or rather, the socio-textual place, since social status, language use and textual production are so closely intertwined. The situation is exacerbated by the phenomenon of diglossia (with a high register and a vernacular version of Egyptian in concomitant use) from the Middle Kingdom to the late 18th dynasty; and the presence of several Egyptian linguistic varieties for different types of textual production side by side from the 19th dynasty on. A wide range of motivations facilitate bor-rowing, in particular onomasiology (lexical gaps), linguistic economy (more precise terminology), and reasons of communication (code switching, style and fashion, social and ideological motivations such as prestige, erudition, exotism). The range of use of loanwords affect their phonological, morphological and semantic integration. E.g., the probable Second Intermediate Period loanword *wrry.t* "chariot" (see p. 80) was fully integrated in Egyptian in the early New Kingdom and appears in stylistic variation with the new borrowing, Northwest Semitic *markabat* (*m-r-k-ꜣ-b-w-tı͗,* Hoch 1994, 146). In the Late Period, it assumes the meaning "wagon, cart (for transport)" und so enters into competition with another Semitic loanword *'agālat* (*ꜥꜣ-g-ꜣ-r-tı͗*, Coptic ^{S}ⲁϭⲟⲗⲧⲉ, ^{B}ⲁϫⲟⲗϯ, "wagon, cart [for transport]"; Hoch 1994, 83).

In Egyptian New Kingdom texts, c. 350 loan words of probably or possibly Semitic origin are attested (Hoch 1994; Sivan and Cochavi-Rainey 1992; Winand 2017); I present a new review of that material on pp. 91-5. Additionally, these texts yield c. 300 loanwords of likely non-Semitic provenance (Schneider 2004; for loanwords from 'African' and 'Mediterranean' languages, see 2.2.2 and 4.3, respectively). In terms of the attestation of these words, it is important to notice that $^{2}/_{3}$ of the terms are from texts of the elite culture (wisdom texts, onomastica, religious texts, autobiographies, royal texts) and just $^{1}/_{3}$ from texts close to the vernacular (letters, judicial, business, fiction and lyric texts) (Winand 2017). The notation of these words uses a specialized Egyptian transcription system, the so-called "syllabic orthography" (after William F. Albright) or "group writing" (Hoch 1994, 498-502; for a recent new assessment, Kilani 2019), which was equally used for the large corpus of foreign toponyms and personal names (Schneider 1992) but was also in use for a number of genuinely Egyptian words (Winand 2017). By contrast with the older transcription system that mainly used one-consonant signs, most hieroglyphs employed in the new system are old biliteral signs that are now used for *Cv* sequences, and additionally, monosyllabic Egyptian words (such as *'i* "island"; *ʿa "great"*) that could represent a foreign syllable (Hoch 1994, 498-502).

One of the more important corollary results of the analysis of loanwords in Egyptian transcription is the information it provides on the donor languages. The majority of Semitic loanwords attested in the New Kingdom seem to be Northwest Semitic (see in detail, pp. 89-96). To Semitic donor languages can be added non-Semitic ones from the Near East, in particular Hittite (see below pp. 96-7) and Hurrian (see below pp. 97-8).

In terms of semantic categories, the largest group of terms is that of military language (cf. the detailed analysis by Schneider 2008a, with the subcategories *technology of the chariot and its equipment* (30 terms), *military equipment, weaponry and infrastructure* (27 terms), *military titles and functions* (14 terms), *military behaviour and activities* (14 terms) and *violence, intimidation and flight* (26 terms). Of these terms, only a very limited number (c. 3) are attested prior to the 18th dynasty (>1550 BC), 10% are attested since the 18th dynasty, and the majority in Ramesside times. In terms of the frequency of loanwords, hapax legomena account for more than 40% of the attested lexemes, words attested up to eight times account for 90% (Winand 2017). The most frequent terms in the New Kingdom are interestingly Hurrian words: the title *kuzine* "charioteer" (written *kꜣ-č̣-n* and *kꜣ-čꜣ-n-ꜣ*: Hoch 1994, 341-345; with the Hurrian 'article' *–ne*: Schneider 2008a, 194) and the adjective *t-l* "valiant" (if < Hurrian *adal*, Schneider 1999) with each more than 125 attestations. The number of attestations across different text genres is at least partially a reflection of the genuine diffusion of these words, as the 65 Semitic loan words from New Kingdom texts that have survived into Coptic are mostly such attested frequently in the New Kingdom (Winand 2017).

With regard to word classes, 83% of the attested Semitic loanwords are nouns, 16% verbs, and just 1% other word classes. One exceptional case from the last group is the Northwest Semitic interrogative particle *'ēḏæ* "which" (Hoch 1994,

43-4, written with the classifier of the speaking/asking man), used by the scribes as a stylistic device to display their erudition and give the text exotic flavor (Winand 2017). In the same way, the abundance of loanwords in specific compositions such as the 'Hymn to the King in His Chariot' were "for the ancient Egyptian scribe a way to craft poetry from exotica"; "just as the Egyptian armies conquered foreign lands, so did Egyptian poets use foreign words verbally to curb Egypt's foes" (Manassa 2013, 151, 153). Pap. Anastasi I, 23, 2-7 may be an example of such an erudite text (Schneider 2008a, 198-202); it could also be seen as a text using linguistic indexes that point to the author's ethnic or professional identity (see p. 155). I give here my own translation of the text (after Schneider 2008a, 199; note the abbreviation *NWS* = Northwest Semitic):

You are a *māhîr* (NWS, elite soldier), experienced in the arts of the hero!
A *māhîr* like you is called upon to *šāq* (NWS, charge) ahead of the troops!
O *Marianni* (Hurrian, maybe < Indo-Aryan), (23,3), forward to shoot!
(Task:) To protect against the *mūrādat* (NWS, fallen rocks) at the *šātōt* (NWS, feet of the mountains), filled with boulders and debris of 2000 cubits depth.
(Solution:) (23,4) You order a *ṯōbēb* (NWS, retreat).
You lift the bow and make a *pirṣ* (NWS, breach) on your left.
You let the chieftains – (23,5) whose eyes are good – see
if there is any negligence in your actions –
"*hēbī'tā [or Phoenician: 'ēbī'tā?] kamā 'arī māhîr nā'îm*"
(NWS: "You have led [the troops] across like a lion, lucky Mahir").
That way you make the reputation of (23,6) every Mahir and *kuzine* (Hurrian, charioteer) of Tameri (Egypt)!
Your name is like (that of) *Gauzal-diy* (NWS, young bird of prey), the chieftain of Aseru,
after the mother bear (23,7) found him in the *bākā'* (NWS, pear tree?)

- Note that no consensus exists even regarding the translation of a sentence like the one in 23,5, said about the Mahir (*ỉ-bꜣ-tʿ* [SPEAK] *kꜣ-m* [SPEAK] *ỉ-ꜣ-r* [ANIMAL.PLURAL]). Presumed to be in Canaanite, interpretations have produced the renderings "I perish like a lamb" (Albright) vs. "You are straying like a sheep" (Fischer-Elfert) vs. "You are murdering like a lion" (Burchardt,

Helck) vs. "I have destroyed (you) like a lion" (Hoch) vs. "You have led (the troops) across like a lion" (Schneider 2008a, 201 with a discussion of the different proposals).

Only short texts exclusively in a foreign language and transcribed in the Egyptian script are known from New Kingdom Egypt (for an overview, Helck 1971, 528-30; Quack 2010a; Allon 2010). These few (mostly Semitic) texts are:

- incantations in the London Medical Papyrus (Pap. BM EA 10059, Steiner 1992). Here one spell is explicitly said to be an "incantation of the disease of the Asiatics in the language of Crete" (Haider 2004; Redford 2005-6; Lange 2007; for the possibility of an identification of the language of Linear A with Luwian, see Mouton, Rutherford and Yakubovich 2013, 5-6);
- incantations in Magical Pap. Harris (Pap. BM EA 10042; Schneider 1989);
- three lines noted down on Ostracon CG 25759 from Deir el-Medineh (Shisha-Halevy 1978).

Allon has recently demonstrated that the Semitic texts in Egyptian transcription show a specific use of the Egyptian system of classifiers, including a metatextual function of the 'speaking man' (Gardiner Sign List A2) and other determinatives to indicate the un-Egyptian linguistic origin of words (Allon 2010). It must be assumed that the Egyptian occupation of the Levant and Egypt's cultural influence also had a lexical impact on Northwest Semitic vocabulary (for proposed Egyptian words in the Ugaritic lexicon, see Watson 2010 [and the earlier installments 1-7 of his series of contributions]; Mahlich 2022, 273-93).

3.2.4.1.1 Semitic languages

The debate on the internal classification of the Semitic languages continues. There is consensus that, genetically, the language family consists of an *East Semitic* subgroup (also attested earlier and thus, sometimes labeled, "Old Semitic") and a *West Semitic* subgroup (sometimes labeled "Young Semitic"). I give here the basic genetic classification of a more comprehensive list provided in Huehnergard and Pat-El (2019, p. 3 fig. 1.1; similarly Huehnergard and Rubin 2011, 263), comprising 60 individual language/ dialect specimens (among which Amurrite/Amorite is missing):

- East Semitic
  - Akkadian
    - Assyrian, Babylonian
  - Eblaïte
- West Semitic
  - Ethio-Semitic
  - Modern South Arabian
  - Central Semitic
    - Ancient Arabian
    - North Arabian (including Classical Arabic)
    - Northwest Semitic
      - Ugaritic
      - Samalian
      - Aramaeo-Canaanite
        - Canaanite (incl. Phoenician-Punic, Hebrew)
        - Aramaic

As Huehnergard and Rubin emphasize, genetic (tree) models do not reflect sufficiently the complex linguistic development over time where inherited features are combined with internal changes and traits received through areal diffusion (Huehnergard and Rubin 2011, 263-7).

Semitic loanwords represent the best-attested segment among the loanwords of the New Kingdom (1530-1070 BCE), a situation which probably reflects the fact that borrowings ocurred very often from Semitic donor languages. However, this status of research is also owed to the fact that we have at our disposal a large contemporary lexicon for comparative purposes – which privileges the establishment of Semitic etymologies over those from other source languages. Hoch's 1994 standard reference work – which is not entirely exhaustive (see the reviews by Quack 1996; Schneider 1996; Meeks 1997; Vittmann 1997) – lists c. 330 words as presumably Semitic, transcribed in a variety of the hieroglyphic script known as "group writing" or "syllabic orthography" (see p. 86).

Winand (2017) has recently emphasized that, of these Semitic loans, two-thirds stem from texts of the elite culture (royal texts, autobiographies, wisdom texts, onomastica, religious texts) and just one-third from texts closer to the vernacular domain (letters and judicial, business, fiction, and lyric texts).

For the purpose of this overview, I have revisited the etymologies given by Hoch (1994) and frequently made different assessments, excluding some etymologies considered by Hoch as 'certain' (his category '5') as not warranted, and conversely, upgrading some of his 'uncertain etymologies' to certain ones. I have retained a total of 110 fairly certain Semitic loanwords from the period of the New Kingdom. They are listed here in the sequence of Hoch's (1994) entries with his entry numbers, in transcription (see the note on p. 4), with Semitic reference terms (languages abbreviated; H. = Hebrew) and a translation:

i̓-ꜣ-y-r ANIMAL (1)	ʾayyāl (H. etc.)	stag
i̓-bꜣ-r HORSE (3)	ʾabbīr (H.)	stallion
i̓/y-bꜣ-š-ti̓/tw BREAD (5)	yabbīšat (Sem.)	biscuit
i̓-pꜣ-ti̓ BREAD (7)	ʾap̄īt (Sem.)	cakes, biscuits
i̓wn-rw-nꜣ TREE (11)	ʾallōn (H.)	oak tree
i̓-r-q-ꜣ-bꜣ-sꜣ STONE (22)	i̓lgbṯ (Ug.), ʾælgab̲īš (H.)	(a precious stone)
i̓-h-ꜣ-r STRING.HOUSE (24)	i̓hl (Ug.)	tent
i̓-ś-b-t WOOD/SEAT (30/31)	ʾašbatu (Akk.)	chair, throne
i̓-ś-pꜣ-ti̓ ANIMAL (34)	ʾašpā (H.), išpatu (Akk.)	quiver
i̓-čꜣ SPEAK (38)	ʾēd̲æ (H.)	which (interr. part.)
i̓-čꜣ-r CROSS.FORCE (40)	ʾasīr (Sem.)	captive
y-w-bꜣ-r WATER.STREAM (49)	yūb̲al (H.)	stream
y-m WATER.STREAM (52)	yām (H.)/yamm (Sem.)	sea
y-ṭ-i̓-ʿ FOREIGN.MAN (64)	yādiʿ (NWSem.)	skilled, learned
ʿ-p-r FOREIGN.MAN. PLURAL (70)	ʿprm (Ug.), ḫabiru (Akk.)	ʿApiru/Habiru
ʿ-p-šꜣ-y-t SCARAB/INSECT (72)	ḥippušit (Aram.)	beetle, scarab
ʿ-m-q PENIS.FORCE (75)	ʿmq (Aram.)	to penetrate (sexually)
ʿ-m-ṭ-i̓ FORCE (76)	ʿmd (H.)	to stand firm
ʿ-m(ꜣ)-ṭ-i̓(-y) ANIMAL/TREE (77)	ʿammūd (H.)	support (part of the chariot)
ʿ-r-šꜣ-n-ꜣ GRAIN.PLURAL (84)	ʿ^{a}dašim (H.), Aram. pl.?	lentils

ʿ-r-tỉ HOUSE (86)	ʿalīt (Ph., Amor., Aram., Akk.)	upper chamber
ʿ-w-r-č̣ꜣ-w-t FORCE.MAN (87)	ʿorəṭōt (Ug., H.)	the terrifying ones
ʿ-š(ꜣ)-q/g(ꜣ) CROSS.VIOLENCE (92) verb; also noun (93)	ʿašaq (H., Aram.)	extort, defraud; oppress
ʿ-gꜣ-r- tỉ WOOD (100)	ʿagalat (Sem.)	wagon, cart
ʿ-ṭ-w-tỉ ENEMY.FORCE.MAN (105)	ʿēdōt (H., Ug.)	(conspiratorial) assem-blies
ʿ-w-č̣ꜣ-r FORCE (108)	ʿōḏer (H., Phoen., Ug.)	saviour
b-ʿ-r WATER.STREAM.LAND (114)	baḥr (Arab., S.Arab., Eth.)	sea, lake
b-ʿ-r SETH ANIMAL (115)	baʿl (NW Sem.)	divine name ‚Baʿal'
b(ꜣ)-r-q/g-ꜣ (126)	brq (Sem.)	to sparkle
bꜣ-r-kꜣ FORCE (127), also nouns "greetings; gifts" (128, 129)	brk (Sem.)	to kneel, bow, bless
bꜣ-r-k-ꜣ-tỉ WATER.STREAM. LAND (131)	birkat (Sem.)	pool, pond
bꜣ-r-g-ꜣ WEARY.BAD (133)	blg (H., Arab.)	be happy, content
bꜣ-r-tỉ WATER.STREAM. LAND (135, 124)	bərīt (H.)	obligatory service, treaty
p-w-r(-i-ꜣ/y) GRAIN.PLURAL (150)	pūl	beans
p-r-ḫ FLOWER (151 vb/152 noun)	prḫ (Sem.)	blossom
mw-ʿṭ LAND (161)	mōʿēd (Sem.)	assembly
mn-nw GRAIN.PLURAL (162)	manû (Akk.), mānæ (H., Aram.)	mina (weight unit)
mn-ḥ-tỉ PLANT (165)	manḥat (Sem.)	gift, tribute
mn-ṭ-ꜣ-tỉ GRAIN (170)	mandat (Aram., Akk.)	tribute, tax
m-r-ḥ INGOT/WOOD (179)	mrḥ (Ug.)	spear, lance
m-w-r-ḥ-m-ꜣ WALK.FORCE.MAN (179)	mōləḥim (H., root Sem.)	salt workers
mr-św VESSEL (183, also 184?)	mrṯ (Ug.)	new wine, must
m-r-k-ꜣ-b-w-tỉ WOOD (189)	markabat (Sem.)	chariot
m-h-ꜣ-r CHILD.FORCE (190)	mahīr (Sem.)	skilled, expert
m-śꜣ-ḫ-ỉ VESSEL (198/9)	mašḫu, mašīḫu (Akk.)	large vessel (for wine/oil)
m-š-ꜣb-w WATER.STREAM.LAND (205)	mašʾaḇ (H.)	watering place

m(ꜣ)-q-ꜣ-r/n.t ^{WOOD} (217)	maqqēl (H.)	staff, stick, rod
m-k-m-rw-tꞽ ^{STRING} (222)	mikmarōt (H.)	fishnets
m-k-ꞽ-rw-ꞽ-w-ꞽ $^{\text{ABSTRACT.FORCE.MAN}}$ (223)	mākiru (Akk., Ug., H.)	merchant
m(ꞽ)-k-tꞽ-r $^{\text{WALL.HOUSE}}$ (224)	migdāl (NWSem.)	tower
m-g-ꜣ-r-tꞽ ^{STONE} (228)	maġārat (Sem.)	cave
m-č̣ꜣ-r-n-ꜣ ^{INGOT} (241)	mḏrn (Ug.)	(a type of weapon)
n-ʿ-m-w $^{\text{WALK.SPEAK}}$ (244)	nāʿim (NWSem.)	pleasant
n-ꜣ-ʿ-rw-n-ꜣ $^{\text{FOREIGN.MAN.PL}}$ (245)	naʿarūna (H., Ug.; ending -n-ꜣ Aram.?)	(special kind of) soldiers
n-ḫ-r $^{\text{WATER.STREAM.LAND}}$ (258)	naḫal (Sem.)	wadi, seasonal river
n-k-pꜣ-tꞽ ^{PLANT} (260; also 261)	nikiptu (Akk.)	the nikiptu plant/oil
r-b-w-y ^{ANIMAL} (273)	lāḇiʾ, ləḇiyyāʾ (H., also Sem.)	lioness
r-bꜣ-šꜣ-y ^{ANIMAL} (274)	ləḇuš (H.), ləḇu/išā (Aram.)	cuirass, leather armour
r-bꜣ-k-ꜣ-y ^{PASTRY} (276)	rəḇikā (MH., Aram.)	(a type of pastry)
r-h-ṭ-t ^{VESSEL} (279)	rah(ā)ṭ (H., Aram., Akk.)	trough, vessel
r-ḥꜣ-b-w $^{\text{VESSEL/INGOT}}$ (281)	rḥb.t (Ug.)	amphora, basin
rw-šꜣ-ꞽ-w ^{HEAD} (285)	rōʾš (Sem., vocalization H.)	peak, summit
r-k-ś-w ^{FORCE} (286)	rəkūš (H.)	outfit, equipment, gear
h-r ^{FORCE} (294)	har (H.)	mountain
h-ꜣ-r-f-ꞽ ^{FORCE} (295)	hārəpōʾ	the healing
h-(ꜣ)-ṭ-m(-)w ^{WOOD} (304)	h^{a}dom (H., Ug.)	footstool
ḥ-f-č̣ꜣ $^{\text{LEG.WALK}}$ (310)	ḥpz (H.)	to hurry
ḥꜣ-m-r ^{ANIMAL} (312)	ḥimār (Sem.)	ass, donkey
ḥ-m-č̣ꜣ $^{\text{VESSEL/BAD}}$ (316)	ḥumḏ (Sem.)	vinegar, sour wine
ḥ(-)n-y-t ^{SPEAR} (318)	ḥ^{a}nit (H.)	spear, javelin
ḥ-r-p-w ^{INGOT} (324)	ḥarb (Sem.)	dagger, short sword
ḫꜣ-r-b-w $^{\text{FOREIGN.FOREIGN LAND}}$ (346)	ḫarbu (Akk.)	desert
ḫ-ꞽ-čꜣ-n-ꜣ ^{PLANT} (355)	ḫazannu (Akk.)	garlic
ś-ʿ-r(w)^{PLANT}/ś-ʿ-r-tꞽ^{HAIR} (355, 356)	śaʿr(at) (Sem.)	barley/scrubs; hair/wool

s-n-n-ꞽ ARROW/WALK/FORCE.MAN (371)	ṯannānu (Ug.)	charioteer
śꜣ-r-q-w SNOW FLAKES/RAIN (375)	ṯalgu (Sem.)	snow
ś-g-ꜣ-r WALL.HOUSE (385)	ṯġr (Sem.)	gate
šꜣ-ꜥ-r SPEAK (387-9)	šꜥr (Aram., Arab.)	measure, estimate
šꜣ-b(-w)-ṯ-t/ṯꞽ/tꞽ WOOD (397)	šiḇṭ (H., Aram.)	staff, rod
šꜣ-r-m(ꜣ) PRAISE (406-8) šꜣ-r-m(ꜣ)-tꞽ BREAD (409)	šlm (Sem.) šlm.t	to greet, surrender peace gift
šꜣ-ḥ-qꜣ ABSTRACT/RAIN/BREAD (411)	šaḥaq (H.)	cloud of dust or flour
šꜣ-ṯ-ꜣ NEGATIVE.VIOLENCE (418)	šod (H.)	violence, destruction
q-ꜣ-rw(-ꞽ-ꜣ/ ꞽ/w) LEG.WALK (428-9)	grʾ, gēr	to be an alien; alien
q-r-ꜥ-w SHIELD q-r-(ꞽ-)ꜥ-w (FORCE.)MAN (432-4)	qlʿ (Ug.)	shield, shield-bearer
q-ꜣ-r-n-ꜣ-tꞽ FLESH (436)	ġurlat (H., Aram., Arab.)	foreskin; uncircumcised phallus
q-ꜣ-r-č̣-ꜣ/ꞽ-n-ꜣ INGOT (438)	garzæn (H.)	(pick-)axe
q-ꜣ-ṯ-ꜣ-rw-tꞽ GRAIN (440)	qṭōræt (H.)	incense
q-ꜣ-č̣-ꜣ(ꞽ-w/ꞽ) GRAIN/STONE/VESSEL (442; cf. also derived 443)	gaṣṣu (Akk.), gēṣ (H., Aram.)	gypsum
k-ꜣ-bꜣ-r-tꞽ FIRE (458)	Akk. kibrītu, Aram. keḇrīṯā, Arab. kibrit	sulphur, brimstone
kꜣ-b-w-śꜣ/św HOBBLE (456)	kōp̄æš (MH., < kupṯ)	basket
k(ꜣ)-p-w HAND (457)	kapp (Sem.)	palm (of the hand)
k-ꜣ-m SPEAK (458)	kamā	like, as
kꜣ/k-ꜣ-m-rw DANCERS/LEG.WALK.MAN (462)	kōmær (H.)	the ardent, agitated one (term for type of dancer)
k-n-ꞽ-n-ꞽ-w-rw WOOD (467)	kinnōr (H., Sem.)	lyre
k-ꜣ-r-čꜣ-r STONE (485)	gilgāl (H.)	stone pile
k(-)ꜣ-r-čꜣ STRIP (485)	kurussu (Akk.)	whip cords
g-ꜣ-r-b/p-w FINGER/CROSS.FORCE (515)	glb (NWSem., Akk.)	to shave, plane (wood)
g(ꜣ)/k(ꜣ)-r/nꜣ-(ꞽ)-tꞽ FLESH (520)	Akk. kalītu, Sem. with -y	kidney
t-r/ tꞽ-n-r LAND (527)	tl (Sem.)	mound

tỉ-r-tỉ (533, also 528?)	dælæt (H.), daltu (Akk.)	door
tỉ-ḫ-r ANIMAL (538)	taḥrā (H.)	leather panels of chariot
č-w-pꜣ-r SCRIBAL KIT.MAN (540)	sōp̄er (H.)	scribe
čꜣ-p-w-r VESSEL (541; also 547?)	spl (NWSem., Akk.)	drinking bowl
č(-w)-p-r(-t) CHARIOT/INGOT (542)	saparru (Akk.)	chariot (w/ copper plat-ing)
čw/čꜣ-rw/r-tỉ GRAIN MEASURE/ BREAD (550)	sōlæt (H.), siltu (Akk.)	fine wheat flour
ṭ-bꜣ-r WOOD.HOUSE (561)	dəḇīr (H., Phoen.)	holy of holies
ṭ-p-ḥ-w TREE/PLANT/PEBBLE (563)	tappūḥ (Sem.)	apple
č̣ꜣ-ʿ-w-q SPEAK (verb 570; noun 571)	ṣ/zʿq (Sem.)	to cry out
č̣ꜣ-bꜣ-ỉw FOREIGN/FORCE. MAN; MERCENARY (573)	ḍābaʾ/uʾ (Sem.)	army, troops
č̣ꜣ-m-ʿ BAD (581)	ṯmʾ (Sem.)	to be thirsty
č̣ꜣ-r-ʿ(-t-)w WOOD (592)	ḏ̣ēlaʿ, pl. ḏ̣əlāʿot (H.)	plank, board
Č̣Ṭ(= /zi/)-t-w TREE.WOOD (594)	zēt (Sem.)	olive, olive tree, olive oil
č̣-ỉ-č̣-ỉ (595)	ṣiṣ (H., Aram.)	flower, flower ornament

According to Hoch's assessment, the inventory of phonemes visible in these borrowings seems rather reminiscent of the phonological situation in Aramaic and South Arabic. The conclusion could be that a richer phoneme inventory needs to be postulated for Phoenician and Hebrew than the short alphabet of 22 signs would suggest (Hoch 1994, 479-486). Within the Late Bronze Age Levant, Egyptians maintained a strong presence, and to judge by excavated cemeteries, some Egyptians may have settled permanently at the Egyptian military bases (Morris 2005, 826-7); an authentic recording of terms from speakers in the Levant was therefore certainly well possible. On the other hand, it is reasonable to assume that many of these terms were borrowed within Egypt from native speakers of Semitic languages of different backgrounds and that the existing evidentiary basis obscures a much more complex transfer situation in Egypt. Most of the Semitic borrowings have parallels in several branches of Northwest Semitic, some in individual Northwest Semitic languages only (e.g.,

Ugaritic or Aramaic). A small number were taken from East Semitic Akkadian, e.g., *mn-ṭ-ꜣ-tỉ* VESSEL = *mandattu*, “tribute” (Hoch 1994, no.170*); m-sꜣ-ḫ-ỉ* VESSEL = *mašḫu, mašīḫu*, “large vessel” (Hoch nos. 198/199), or *n-k-pꜣ-tỉ PLANT* = *nikiptu*, “an aromatic, gum-yielding plant” (Hoch no. 260). Some of the loan histories are complex (see below pp. 127-8 for *tꜣ-ḫ-b(w)-s/šꜣ-tỉ* as an example). The variation visible in the writing of some terms may be due to post-transfer integration, including the adaptation by native Egyptian speakers.

3.2.4.1.2 Anatolian languages

Anatolian languages (see map 4) are a subgroup of Indo-European languages in Asia Minor, where they replaced autchthonous languages following the immigration of Indo-European populations (for models about the Indo-Europeanization of Anatolia, see below 4.2). The internal classification of Anatolian languages is still a matter of debate (see Popko 2008; ten Cate, van den Hout and Melchert 1999/2009; Rieken 2017; for the Carian evidence in the 1st millennium BCE, see pp. 106-7). In the 19th dynasty, the royal courts of Egypt and the empire of Hatti entertained close diplomatic, scientific and economic contacts (see the comprehensive survey by Breyer 2010a). These contacts are also reflected in intense linguistic engagement, best visible in Egyptian-Hittite mutual translation (see pp. 101-2). They also left an impact in the form of loanwords in Egyptian from Anatolian languages, of which Hittite and Luwian are relevant for the 2nd millennium. Some of the better established loanwords are:

- *p-ṭ-ỉ-r* “woven container” < Hittite *pattar*, Lycian πατάρα “basket” (Schneider 2004, 16)
- *mꜣ-ỉ-w-r-tỉ* (in list of food items after honey, goose fat, cream, milk) = Hittite (etc.) *milit* “honey” (Schneider 1996)
- *h-ꜣ-r-n-ꜣ-tỉ* (a kind of grain) = Hittite / Luwian *ḫarnant-* “risen, ferment ed (dough)” (with assimilation; Breyer 2010a, 360)
- *ḫ-bꜣ-ỉ-r* “business, trade” < Hittite heth. *ḫappar* “business, trade, payment, price” (Schneider 2004, 23)
- *ḫꜣ-pw* “a body of water, river?” = Luwian *ḫāpa*, Hittite *ḫapa* “river” (Schneider 2004, 24)

- *ḫꜣ-rw-p-w-sꜣ-t* (a kind of pastry) < Hittite *ḫar(a)špau̯ante* "type of bread or cake made of meat or mushrooms" (with post-transfer metathesis? Schneider 2004, 21)
- *ḫꜣ-rw-rw* (a mineral) = Hittite *ḫulala* "onyx, agate ?" (Breyer 2010a, 363)
- *šꜣ-kꜣ-n-ꜣ* "watering place" = Hittite *šaku(u̯a)nni* "spring, pool" (Breyer 2010a, 364-5)
- *kꜣ-r-sꜣ* "sack" < Hittite kurša "(sack of) leather, skin" (Schneider 2004, 26-7; also attested in Ugaritic and Akkadian).

3.2.4.1.3 Hurrian

Hurrian, the language of the empire of Mitanni, constitutes with Urartian as its only confirmed cognate an isolated language group of the Near East (see Campbell 2020). Competency in Hurrian on Egyptian soil is most famously attested through the "Mitanni letter" from Amarna (EA 24). Only a small number of Hurrian loanwords in Egyptian texts of the New Kingdom have so far been established with a certain degree of certainty. This is conspicuous, given that the Hurrian country name *ḫurri* (Richter 2012, 171) was adopted as a regular term for 'Syria' in the New Kingdom *(ḫꜣ-rw*; with the Egyptian article also as a frequent ethnonym: *pꜣ ḫꜣ-rw* "the Syrian"), and that the most frequently attested loanwords in Late Egyptian seem to be Hurrian terms:

- the title *kuzine* "charioteer" (Hoch 1994, 341-345; *–ne* is the Hurrian 'article': Schneider 2008a, 194)
- the adjective *tl* "valiant" (if < Hurrian *adal*, Schneider 1999)

with each more than 125 attestations. The limited number of Hurrian loanwords is therefore likely a reflection of our limited knowledge of Hurrian vocabulary and will increase in future research. Possible loanwords are:

- pw-tꜣ-rw < Hurrian *pedari* "cattle") (Schneider 2004, 16)
- ḫꜣ-rw, Coptic ϩιⲣ "street, quarter" < Hurrian *ḫari* (Urartian *ḫarə*) "street, way" (or Hittite *ḫaruwa*, Hierogl.-Luwian *ḫarwa* "street, way"?) (Schneider 2004, 21; a problem is the vocalization, see Schweitzer 2005)
- śꜣ-i͗-ꜣ WATER.CANAL < Hurrian *šie/a, šiye/a* "water, water course, river"

(Schneider 2004, 22; cf. Richter 2012, 366-7)

> The latter term appears in one of the tomb robbery trials (Pap. Turin 10052, 14, 8), probably in a metaphorical sense "torrent" ("Fill yourself with my courage in this *torrent* of investigation").

An interesting case of implicit translation of a Hurrian term may occur in the description of the chariot in Pap. Anastasi IV 16,8: "their supports (Semitic ʿmd) are made of gold, their *ḫiaroḫḫe* (Hurrian: "golden ones") are of gold" (Schneider 2003d; Schneider 2004, 21).

3.2.4.1.4 Other Near Eastern languages of the Late Bronze Age

It is very likely that other languages of the Near East that are currently attested only marginally or unattested (see the comments on p. 72) are also represented in the borrowed lexicon of Egyptian. Additional loanwords may originate in languages from outside the Near East. One such example is the Hurrian military title *marianni* "charioteer, knight" which may ultimately be of Indo-Aryan origin (Sanskrit *marya*, "hero"), although the term spread widely across the Near East (see Hoch 1994, 135-7; Richter 2012, 244-5).

3.2.4.2 Bilingualism and Interpreting

While a comprehensive appreciation of linguistic interference between ancient Egyptian and Near Eastern languages in the Late Bronze Age escapes us, information on the extent of oral, written and scribal interaction can be gained from different types of evidence. Foreign linguistic communities are attested throughout Egypt (cf. Schneider 2010), so that bilingualism must have been a frequent phenomenon. It can be assumed that bearers of non-Egyptian personal names may be an indicator of non-Egyptian heritage, and possibly foreign language expertise. Among the Near Eastern personal names preserved for residents of Egypt in the New Kingdom, almost 80% can be explained as Semitic and 20% as of other provenance (Schneider 1992, 357). While the majority of

the Semitic names can be classified as Northwest Semitic, a number of names are clearly Akkadian (Middle Assyrian; c. 2%) and some also possibly early North Arabic (c. 3%; Schneider 1992, 358; further developed by Israel 2006, 33-36). In some cases, Semitic personal names are attested in subsequent generations of a family or for both husband and wife, thus pointing to the presence of Semitic communication in a private context (Schneider 2006, 207). A certain presence of Hittite, Middle Babylonian and Hurrian within the Egyptian royal family is certain through the diplomatic marriages of Egyptian kings with Hittite, Babylonian and Mitanni princesses (Roth 2002) who moved to Egypt with their entourage and, arguably, also literary texts for their personal perusal. The knowledge of the Semitic languages of the Levant seems to have been a prerequisite for higher military posts in the New Kingdom (as exemplified by the military handbook of Papyrus Anastasi I; Schneider 2008a). In the Levant, Egyptian may have had the status of *lingua franca* (Helck 1971, 436). Interpreters of foreign languages are depicted on the reliefs from the Saqqara tomb of the later king Horemheb (Martin 1989); under Merenptah, the high priest and former army scribe of the chariotry Onurismes declares in his funerary biography: "I spoke in the [appropriate] foreign language for any foreign language in attendance before my lord" (Meyrat 2015, 332; Starke 1993, 38 n. 63).
Interpreters proficient in Egyptian are also mentioned for foreign states (e.g., for Babylonia, in Amarna letter EA11; for Cyprus, in the 21st dynasty *Tale of Wenamun*); an Egyptian interpreter Ramose (Riamassi) served for 13 years in Hittite diplomatic service (Starke 1993, 37). The fact that interpreters and translators are hardly ever explicitly mentioned in our texts is a case of *implicit communication*, similarly to Mesopotamia (von Soden 1989; Starke 1993, 37-8; for a comprehensive view, Tarawneh 2011), testament to the ubiquitous use of language specialists and also the presence of bilingualism. Royal envoys abroad (for a list of Egyptian envoys in Cuneiform sources, see Helck 1971, 437-442) were accompanied by interpreters, and specialized interpretation can be assumed for the Egyptian physicians at the Hittite court and other occasions

of cultural and technological exchange (see Breyer 2010, 247-307), such as the Hittite specialists working in Piramesse (Herold 1998).

3.2.4.3 Interference in texts: interlanguage and translation

3.2.4.3.1 A presumed interlanguage: 'Akkadian by Egyptians'

The Amarna letters from c. 1350 BCE and the correspondence between the Ramesside and Hittite royal courts from the reign of Ramesses II attest to the existence of scribes trained in corresponding in Akkadian, Hittite, Hurrian and other languages of the Near East (for the training in Cuneiform, see Mynářová 2015). Important literary texts from abroad were used for scribal and cultural instruction, and one tablet (EA368) represents an Egyptian-Akkadian vocabulary (Tarawneh 2011, 276; Meyrat 2015, 326). The presence of a "gloss marker" in these texts to gloss Akkadian words and logograms by Canaanite terms must have supported the writing or the translation process (Tarawneh 2011, 277f.). The Egyptians also knew as early as the 18th dynasty of the Semitic alphabet sequences (Haring 2015; Schneider 2018).

Two groups of texts display linguistic interference between the native Egyptian language of the scribes and the normative Akkadian language of diplomacy:

(1) the mid-14th century letters dispatched from Egypt (ten found at Amarna; two at Egypt's administrative center Kumidi/Kamid el-Lōz in Lebanon) and the copies of literary texts, syllabaries and wordlists from Amarna;

(2) c. 100 texts (mostly letters, but also two versions of the Egyptian-Hittite peace treaty) from the first half of the 13th century.

Matthias Müller has defined this "Akkadian from Egypt" as an interlanguage (Müller 2010; Müller 2015) with a number of linguistic peculiarities that could be explained by the situation in Egyptian:

- on a graphemic level, a tendency to use fewer Cuneiform signs than in Mesopotamian texts and to mark the plural by the plural marker MEŠ after the noun, as in Egyptian;
- on a phonological level, e.g., no discrimination in the rendering of stops

(<TA> for /ta/, /da/ and /ṭa/) and some other features;

- on a morphological level, the occasional disregard for case endings (e.g., nominative *–u* instead of Genitive *–i*), the absence of causative and passive, as well as a number of features that appear to replicate Egyptian linguistic laws: the use of the particle *ana* to introduce a dative pronoun and the avoidance of direct suffigation of a pronoun to the stative; an indirect expression of possession after indefinite nouns; and the use of adverbs to grade adjectives and to express excessiveness by iteration.
- On a syntactical level, features of interference are visible in the word order (sometimes demonstrative pronouns before nouns) and particularly the replication of Egyptian sentence patterns: e.g., the future tense makes use of the preposition *ana* "to", followed by an infinitive, as in the Egyptian *Future III*; the verb is placed in initial position like in Late Egyptian past and prospective sentences; the stative forms are used with verbs of motion in the past. Further interference can be detected in several types of nominal and adverbial sentences, in the use of predicative adjectives in initial positions, and within the Amarna letters, also in the use of relative clauses without the particle *ša*. Egyptian Akkadian also shows new syntactic developments such as *subject-verb-object* as the unmarked word order and idiomatic borrowings from Egyptian ("to give the face to" in the sense of "to give attention to sth").

3.2.4.3.2 Translation and the adaptation of texts

The full translation of entire texts into Egyptian (cf. Schneider 2011) is best known from the Egyptian version of the Hittite-Egyptian peace treaty between Hattusili III and Ramesses II, from 1269 BCE (the 21st regnal year of Ramesses II). The translation used the text on the silver tablet brought to Egypt and was engraved on the walls of the Karnak Temple and the Ramesseum; it has been the focus of extensive scholarship (Edel 1997; Allam 2011; Davies 2018, 25-43). In the Egyptian version the Egyptian term *mỉty* "copy" most likely means "translation" (Meyrat 2015, 330-2; for a comprehensive treatment with a comparison of the textual versions, see Edel 1997; Breyer 2010a). In the case of the Egyptian description of the Hittite royal seal of the peace treaty, translation is explicitly described:

> "What is written in the middle of this silver tablet on its other side: a representation with the image of the goddess of Hatti embracing the princess of Hatti, accompanied by a legend of this meaning: 'The seal of the sun deity of the city of Arinna, of the country's lord, the seal of Pudukheba, the princess of the country of Hatti, the daughter of the country of Kizzuwatna, the priestess of the sun deity of the city of Arinna (etc.)."

Particularly interesting is the translation of divine terms (including even the translation of Cuneiform classifiers) with regard to the treaty's Hittite witness deities (Singer 2013; Mouton and van den Hoven 2015).

Another translation into Egyptian occurs in magical Pap. Leiden 345+348, for the Ugaritic divine pair *Šaḥar* "Dawn (morning star)" and *Šalim*, literally "the healthy, intact one" (dusk; evening star; Olmo-Lete and Sanmartin 2015, 809). The first divine name was rendered as *pꜣ nčr ṭwꜣ*, "the god (of) Dawn", the second was lexically explicated as *wč̣ꜣ śnb*, "the intact and healthy one" (Quack 2019, 81-2).

Near Eastern mythological texts were often adapted for Egyptian purposes rather than outright translated; nevertheless, through loanwords in the Late Egyptian texts and other interference phenomena, the transfer process is quite apparent. The Egyptian *Myth of the Weather God's Battle with the Sea* (traditionally known as the "Astarte papyrus", see Collombert and Coulon 2000; Schneider 2003b; Schneider 2011-12; Pehal 2014) was adapted from Levantine and Anatolian *Vorlagen* – thematically closest is the Hurrian-Hittite text KBo XXVI 105. I have suggested that the prominence that the text accords to the weather god's victory over the sea god Yam – the weather god prevented the earth from being destroyed in a flood –, should be understood in the context of the installation of Seth-Baal as a new patron of Egyptian kingship at the transition to the 19th dynasty and the foundation of Piramesse as a new Egyptian residence city, parallel to the foundation of Tarhuntassa as a new Hittite capital consecrated to the weather god after 1300 BCE (Schneider 2011-12).

> The adaptation is obvious from sentences such as *i͗w=tw ḥr rṭi͗.t n=s tꜣy=s i͗sb.t i͗w=s ḥr ḥms* = "one brought her her throne and she sat down" which appears to emulate the Ugaritic original, *tʕdb ksu͗ wyṯṯb* "a throne was prepared and they seated (him)" (Gaster 1952). The text not only contains the first attestations of the divine names Teššob as *ti͗-ś-b-w*$^{\text{RETURN.GOD}}$ (Schneider 2003c, 612 with n. 25; 2011-12, 180 with n. 25) and Yam (the latter would become the regular Egyptian word for 'sea', see Winand 2017), but also new lexical terms. An interesting case here is *šꜣ-q-ꜣ*, probably "cupbearer" (< Akk. *šāqû*, Ugar. (< akk.?) *šqy*, Aram. *šāqyā*), in a sentence "Then they [the gods] were bowing like a cupbearer", which recalls the scene from Ugarit (KTU 1.2 i 21-26) where the gods knuckle under to Yam when threatened.

An Ugaritic text may also have been the source of the second part of the 'Tale of the Two Brothers' (Pap. BM 10183), if it was indeed modeled on the plot of the Ugaritic myth and water ritual about Baal and his elder brother KTU 1.12 (Schneider 2008b). This tale may contain possible calques between Ugaritic and Egyptian (Eg. *ʿḥꜣwti͗ nfr,* "perfect fighter" < Ugar. *aliy qrdm,* "mightiest of warriors"; maybe Egyptian *m wnw.t bi͗n.t*, "in the worst moment" < Ugaritic *b adn adnm*, "in the moment of moments, at the most crucial time"; Schneider 2008b, 4; for Ugarit-Egypt relations, now Eßbach 2021).

These two texts are examples of a quite certainly rich tradition of Near Eastern religious texts that were adopted into the Egyptian textual repertoire of which, however, only a very small part has been preserved (for various texts about Anat and Hauron, see Silverman and Houser Wegner 2007; Quack 2022a).

3.2.5 Iron Age

The Near East at the end of the Bronze Age witnessed significant changes in the political, demographic and linguistic geography of the Near East. Ancient Egypt lost its province of Palestine-Syria, and for 250 years, did not wage any wars in the area, which reduced the extent of language contact through external engagement. Regional statehood proliferated across Palestine, Syria, and Anatolia, a system eliminated by the Neo-Assyrian empire which in turn was continued by the Neo-Babylonians and Persians. The linguistic situation across the Near East was complex (see Streck 2005; Popko 2008; Gzella 2009). Most consequential in this respect was the expansion of the Aramaeans since the 11th c. BCE (Lipiński 2000), leading to the adoption of Aramaic as a *lingua franca* from the Neo-Assyrian period on. This entailed a continuous situation of bilingualism for everyday and business use in Egypt itself (Demotic Egyptian and Aramaic), and multilingualism in the case of many individuals and communities from other linguistic areas (for the multilingual situation in Egypt in the 1st millennium, see Vittmann 2003; Winnicki 2009; in particular with regard to Elephantine, see Botta 2009, 8-13). The multilingual context could even affect conservative textual registers such as funerary texts – supplementary chapters with 'Nubian' spells were added to the Book of the Dead (see pp. 33-4).

3.2.5.1 Hebrew, Aramaic, Phoenician, Arabic, Akkadian

Lexical transfer is visible between Egyptian and several Semitic languages. A limited number of terms were borrowed into Hebrew (Muchiki 1999, 236-258; Arnet 2014; Breyer 2019), mostly for items that are Egyptian in nature, such as:

- commodities (e.g., *nætær* "natron" < *nčrỉ (ntrỉ)* [Breyer 2019, 145-6; Noonan 2019, 156-7]; *šēš* "fine linen" < *šś* [Breyer 2019, 173; Noonan 2019, 215-6], *tēḇā* "box, ark" < *č̣bꜣ.t, tb.t* "chest, shrine" [Breyer 2019, 173; Noonan 2019, 217], *qæsæt* "scribal equipment" < *gś.tỉ* "scribal palette" [Breyer 2019, 162-3; Noonan 2019, 194], *ʿeṭ* "rush pen" [Quack 2022b]);
- technical terms (the units of volume *ʾêpā* < *ỉp.t* [Breyer 2019, 121-2; Noonan 2019, 60], *hîn* < *hn.w* [Breyer 2019, 127-8; Noonan 2019, 95]);
- plants (*šiṭṭāh* "acacia" < *šnč̣.t, šnṭ.t* (with later assimilation *nṭ* > *ṭṭ*) [Breyer 2019, 168; Noonan 2019, 208-9]; *šûšān* "lotus" < *sšn,* later *ššn* [Breyer 2019, 167-9; Noonan 2019, 206-8);
- elements of Egypt's riverine environment (*ʾî* "island, coast" < *ỉw* [Breyer

2019, 120]; *y*[e]*'ōr* "Nile" < *ỉtr.w,* demot. *yr, y'r* [Breyer 2019, 137-9; Noonan 2019, 112], *ṣî* "ship" " < *č̣ꜣy,* demot. *č̣y* [Breyer 2019, 160; Noonan 2019, 189]).

- More rare are other terms, e.g. religious ones such as *ḥarṭōm* "magician, diviner" < *(ḫr.ỉ-ḥb.t)-ḥr.ỉ-tp* (Breyer 2019, 130-2; Noonan 2019, 102-3); for the festival name *pæsaḥ* < *pꜣ-sḫ* "the striking" see Schneider 2015, 550 n. 43 (cf. Breyer 2019, 153-4).

Conversely, Joachim Quack has proposed that a number of Egyptian words attested only in Coptic may actually be earlier loans from Hebrew predating the Persian Period, even though they are not currently attested in earlier Egyptian texts (Quack 2005, 329-30). These words include ⲉⲃⲓⲏⲛ "miserable, poor" < *'æbyōn*, ⲗϩⲱⲃ "steam, vapour" < *lahab̲* "flame", ϩⲙⲟⲧ "grace, gift" < *ḥæmæd* (< *ḥamd*), ϭⲗⲏⲃ "muzzle [device]" < *k*[e]*lūb* "basket", or ϭⲁⲙⲟⲩⲗ "camel" < *gāmāl* (Quack 2005, 310, 313, 319, 320, 321).

A similar semantic situation as with Egyptian loans into Hebrew can be determined for the Egyptian loans into Egyptian Aramaic (Muraoka and Porten 1997, 352-3; Folmer 2011, 595), the administrative language of Egypt under Persian rule. From the 46 attested loanwords, 13 are terms for ships or parts of ships, 9 terms for buildings or building materials, 5 are religious terms found on funerary stelae, and the rest covers certain commodities, legal and economic terms and titles, and the flora. Some of them (e.g., the religious term *nm' ty* = Egyptian *nꜣ mꜣ'.tyw*) are attested just once and could rather be examples of code-switching. In one text, the phrase 'wall of *hanpāna*' (a Persian term, "protection") is glossed by an Egyptian term in Aramaic transcription, *tmw'nty* = *tꜣ my.t nt (< nṯr)* "the way of the god".

Aramaic loanwords in Egyptian before the Persian period can only rarely be ascertained, such as ⲕⲉⲗⲱⲗ "vessel"; ⲙⲁⲛϭⲁⲗⲉ "hoe" (Quack 2005, 311, 314). Starting in the late 6th/early 5th c. BCE (spell from the Wadi Hammamat: Vittmann 1984; Steiner 2001), we have numerous Aramaic texts written in Demotic script, most famously Papyrus Amherst 63 from probably the 4th c. BCE

(Steiner 1997; Vittmann 2003, 84-119; Quack 2010b, 83-5; for Papyrus Amherst 63 see now van der Toorn 2018; Na'aman 2022). In the 5th and early 4th centuries BCE, the Jewish community at Elephantine (and a similar community at Saqqara) is the best-documented case of an Aramaic language group on Egyptian soil (see Vittmann 2003, 84-119; Joisten-Pruschke 2008; Botta 2009; for an Aramaic loanword for the 1st cataract on the Ptolemaic famine stele, see Breyer 2003b). There is little evidence about Northwest Semitic language communities other than Aramaic ones, although Phoenicians were certainly present (Vittmann 2003, 44-83; for a Phoenician graffito in Middle Egypt, Vittmann 2011, 301).

A few Akkadian loanwords in Egyptian may date to the Neo-Assyrian period, such as Demotic *mtgṱ(.t)* (CDD M, 297-8), Coptic ⲙⲁⲧⲉϭⲧⲉ "army" < Akkadian *madaqtu* "army camp" (Vittmann 1996; Quack 2005, 314; for Akkadian names in Aramaic sources from Egypt, see Porten, Zadok and Pearce 2016). Through the deportation of Egyptians as a consequence of the Assyrian conquest of Egypt, Egyptian language communities are also attested in Mesopotamia (for the Assyrian deportations, see Koch 2022; for Egyptian, Nubians and Libyans in Neo-Assyrian sources, Karlsson 2022; for the renderings of Egyptian names in Neo-Assyrian, Neo-Babylonian and Achaemenid sources, see the new analysis in Mahlich 2022, 471-521).

It is likely from the outset that language contact between Egyptian and Old North Arabian dialects as well as Old South Arabian existed (for the rich documentation in first millennium BCE Egypt of people originating from Arabia, see Vittmann 2003, 180-193; Winnicki 2009, 294-362), although the most visible testimony for this is only the Minaean inscription on the merchant Zayd'il's coffin, from Ptolemaic times (Swiggers 1995; Robin 2015, 117).

3.2.5.2 Carian

Attested as mercenaries since the early 26th dynasty (around 650 BCE), the Carians are a particularly interesting case of an Anatolian language group living in Egypt. Preserved are c. 200 documents from Egypt between the 7th and the 4th c. BCE, in particular bilingual, or better: 'digraphic' stelae from Saqqara with Carian script and Egyptian iconography. The scholarship on the decipherment of Carian and the documentary evidence is substantial (Höckmann 2001; Vittmann 2001; Kammerzell 2001b; Vittmann 2003, 155-179; Knigge 2004, 36-40; Adiego 2007; Popko 2008, 103-108; Villing 2022, 16-21).

In one inscription (E.Me.8; Adiego 2007, 40-1, 355), there is an interesting equivalence of a title – of Carian *armon-ǩi* (with suffixed Carian article *-ǩi*) and Egyptian *pꜣ wḥm* "the interpreter, dragoman". As Yakubovich suggested, Carian *armon* may go back to a pre-Carian form **armān*, which would also be the origin of Greek ἑρμηνεύς "interpreter" (Yakubovich 2012: 133; accepted by Simon 2019; Herda 2013, 469-70; differently explained by Janko 2014 [both terms < Akkadian *targumānu*]).

3.2.5.3 Old Persian and Median

Despite the two Persian periods of overlordship in Egypt (Vittmann 2003, 120-154), Persian terms in ancient Egyptian documents are rare (an overview in Knigge 2004, 41-51). From the 14 attested words (five additional loans are attested in Demotic and Coptic, see Schweitzer 2005, 287), only very few occur before the Graeco-Roman period (Vittmann 2004, 168; Demotic *wrṯ* "rose" [Knigge 2004, 47] was more likely borrowed < Aramaic *wardā*):

- *wsỉpwtr* = *vis(a)puθra* "king's son" (Vittmann 2004, 131);
- *Mṭỉ* = *māda*, "Mede, soldier" (Vittmann 2004, 141-3);
- the volume unit *kpč̣* (maybe a *Wanderwort,* Vittmann 2004, 136-7);
- the title *qppš* (Vittmann 2004, 131-2);

The term *ꜣbỉkrm* "penalty" demonstrates the role that Aramaic played in linguistic transfer – attested in the Ptolemaic period, it seems a new adoption into Egyptian of Aramaic *'b(y)grn*, the rendering of Old Persian **abigarana-* ultimately harking back to the Persian codification of Egyptian law under Darius I (Vittmann 2004, 135-6; Knigge 2004, 47).

An interesting calque on Old Persian **haxāya-šai*, "his colleagues", is Demotic *n ꜣy=f iry.w* in Pap. BM EA 76274, referring to the Persian governance practice whereby government officials had companions who assisted them in their decision-making (Martin 2019, 182). In turn, a Median (rather than Old Persian) title, **vastra-bara* "chamberlain" (> Babylonian *ustbaru*), is attested in the early Demotic transcription *wsṯbr* (Martin 2019, 181 with n. 34).

An alabaster cosmetic bottle at Yale shows the titulary and name of Xerxes equally in hieroglyphic Egyptian as well as Cuneiform Old Persian, Elamite, and Akkadian, but also carries a Demotic label indicating the volume unit *kpḏ* of the vessel (Ritner 1996). Vessels with quadrilingual inscriptions are also attested from Darius and Artaxerxes (Westenholz and Stolper 2002, 7-10). This multilingualism was given monumental expression on the stelae erected along the precursor of the Suez Canal by Darius I, where four languages – Persian, Elamite, Babylonian and Egyptian – and two script traditions (Egyptian hieroglyphs and Cuneiform, confirmed for two of the known four stelae) were put on official display side by side (Wolze 2019; the most comprehensive treatment is Mahlich 2020).

It is likely that many linguistic interference phenomena are of a complex nature. An intriguing example of interlinguistic dialogue involving multiple language and writing traditions is visible on the Maskhuta stela. The Egyptian expression *prs-nw.t* "*Pārsa-*(*the-*) *city*" appears here as an obvious equivalent of the Greek city name Περσέπολις (Klotz 2015, 272; Mahlich 2020b). Mahlich posits that the Greek term, first attested in Aristophanes' *The Clouds* (which premiered in 423 BCE), might have been modeled after the Egyptian expression which in turn would have been a clarification of the ambiguous Persian term *Parsā* (for both the region and the city) by the Egyptian composer of the stela. The opposite may still be the more likely option, however – a more widely used Greek toponym Περσέπολις emulated by the Egyptian *prs-nw.t* "*Pārsa-*(*the-*) *city*".

4. LANGUAGE CONTACT WITH ANCIENT MEDITERRANEAN LANGUAGES

This chapter focuses on linguistic interference between ancient Egyptian and the languages of the Eastern Mediterranean basin that were concurrent with ancient Egyptian in the 3rd, 2nd and 1st millennia BCE. These languages comprised both non-Indo-European (4.1) and Indo-European languages (4.2), in addition to the Levantine and Anatolian languages discussed separately in the previous chapter. The Indo-Europeanization of the Mediterranean basin and Europe at the expense of the earlier paleo-languages occurred during the time period covered in this introduction – late 4th millennium to the 4th c. BCE. I will therefore discuss briefly the evidence and methodological problems with a focus on those languages that are more relevant for this topic.

4.1 Non-Indo-European paleo-languages of the Mediterranean

Most of the paleo-languages of the Mediterranean basin and adjacent regions to its north are scarcely known, often only in a fragmented way as *Trümmersprachen* ('debris languages'; see Untermann 1989, 15–19). Haarmann (2014, 22-3) provides a list of non-Indo-European paleo-languages of Europe that can be identified as "individual linguistic complexes"; except for Basque, they all succumbed to the Indo-Europeanization of the macroregion and became extinct:

- Old European (the language associated with the Danube civilization): SE Europe
- Minoan: ancient Crete
- Lemnian (closely related to Etruscan): island of Lemnos
- Etruscan: Etruria (Tuscany)
- Non-Indoeuropean (Pre-Greek) languages of Sicily
- Paleo-Sardinian: Sardinia
- Camunic: Alpine region of Northern Italy
- Rhaetic: Swiss Alps (by some grouped with Etruscan and Lemnian as "Tyrsenian")
- Ligurian: region of Genoa
- Aquitanian: SW France
- Basque: SW France and Northern Spain
- Iberian: NE Spain

- Cantabrian: Northern Spain
- Tartessian: Southern Spain
- Lusitanian: Southern Portugal

There is extensive scholarship on these languages that is beyond the scope of this volume. E.g., research on Paleohispanic – the languages and scripts used in the Iberian peninsula and southern France between the 5th century BCE and the early Roman Empire – comprises the epigraphic and linguistic study of more than 3000 inscriptions preserved in Phoenician, Greek and Latin as well as at least four writing systems used to write Tartessian, Iberian, Celtiberian, and Lusitanian (see Sinner and Velaza 2019).

I will touch on some of the non-Indo-European paleo-languages insofar as they are relevant for Egyptian-Mediterranean language contact (Minoan: 4.3.2; Tyrsenian: 4.3.5; unknown substrate languages of the Mediterranean: 4.3.1).

4.2 The Indo-Europeanization of Europe and the Mediterranean

4.2.1 Indo-Europeanization hypotheses

Models for the expansion of Indo-European languages across Europe and the Mediterranean have been proposed by archaeology and archaeogenetics (for a recent summary and critique, see Hajnal 2012 [who does not include Anthony 2007]; Leach 2016, 87-92; Danino 2019; earlier Raulwing 2000, 69-75). They are relevant to the question of the linguistic interference with Egyptian during the 3rd–1st millennia but have also been adduced for hypotheses of a presumed influence of Indo-European on an early stage of Egyptian during the 4th millennium (see below 4.2.2, pp. 113-6).

According to Marija Gimbutas' "Kurgan hypothesis", Proto-Indoeuropeans infiltrated, from their presumed homeland in the Pontic-Caspian steppe, both Eastern Central Europe and the Balkans as well as, across the Caucasus mountains, Iran. She posits this to have occurred in three waves between 4300 and 2800 BCE. By contrast, Colin Renfrew assumed a gradual expansion of Proto-Indo-European farmers and farming from their Near Eastern homeland into Europe, Central and South Asia, between 7000/6500 BCE and the early 3rd millennium BCE (for a critique, see Anthony 2007, 75-82; Hajnal 2012). Archaeogenetics has attempted to reconcile the two hypotheses with genetic evidence; the Neolithic farmers would have reached the Ukraine through the Balkans towards the later 4th millennium BCE, establishing there the Yamnaya culture as a second Proto-Indo-European homestead. Renfrew has accommodated these hypotheses by assigning the Balkans an important role in the development of Indo-European and by viewing the speakers of the Indo-European languages of Anatolia as the remainder of the presumed Near Eastern Proto-Indo-Europeans. The twofold scenario of a Proto-Indo-European homestead in the Near East and a secondary one in the Southern Ukraine was believed to be confirmed by glottochronological calculations. Hajnal (2012, 274-8) has criticized a number of assumptions underlying these hypotheses, e.g., that of very little linguistic differentiation over the first 3000 years vs. very rapid diversification thereafter; the unlikelihood of a Balkan linguistic area (cf. Sowa 2005) as opposed to the Ukraine; the more archaic features at the margins of the Indoeuropean areas whereas they should be less archaic according to Renfrew's model; also the assumption that the Near Eastern immigrant farmers were already speakers of Proto-Indo-European – conversely, Indo-European could have developed later through contact in the subsequent areas of settlement.

In Anthony's revised Kurgan hypothesis of 2007, he posits the dissemination of Indo-European to have occurred as follows:

(1) The Suvorovo migrants, speakers of Pre-Anatolian, would have moved to the lower Danube valley and perhaps the Balkans around 4200-4000 BCE (Anthony 2007, 262). The date of the settlement of Anatolia by speakers of Proto-Anatolian is uncertain but happened before the separation of Tocharian, probably before 3500 BCE (with a latest possible date of 2800-2300 BCE; Anthony 2007, 43-57, 229-30).

(2) Around 3500 BCE, a section of the Volga-Ural steppe population (Afanasievo culture) would have migrated more than 2000 km east across the Kazakh steppes to the Altai mountains, leading to the development of the

Tocharian languages (Anthony 2007, 264-5).

(3) The Yamnaya horizon would have spread across the Pontic-Caspian steppes around 3300 BCE. Between 3100 and 2600 BCE, migrations into the Danube valley and the East Carpathian piedmont would have occurred, providing the foundations for the 'older western IE branches' (Pre-Italic, Pre-Celtic, and Pre-Germanic), whose separation happened after that of Tocharian (Anthony 2007, 344-5). Western Indo-European languages may have been limited to islands scattered across eastern and central Europe until after 2000 BCE (Anthony 2007, 370; for a recent discussion of the assumed migration of the Yamnaya culture into Europe, see Klejn et al. 2018).

(4) Greek remains "the only major post-Anatolian branch that is difficult to derive from the steppes" (Anthony 2007, 368). Anthony moots that "the people who imported Greek or Proto-Greek to Greece might have moved several times, perhaps by sea, from the western Pontic steppes to southeastern Europe to western Anatolia to Greece, making their trail hard to find," likely during the Early Helladic II/III transition 2400-2200 BCE (Anthony 2007, 369). After the Greek split some time after 2500 BCE, Indo-Iranian separates by 2000 BCE.

While Philip Kohl has praised the magisterial synthesis that Anthony presents, he has also criticized its methodology in which "the archaeological record is consistently manipulated to fit the linguistic model that it is meant to confirm" (Kohl 2009, 109), and its key assumption, namely:

> "that Indo-Europeans exclusively or nearly exclusively practiced certain cultural features, including technologies and even religious rituals. Was such exclusivity characteristic of the late prehistoric world or, rather, were peoples who spoke different languages continuously interacting with each other, adopting and transforming other peoples' practices and beliefs? Herodotus believed that most of the Greek gods came from ancient Egypt. The Greek myth of Prometheus chained to a mountain in the Caucasus – recounted by Hesiod and Aeschylus – greatly resembles the myth of Amirani, a hero widely claimed by different Caucasian peoples, some speaking Indo-European and some speaking local Caucasian languages. Such examples abound

> in the early historical record. Given such borrowings, why is it accurate or even important to identify particular cultural traits as uniquely Indo-European?" (Kohl 2009, 110).

Other scholars have equally criticized Anthony's methodological approach, his treatment and integration of linguistic and archaeological data, as well as our general ability to identify a Proto-Indo-European homeland, and the precise stages of the expansion of respective populations and their languages (e.g., Klejn 2008; Kaiser 2010). As Raulwing states regarding the hypotheses by Gimbutas, Gamkrelidze and Ivanov, and Renfrew: "Nearly every single argument is applicable on several prehistorical cultures which leads to the result that the Indo-European *homeland* problem is not solvable with the linguistic and prehistorical data we are forced to work with" (Raulwing 2000, 72).

This assessment is also relevant to the proposed prehistorical linguistic interference between Proto-Indo-European and Pre/Proto-Egyptian (see 4.2.2).

4.2.2 A Proto-Indo-European adstrate in early Egyptian?

In the context of a presumed expansion of Proto-Indo-European from the Near East, Frank Kammerzell has advanced the idea that Proto-Indo-European influenced the early Egyptian language in a direct or indirect way (Kammerzell 1999, 261-2; Kammerzell 2005, 224-9; critical assessment by Zeidler 2004). He considers different scenarios for this influence:

> **(1)** A population in Northern Egypt of the late 4th millennium BCE spoke a non-Afroasiatic language that shared structural and lexical features with Indo-European. This language acquired Afroasiatic features through a contact situation with an Afroasiatic language ("Pre-Old Egyptian", the language of the oldest hieroglyphic records) before those speakers adopted the Old Egyptian language. Kammerzell himself considers this hypothesis not very plausible.
>
> **(2)** The second scenario assumes the existence of the same hypothesized languages as (1) but posits the development of a pidgin which later developed into a creole or creoloid language (Pre-Old Egyptian). Due to the absorption of more Afroasiatic features, the language became decreolized (the historical

Old Egyptian language). Kammerzell assesses this model as another possibility that cannot be proven.

(3) The third scenario posits the existence of an Afroasiatic Proto-Egyptian in Lower Egypt in the late 4th millennium. The oldest hieroglyphic documents would not display this Proto-Egyptian but a contact language ("Pre-Old Egyptian) that came about through a language related to Indo-European. The speakers of this latter language might have been a minority group but were represented in the higher social echelons and instrumental in the creation of the hieroglyphic writing system. Ultimately, Pre-Old Egyptian and its speakers would have been absorbed into the majority language which became Old Egyptian. Kammerzell sees this scenario as the most promising.

While any Indo-European linguistic influence on early Egyptian from Anatolia (Peust 2001, 352) is difficult to pitch historically – the Proto-Indo-European settlement of Anatolia is variously dated from before 3500 BCE to 2300 BCE, while the oldest Pre-Old Egyptian documents date to 3250 BCE –, some of the proposed lexical isoglosses (Kammerzell 1999, 250-4; Peust 2001, 352-3; Peust 2003, 347; Kammerzell 2005, 210-23; Peust 2008, 395) are particularly striking. The possibility of an Indo-European adstrate in early Egyptian, which might be visible in such cognates, has also been endorsed by other Egyptologists (Müller 2020, 110). However, Afroasiatic cognates are available in most of these cases. I list here 13 proposed cognates with alternative etymologies:

Egyptian lexeme & phonological value	Proposed Proto-IE or IE cognate	Alternative AA etymology
(1) *ỉw* / *ʾw* / "come; go"	hitt. *uwa*	Arab. *ʾawā* "to betake oneself to (a place), to go" (Schneider 1997, 195) or also *ǧāʾa* "to come"
(2) *ỉrč.t* / $^{y(ʾ,g)}$*lk.t* / "milk", equally variant form *ỉr.t* without <č>	PIE ***galakt-*	Cf. Arab. *libaʾ*, Syriac *ʾalwā/ʾalō* "first milk, colostrum"? Note that <r> and <b> for a presumed form **(ỉ)rb.t* are incompatible in Egyptian (> elision in *ỉr.t*, substitution in *ỉrč.t*?)

(3) *ꜥꜣ* / *d-$^r/_l$* / "door (leaf)"	PIE **dʰu̯er, dʰur*	Semit. *dalt (f.) etc.* "door (leaf)" (Rössler 1971, 286, 311)
(4) *bꜣk* "servant; to work"	PIE **u̯erǵ* "work" (Peust 2003, 347)	Semitic *brk* "kneel down, bend to sb. (= to be subservient")?
(5) *pꜣꜥ.t* "quail"	πέρδιξ "partridge" (Peust 2003, 347)	Berb. *frḍ* "to flutter about" *ferṭiṭu, ferṭeṭṭu* "bat; swallow; butterfly"
(6) *pr* /*pl*/ "house"	hitt. *pir*	Common berber *fella* "upper floor; roof; terrace"
(7) *fꜣꞽ* /*br*/ "carry"	PIE **bher*	Tuar. *aber* "grasp with the hand, hold" (Schneider 2003b, 195)
(8) *mn* /*mn, ml*/ "stay, remain"	PIE **men*	Berber *emel* "to be (in a place) (Tuareg)", "to occur" (Kabyle) (Schneider 1997, 198)
(9) *mnꜥ.t* *"wet nurse"*	Armenian *mënd* "to suckle", *mëndeshë* "wet nurse" (Kammerzell 2005, 213)	Tuareg *te-melḍ-eṭ* (with assimil. ending -t > ṭ) "woman suckling animals" (other dialects, "wet nurse" – root *ḍḍ/ṭṭ* "to suckle")
(10) *ḥꜣtꞽ* /ʿ/$_{\dot{g}}$-$^r/_l$-t / "heart (as organ)"	PIE **k̂erd*	Traditionally seen as Egyptian nisba "the frontal (organ)" < *ḥꜣ.t* "front"
(11) *ḥwn* /ʿ/$_{\dot{g}}$-w-$^n/_l$/ "young"	*PIE **h₂iu-h₁en*, Skr. yúvan, lat. *iuvenis* (cf. de Vaan 2008, 317)	Sem. *ʿwl* "child, infant" (hebr. *ʿawīl etc.)* (Rössler 1971, 298)
(12) *ḫnt* /ʿ/$_{\dot{g}}$-n-t/ "face, forehead, front"	PIE **h₂nt*, hitt. *ḫant* "forehead, front", hitt. *ḫanti*, gr. ἀντί "opposite"; lat. ante "before"	Isolated (with a different 3rd radical) is Modern South Arabian (Jiballi) *ḫanṭí* "front", *ḫunṭ* "outside" (Takács 2006, 153-4; Takács 2008, 511)
(13) *tꜣ* /*tr, tl*/ "land, earth"	lat. *terra* (impossible since *terra* < Proto-Italian **tersā, PIE *ters-h₂-* "dry land") (de Vaan 2008, 616)	If *tꜣ* < * *čꜣ*, cf. common Berber *kal* "land, earth" (for which, Kossmann 1999, 175)

Additional similarities have also been posited for the phonologies of Proto-Indo-European and Pre-Old Egyptian (Kammerzell 1999, 256) as well as morphosyntactic features (such as the Old Egyptian stative and the Indo-European Medio-Passive; Schenkel 1971; Kammerzell 1999, 257-8). While the question deserves a more detailed interdisciplinary study, at present no historical constellation seems conceivable in which speakers of Proto-Indo-European would have been in contact with speakers of a Proto-Egyptian language.

4.3 Contact with individual languages and language groups since the 3rd millennium BCE

Interconnections between Egypt and civilizations of the Aegean, the Greek mainland and Cyprus are well attested since the early 3rd millennium BCE, showing the trade of commodities and also cultural contact (for an overview of these contacts, Pfeiffer 2013; Spier, Potts and Cole 2018). Military engagement is first known from the annals of Amenemhet II (1911-1877 BCE) when Egypt conquered Cyprus (for a discussion, Marcus 2022, 792-803). Knowledge of the geography of mainland Greece and the Aegean islands can be inferred from a topographical list on a statue base found at Amenhotep III's funerary temple at Kom el-Hetan; the hieroglyphic transcriptions of place names include Amyklai, Mycenae, Messenia, Nauplion (on the Peloponnes), Thebes (in Boeotia), Knossos, Amnisos, Lyktos, Kydonia, Phaistos (on Crete), as well as the island of Kythera (see, e.g., Lehmann 1991, 107-10; Cline and Stannish 2011).

4.3.1 Unknown Mediterranean substrate languages

It is likely that several of the unknown paleo-languages of the Mediterranean basin and its northern shore influenced the vocabulary of Egyptian during different of its stages. The importance of those languages is visible in the lexicon of ancient Greek which still comprises c. 1100 lexemes that appear to be of Pre-Greek origin (Beekes 2014). By way of example, I single out two terms from the Egyptian lexicon that may be related to such lexemes:

- An Egyptian term for trumpet, attested between the 20th and 25th dynasty, *šꜣ-n-b-ỉ* ^{INGOT} (= /*šanbi, šalbi* /) is likely related to the Greek term for "(war) trumpet" of apparently pre-Greek origin, σάλπιγξ (Hoch 1994, 281-2; for the Greek term, Beekes 2010, 1304; 2014, 136; like σῦριγξ, "flute", and φόρμιγξ, "lyre", with a suffix –ιγξ). For the instrument, see Holmes 2008.
- I wonder whether the Late Egyptian word *bč̣l* (*bꜣ-č̣ꜣ-r/n-ꜣ* ^{WOOD}) "staff, stick, cudgel" (Hoch 1994, 116-7; used for the punishment of beating) might be related to the "European loanword" **bak-tlo* "staff, stick, cudgel": lat. *baculum* (> *bacillum* "small stick"), Greek *βάκτρον, βακτηρία, βακτήριον,* Cypriote *pa-ka-ra* (Beekes 2010, 194; de Vaan 2008, 67)?

4.3.2 Languages of ancient Crete

The language of the Minoan civilization on Crete, written with the Linear A script, has not yet been identified (maybe Luwian, see Mouton, Rutherford and Yakubovich 2013, 5-6); equally unintelligable is Eteocrete, the non-Greek language of short texts from the 7th-4th c. BCE (Neumann 2006, 160).

The magical-medical papyrus London BM 10059 from the time of Amenhotep III (1390-1352 BCE) lists in rt.7, 1–7 seven apparently non-Egyptian spells (Leitz 1999, 61–63 and pl. 32; Quack 2010a, 318); one is explicitly singled out as being a "conjuration of the [disease] of the Asiatics in what the *kftỉw* [the Cretans; on the term and concept of *kftỉw*, Matić 2012; 2014a] say to him (the patient)" (see Vercoutter 1956, 83 n. 2, 123 on the "orthographie aberrante" of the toponym and the grammatical difficulties with this understanding). This spell and the subsequent one (held by some scholars to be in the same language, although this is by no means certain) remain unintelligible, although they have received significant attention (e.g., Kyriakidis 2000; Haider 2004; Lange 2007).

4.3.3 Languages of ancient Cyprus

For Cyprus, several local, non-Greek languages appear to be represented in the corpus of Cypro-Minoan inscriptions, mostly from the Late Bronze Age and some from the Early Iron Age (Steele 2013, 9-98), as well as in the later so-called "Eteocypriote" corpus of inscriptions from Amathous and other localities between the 7th-3rd c. BCE (Steele 2012; Steele 2013, 99-172). The languages written in these inscriptions cannot at present be determined (Steele 2013, 78-83; 158-60; Steele 2012). In the 1st millennium, Phoenician as a Semitic language marks its presence on the island in addition to the local non-Greek languages and Greek (Steele 173-235). The only element that the Egyptian documentation can add to the linguistic debate is the name of the female ruler of Alasiya in the Tale of Wenamun (c. 1070 BCE). The Egyptian envoy is sent off by the ruler of Byblos and reaches Cyprus ("the land of Alasiya") where an inhabitant conversant in Egyptian translates between Wenamun and the princess – one of the few references to translation in Ancient Near Eastern sources:

> "He had me board and sent off from the harbor of the sea. And the wind drove me to the land of Alasiya. Then the town's people came out against me to kill me. But I forced my way through them to where Hatiba, the princess of the town was. I met her coming from one of her houses to enter another. I saluted her and said to the people who stood around her: "Is there not one among you who understands Egyptian?" And one among them said: "I understand it." I said to him: "Tell my lady that I have heard it said as far away as Thebes, the place where Amun is: 'If wrong is done in every town, in the land of Alasiya right is done.' Now is wrong done here too every day?" She said: "What is it you have said?" I said to her: "If the sea rages and the wind drives me to the land where you are, will you let me be received so as to kill me, though I am the envoy of Amun? Look, as for me, they would search for me till the end of time. As for this crew of the prince of Byblos, whom they seek to kill, will not their lord find ten crews of yours and kill them also?" She had the people summoned and they were reprimanded."
> (Translation Lichtheim 1973, 228-9)

The name of the female ruler of Alasiya – *ḥꜣ-ti͗-bꜣ* (marked as foreign by the 'foreign' classifiers [Gardiner sign list T14, N25]) – is maybe to be explained as a feminine participle *ḥāṭiba*, "wood collector", from the Semitic root *ḥṭb*, "to cut/collect wood" (the presence of a vocalic ending for the feminine participle in c. 1070 BCE would be noteworthy), which is also attested onomastically at Ugarit as well as in Safaitic and Nabatean inscriptions (female name *ḥṭbt/ḥāṭiba*, Schneider 1992, 173; differently Di Biase-Dyson 2013, 322, who posits an unknown Cypriot-Minoan lexical basis). A Semitic name for a member of the ruling elite of Alasiya at the end of the Late Bronze Age would not necessarily be surprising in the context of the 11th c. BCE (cf. Negbi 1992, 603-6).

4.3.4 Mycenean Greek and later Greek

Ancient Greek is the largest attested corpus language from antiquity (Peust 2000, 253; see p. 71); it replaced earlier non-Indo-European languages of which c. 1100 words are still preserved in the Greek lexicon (see Beekes 2014; Beekes 2009, xiii-xlii). A number of loanwords from Mycenean Greek, the earliest attested stage of Greek, may have entered the vocabulary of Late Egyptian during the Egyptian New Kingdom, such as:

- *ỉ:-r-rw-ç̌ꜣ-w* ^{JUG} for a vessel or cup at a banquet = Myc. Greek *a-re-so/* **aleiso-*, Greek ἄλεισον "drinking vessel with two handles" (Schneider 2004, 17)
- *m-rw-rw* ^{PASTRY} = Myc. Greek *me-re-u-ro/* **meleuron*, Greek μάλευρον "flour" (Schneider 2004, 21)

Based on finds such as the depiction of Mycenean warriors wearing boar tusk helmets on a papyrus from Amarna (Schofield and Parkinson 1994; Kelder 2022, 9 with figs. 15a-b) and the rests of an actual boar tusk helmet from Piramesse (Pusch 1989, 254l Kelder 2022, 9), it is possible that Mycenean soldiers fought on behalf of Egypt since the 18th dynasty, and there is ample evidence of cultural contact (see Creasman and Wilkinson 2017, passim). In the first millennium, there is more significant evidence for Egyptian-Greek historical and cultural contacts which also entailed intense linguistic contact, although the scope of that contact is not reflected in the lexicon of loanwords in Egyptian which remained limited in number and type. I mention here Demotic *ʿngn* "vessel" (CDD ʿ p. 92) < Greek ἀγγεῖον (Quack 2010b, 85) and *gʿwmʿ* "fever" (CDD g p. 13) < Greek καῦμα (Loprieno and Müller 2012, 144). Ptolemaic *ʿrq-wr* "the great bent one" may be a possible pseudo-etymological rendering of Greek ἄργυρος "silver" (Quack 2010b, 87).

The situation is much different on the Greek side which comprises a significant number of Egyptian loanwords of wider usage in ancient Greek as well as more specialized terms, mostly designating items of the Egyptian flora and fauna as well as Egyptian products and objects (see Fournet 1989[10]). From the latter, cf.:

- βωρεύς "mullet" (< Egyptian *br,* Coptic S ⲃⲱⲣⲉ, Egyptian Arabic *būri* "mullet", Fournet 1989, 58; Beekes 2009, 251);
- ἔρπις "wine" (< Egyptian *ỉrp,* Coptic ⲏⲣⲡ "wine"; Fournet 1989, 59; Beekes 2009, 463);
- ζῦθος / ζῦτος "Egyptian wine" (< Egyptian *ỉtỉ* "barley" according to Ernštedt 1953, 27-32 and Schenkel 2006, 557, but phonologically and semantically not convincing; see also Beekes 2009, 503);
- κῖκι "castor oil" (< Egyptian *kꜣkꜣ/kỉkỉ,* "castor, ricin ?"; Fournet 1989, 61)
- κοῦκι "name of a palm-like tree, *Hyphaena thebaica*" (< Egyptian *qwqw*, Demotic *kk* "fruit of dōm-palm", Coptic ⲕⲟⲩⲕ; Fournet 1989, 62);
- στῖμι, στίμμι "powdered antimony, kohl, black make-up", Latin *stibium* (< Egyptian (*mśṭm.t* and) *śṭm*, Demotic (*mstmy* and) *smty, stm*; Coptic ⲥⲧⲏⲙ; Beekes 2009, 1406; Fournet 1989, 65; Schenkel 2006, 555);
- ψάγδης (var. ψάγδας, σάγδας), name of an Egyptian ointment (< Egyptian with definite article *pꜣ-śgnn,* Demotic *pꜣ-sgn,* Coptic ⲡⲥⲟϭⲛ; Fournet 1989, 66; Beekes 2009, 1657; CDD S 479-81).

From the loanwords of wider usage, several had a successful history in post-antique modern languages (Peust 1999a, 71), to mention only:

- *wḥꜣ.t "oasis"* (Coptic S ⲟⲩⲁϩⲉ; Greek *ὄασις*, English etc. *oasis;* Fournet 1989, 67);
- *br* "cargo boat" (> Greek *βᾶρις*; Latin **bārīca* > *barca,* English (etc.) *bark, barque, barge*; see Fournet 1989, 57; Kramer 2018);
- *nčrỉ* > *nṯrỉ* "natron" (> Greek *νίτρον*, Arabic *naṭrūn,* English etc. *natron;* Fournet 1989, 64);
- *hbỉ* "ibis" (> Greek ἶβις, Latin etc. *ibis;* Fournet 1989, 60);

---

[10] Fournet's assessment ("Faut-il citer l'ouvrage en russe de P.V. Jernstedt, Mots d'emprunt égyptien au grec, Moscou 1953, illustrant le 'pan-égyptianisme' fantaisiste dans tout son excès?" 1989, 55-6 n. 1) is not appropriate, see Schenkel's vindication (Schenkel 2006).

- *hbny* "ebony" (> Greek *ἔβενος, ἐβένη,* English (etc.) "ebony"; Fournet 1989, 59);
- *šnč̣.wt > šnṭ.wt* "kilt" (Coptic [S]ϣⲛⲧⲱ, [B]ϣⲉⲛⲧⲱ; > Greek σινδών "fine woven cloth, blanket" [the Egyptian etymology not in Beekes 2009, 1333-4] > Ital. *sindone* "burial shroud [particularly the Shroud of Turin]; Fournet 1989, 73-4; Schenkel 2006, 555);
- *qmy.t* "resin, gum" (Demotic *qmꜣ*, Coptic ⲕⲟⲙ(ⲙ)ⲉ, ⲕⲟⲙ(ⲙ)ⲓ) > Greek *κόμμι*, Latin *cummi/gummi/gumma*, English etc. *gum* (see Fournet 1989, 62; Kramer 2011);
- The New Kingdom compound noun *gr n p.t* "*gr* of the sky," which survived in Demotic as *grmp*, Coptic as [S]ϭⲣⲟⲙⲡⲉ, [B]ϭⲣⲟⲙⲡⲓ "dove", is a possible etymology of Greek *κόλυμβος*, Latin *columba*, and Church Slavonic *golǫbĭ* (Peust 1999a, 280, n. 356; CDD G p. 43; opposed Buzi and Soldati 2021, 73 who surmise in the Demotic and Coptic term the oldest Latin borrowing in Egyptian). The basic term *gr* "(a type of) bird (pigeon?)", may be onomatopoeic, imitating the sound of doves (cf. English *curr*; German *gurren*; Berber *gurr*, *gerger*, etc. "to curr"; see Schneider 2018, 108).

A large number of additional Egyptian etymologies have been proposed for other Greek names and terms, to mention only λαβύρινθος and 'Ατλαντίς (Schenkel 1979; Schenkel 1997; Schenkel 2006; for Atlantis also Bichler 2008, 96-7 [if not from the name *Atlas*]).

A culturally significant case would be the word *myth,* Greek *μῦθος*, which has no Greek or Indo-European etymology (Beekes 2009, 976: "There are no comparanda; the word is quite possibly Pre-Greek"). With a wider range of meanings in Greek ("word, discourse, story, saga, myth"), Ernštedt derived it from Egyptian *mṭw,* "word, speech" (Ernštedt 1953, 55-7). Schenkel (2006) subjected this etymology to a close review and rejected it, as the phonological rules would require the Greek word to contain an unaspirated /t/, **μῦτος*.

An intriguing case of a Greek/Egyptian calque is the rendering of 'Persepolis' by Egyptian *prs-nw.t "Pārsa-(the-)city"* on Darius I's canal stele from Tell el-Maskhuta (Klotz 2015, 272; Mahlich 2020b – who gives primacy to the Egyptian form; see also above p. 108).

4.3.5 The languages of the Sea Peoples and "Tyrsenian"

Of major relevance for the question of Egyptian-Mediterranean language contact is the question of the origin and the languages of the "Sea Peoples". In a recent contribution, Nathan Meyer and A. Bernard Knapp lowercase the term as "sea peoples" and emphasize that "the traditional capitalisation of this term perhaps suggests something rather too distinct" and that, "to the extent that any 'sea peoples' existed, such social formations, however they were actually constituted ethnically or otherwise, were not merely aggressors but victims of the same disintegration of interconnected cultures in the LBA eastern Mediterranean" (Meyer and Knapp 2021). A recent DNA analysis of skeletal material from Ashkelon determined a genetic distinction "due to a European-related gene flow introduced in Ashkelon during either the end of the Bronze Age or the beginning of the Iron Age" (Feldman et al. 2019). However, the precise provenances and identities, as well as the languages spoken by the different Sea Peoples, continue to be elusive and the subject of intense speculation. While the similarity of their ethnonyms with placenames has often been adduced as an indication of either their provenance or ultimate settlement (Lehmann 1985, 42-3; 47), Yasur-Landau emphasized that "the etymological evidence for the origin of the Philistines and other Sea Peoples can be defined as unfocused and ambiguous at best" (2010, 180, 182). A full discussion cannot be conducted here; I provide merely a list of the attested terms (cf. Winnicki 2009, 79-85; Adams and Cohen 2013) with brief notes regarding some of their potential etymologies. The etymologies of the ethnonyms and the diverse comparanda adduced in past scholarship seem often rather haphazard; a comprehensive linguistic assessment remains a desideratum of future research.

- *ỉ-q-ꜣ-wꜣ-šꜣ* "Ekwesh": This term is often equated with the term *Achaeans* ('Αχαιοί)/Aḫḫiyawa; e.g., Helck 1995, 112; Lipiński 2004, 124; on the probable identity of the two and their reference to the Mycenean civilisation see Fischer 2010; Beckman, Bryce and Cline 2012; Kelder 2018). This equation is problematic on account of the Egyptian <q>. Other etymologies seem in principle possible for *ỉ-q-ꜣ-wꜣ-šꜣ*, cf. – for the sake of demonstration – Mycenean Greek **hikwēwes* (cf. Bartonek 2003, 279-92) > *Homer.* ἱππῆες *(>* ἱππεῖς) "horsemen, knights";

- *wꜣ-šꜣ-šꜣ* "Weshesh": The name is of obscure etymology (Strobel 1976, 208);
- *p-w-r-śꜣ-tỉ* "Peleset, Philistines": Connected with toponyms such as *Palaiste* (Adriatic/Illyrian coast) and ethnonyms such as *Pirustae* (Lehmann 1985, 45) and recently, the Hieroglyphic-Luwian toponym *Palastin/Walastin.*[11] I suggested to see in the term a Mycenean exonym πλώϝιστοι, "sea farers, sailors" (Schneider 2011a, 570-1);
- *Rw-kꜣ* "Lukka": Related to the toponym "Lukka" (Gander 2010);
- *šꜣ-r-ṭ-ỉ-n-ꜣ* "Shardanu, Sherden": The name has been connected with toponyms in Lydia (*Sardeis*, mountain *Sardene* etc.; Helck 1995, 112) and also that of Sardinia (Lehman 1985, 42; maybe identical with *Šrdn* on the Phoenician stele of Nora, Sardinia, from c. 800 BCE), and the later ethnonym *Σαρδονιοί* or *Σαρδιανοί*: Lipiński 2004, 234-247, 242-3);
- *šꜣ-k-rw-šꜣ* "Shekelesh": This term must be kept separate from the one spelled *čꜣ-k-r* (cf. Edel 1984; Lehmann 1985, 33-5). Etymologies have been proposed (e.g., connection with the Pisidian city *Sagalassos* [Strobel 1976, 195]) but other hypothetical possibilities exist, such as – for the sake of demonstration – the epic epithet σιγαλόεις "shining, brillant";
- *t-w-r-ỉ-šꜣ* "Tereš, Turša": Usually identified with the Τυρρηνοί / Τυρσηνοί *Tyrheni* (Lehmann 1985, 43, 59-60; Drews 2000, 177-182);
- *čꜣ-k-r* "Tjeker": Connected with ethnonyms 'Sikeloi/Siculi' (Sicily, Italian peninsula, Adriatic/Dalmatian coast; Lehmann 1985, 33-5, 45, 47);
- *ṭ-ꜣ-ỉ-n-ỉ-w* "Denyen, Tanayu": This term has often been identified with the Δαναοί (for which term, Beekes 2014, 163), e.g., Strobel 1976, 201-206; Lehmann 1991, 110).

From these population groups, the language of the Philistines is attested through a very small number of words and names preserved in the Hebrew Bi-

---

[11] For a caveat that this new toponym and the ethnonym 'Philistine' are related, see Schneider 2011a, 571-2; Adams and Cohen 2013, 662-3 with n. 19. Bányai 2020-1 regards the language of the inhabitants of the kingdom of Palastin as Palaic.

ble and epigraphically (Ekron). A potential hint at their provenance is the Philistine administrative title *srn* /t͡srn/, attested in the Hebrew Bible (pl. *s*^{e}*rānîm*; pl. cs. *sarnē*) – probably not the Philistine royal title but the designation of a subordinate military official (see Wagner 2008). I have proposed that it may be related to the Lemnian administrative title *zerona* (Schneider 2011a, 572; on the Lemnos stele and the term *zerona* "chief magistrate", Eichner 2012, 18, 22, 24; Eichner 2013, 8, 11, 36-7; Eichner 2019, 114) rather than the traditionally compared title *tarwanis/tyrannos* (so still Michałowski 2017, 39). Schmitz recognizes contact effects of Indo-European (probably Greek) in the Ekron Dedicatory inscription (Schmitz 2016). Even in the case of the divine name of this inscription, *ptgy*, no consensus has been reached, with Greek interpretations including *πυθο-γαια "Pythian Gaia" (Schäfer-Lichtenberger 2000), *ποτ(ν)ια-γαια "lady Gaia" (Yasur-Landau 2001), *φυτι-γαια "Who makes the earth grow" (Schneider 2011a), *πενταγαια 'five lands' (Schmitz 2016).

4.3.6 Italic languages

Lexical interference between Egyptian and Italic languages (on which see the different contributions in Klein, Joseph and Fritz 2017, 733-873) seems in principle possible. As an example of a possible borrowing from Italic, I would like to suggest that a term studied in detail by Satzinger (2008) – the loanword *q-ꜣ-r-m-tỉ* (Hoch 1994, 301-2; 19th dynasty) > Demotic *krm/krb* "ashes" (CDD K, p. 30), Coptic ^{S}ⲕⲣⲙⲉⲥ, ^{B}ⲕⲉⲣⲙⲓ "ash, soot, dust" could be related to lat. *cremō* "to burn" and *carbō* "coal" (see de Vaan 2008, 142 for the possible relationship between the latter two and their relatively isolated status in Proto-Indo-European). While Satzinger (2008) posits that *q-ꜣ-r-m-tỉ* may be a genuine but "non standard" Egyptian lexeme – unattested before the New Kingdom and written down in syllabic orthography in the New Kingdom for lack of an inherited Egyptian orthography – and also considers it an isogloss between Egyptian and Chadic, the possibility of a loan from an Italic predecessor of Latin *cremō/carbō* may deserve serious consideration.

5. Phenomena of Language Contact – An Analytical Overview

This chapter provides an analysis and summary of the evidence on language contact according to linguistic categories. The chapter complements the diachronic presentation relating to language families presented in chapters 2-4.

5.1 Loanwords

Most evidence about language contact in ancient Egypt occurs in the form of loanwords. Lexical borrowing has been studied extensively (see Haspelmath and Tadmor 2009[12]). Lexical transfer is most visible during the New Kingdom and in borrowings from Semitic languages (Hoch 1994; pp. 85-96); however, our knowledge is biased by the preserved evidence and our acquaintance with donor languages. Thousands of attestations of hundreds of loanwords from dozens of donor languages show up in specific socio-textual places – texts of different genres and registers, reflecting different users and varying motivations for the use of loanwords. Motivations for borrowing include onomasiology (lexical gaps in the receiving language), linguistic economy (more precise terminology), and communication (code switching, style, fashion, social/ideological identity, prestige, erudition: Schneider 2004, 11-31; Haspelmath 2009).

5.1.1 Loanwords prior to the New Kingdom

Attestations of loanwords prior to the New Kingdom are relatively rare. Similarly lacking is scholarship analyzing this situation of the evidence, which is owed to a dearth of certain categories of sources in comparison to those of the New Kingdom; the possibility of different sociolinguistic parameters facilitating the display of loanwords; and a highly controversial debate about the historical phonology of Egyptian in its earlier periods, which makes it more difficult to identify borrowings. An example of the latter dissent is a recent proposal by Kilani to see in Egyptian *ʿš* (type of conifer or conifer wood) a particularly ancient, fourth millennium BCE borrowing from Proto-Semitic ᶜṣ́

[12] The associated World Loanword Database [WOLD] is available at https://wold.clld.org/

[ʕɬ’] (Kilani 2016, 51-52). Conventional historical phonology of Egyptian would allow for the first sound correspondence but not the second; Otto Rössler's "New Comparatism" (Rössler 1971; Schneider 1997; Peust 1999a) would disqualify both. In addition, early loans are difficult to recognize prior to the establishment, by the Middle Kingdom, of a coherent subsystem of the hieroglyphic script used to render foreign names and words, with *matres lectionis* after monoconsonantal signs for the rendering of the vowels /u/ and /i/ and the occasional use of *CVC* signs (Hoch 1994, 488-504). The most detailed use of this system is visible in the Middle Kingdom *Execration Texts* from the 12th Dynasty, which list the names of Levantine princes and their cities and territories (Wimmer 2010, 33-50). With these limitations in mind, a few proposed loanwords may serve as examples:

1) Early Dynastic Period and Old Kingdom:

- *ʿꜣm* "Asiatic (inhabitant of areas to the NE of Egypt)" < *drmj* "inhabitant of the south (of Palestine)" (Schneider 1997, 194-195; see pp. 74-5);
- *wnš* "wolf" < Proto-Berber (Berber *uššen* , "wolf"; see above p. 66);
- *nsw* "king" < Sumerian *ensi* "king" (Peust 2007; see above p. 73);
- *stỉ* "(red) ochre" < Beja/Tu-beḍawiye adjective *sōtay, sūtay* "dark-colored, dark green/brown/grey" (see above p. 22).

2) First Intermediate Period and Middle Kingdom:

- *ỉśb.t* "quiver" (Papyrus Kahun 19.16 and 20.47) < Northwest Semitic *'aṯbāt* (also attested in the New Kingdom; see pp. 80, 91);
- A number of Middle Egyptian terms have been proposed to be potential loanwords from Ethio-Semitic, such as *ʿꜣg* "hit, beat", *wʿꜣ* "slander, defame", *śčꜣ* "weave, spin", *č̣bꜣ* "clog, bar", *fnč̣* "nose" (p. 47; for the discussion of the homeland of the (Ethio-)Semitic languages, pp. 46-7).
- In turn, Northwest Semitic likely borrowed an earlier form of Hebrew *dəyō* "ink" from Egyptian *ry.t* (Rössler 1966, 227) as well as other terms of scribal and sealing practice, such as precursors of Hebrew *ṭabbaʿat* "signet ring" and *ḥôtām* (< ḫtm), "seal" (Noonan 2019, 108-110).

5.1.2 Loanwords in the New Kingdom

In Egyptian New Kingdom texts, approximately 350 loanwords presumed by Hoch (1994; see also Sivan and Cochavi-Rainey 1992; Winand 2017) to be of Semitic origin are attested (Hoch 1994). The reassessment of those lexemes (see above, pp. 91-4) posits that c. 110 of them are quite definitely of Semitic origin. Additionally, texts of the New Kingdom comprise also at least 300 loanwords of likely non-Semitic provenance (Schneider 2004). The notation of those words uses a specialized Egyptian transliteration system, "syllabic orthography" (after William F. Albright) or "group writing" (Hoch 1994, 498-502; for a new interpretation, Kilani 2019). In contrast with the older transcription system that mainly used monoconsonant signs, most hieroglyphs employed in the new system are old biliteral signs that are now used for *Cv* sequences and, additionally, monosyllabic Egyptian words – such as *ỉw* "island"; *ʿȝ* "great" – that could represent a foreign syllable (Hoch 1994, 498-502).

Winand (2017) has recently emphasized that, of the Semitic loans, two thirds stem from texts of the elite culture (royal texts, autobiographies, wisdom texts, onomastica, religious texts) and just one third from texts closer to the vernacular domain (letters and judicial, business, fiction, and lyric texts). Most of the Semitic borrowings have parallels in several branches of Northwest Semitic, some in individual Northwest Semitic languages only (e.g., Ugaritic or Aramaic). A small number were taken from East Semitic (Akkadian; see p. 96). Some of the lexical transfers can be shown to have been complex, as in the case of the term *tȝ-ḫ-b(w)-s/śȝ-tỉ* BASKETRY. This word – ultimately a Hurrian term for "horse blanket" which was also borrowed by Akkadian and Ugaritic –underwent a semantic expansion in Egyptian:

> "Most likely, however, the word *tḫbs(t)* originally entered the Egyptian language as a term related to a covering for equids, perhaps as a term for—or at least encompassing the item—'packsaddle'; if the Egyptians then substituted baskets for woolen bags attached to the horse (or other equid) covering called *tḫbs(t),* then a term for a woolen object may have transformed into a term for basketry. Subsequently, the Egyptian lexicon employed *tḫbs(t)* to

> refer to any large basket, including transport containers slung over carrying poles rather than those loaded onto equids. This theory enables the word to keep its same function—a covering of some sort—but would enable a change in material, from wool to basketry. The transformation of the term *tḫbs(t)* in ancient Egyptian, a word used in genres as diverse as administrative texts and works of literature, provides a single example of the complexities of language contact and the adoption of loan words." (Manassa 2012, 110; cf. Richter 2012, 425-6).

As to non-Semitic languages, the situation presents itself differently. Only a very small number of borrowings from Hurrian can be identified with some degree of certainty (Schneider 2004; for probable loanwords see pp. 97-8), impeded by the still limited knowledge of the Hurrian vocabulary. This stands in striking contrast to the fact that the country name *ḫurri* (Richter 2012, 171) was adopted in Egypt as a regular term for "Syria" in the New Kingdom (*ḫꜣ-rw*; with the Egyptian article also as a frequent ethnonym: *pꜣ-ḫꜣ-rw* "the Syrian") and that the most frequently attested borrowings in Late Egyptian might ultimately come from Hurrian: the title *kꜣ-č̣(ꜣ)-n*/*kꜣ-č(ꜣ)-n-ꜣ* "charioteer" (Hoch 1994, 341-345) = *kuzine* (where -*ne* is likely the Hurrian "article", Schneider 2008a, 194) and the adjective *tl* "valiant" (if < *adal*: Schneider 1999), each with > 125 attestations. A somewhat larger number of loanwords may be traced to Anatolian languages, although some may have reached Egyptian through intermediary languages (for examples of probable loanwords, see pp. 96-7).

In terms of semantic categories, the largest group of terms is that of military language (cf. the detailed analysis by Schneider 2008a, with the subcategories *technology of the chariot and its equipment* [30 terms], *military equipment, weaponry and infrastructure* [27 terms], *military titles and functions* [14 terms], *military behaviour and activities* [14 terms] and *violence, intimidation and flight* [26 terms]). Of these terms, only a very limited number are attested prior to the 18th Dynasty (> 1550 BCE), 10% are attested after the 18th Dynasty, and the majority in Ramesside times. In terms of the frequency of loanwords, *hapax legomena* account for more than 40% of the attested lexemes, while words attested up to eight times amount to 90% (Winand 2017). The number of attestations across different text-genres is at least partially a reflection of the genuine diffusion of these words – the 65 Semitic loanwords from New Kingdom texts that have survived into Coptic are in their majority ones frequently attested in the New Kingdom (Winand 2017). With regard to the word classes of the attested Semitic loanwords, 83% are nouns, 16% verbs, and just 1% belong to other word-classes. One exceptional case from the last group is the Northwest Semitic interrogative particle *'ēḏæ* "which" (ỉ-čꜣ; Hoch 1994, 43-44), a term possibly used as a stylistic device to display erudition and give the texts an exotic flavor (Winand 2017; perhaps also reflecting the idiolect of a scribe *Yns*, who may have been of Semitic provenance).

While contact with populations in North and Northeast Africa to Egypt's west, south, and southwest is amply attested, and language contact is thus obvious, only a limited number of loanwords from African languages can be easily identified in the evidence (see Cooper 2020a for an overview). I refer here to the detailed discussion above, in particular

- 2.2.2.2 (Nilo-Saharan languages, including Northern East Sudanic to which both Meroïtic and Old Nubian belong);
- 2.2.2.3.1.1 (Old Beḍawiye/Blemmyan);
- 2.2.2.3.1.2 (other Cushitic languages and Omotic);
- 2.2.2.3.2 (Ethio-Semitic languages);
- 2.2.2.3.4 (Proto-Berber).

There can be no doubt that other donor languages that are poorly known to us or entirely unattested in the preserved evidence were the source of borrowings in the second millennium (cf. pp. 125-6). In turn, a number of Egyptian loanwords in Old Nubian show a Paleo-Coptic vocalization (see p. 39). This indicates that these words must have been borrowed into a local form of Nubian during the New Kingdom, at the latest, and thus preserved the archaic vocalization pattern (alternatively, they may reflect more recent borrowings from a dialect characterized by an archaizing vocalization or a transfer via early Meroïtic or Napatan Egyptian). The same possibilities of transfer apply to a number of divine names in Meroïtic (see pp. 34-5).

5.1.3 Loanwords between the New Kingdom and the Greco-Roman Period

In the first millennium before the Ptolemaic and Roman Periods, lexical transfer into and from Egyptian is well attested, although the number of attested borrowings is limited as is the number of identified source languages. This is likely a reflection of the textual and documentary evidence and not the actual situation of past linguistic interference. I refer here to the detailed discussion in the specific sections of chapter 3:

- Hebrew (for details, see pp. 104-5): While hundreds of Egyptian etymologies have been proposed for Hebrew terms, only about 20 terms are undisputed, particularly of commodities, units of measurement, plants, elements of Egypt's environment, and religious terms. In turn, Joachim Quack has pointed to potential borrowings from Hebrew into Egyptian from before the Persian Period that are not yet attested in pre-Coptic stages of the language. It is possible that some of these borrowings might be due to interference of Egyptian with Phoenician (rather than Hebrew).
- Aramaic (for details, see pp. 105-6): A semantic situation similar to that of Egyptian loans into Hebrew applies to Egyptian loans into Egyptian Aramaic (Muraoka and Porten 1997, 352-353; Folmer 2011, 595), the administrative language of Egypt under Persian rule. Less than 50 loanwords are attested; they comprise terms for (parts of) ships, terms for buildings and building materials, and religious terms (documented on funerary stelae), with the remaining terms including commodities, legal/economic expressions and titles, and designations of the flora.
- For interference with other Semitic languages during the Late Period (Akkadian, Ancient North Arabian, Old South Arabian, see p. 106).
- Despite the two Persian periods of overlordship in Egypt (Vittmann 2003, 120-54), only few Persian and Median terms are attested in ancient Egyptian documents (see pp. 107-8).

- Texts of the Ptolemaic and Roman Periods also show definitive evidence for Egyptian loanwords from Proto-Berber (pp. 55-6).
- There are a significant number of Egyptian loanwords in Greek, some of which likely derive from pre-Hellenistic times (for an overview, see Fournet 1989; cf. also Schenkel 2006); very few Greek borrowings are attested in Demotic Egyptian and Ptolemaic (see pp. 119-21).

5.2 Calques (loan translations)

Calques (an important form of *structural borrowing,* Haspelmath 2009, 39) denote literal translations of specific phrases from a host language to a recipient language. I thus exclude cases where entire texts were translated (such as the Egyptian version of the Hittite-Egyptian peace treaty, which also includes a rendering of the Hittite witness deities; Singer 2013; Mouton and van den Hoven 2015). Also a sentence such as *i͗w=tw ḥr rṭi͗.t n=s tꜣy=s i͗sb.t i͗w=s ḥr ḥms* "one brought her her throne and she sat down" in the Astarte Papyrus is an entire sentence emulating the Ugaritic original, *tʕdb ksů wyṯṯb* (Gaster 1952), not an independently used translation of a phrase. Examples of actual calques are:

- Northwest Semitic to Late Egyptian: An early example is *nb.t kbn* = *bʿl.t gbl,* "Lady of Byblos" (Zernecke 2013: 227-230). I proposed the Ugaritic text KTU 1.12 as a source for the second part of the *Tale of the Two Brothers* (Papyrus BM 10183), with a possible calque in the expression *ʿḥꜣwti͗ nfr,* "(most) perfect fighter" < Ugaritic *aliy qrdm* "the superior of fighters" (Schneider 2008b, 4). Another example of an Ugaritic/Egyptian loan translation occurs in magical Papyrus Leiden 345+348 (Beck 2018, 41, 46), for the Ugaritic divine pair *Šaḥar* "Dawn (morning star)" and *Šalim*, literally "the healthy, intact one" (Dusk, evening star; cf. del Olmo-Lete and Sanmartin 2015: 809). The first divine name in the pair was rendered in Egyptian as *pꜣ nčr ṭwꜣ*, "the god (of) Dawn," while the second was lexically explicated as *wč̣ꜣ śnb,* "the intact and healthy one" (Quack 2019, 81-2).

- OLD PERSIAN TO EARLY DEMOTIC: In Papyrus BM EA 76274, Old Persian **haxāya-šai*, "his colleagues," is rendered by Demotic *nꜣy=f iry.w*, referring to the Persian governance practice whereby government officials had companions who assisted them in their decision-making (Martin 2019, 182). Cf. also the rendering of "Persepolis" by Egyptian *prs-nw.t* "*Pārsa-*(*the-*) *city*" on Darius I's Tell el-Maskhuta stele (Klotz 2015, 272; Mahlich 2020b posits that the Greek term emulated the Egyptian form – see p. 108).
- CARIAN AND EGYPTIAN: From the Carians attested in Egypt since the early 26th Dynasty (around 650 BCE), bilingual ("digraphic") stelae from Saqqara with Carian script and Egyptian iconography are preserved (see p. 107). In one inscription (E.Me.8; Adiego 2007, 40-41, 355), the Carian title *armon-k̆i* (with suffixed Carian article *-k̆i*) is equated with Egyptian *pꜣ wḥm* "the interpreter, dragoman" (Yakubovich 2012, 133; accepted by Simon 2019; Herda 2013, 469-470; differently explained by Janko 2014 [both terms < Akkadian *targumānu*]).
- AKKADIAN TO NAPATAN EGYPTIAN: On the Nastasen stela (327 BCE), we find an apparent Akkadianism in Napatan. The phrase *nsw n pꜣ 4 qꜥḥ* "*king of the 4 corners = the world*" is a calque from Akkadian *šar kibrāti erbetti* "king of the four corners" (see above, p. 31).
- A graphemic/phonological calque between Proto-Meroïtic and Egyptian may exist between the proper name of Shabaqo and the Kushite king's Horus, Nebti and Gold name, *sbꜣq-tꜣwỉ*, "*the one who brightens the two lands*". While the meaning of the two names is different – *Šꜣ-bꜣ-kꜣ* is probably to be understood as *šb-qo* "the noble prince" (Zibelius-Chen 2011, 217) –, *śbꜣq-tꜣwỉ* may emulate the writing and sound of the proper name.

5.3 Non-Egyptian texts in Egyptian script

The Egyptian evidence comprises a rather small number of non-Egyptian text passages rendered in hieratic and, rarely, hieroglyphic script (Helck 1971, 528-530; Quack 2010a; Allon 2010) and, in the first millennium BCE, also in the

Demotic script. They appear to represent different language families and are likely indicative of a larger, mostly undocumented phenomenon.

- Semitic texts of the Late Bronze Age (see p. 89).
- Aramaic: starting in the late sixth and early fifth centuries BCE numerous Aramaic texts are preserved in Demotic script, most famously Papyrus Amherst 63 from probably the fourth century BCE (see pp. 105-6).
- A spell "in the language of Crete" in Pap. BM EA 10059 (see pp. 89, 117).
- Proto-Berber: An unpublished papyrus in the Egyptian Museum in Torino (CGT 54030; Cat. 2106/380) contains a spell against snakes (see p. 58).
- The "supplementary chapters" (chapters 162-167) of the *Book of the Dead*, attested since the 21st Dynasty, of which chapter 164 claims to be in the language of "Nubians and Nomads of 'Nubian Land' [the 1st Upper Egyptian nome]"; similar foreign terms also occur in the isolated *Book of the Dead* spells of Papyrus Berlin 3031 (see pp. 33-4).
- (Proto-)Old Beḏawiye: Pap. BM EA 75025 *recto* (late 20th Dynasty) contains a probably magical spell which has been proposed to be in (Proto-) Old Beḏawiye (for a discussion, see pp. 44-5).
- "Puntite": In the texts of the Min festival at the Ramesseum and Medinet Habu (with another two versions preserved at Athribis), a spell claims to be "what the African (*nḥśỉ*) from Punt says." For a discussion and a possible Ethio-Semitic suggestion, see p. 50.

5.4 Bilingualism, multilingualism, interpreting, translation

Information on the extent of bilingualism and multilingualism can be inferred from different types of evidence. From the third through the first millennia BCE, non-Egyptian speakers are attested on all socio-economic levels and foreign linguistic communities are equally well documented; thus, bilingualism and multilingualism must have been frequent phenomena (cf. Schneider 2020; for a case study of foreign language use in the military, see pp. 139-52; for the scribes at Amarna, see p. 135). Proficiency in the Semitic languages of the

Levant seems to have been a prerequisite for higher military posts in the New Kingdom (Schneider 2008a); in turn, Egyptian may have had the status of a *lingua franca* in the Levant of the New Kingdom (Helck 1971, 436).

Interpreters of foreign languages are attested from the Old Kingdom onward, e.g., in the title *mr iʿꜣw* "commander of Egyptianized Nubians/Nubian interpreters" (Bell 1976). A Nubian military officer at Gebelein in the 13th dynasty bears the epithet "who resolves the language of any foreign country" (Morenz 2010, 530). Depictions of sea-going ships from the funerary temple of Sahure and the Unas causeway depict translators that accompanied the Levantine and Egyptian crew (Bietak 1988; Ćwiek 2003, 254-255). Another famous depiction of interpreting can be found on reliefs from the Saqqara tomb of the later king Horemheb (Martin 1989). Under Merenptah, the high priest and former army-scribe of the chariotry Onurismes states in his funerary biography: "I spoke in the [appropriate] foreign language for any foreign language in attendance before my lord" (Meyrat 2016, 332; Starke 1993, 38 n. 63). Interpreters proficient in Egyptian are also mentioned for foreign states (e.g., for Babylonia, in Amarna letter EA11; for Cyprus, in the 21st Dynasty *Tale of Wenamun*); an Egyptian interpreter Ramose served for 13 years in Hittite diplomatic service (Starke 1993, 37). Still, interpreters and translators are rarely mentioned explicitly in our texts, which suggests a case of *implicit communication*, similar to that of Mesopotamia (von Soden 1989; Starke 1993, 37-8; Tarawneh 2011), a token of the ubiquitous use of language specialists and also the presence of bilingualism. Royal envoys abroad (for a list of Egyptian envoys in Cuneiform sources, see Helck 1971, 437-442) were accompanied by interpreters, and specialized interpretation can be assumed for the Egyptian physicians at the Hittite court and other cases of cultural and technological exchange (Breyer 2010a, 247-307), such as the Hittite specialists working in Piramesse (Herold 1998). There is extensive evidence on the translation of texts into Egyptian and also the adoption and adaptation of texts for an Egyptian context. I refer here to the detailed discussion above (pp. 101-3; 133).

5.5 Language education and re-education

There is significant evidence from the Amarna and Ramesside Periods for the training of specialists in languages of the Near East, particularly the diplomatic *lingua franca*, Akkadian. It appears that scribes in charge of international correspondence in the 18th Dynasty were proficient in both Egyptian and Akkadian (Mynářová 2007, 43-44; 2014); initially, they may have been trained in the tradition of Babylonian Akkadian, which during the Amarna Period may have been replaced by a curriculum informed by a Hittite milieu (Mynářová 2015, 98-99). The epistolary traditions visible at Amarna and in the Ramesside correspondence are again different (Mynářová 2009, 116-7), pointing to continuous adaptation of the literary education. The Amarna tablets comprised a "scholarly library", with an Egyptian-Akkadian bilingual lexical list (EA 368) and literary texts of Mesopotamia (Izre'el 1997). Texts of this kind were also part of the scribal training in Cuneiform attested in Canaan (Cohen 2019, 247-251). Except for the correspondence from Amarna and from the early 19th dynasty, the official correspondence of the Egyptian Bronze Age with the Near East is lost; however, a fragment of a letter from the end of the Old Babylonian Period sent to the Hyksos residence at Avaris (Mynářová 2015, 90) points to the existence of diplomatic exchange. The overall historical probability indicates that versatility in Akkadian Cuneiform diplomacy must be posited for this entire period. Both the development of the system of New Kingdom syllabic orthography or group-writing (Hoch 1994, 498-502; now Kilani 2019) and the discovery of an ostracon of the early 18th Dynasty containing one or two Semitic alphabet sequences (Haring 2015; Schneider 2018) point to a much more comprehensive ancient knowledge of and engagement with writing systems from the Near East than is currently attested.

Conversely, in the case of prisoners of war, we also learn about state efforts to suppress the continued use of communication in languages other than Egyptian and to re-educate prisoners of war (see pp. 58, 140).

It may be added here that there is evidence of the use of Egyptian language and writing abroad. At Egypt's trade emporium, Byblos, on the Lebanese coast, the local rulers adopted the hieroglyphic script for their official stelae and reliefs, where their names appear in Egyptian transcription. We also see Egyptian hieratic writing used at Byblos (the pseudo-hieroglyphic stela "L"), although "it is ... not clear whether this is an Egyptian hieratic tradition, a local Byblian adaptation of Egyptian forms, or a reflection of less than total competence with the language and standard Egyptian usage" (Hoch 1994, 65). Egyptian inscriptions also appear as legends on some seals from the Middle Bronze Age Levant (Eder 1995, 51-57; see p. 79). The influence of Egyptian language and writing in the Sudan of the 1st millennium BCE is visible in the case of Napatan Egyptian and the two (monumental-hieroglyphic and cursive) script systems of Meroïtic, the language of the kingdom of Meroë (3rd c. BCE to 4th c. CE), both derived from the Egyptian writing system (Rilly 2007, 71-229).

5.6 Interlanguages, mixed languages, pidgins

Mixed languages (such as bilingual mixed languages or possibly, pidgin languages) are likely to have existed in Egypt's large urban hubs, port cities, and garrison cities (for a useful discussion of the question of "mixed languages" in antiquity, see Mullen 2013 and Andrason and Vita 2016; for pidgins, Ansaldo and Meyerhoff 2021). Torallas Tovar has posited the existence of a pidgin language for the merchants of the Greek trade emporium of Naukratis in 6th c. BCE Egypt (Torallas Tovar 2010, 255). On the basis of our knowledge of the hybrid populations of cities such as Avaris or Piramesse, we can not only presume that bi- and multilingualism existed there but quite possibly also a form of (bilingual) mixed language or pidgin (see the case study on Avaris, pp. 81-4). The existence of an interlanguage and a creole language, respectively, has been proposed for two cases of language use more peripheral to the Egyptian evidence, "Akkadian from Egypt" and Napatan Egyptian:

(1) "Akkadian from Egypt": Matthias Müller defined the variety of the Akkadian language used by the Egyptian scribes of Amarna and the early 19th Dynasty as an interlanguage (Müller 2010, 2021; also Mynářová 2007), displaying a number of linguistic peculiarities that could be explained by interference from Egyptian (see in detail above, pp. 100-1).

(2) Napatan Egyptian: a variety of the ancient Egyptian script and language attested in the Sudan. Napatan Egyptian has received very different linguistic assessments, as an ancient Sudanese dialect of Egyptian (Peust 1999b), "peripheral Demotic" with the influence of a substrate language (Quack 2002, 394) or else as a creole language with a Meroïtic substrate (Breyer 2008). I refer here to the detailed treatment above, pp. 28-31.

5.7 Language convergence through a *sprachbund* situation

It is *a priori* likely that the linguistic development of Egyptian also provides examples of linguistic features induced through areal proximity with other languages or even more far–reaching shared linguistic patterns owed to a *sprachbund* situation (for areal linguistics, see Matras, McMahon, and Vincent 2006; Muysken 2008). Despite the fact that ancient Egyptian was embedded for millennia within other languages, particularly Afro-Asiatic languages and to its south, also Nilo-Saharan languages, linguistic convergence as a result of language contact – distinct from genetically shared features and also extending beyond cognate languages – has never been studied in full depth.

Noteworthy of mention are three cases where some debate has occurred:

(1) Areal interference with African languages, studied by scholars such as Helmut Satzinger and Carsten Peust who recast "Egyptian as an African language" (see in detail above, pp. 69-70). On the assumption of a particular degree of lexical parallels shared between ancient Egyptian and Hausa and the additional postulate of cognates of Egyptian lexemes in non-Afroasiatic African languages, Gábor Takács (Takács 1999, 38-46 and 46-8) and more recently, Hermann Jungraithmayr (2021, with a contribution by Gábor Takács) advanced a hypothesis about an original homeland of the Afroasiatic languages in the Eastern Sahara where areal interference could have taken place.

(2) Indo-European languages were adduced since the 1970s for presumed lexical and typological parallels, in the context of debates about the expansion of Proto-Indo-European from the Near East (see in detail above, pp. 113-6).

(3) An assessment of a *sprachbund* situation between Egyptian and Semitic languages – including Ethio-Semitic languages on the assumption that their historical home was Ethiopia, see above pp. 46-8 – has never been conducted, although various hypotheses have been advanced, particularly regarding the position of Egyptian within Afroasiatic and its precise relationship to the Semitic languages (see Almansa-Villatoro and Štubňová 2022). Recently, Alexander Borg posited a "close symbiotic relationship between Ancient Egyptian and a preclassical Old Arabic phenotype", which would have yielded the modern Arabic vernaculars (Borg 2021, 4-5). Shared linguistic and lexical features would be the "evolutionary outcome of ecological convergence between these two ancient Afroasiatic idioms, plausibly transpiring during the second millennium BC" (Borg 2021, 5). Unfortunately, Borg's study does not account for the recent debates on Egyptian historical phonology and also disregards any lexical assessments of the discussed terms.

A comprehensive interdisciplinary assessment of Egyptian–Semitic areal relations remains an urgent desideratum of future research.

6. CONFLICT AND COMMUNICATION: FOREIGN LANGUAGE COMMUNITIES IN THE EGYPTIAN MILITARY

The evidence for the presence of speakers of non-Egyptian languages is ubiquitous in all periods of Egyptian society. On an individual basis, thousands of persons with non-Egyptian personal names are attested in Egypt throughout the 3rd millennium BCE (Schneider 1998a, 1-23; Scheele-Schweitzer 2014, 123-5; El-Sayed 2011), the 2nd millennium BCE (Schneider 1992; Schneider 1993; Schneider 2003a, 112-176; El-Sayed 2011; Zibelius-Chen 2011) and the 1st millennium BCE (Vittmann 2003; Winnicki 2009). From the Middle Kingdom to the Egyptian Late Period, we are able to document the presence of people of different ethnic origin and their descendants on all socio-economic levels and throughout all professional segments, including high offices of the state administration, the military, the royal court and the priesthood (Schneider 2003a, 201-290; Schneider 2006; Schneider 2010).

In addition to individuals, the presence of groups and communities of speakers of foreign languages is amply documented. Immigration to Egypt comprised prisoners of war and the systematic deportation of population groups (Langer 2021), state-induced conscription for work (cf. Di Teodoro 2018 for the system of state labor in the Middle Kingdom[13]), "slave trade" (Helck 1972, 347-50; Loprieno 2012 [also for the terminological issues]; Bussmann 2014) and voluntary immigration (e.g., for labor).

The actual language use and communicative behavior of these people cannot be traced or reconstructed for lack of the necessary documentation. However, this chapter will attempt to take a closer look at foreign language communities within one sector of major demographic and linguistic influx: the military. I will attempt – somewhat speculatively – to sketch three situations of language development: language preservation, language attrition, and multilingualism.

---

[13] Mark Lehner has surmised that foreigners might already have been employed in the construction of the Giza pyramids (Lehner 2015, 431, 477, 489, 497).

Foreign groups within the Egyptian military have been identified in the past literature, albeit not from a linguistic but rather ethnic or cultural viewpoint. They would have operated within the institutional system of state violence (see Bestock 2017) which would also use coercive measures of integration. In a unique statement about state-enforced measures to expunge the language of prisoners, on a stele from chapel C at Deir el-Medineh (KRI V 90-1; Zinn 1998, 80-1), the captivated Libyans (the Libu and Meshwesh tribes) are said to have been placed "into strongholds of the victorious king, that they might hear the speech of the (Egyptian) people while serving the king. He makes their speech disappear; he overturns ther tongues" (Sagrillo 2009, 344, who speaks about "military re-education centers"). Here the Libyan language is flagged as a domain of identity and resistance. Foreign language communities in the military raise the problem of loyalty to the state; thus, they provide the opportunity to frame the discussion of language contact and contact linguistics differently, from the viewpoint of *language conflict* and *conflict linguistics* (see Schneider-Mizony 2014, 80-3; these terms have not yet been used within Egyptology).[14]

6.1 The military and the "mercenary" terminology

Since the inception of an Egyptian military system (on which, Spalinger 2005) in the Old Kingdom, the Egyptian state relied on the use of troops of different ethnicity. Contingents of such troops are also attested by the titles of the military officers in charge of them (e.g., Schneider 2003a, 193-4). Ellen Morris has touched upon the role of the army as an agent aiding in the melding of disparate cultures, and compared the situation in Egypt to that in the early Roman

[14] There also existed mixed language communities abroad, to mention only those in Egypt's Nubian colony during the Middle and New Kingdoms (Morris 2018a, 90-99; Smith 2018) and the Egyptian diaspora in Mesopotamia following the Neo-Assyrian and Persian conquests of Egypt (e.g., Huber 2006; Henkelman 2017). For the Assyrian deportations, see Koch 2022; for Egyptian, Nubians and Libyans in Neo-Assyrian sources, Karlsson 2022; for the renderings of Egyptian names in Neo-Assyrian, Neo-Babylonian and Achaemenid sources, see the new comprehensive analysis in Mahlich 2022, 471-521.

empire (Morris 2018a, 98-100). The presence of these foreign troops as well as the accoutrement of the Egyptian army with weaponry must have led to significant linguistic interference that is visible to a limited degree in the military vocabulary and texts of warfare (Schneider 2008a). I have suggested to distinguish between different varieties of language use for communicative situations and text production relating to the Egyptian military. "Military language" in the narrower sense would relate to the specialized language of the institution, and "soldiers' slang" or "military slang" would mean the sociolect of the troops, comprising again different varieties according to military units and hierarchy (Schneider 2008a, 182-3; taken up by Spalinger 2020, 29-30). The military slang, but also technical terms, are poorly documented. Many of these term were borrowings from foreign languages; they relate to weaponry and military infrastructure, titles and functions, behavior, the application of violence, intimidation, and flight (see pp. 87, 128).

While the presence of different ethnic components of the Egyptian army has often been discussed, the fact that they at the same time constituted different *linguistic communities* – both as parts of the army in action and as members of garrisons throughout the country – has not been addressed much. Scholarship saw these troops in opposition to – rather than, part of – the Egyptian population due to the simple fact that they displayed non-Egyptian ethnicity. This lack of acknowledgment may stem partially from the use of a misleading terminology. These troops are mostly labeled "mercenaries" in the literature (e.g., Manassa 2003, 81-2; Morenz 2010, 527-30, Spalinger 2010, 429 for the Nubian "mercenaries" from Gebelein; Morris 2018a, 7, 98, 214-6; Spalinger 2020 *passim* for Nubian, Libyan, Sherden mercenaries), insinuating that these troops were not permanent or long-term members of Egyptian society. While this terminology is widely accepted in Egyptology, I would advocate for a more differentiated use. The definition of a mercenary contains elements that often do not apply to the Egyptian evidence, at least not before the 7th c. BCE. As per the *International Convention against the Recruitment, Use, Financing and*

Training of Mercenaries (article 1, 1; see Percy 2007; *https://treaties.un.org*):

> 1. A mercenary is any person who:
> (a) Is specially recruited locally or abroad in order to fight in an armed conflict;
> (b) Is motivated to take part in the hostilities essentially by the desire for private gain and, in fact, is promised, by or on behalf of a party to the conflict, material compensation substantially in excess of that promised or paid to combatants of similar rank and functions in the armed forces of that party;
> (c) Is neither a national of a party to the conflict nor a resident of territory controlled by a party to the conflict;
> (d) Is not a member of the armed forces of a party to the conflict; and
> (e) Has not been sent by a State which is not a party to the conflict on official duty as a member of its armed forces.

Criteria (b)-(d) cannot be assumed or can often be outright excluded for the Egyptian evidence before the Late Period. E.g., the Nubian warriors at Gebelein are clearly residents of the town; (c) can thus certainly be excluded. We do not have evidence of "compensation substantially in excess of that promised or paid to combatants of similar rank and functions in the armed forces of that party" (b; but see Manassa 2003, 61, 82). (d) is not a valid argument, either, if we assume that Egypt's army relied on people of foreign ethnicity who may have been regular inhabitants of Egypt. About the circumstances of the recruitment of these soldiers (a) we are not informed; in some cases (such as the Sherden), they seem to have been prisoners of war turned into auxiliary troops.

For the situation in Gebelein, Morenz (2010, 526-7) adduces as evidence for the recruitment of mercenaries the tomb of the troop commander Iti in Gebelein. It shows armed Nubians as well as a captive and a Nubian being brought before Iti, as well as a statement on the stele of a troop commander and overseer of foreign troops (*mr ỉꜣ ʿ.w*), Djemi, where he says to have made subservient (*bꜣk*) the inhabitants of Lower Nubia. Neither the scene nor the statement seem particularly conducive to the interpretation of military recruitment. Rather than the latter (Morenz 2010, 320), *bꜣk* seems to convey the meaning of "taxing" (Schenkel 1965, 116; Goedicke 1960, 289 and 290 n. [m]). The Nubian (*nḥśỉ*) soldier Tjehemau reports in his inscription in monumental Hieratic at Abisko in Lower Nubia (Darnell 2003) how he joined king Mentuhotep II's regular army when the king was on a visit to the region – as an "Egyptianized Nubian" (Darnell), not a mercenary.

As a matter of fact, then, such troops may have constituted regular members of the Egyptian military and general population that were of foreign ethnic origin. In this respect, the *Légion étrangère* (a regular part of the French army) or the *Ostlegionen* of the German Wehrmacht in the Second World War may be comparable in nature, if not in scale.

6.2 Case studies of military foreign language communities

6.2.1 Language preservation: Cushitic-speaking troops of the First Intermediate Period

Nubian troops are a frequent topic of the 1st Intermediate Period, mentioned in texts and represented in art (Meurer 1998, 94-5; Schneider 1998a, 21-2; Spalinger 2010, 428-30). The representations pertain to Nubian archers in the service of different rulers of this period, the Heracleopolitan (9th-10th) and the Theban (11th dynasty) dynasties. They include depictions in the tombs of the nomarch Ankhtifi at Moalla and of Setka at Assuan (Fischer 1961, 62-4, 77-8; Meurer 1998, 94-5), the wooden model of 40 Nubian archers from the tomb of the nomarch Mesehti at Assiut (Bietak 1985), depictions in the Theban tomb of Antef (TT386) and in the tomb of the aforementioned troop commander Iti at Gebelein (p. 142; Spalinger 2010, 428-30). Nubian troops may also be attested by the frequent military title *mr iꜥꜣw* "commander of the *iꜥꜣw*" (Bell 1976) among whom figures the individual Djemi mentioned above (p. 142).

> The much-discussed term *iꜥꜣw* had most likely the significance βάρβαροι, ἀλλόγλωσσοι (see p. 150 for the latter term's use for Carian and Greek troops in Egypt). It was used for Egyptianized Nubians and also individuals serving as interpreters (Schneider 2003a, 110-1). In this context, it is noteworthy to point out that a Nubian 'superintendent of bodyguards' (for the title, Schneider 2003a, 247-8) attested at Gebelein in the 13th dynasty carries the epithet "who resolves the language of any foreign country" (Morenz 2010, 530).

A key site for the stationing of these troops appears to have been the city of

Gebelein in Upper Egypt (Fischer 1961; Kubisch 2000; Morenz 2010, 527-30; Spalinger 2010, 429; Moreno García 2018, 166). In his autobiography from Gebelein (stele Berlin 24032; Schenkel 1965, 61; Meurer 1998, 95), the soldier Qedes makes explicit reference to both Nubian and Upper Egyptian population segments within the city when he boasts: "Moreover, I surpassed this entire city in swiftness, its Nubians and Upper Egyptians" (Lichtheim 1973, 90). Six funerary stelae from Gebelein are known that represent individual Nubian soldiers and their families. Showing the Nubians with large eyes and a protruding mouth, they are of an artistically distinct style and were executed clumsily, maybe manufactured by a 'Nubian workshop' (Kubisch 2000, 247). The owners carry either the title *nḥśỉ* "Nubian" (see above pp. 19-21 for the discussion of ethnic and linguistic correlations of this term) or the epithet *ỉqr* "the capable, proficient one". It has been suggested that the ethnonym (which is sometimes followed by the 'soldier' classifier) may denote more precisely a "Nubian soldier" (Kubisch 2000, 248 n. 45; Morenz 2010, 526). These Nubians are presumed to have lived in a garrison (Morenz 2010, 526-7) although this assumption is conjectural. A precise dating of the stelae within a range of 100 years is not possible; the troops could thus belong either in the context of the Nubian troops of Ankhtifi in the earlier 1st Intermediate Period (Fiore Marochetti 2013; Ejsmond 2017: 9th dynasty) or the rise of Thebes under Mentuhotep II in the 11th dynasty (both dates admitted by Kubisch 2000, 264; Morenz 2010, 529).

I have discussed in detail the disputed scholarship on the ethnic and linguistic attribution of Pan-grave, C-group and Kerma 'Nubians' (see pp. 48-9). Their linguistic affiliation seems in any case a branch language of Cushitic. The ethnic affiliation of the Nubians of the Gebelein stelae is not *a priori* certain, nor is it clear that these people had necessarily the same origin (El-Sayed 2011, 77-8). However, on the basis of the very persuasive interpretation of one of the foreign names from the Gebelein stele Turin 1270 – that of the brother *ỉ-h-t-k* of the stele owner Čnnw (Blemmyan name ⲉⲓⲁϩⲁⲧⲉⲕ *yahatek* = *(y)ihattak* with assimilation < **(y)ihā́m-tak "leopard man"* [see p. 43]) –, the most plausible linguistic affiliation for at least some of the *nḥśỉ.w* here is (Proto-)Old Beḍawiye. Zibelius-Chen also points to the fact that some features – the chin beard of *Nnw* on the Turin stele; the hair needle in his son's headdress – are typical for the Beja until today (2007, 395). Given the fact that 'Nubians' are attested here since the 4th dynasty (El-Sayed 2011, 77) and into the 2nd millennium (Morenz 2010, 530), it is possible to see Gebelein as an Egyptian military hub for the conscription and training of Beja living adjacently in the Eastern desert. This would make it likely that these troops maintained proficiency in their language of origin and acquired some degree of bilingualism through their Egyptian military service and their later settlement in Egypt.[15]

6.2.2 Language attrition: The language of the Sherden troops in Ramesside Egypt

The best-documented group of the Sea Peoples within the Egyptian evidence (see p. 123) is that of the Sherden (Cavillier 2005, 2010, 2015; Winnicki 2009, 81-3; Emanuel 2013; Adams and Cohen 2013, 649-50; Abbas 2017) – for the very reason that they were employed in the Egyptian army over a period of two centuries (1300-1100 BCE) and also settled in Egypt on fiefs of land received in compensation for their service (for a discussion of this land-for-service practice, see van der Toorn 2019, 92-4). The attested initial step of their integration was in the reign of Ramesses II (1279-1214) when they served as an elite component of Ramesses II's personal guard (Abbas 2017, 10). In his second regnal year, the king had thwarted attacks of "warriors of the sea", "so Lower Egypt could again sleep in peace", describing their martial nature as follows:

---

[15] A military context has also been proposed for the *nḥśỉ.w ḥtp.w* "settled/pacified Nubians" of the 6th dynasty (Fettel 2010, 155 n. 1327 translates "compensated Nubians" [sg., "bezahlter Nubier"]), possibly auxiliary troops constituting a military colony (Schneider 1998a, 22; Kubisch 2000, 248 n. 45; Lehner 2015, 487-9). For the controversial discussion about the presence of Kerma people at Deir el-Ballas and Tell el-Dabʿa, see Matić 2014b; Walsh 2018; and the overview of Nubian material evidence at Egyptian sites in Raue 2018.

> "(Regarding) the Sherden whose heart is rebellious, from time immemorial one did not know how to fight them when they came boldly after sailing in their war-ships from the midst of the sea, and one did not know how to bear up against them." (KRI II 290: 2-3; my translation).

Ramesses II seems to have turned captured Sherden into specialized foreign troops. Just three years later (year 5 of Ramesses II), Sherden are attested as an Egyptian elite corps in the Battle of Kadesh against the Hittites (Spalinger 2003, 171-5; 187-9; according to Manassa 2003, 78 n.9 and Abbas 2017, 10, already as infantry or chariot 'runners'; after Spalinger 2021, 113, as a regular component of the army besides infantry and chariotry). In regnal year 10, they appear as fighters in the attack on Dapur (Abbas 2017, 10-1). In the wars of Merenptah (Abbas 2017, 11-2) and those of Ramesses III – the later 13th and the early 12th c. BCE – , the Sherden were a regular part of the Egyptian army. This is also confirmed by Pap. Anastasi I (17.4) from c. 1200 BCE, where a Sherden contingent of 520 soldiers leads a list of foreign auxiliary troops of the Egyptian army. During the reign of Ramesses III, a fort "Ramesses, Ruler of Heliopolis, Beloved of his Army" at the entrance to the Fayyum contained Sherden (Abbas 2017, 8).

In the Great Papyrus Harris, an accountability report on the reign of Ramesses III commissioned by his successor, Ramesses IV, Sherden are mentioned among the adressees of the king's speech (75.1-2) and among the military forces (76.5-10). A description of the peaceful state of Egypt when troops could rest includes an explicit reference to Sherden 'towns': "the Sherden and the (Libyan) Qeheq were in their towns, laid out on their backs" (78.9-10; cf. Grandet 1994, 203-4). The existence of Sherden contingents is also obvious from the 20th and early 21st dynasties, through the term "Sherden of the fortresses" – probably Sherden stationed in garrisons – as well as the titles "commander of the great fortresses of the Sherden" and "commander of the five fortresses of the Sherden" (Cavillier 2005; Manassa 2003, 130 with n. 32; Bennett 2019, 223-5). Pap. Amiens (reign of Ramesses VII, 1100 BCE) lists grain provisions "to (?) the Sherden people" and "the house of the Sherden" (Cavillier

2005; Emmanuel 2013, 19).

A unique document for the question of the Sherden presence in Egypt is the land register of Papyrus Wilbour from c. 1150 BCE which lists land allotments for smallholders in Middle Egypt. Among the dozens of occupations are many military ones, including Sherden (Katary 1989, 16; Antoine 2014, 26), as well as "standard bearers of the Sherden" and "retainers of the Sherden". A last attestation, listing "the fields of the Sherden", is a donation stele from Helwan from the reign of Osorkon II (c. 860 BCE; Cavillier 2005; Emmanuel 2013, 21). The available evidence indicates that the genesis of the Sherden contingents goes back to the integration of captives from the Sherden segment of the Sea Peoples in the Egyptian military forces in the 13th century. We do not have any evidence in support of the assumption that in the 150 years after their initial conscription, those contingents would have been replenished from any remaining Sherden population groups outside Egypt. Moreover, the notion of 'Sherden' seems to have shifted from an ethnically marked term for military personel to a mere designation of a military unit or function, comparably to the shift in meaning of the ethnic term Medja to denote 'policemen' (see p. 18).

It is thus likely that the knowledge of the Sherden language and culture within Egypt declined – and probably disappeared – after 1200 BCE (cf. Emmanuel 2013, 20-2). A linguistic body that might support this hypothesis is provided by the onomastics of the Sherden listed in Papyrus Wilbour and contemporary documents (listed by Cavillier 2005, *Appendice onomastico*). They do not contain any proper name that might be seen as stemming from the Sherden language, whereas the names are Egyptian and Semitic and emphasize attributes of military prowess. It is true that the absence of names in a given language cannot be taken as proof that the language itself was no longer practiced; Egyptian personal names – often the only indicator of a person's ethnic or linguistic heritage (Schneider 2010, 148) – were at all times adopted readily by immigrants. However, these names do not indicate positively the preservation of the Sherden language:

Of the c. 60 names attested, 90% are Egyptian; c. 7 foreign names seem to be Semitic (*Bʿl-nʿm* "Baal is pleasant"; *čꜣ-r-b-w* "the pot" (2x), *m-h-r-y-t* "(the god NN is) a warrior", *h-ꜣ-ỉ-t-b-ỉ*, maybe *pꜣ-q-ꜣ-hꜣ; ṭ-ỉ-ṭ-ỉ*), and two names have the meaning "(the) Syrian" (*ẖꜣ-r-w-y* [2x, same person?], *pꜣ-ẖꜣ-rw* [F]) – cf. here also the names *pꜣ-qꜣrw-ỉ-w* "the vagabond, foreigner", *pꜣ-wʿr* "the fugitive" and even *pꜣ-nḥśỉ*, "the Nubian". It is conspicuous that several of the Egyptian names (in addition to the Semitic one quoted) contain the divine name Seth–Baal, the patron god of Ramesside Egypt and god of warfare, and that a majority of names reference strength, bravery and military command: *ꜣčw mšʿ* "troop commander", *ʿḥꜣwtỉ ʿꜣ* "great fighter", *ʿčṭ* "boy, young man", *pꜣ-ʿꜣ-n-nn-nsw* "The great one of Heracleopolis", *mntw-ḥr-ḫpš* "Montu is striking power", *nḫt-ʿꜣ* "great strongman", *nḫt-km.t* "the strong one of Egypt", *qny*, "the brave one", *qnỉ-ḥr-ḫps=f* "brave through his strength", *qnỉ-śʿnḫ* "the brave one enlivens", *tly* "the valiant one".

A full integration of these Sherden in Egyptian society is apparent from documents of the late 20th dynasty. In the Adoption papyrus from the reign of Ramesses XI, two Sherden with Egyptian names appear as witnesses in a legal trial; in a stela from Herakleopolis (Ehnasya el-Medina), a Sherden Padjesef "of the fort of Weser-Maat-Re" appears as offering to the Egyptian deities Herishef and Hathor (Emmanuel 2013, 21-2). A reference to *Pr-nṯr n Šrdn* "the temple of the Sherden" in Pap. Wilbour B (9.x+2) likely refers to a local cult place utilized by Sherden troops.[16]

6.2.3 Multilingualism at war and peace: Greeks, Carians and other linguistic units in the Saïte army

The Egyptian administration, and in particular the military, saw an increase of officials of Libyan descent since the 20th dynasty, a development that led to the Third Intermediate Period in Egyptian history (1075-664 BCE) and a feudalistic system of state power inspired by Libyan practices (Sagrillo 2013). This system was abolished with the invasion of Egypt by the Kushite ruler Piye/Pi-

[16] It does not mean "temple of the god of the Sherden" (as Cavillier 2015, 637, insinuates) and thus is not an indication of a god of presumably Sea People origin.

ankhy (see p. 44) around 724 BCE and the establishment of the Kushite 25th dynasty (for the question of Kushite cultural identity in an Egyptian context, Budka 2019), only to be replaced once again by a dynasty of ultimately Libyan heritage, the 26th or Saïte dynasty (664-525 BCE).

The military efforts of this system need to be seen within a global context. The 26th dynasty witnessed the end of the Neo-Assyrian empire, the rise of the Neo-Babylonian empire (605 BCE: Battle of Karkemish; 601 and 569 BCE: Babylonian attempts to conquer Egypt defeated) and the expansion of the Persian empire. The dynasty tried – with temporary success – to re-establish an Egyptian empire in the Eastern Mediterranean, including the Levant, Cyprus and the Sudan, and to become a maritime power. It relied decisively on foreign troops that were provided by Egypt's political allies and vassals (Vittmann 2003). The military collaboration with Greek polities is part and parcel of the intense system of Greek-Egyptian contacts in the 7th and 6th c. BCE (for which see von Bredow 2017; Manning 2020, 366-7). While the focus of the following remarks is on language contact within the military sector, such contact must have been omnipresent in other sectors, too. E.g., Torallas Tovar has suggested the existence of a pidgin language for the merchants of the Greek trade emporium of Naukratis (Torallas Tovar 2010, 255; for the status of Naukratis, see Agut-Labordère 2012; Masson-Berghoff and Thomas 2019; for Naukratis and other Greek emporia such as Herakleion, Pfeiffer 2005, 165-6).

It is relevant to refer here to a recent study by Jeffrey Rop which reassesses the Greek military service in the ancient Near East during the 4th century BCE, including the use of Greek troops by Egypt's last indigenous dynasties (Rop 2019; Van Regenmortel 2020; Sears 2020). Rop challenges the earlier scholarly hypothesis according to which these Greek troops would have been used because of the alleged military superiority of the Greek *hoplites*. In the 4th century, Egypt's main purpose in recruiting Greek troops was to boost their numbers against the large forces of the Persian empire. Egypt relied solely on troops from its political allies; therefore, their perusal was "part of an international system based on political patronage and reciprocity" (Rop 2019, 2) in which the troops furthered the political interests of the alliances. This situation seems also to apply to the Saïte dynasty; accordingly, the overarching political alliance presents a challenge to the assumption of mercenaries being motivated by personal profit and hired through independent recruitment.

The ethnic and linguistic composition of the Saïte army was complex. Based on Egyptian infantry and archers, it was commanded by generals who often were of Libyan background (Agut-Labordère 2013, 987). It comprised the *kalasiries* – a kind of police force (Agut-Labordère 2013, 987-8; for the hybrid, maybe Nubian-Egyptian etymology of this term, see p. 39) – and developed a cavalry partially composed of "Asian" cavalrymen. Initially employed to guard frontier areas, it was later probably also deployed on the battlefield (Agut-Labordère 2013, 988-9). The Saïte state also established a Mediterranean and Red Sea fleet (Agut-Labordère 2013, 990). The construction of a canal to connect the Nile valley (and thus, the Mediterranean Sea) and the Red Sea under Nekaw II (completed by Darius I, see Mahlich 2020) was part of the maritime and imperial strategy of the Saïte dynasty.

According to Herodotus, Gyges of Lydia sent Ionian Greek and Carian troops to Egypt as early as the reign of Psammetichus I (Agut-Labordère 2013, 989). One of the members of the Greek troops is known to us through a cuboid statue found at Priene – a certain Pedon, son of Amphinneos, who was awarded for his bravery with a gold bracelet and an Egyptian village (Agut-Labordère 2013, 989; Barbaro 2018). The longest Greek inscription engraved on the legs of the Abu Simbel colossi during the Nubian campaign of Psammetichus II in 592 BCE informs us – in Greek, but from an Egyptian viewpoint – that "Potasimto commanded the non-native speakers (ἀλλόγλωσσοι), and Amasis the Egyptians" (Meiggs and Lewis 1969, 7a; Bernand and Masson 1957; Agut-Labordère 2013, 993). Apart from Ionian Greek and Carian soldiers, we know of Dorian Greek, Cypriote, Phoenician and Judean troops as parts of the Saïte army (Schmitz 2010; Kahn 2007, 508, 514; Agut-Labordère 2013, 994; Brown 2020, 231).

Even for foreign troops serving in the Egyptian army for a limited time period, such service would implicate substantial interaction among people of different linguistic affiliation. An example is a revolt of combatants in Elephantine under Apries (589-570 BCE), comprising of "bowmen", "Greeks" and "Asiatics" (biography of Neshor; Agut-Labordère 2013, 1004; Bassir 2016, 45-6, 58).

In Egypt's increasingly Hellenized context of the 6th c. BCE, some proficiency in Greek can be postulated. Bilingualism or multilingualism is explicitly attested for military commanders. A general of the Egyptian army Djedptahiufankh from the reign of Psammetichus also carries the titles "leader of foreign contingents" and "mouthpiece of his Majesty in the middle of the contingents of Asiatics" (Agut-Labordère 2013, 989; De Meulenaere 1963, 23-5), probably a reference to the general's proficiency in Phoenician and/or (the closely related) Hebrew. Psammetichus II's commander Potasimto (= Padisematawy) whose Egyptian background from a priestly family is well-known (Pernigotti 1968) was clearly bilingual in Egyptian and Greek. Similarly, the functions of a military commander Hor (surname Psamtik) who was "admiral of the royal combat vessels in the Mediterranean", "commander of the foreigners of the Aegean" and "confidant of the king for the Aegean countries", seem to implicate that he was bilingual in Egyptian and Greek – the crews of his fleet were probably manned with Greeks (Agut-Labordère 2013, 991).

Herodotus (II.154) provides information about the long-term settlement of the foreign troops of the Saïte army in *stratopeda* (στρατόπεδα) and the language education of Greek-Egyptian interpreters; his statement that they were "the first of foreign speech to settle in that country" is obviously not correct:

> To the Ionians and Carians who had helped him, Psammetichus gave places to live in called "The Camps", opposite each other on either side of the Nile; and besides this, he paid them all that he had promised. [2] Moreover, he put Egyptian boys in their hands to be taught Greek, and from these, who learned the language, are descended the present-day Egyptian interpreters. [3] The Ionians and Carians lived for a long time in these places, which are near the sea, on the arm of the Nile called the Pelusian, a little way below the town of Bubastis. Long afterwards, king Amasis removed them and settled them at

> Memphis to be his guard against the Egyptians. [4] It is a result of our communication with these settlers in Egypt (the first of foreign speech to settle in that country) that we Greeks have exact knowledge of the history of Egypt from the reign of Psammetichus onwards. [5] There still remained in my day, in the places out of which the Ionians and Carians were turned, the winches for their ships and the ruins of their houses. This is how Psammetichus got Egypt. (translation A.D. Godley)

An exemplary case of immigration and cultural integration from this time period, the 26th dynasty, is documented through the Egyptian sarcophagus of a person carrying the Egyptian personal name Wahibraemhat "Apries is in the vanguard" while the names of his Greek parents, transcribed into hieroglyphs, were Alexikles and Zenodote (Grallert 2001).

With regard to the military, the most famous and best-documented example for the settlement of ethnically and linguistically foreign troops in Egypt during the Saïte period, probably in the later 7th century BCE, is the Jewish military colony at Elephantine (latest treatment Becking 2020; Folmer 2022; Kratz and Schipper 2022; on the debate about the date, Botta 2009, 13-6; van der Toorn 2019, 61-88; see also Vittmann 2003, 84-119; Joisten-Pruschke 2008).[17] As Karel van der Toorn (2019, 94) has put it, "the Jews of Elephantine were frontier soldiers attached to a garrison" but "their daily activities were nonmilitary". Hundreds of Aramaic papyri from throughout the 5th c. BCE – letters, legal documents, lists, also the Aramaic version of the Story of Achiqar – show an Aramaic language community within a local Egyptian and, through the presence of other languages, a multilingual community. Apart from the local Egyptians and the Persians, legal documents mention as soldiers of the different detachments on Elephantine and at Syene, the main city to the east of the island, also Aramaeans, Babylonians, as well as speakers of different Iranian languages: Bactrians, Caspians, Khwarezmians, Magians, and Medes (Botta 2009, 9-10).

[17] Similarly, on Egypt's western border garrison of Khastem (aram. ḤSTMḤ = *ḫ ꜣs.t Ṯmḥ.w*, "Country of the Libyans"; = Mareia, west of Lake Mareotis), an Egyptian official Sematawy -Tefnakht was "agent at the gate of the foreign countries of Libya" and "chief of Asiatic foreigners (= Aramaean troops)" (Aramaic stele Berlin ÄM 7707; Agut-Labordère 2013, 1004).

7. CONCLUSION: MULTILINGUALISM, INDEXICALITY, LINGUISTIC IDENTITY

Linguistic identity constitutes a pivotal element of human identity, and multilingualism is today seen as the norm, rather than the exception among human societies and individuals (see Zarate, Lévy and Kramsch 2011; Martin-Jones, Blackledge and Creese 2012; Weber and Horner 2012; Maher 2017; Coulmas 2018). The significance of these multiple linguistic voices in ancient societies has recently been demonstrated by key studies such as Mullen (2013) or Hasselbach-Andee (2020). The survey in this book has demonstrated the omnipresence of non-Egyptian languages in pre-Hellenistic Egypt, despite the fact that only a minute fraction of the ancient linguistic diversity has been preserved. John Ray's conjecture of a cosmopolitan Egypt becomes a multilingual Egypt if we replace his dated term 'different nationalities' by "different languages":

> „Is this kaleidoscope of different nationalities which seems to characterise New-Kingdom Egypt merely an accident of time and place, or is it a phenomenon which, if we had the information, would turn out to be true in earlier dynasties? The evidence of Manfred Bietak's work at Avaris suggests that the cosmopolitan picture that we have been proposing holds for that site as well. However, Avaris is in the Delta, and the Delta, as we comfortingly tell ourselves, was always untypical; but can we be sure that contemporary Memphis, to give an example, was so different from Avaris? And if this is true of the Second Intermediate Period, the New Kingdom, and the Late Period, may it not also be true of the Middle Kingdom, the Old Kingdom, and for that matter the rise of Dynasty I?" (Ray 1998, 11)

The pervasiveness of multilingualism in Egypt does raise the question of where the communicative spaces of those languages were besides the Egyptian space of languages and scripts – where the latter may have exercised a boundary-maintenance function (cf. Portes and Rumbaut 2001, 115). Egyptian linguistics has traditionally focused on the study of aspects of inner-Egyptian linguistic diversity (such as dialects, diglossia) but has not surveyed systematically, and analyzed the presence and use of, Egyptian vis-à-vis other languages. Broadening the traditional approach to a full range of linguistic codes that would encompass different languages, language varieties, or language registers, will open a new avenue for the study of language in ancient Egypt.

The use of foreign languages and mixed languages, and the selective use of loanwords and loan translations within Egyptian, provided a means for past groups or individuals to "index" their (social, ethnic, professional, etc.) identity in specific contexts or "domains" (Adams 2003, 595). By indexicality we understand the way individuals use and evaluate their access to linguistic resources and linguistic codes to 'tag' their (social, ethnic, professional etc.) identity (for the concept, see Bassiouney 2015, 58-62). Riggs and Baines (2012) are among the few scholars in Egyptology that have pointed to language as a component of ethnicity.

Linguistic resources can be *discursive* – (ethnic, social etc.) identity categories of the speakers, forms of speech, presuppositions, intertextuality etc. – or *structural* (grammatical, lexical, phonetic etc. features) (Bassiouney 2015, 66) and combine phenomena such as *code-switching* and *code-choice*. Linguistic codes refer to different languages, language varieties (such as dialects) or language registers ('high' vs. 'low' registers). Egyptian linguistics has studied indexicality for the different written language varieties, including the diglossia situation between the Middle Kingdom and the Amarna Period (Jansen-Winkeln 1995; Vernus 1996; Stauder 2013, 2020; Paksi 2020) but has not researched the presence and use of spoken Egyptian vis-à-vis other languages.

In this respect, documented multilingual contexts from later times (cf. Richter 2010, Boud'hors 2020, Bassiouney 2015) are highly instructive. The trilingual (Arabic, Greek, Coptic) Qurra archive from 8th c. CE Aphrodito demonstrates the use of Greek as a *lingua franca* between different segments of society – the Coptic-speaking milieu of the villages and the local elite, the Hellenized provincial and urban elite (with either Greek/Coptic or Greek/Arabic bilinguals) and the Arabic-speaking government at Fusṭāṭ. Intriguingly, it does not provide

evidence for individual trilingualism or Coptic/Arabic bilingualism (Richter 2010). Bassiouney (2015) provides a highly instructive analysis of the linguistic indexicality of Standard Arabic, Egyptian Colloquial Arabic, English as well as other modern languages in contemporary Egypt.
From this perspective, a text such as Pap. Anastasi I – a polemic Late Egyptian text from the early 19th dynasty about the duties of a military officer, framed as a letter sent from a military scribe Hori to a fellow scribe Amenemope in the state administration – can be seen as *highly indexed linguistically* to convey socio-professional and maybe, ethnic identity. The passage of the text quoted earlier (22, 2-7; p. 88) shows Late Egyptian interspersed with specialized Northwest Semitic and Hurrian lexical terms from the military language, including a complete and untranslated sentence in Northwest Semitic, as well as Levantine topographical information. It foregrounds tactical expertise, appeals to heroic action, and presumes knowledge of local stories and realia. The specific linguistic identity of the text presents us with the profile of a military specialist who grew up and was trained in a situation of cultural hybridity and language contact. It is a text that may not necessarily reflect a military register or norm that was in wider use but, more probably, an individual's expression of identity.

Any future study of language contact in Egyptology will comprise the publication of additional textual evidence and the new analysis of published material. It will also need to apply more thoroughly theoretical models to the unwieldy and complex evidence. Scholarship will be able to foster – and to benefit from – a true interdisciplinary dialogue between theoretical linguistics (contact linguistics, sociolinguistics and the sociology of language) and the particular linguistics of Egyptian as well as ancient and modern Near Eastern, African and Mediterranean languages.

8. Bibliography

Note that German Umlaute and other modified letters are arranged according to English convention like their nearest basic equivalent letters in the English alphabet.

ABBAS 2017 = Mohamed Raafat Abbas, A Survey of the Military Role of the Sherden Warriors in the Egyptian Army during the Ramesside Period. *Égypte Nilotique et Méditerranéenne* 10, pp. 7-23.

ADAMOU AND MATRAS 2020 = Evangelia Adamou and Yaron Matras, *The Routledge Handbook of Language Contact.* London and New York: Routledge.

ADAMS, JANSE AND SWAIN 2002 = James Noel Adams, Mark Janse and Simon Swain, *Bilingualism in Ancient Society: Language Contact and the Written Text.* Oxford: Oxford University Press.

ADAMS 2003 = James Noel Adams, *Bilingualism and the Latin Language.* Cambridge: Cambridge University Press.

ADAMS AND COHEN 2013 = Matthew J. Adams and Margaret E. Cohen, The "Sea Peoples" in Primary Sources. In *The Philistines and Other "Sea Peoples" in Text and Archaeology*, ed. Anne Killebrew and Gunnar Lehmann, pp. 645-664. Atlanta, GA: Society of Biblical Literature.

ADIEGO 2007 = Ignacio Adiego, *The Carian Language.* With an Appendix by Koray Konuk. Leiden and Boston: Brill.

ADIEGO 2010 = Ignacio Adiego, Recent Developments in the Decipherment of Carian. In *Hellenistic Karia. Proceedings of the First International Conference on Hellenistic Karia, Oxford, 29 June-2 July 2006,* ed. R. Van Bremen and J.-M. Carbon, pp. 147-76. Bordeaux.

AGHALI-ZAKARA 2003 = Mohamed Aghali-Zakara, Anthroponymie touarègue. Dénominations multiples des individualités. *Nouvelle revue d'onomastique* 41-42, pp. 221-29.

AGUT-LABORDÈRE 2012 = Damien Agut-Labordère, Le statut égyptien de Naucratis. In *Entités locales et pouvoir central: La cité dominée dans l'Orient hellénistique*, ed. V. Dieudonné et al., pp. 353-73. Nancy: De Boccard.

AGUT-LABORDÈRE 2013 = Damien Agut-Labordère, The Saite Period: The Emergence of a Mediterranean Power. In *Ancient Egyptian Administration.* Handbook of Oriental Studies. Section 1: The Near and Middle East, 104, ed. Juan Carlos Moreno García, pp. 965-1027. Leiden and Boston: Brill.

AHRENS 2006 = Alexander Ahrens, A Journey's End: Two Egyptian Stone Vessels with Hieroglyphic Inscriptions from the Royal Tomb at Tell Misrife/Qatna. *Egypt and the Levant* 16, pp. 15-36.

ALLAM 2011 = Schafik Allam, Le traité égypto-hittite de paix et d'alliance entre les rois Ramsès II et Khatouchili III (d'après l'inscription hiéroglyphique au temple de Karnak). *Journal of Egyptian History* 4, pp. 1-39.

ALLAM 2019 = Schafik Allam, *Hieratischer Papyrus Bulaq 18.* Tafeln + Index; Kommentar

+ Übersetzungen. 2 vols. Tübingen: Im Selbstverlag des Herausgebers.

ALLEN 2005 = James P. Allen: *The Ancient Egyptian Pyramid Texts, Translated with an Introduction and Notes.* Atlanta, GA: Society of Biblical Literature.

ALLEN 2008 = James P. Allen, The Historical Inscription of Khnumhotep at Dashur: Preliminary Report. *Bulletin of the American Schools of Oriental Research* 352, pp. 29-39.

ALLON 2010 = Niv Allon, At the Outskirts of a System: Classifiers and Word Dividers in Foreign Phrases and Texts. *Lingua Aegyptia* 18, pp. 1-17.

ALMANSA-VILLATORO AND ŠTUBŇOVÁ 2022 = M. Victoria Almansa-Villatoro and Silvia Štubňová (eds.), *Rethinking the Origins: Ancient Egyptian in the Afroasiatic Phylum.* Languages of the Ancient Near East. University Park, PA: Eisenbrauns.

ALTENMÜLLER 2015 = Hartwig Altenmüller, *Zwei Annalenfragmente aus dem frühen Mittleren Reich.* Studien zur altägyptischen Kultur, Beihefte 16. Hamburg: Buske.

ANDRASON AND VITA 2016 = Alexander Andrason and Juan-Pablo Vita, Contact Languages of the Ancient Near East: Three More Case Sudies (Ugaritic Hurrian, Hurro-Akkadian and Canaano-Akkadian). *Journal of Language Contact* 9, pp. 293-334.

ANFINSET 2010 = Nils Anfinset, *Metal, Nomads and Culture Contact: The Middle East and North Africa.* London: Equinox.

ANSALDO AND MEYERHOFF 2021 = Umberto Ansaldo and Miriam Meyerhoff (eds.), *The Routledge Handbook of Pidgin and Creole Languages.* London and New York: Routledge.

ANTHONY 2007 = David Anthony, *The Horse, the Wheel, and Language: How Bronze-Age Riders from the Eurasian Steppes Shaped the Modern World.* Princeton: Princeton University Press.

ANTOINE 2014 = Jean-Christophe Antoine, Social Position and the Organisation of Landholding in Ramesside Egypt. An Analysis of the Wilbour Papyrus. *Studien zur altägyptischen Kultur* 43, pp. 17-46.

APPLEYARD 2012 = David Appleyard, Cushitic. In *Semitic and Afroasiatic: Challenges and Opportunities.* Porta Linguarum Orientalium. N.S. 34, ed. Lutz Edzard, pp. 199-292. Wiesbaden: Harrassowitz.

ARNET 2014 = Samuel Arnet, Lehnwörter im biblischen Hebräisch. http://www.bibelwissenschaft.de/stichwort/18569/

ARNOLD 1976 = Dieter Arnold, *Gräber des Alten und Mittleren Reichs in El-Tarif.* Archäologische Veröffentlichungen 17. Mainz am Rhein: Harrassowitz.

ASSMANN 1994 = Jan Assmann, Die ägyptische Schriftkultur. In *Schrift und Schriftlichkeit: Ein interdisziplinäres Handbuch internationaler Forschung.* Handbücher zur Sprach- und Kommunikationswissenschaft 10.1, ed. Hartmut Günther and Otto Ludwig, pp. 472-91. Berlin and New York: De Gruyter.

ASTON AND BIETAK 2017 = David Aston and Manfred Bietak, Nubians in the Nile Delta. À propos Avaris and Peru-Nefer. In *Nubia in the New Kingdom. Lived Experience, Pharaonic Control and Indigenous Traditions*, ed. Neal Spencer, Anna Stevens and

Michaela Binder, pp. 491-524. Leuven: Peeters.

BADER 2013 = Bettina Bader, Cultural Mixing in Egyptian Archaeology: The 'Hyksos' as a Case Study. *Archaeological Review from Cambridge* 28, pp. 257-286.

BADER 2021 = Bettina Bader, *Material Culture and Identities in Egyptology. Towards a Better Understanding of Cultural Encounters and their Influence on Material Culture.* Archaeology of Egypt, Sudan and the Levant, Volume 3. Vienna: Austrian Academy of Sciences.

BAHUCHET 2006 = Serge Bahuchet. Languages of African Rainforest "Pygmy" Hunter-Gatherers: Language Shifts without Cultural Admixture. *Historical Linguistics and Hunter-Gatherers Populations in Global Perspective.* Max-Planck Institut, Leipzig, August 2006. https://hal.archives-ouvertes.fr/hal-00548207

BALLENTINE 2019 = Debra Ballentine, Foreignization in Ancient Competition. *Journal of Religious Competition in Antiquity* 1, pp. 18-36.

BÁNYAI 2020-1 = Michael Bányai, The Northern Philistines Reconsidered. *Jaarbericht Ex Oriente Lux 48,* pp. 9-27.

BARBARO 2018 = Nicolò Barbaro, Dedica votiva del mercenario Pedon. *Axon* 2/1, pp. 19-30.

BARNARD 2009 = Hans Barnard, The Archaeology of the Pastoral Nomads between the Nile and the Red Sea. In *Nomads, Tribes, and the State in the Ancient Near East. Cross-Disciplinary Perspectives.* Oriental Institute Seminars 5, ed. Jeffrey Szuchman, pp. 15-41. Chicago: The Oriental Institute of the University of Chicago.

BARTONĚK 2003 = Antonín Bartoněk, *Handbuch des mykenischen Griechisch.* Heidelberg: Winter.

BASSIOUNEY 2015 = Reem Bassiouney, *Language and Identity in Modern Egypt.* Edinburgh: Edinburgh University Press.

BASSIR 2016 = Hussein Bassir, Neshor at Elephantine in Late Saite Egypt. *Journal of Egyptian History* 9, pp. 66-95

BATES 1914 = Oric Bates, *The Eastern Libyans. An Essay.* London: Macmillan.

BECHHAUS-GERST 1984-85 = Marianne Bechhaus-Gerst, Sprachliche und historische Re konstruktionen im Bereich des Nubischen unter besonderer Berücksichtigung des Nil-nubischen. *Sprache und Geschichte in Afrika* (SUGIA) 6, pp. 7-134

BECHHAUS-GERST 1989 = Marianne Bechhaus-Gerst, *Nubier und Kuschiten im Niltal. Sprach- und Kulturkontakte im 'no man's land'.* Afrikanistische Arbeitspapiere: Schriftenreihe des Kölner Instituts für Afrikanistik; Sondernummer. Cologne.

BECK 2018 = Susanne Beck, *Exorcism, Illness and Demons in an Ancient Near Eastern Context: The Egyptian Magical Papyrus Leiden I 343 + 345.* PALMA 18. Leiden: Sidestone Press.

BECKING 2020 = Bob Becking, *Identity in Persian Egypt. The Fate of the Yehudite Community of Elephantine.* University Park, PA: Eisenbrauns.

BECKMAN, BRYCE and CLINE: Gary M. Beckman, Trevor R. Bryce and Eric H. Cline, *The Ahhiyawa Texts.* Writings from the Ancient World. Atlanta, GA: Society of Biblical

Literature.

BEEKES 2010 = Robert Beekes, *Etymological Dictionary of Greek*. 2 volumes. Leiden and Boston: Brill.

BEEKES 2104 = Robert Beekes, *Pre-Greek: Phonology, Morphology, Lexicon*. Brill Introductions to Indo-European Languages 2. Leiden and Boston: Brill.

BELL 1976 = Lanny Bell, Interpreters and Egyptianized Nubians in Ancient Egyptian Foreign Policy: Aspects of the History of Egypt and Nubia. Ph.D. dissertation: University of Pennsylvania.

BENDER 1997 = Lionel M. Bender, *The Nilo-Saharan Languages. A Comparative Essay*. Munich and Newcastle: LINCOM Europa.

BENNETT 2019 = James E. Bennett, *The Archaeology of Egypt in the Third Intermediate Period*. Cambridge: Cambridge University Press.

BERNAND and MASSON 1957 = André Bernard and Olivier Masson. Les inscriptions grecques d'Abou-Simbel. *Revue des études grecques* 70, pp. 1-46.

BESTOCK 2017 = Laurel Bestock, *Violence and Power in Ancient Egypt: Images and Ideology before the New Kingdom*. Abingdon, Oxon and New York: Routledge.

BICHLER 2008 = Reinhold Bichler, Historiographie – Ethnographie – Utopie. Gesammelte Schriften. Teil 2: Studien zur Utopie und der Imagination fremder Welten. Philippika: Marburger altertumskundliche Abhandlungen 18,2, ed. Robert Rollinger. Wiesbaden: Harassowitz Verlag.

Bietak 1985 = Manfred Bietak, Zu den nubischen Bogenschützen aus Assiut. Ein Beitrag zur Geschichte der Ersten Zwischenzeit. In *Mélanges Dr. Gamal Eddin Moukhtar*. Biblio thèque d'Étude LXX, vol. I, pp. 87-97. Cairo: Institut français d'archéologie orientale.

BIETAK 1988 = Manfred Bietak, Zur Marine des Alten Reiches. In *Pyramid Studies and Other Essays Presented to I. E. S. Edwards*. Occasional Publications 7, ed. John Baines et al., pp. 35-40. London: Egypt Exploration Society.

BIETAK 2009 = Manfred Bietak, Near Eastern Sanctuaries in the Eastern Nile Delta. *BAAL Hors-Série* VI, pp. 209-226.

BIETAK 2010a = Manfred Bietak, Le hyksôs Khayan, son palais et une lettre en cunéiforme. *Comptes rendus des séances de l'Académie des Inscriptions et Belles-Lettres*, pp. 973-990.

BIETAK 2010b = Manfred Bietak, The Early Bronze Age III Temple at Tell Ibrahim Awad and its Relevance for the Egyptian Old Kingdom. In *Perspectives on Ancient Egypt: Studies in Honor of Edward Brovarski*, ed. Zahi Hawass, Peter Der Manuelian and Ramadan B. Hussein, pp. 65-77. Cairo: Supreme Council of Antiquities.

BIETAK 2018 = Manfred Bietak, The Many Ethnicities of Avaris: Evidence from the Northern borderland of Egypt. In *From Microcosm to Macrocosm: Individual Households and Cities in Ancient Egypt and Nubia,* ed. Julia Budka and Johannes Auenmüller, pp. 73-92. Leiden: Sidestone Press.

BIETAK and CZERNY 2004 = Manfred Bietak and Ernst Czerny (eds.), *Scarabs of the Second*

Millennium BC from Egypt, Nubia, Crete and the Levant: Chronological and Historical Implications. Vienna: Verlag der Österreichischen Akademie der Wissenschaften.

BINDER 2019 (p. 38) = Michaela Binder, The Role of Physical Anthropology in Nubian Archaeology. In *Handbook of Ancient Nubia*, ed. Dietrich Raue, pp. 103-127. Berlin and Boston: De Gruyter.

BLAŽEK 1994 = Václav Blažek, Elephant, Hippopotamus and Others: Some Ecological Aspects of the Afro-Asiatic Homeland. *Asian and African Studies* 3, pp. 196-212.

BLENCH 2006 = *Archaeology, Language, and the African Past.* The African Archaeology Series, 10. Lanham, MD: AltaMira Press.

BLENCH 2011 = Roger Blench, Beria [Zaghawa] dictionary. Available at https://www.rogerblench.info/Language/Nilo-Saharan/NS%20page.htm

BLENCH 2013 = Roger Blech, Splitting Up Kordofanian. In *Nuba Mountain Language Stud ies*, ed. Thilo C Schadeberg and Roger Blench, pp. 571-586. Cologne: Rüdiger Köppe.

BLENCH 2021 = Roger Blench, Relating Linguistic Reconstructions to the Archeobotany of North Africa. *Journal of Archaeological Science: Reports* 38. DOI: 10.1016/j.jasrep.2021.103009

BOMMAS 2013 = Martin Bommas, *Das ägyptische Investiturritual*. Oxford: Archaeopress.

BONNET 2019 = Charles Bonnet, *The Black Kingdom of the Nile*. Cambridge, MA: Harvard University Press.

BOTTA 2009 = Alejandro F. Botta, *The Aramaic and Egyptian Legal Traditions at Elephantine: An Egyptological Approach.* T&T Clark International.

BORG 2021 = Alexander Borg, *Rewriting Dialectal Arabic Prehistory. The Ancient Egyptian Lexical Evidence*. Studies in Semitic Languages and Linguistics 105. Leiden and Boston: Brill.

BOUD'HORS 2020 = Anne Boud'hors, Situating the Figure of Papas, Pagarch of Edfu at the End of the Seventh Century: The Contribution of the Coptic Documents. In *Living the End of Antiquity: Individual histories from Byzantine to Islamic Egypt*, ed. Sabine Huebner et al., pp. 63-71. Berlin and Boston: De Gruyter.

BOURRIAU and PHILIPPS 2004 = Janine Bourriau and Jacke Philipps, *Invention and Innovation: The Social Context of Technological Change II, Egypt, the Aegean and the Near East, 1650-1150 B.C.* Oxford: Oxbow Books.

BREYER 2003a = Francis Breyer, Die ägyptische Etymologie von griechisch ἐλέφας = "Elefant" und lateinisch ebur = "Elfenbein". Sprachkontakt zwischen Tschadsee und Island vom Neolithikum bis zu den Türkenkriegen. In *Basel Egyptology Prize 1. Junior Research in Egyptian History, Archaeology and Philology*. Aegyptiaca Helvetica 17, ed. Antonio Loprieno and Susanne Bickel, pp. 251-276. Basel: Schwabe.

BREYER 2003b = Francis Breyer, Ein *aramäisches Lehnwort* für „*Katarakt*" in der Beschreibung Elephantines auf der Hungersnotstele und Überlegungen zur Datierung derselben anhand der Nennung eines meroitischen Funktionärs. In *Egyptian and Semito-Hamitic (Afro-Asiatic) Studies in Memoriam W. Vycichl.* Studies in Semitic Languages and

Linguistics, 39, ed. Gábor Takács, pp. 13-31. Leiden: Brill.

BREYER 2008 = Francis Breyer, Das Napatanische: Eine ägypto-meroitische Kreolsprache und ihr Verhältnis zum Altnubischen. *Lingua Aegyptia* 16, pp. 323-330.

BREYER 2009 = Francis Breyer, Art. Punt. In *Encyclopedia Aethiopica*, vol. 5, pp. 239-42. Wiesbaden: Harrassowitz.

BREYER 2010a = Francis Breyer, *Ägypten und Anatolien: Politische, kulturelle und sprachliche Kontakte zwischen dem Niltal und Kleinasien im 2. Jahrtausend v. Chr.* Vienna: Österreichische Akademie der Wissenschaften.

BREYER 2010b = Francis Breyer, Thutmosis III. und die Hethiter: Bemerkungen zum Kurustama-Vertrag sowie zu anatolischen Toponymen und einer hethitischen Lehnübersetzung in den Annalen Thutmosis' III. *Studien zur altägyptischen Kultur* 39, pp. 67-83.

BREYER 2012a = Francis Breyer, Die meroitische Sprachforschung: Gegenwärtiger Stand und richtungssweisende Ansätze. *Mitteilungen der Sudanarchäologischen Gesellschaft zu Berlin e.V.* 23, pp. 117-149.

BREYER 2012b = Francis Breyer, Zu den angeblich semitischen Schlangensprüchen der Pyramidentexte, *Orientalistische Literaturzeitung* 107, pp. 1-6.

BREYER 2012c = Francis Breyer, Zwerg-Wörter und ägyptisch-kuschitischer Sprachkontakt bzw. -vergleich: Zur sprachlichen Situation im mittleren Niltal des 3.-2. Jts. v.Chr. *Studien zur altägyptischen Kultur* 41, pp. 99-112.

BREYER 2014a = Francis Breyer, Äthiopisches in altägyptischen Quellen? Eine kritische Evaluation. In *Multidisciplinary Views on the Horn of Africa. Festschrift in Honour of Rainer Voigt's 70th Birthday*, ed. Hatem Elliesie, pp. 3-23. Köln: Köppe.

BREYER 2014b = Francis Breyer, *Einführung in die Meroitistik.* Einführungen und Quellentexte zur Ägyptologie 8. Berlin: LIT.

BREYER 2016 = Francis Breyer, *Punt: Die Suche nach dem Gottesland.* Culture and History of the Ancient Near East 80. Leiden: Brill.

BREYER 2018 = Francis Breyer, Die Etymologie des ägyptischen Suffixpronomens *=f.* Ein kontaktinduziertes Szenario zur Lösung eines alten Problems der semitohamitischen Sprachwissenschaft. *Lingua Aegyptia,* pp. 1-31.

BREYER 2019 = Francis Breyer, *Ägyptische Namen und Wörter im Alten Testament.* Ägypten und Altes Testament 93. Münster: Zaphon.

BREYER 2021 = Francis Breyer, *Schrift im Antiken Afrika: Multiliteralismus und Schriftadaption in den antiken Kulturen Numidiens, Ägyptens, Nubiens und Abessiniens.* Berlin and Boston: de Gruyter.

BRIANT 2002 = Pierre Briant, *From Cyrus to Alexander: a History of the Persian Empire.* Winona Lake, IN: Eisenbrauns.

BROVARSKI 2016 = Edward Brovarski, Reflections on the Battlefield and Libyan Booty Palettes. In *Another Mouthful of Dust: Egyptological Studies in Honour of Geoffrey Thorndike Martin*, ed. J. Vandijk, pp. 81-89. Leiden: Peeters.

BROWNE 2003 = Gerald M. Browne, *Textus Blemmyicus aetatis christianae*. Champaign (Ill.): Stipes Pub.

BROWNE 2004 = Gerald M. Browne, Blemmyes and Beja. Review of L. Kirwan, *Studies on the History of Late Antique and Christian Nubia,* ed. T. Hägg, L. Török, D. A. Welsby. *The Classical Review* 54, pp. 226-228.

BROWN 2020 = Andrea Brown, Anatolia. In *A Companion to Greeks Across the Ancient World*, ed. Franco De Angelis, pp. 221-245. Hoboken, NJ: Wiley.

BUCK 2019 = Mary E. Buck, *The Amorite Dynasty of Ugarit. Historical Implications of Linguistic and Archaeological Parallels.* Studies in the Archaeology and History of the Levant, Volume 8. Leiden and Boston: Brill.

BUDKA 2019 = Julia Budka, Nubians in the 1st Millennium BC in Egypt. In *Handbook of Ancient Nubia*, ed. Dietrich Raue, pp. 697-712. Berlin and Boston: De Gruyter.

BURKE 2014 = Aaron A. Burke, Entanglement, the Amorite *koiné,* and Amorite Cultures in the Levant. *ARAM* 26, pp. 357-373.

BURKE 2019 = Aaron A. Burke, Amorites in the Eastern Nile Delta: The Identity of Asiatics at Avaris during the Early Middle Kingdom. In *The Enigma of the Hyksos I: ASOR Conference Boston 2017 – ICAANE Conference Munich 2018 Collected Papers.* Contributions to the Archaeology of Egypt, Nubia and the Levant 9, ed. Manfred Bietak and Sylvia Prell, pp. 67-91. Wiesbaden: Harrassowitz.

BURKE 2020 = Aaron A. Burke, *The Amorites and the Bronze Age Near East. The Making of a Regional Identity.* Cambridge: Cambridge University Press.

BUSSMANN 2014 = Richard Bussmann, Krieg und Zwangsarbeit im pharaonischen Ägypten. In *Zwangsarbeit als Kriegsressource in Europa und Asien (Krieg in der Geschichte 77),* ed. Kerstin von Lingen, Klaus Gestwa, pp. 57-72. Paderborn: Schöningh.

BUTZER 1999 = Karl Butzer, Climatic history. In *Encyclopedia of the Archaeology of An cient Egypt*, ed. Kathryn A. Bard, pp. 195-98. London: Routledge.

BUZI and SOLDATI 2021 = Paola Buzi and Agostino Soldati, *La lingua copta*. Milano: Editore Ulrico Hoepli.

CAMPBELL 2020 = Dennis R.M. Campbell, Hurrian. In *A Companion to Ancient Near Eastern Languages,* ed. Rebecca Hasselbach-Andee. Blackwell Companions to the Ancient World, pp. 203-219. Hoboken, NJ: Wiley Blackwell.

CAMPS 1990 = Gabriel Camps, Qui sont les *Dii mauri*? *Antiquités africaines* 26, pp. 131-153.

CAMPS 2002 = Gabriel Camps, Liste onomastique libyque. Nouvelle edition. *Antiquités africaines* 38-39, pp. 211-257.

CAMPS and CHAKER 1986 = Gabriel Camps et Salem Chaker, Akuš (Yakūš/Yuš). In *Encyclopédie Berbère 3: Ahaggar–Alī ben Ghaniya*, pp. 431-2. Aix en-Provence: Edisud.

CANDELORA 2012 = Danielle Candelora, *From Weapons to Wall Paintings: A Reinterpretation of the Chronology of the Tell El Dab'a Frescoes*. Unpublished Master's thesis: University of Chicago.

CARON 2020 = Bernard Caron, Chadic. In *The Oxford Handbook of African Languages*,

ed. Rainer Vossen and Gerrit J. Dimmendaa.
DOI: 10.1093/oxfordhb/9780199609895.013.29

CAVILLIER 2005 = Giacomo Cavillier, *Gli Shardana nell'Egitto Ramesside*. British Archaeological Series 1438. Oxford: BAR Publishing.

CAVILLIER 2010 = Giacomo Cavillier, "Shardana project": Perspectives and Researches on the Sherden in Egypt and Mediterranean. *Syria* 87, pp. 339-345.

CAVILLIER 2015 = Giacomo Cavillier, From the Mediterranean Sea to the Nile: New Perspectives and Researches on the Sherden in Egypt. In *Proceedings of the Tenth International Congress of Egyptologists,* University of the Aegean, Rhodes, 22-29 May 2008. Vol. I. Orientalia Lovaniensia Analecta 241, ed. P. Kousoulis and N. Lazaridis, pp. 631-38. Leuven, Paris, Bristol, CT: Peeters.

CDD = Chicago Demotic Dictionary *Accessible at* https://oi.uchicago.edu/research/publications/demotic-dictionary-oriental-institute-university-chicago

ČERNÝ 1976 = Jaroslav Černý, *Coptic Etymological Dictionary*. Cambridge: Cambridge University Press.

CHAKER 1984 = Salem Chaker, *Textes en linguistique berbère: introduction au domaine berbère.* Paris: Éditions du Centre national de la recherche scientifique.

CHAKER 1995 = Salem Chaker, *Linguistique berbère: études de syntaxe et de diachronie.* Leuven: Peeters.

CHAKER 2003 = Salem Chaker, Le berbère. In *Les langues de France*, ed. Bernard Cerquiglini, pp. 215-227. Paris: PUF 2003.

CLARKE et al. 2019 = Joanne Clarke et al., Climatic changes and social transformations in the Near East and North Africa during the 'long' 4th millennium BC: A comparative study of environmental and archaeological evidence. *Quaternary Science Reviews* 136, pp. 96-121. https://doi.org/10.1016/j.quascirev.2015.10.003

CLINE and STANNISH 2011 = Eric H. Cline and S.M. Stannish, Sailing the Great Green Sea? Amenhotep III's "Aegean List" from Kom el-Hetan, Once More. *Journal of Ancient Egyptian Interconnections* 3(2), pp. 6-16.

COHEN 2019 = Yoram Cohen, Cuneiform Writing in Bronze Age Canaan. In *The Social Archaeology of the Levant: From Prehistory to Present*, ed. Assaf Yasur-Landau, Eric Cline and Yorke Rowan, pp. 245-264. Cambridge: Cambridge University Press.

COLE 2015 = Emily Cole, *Interpretation and Authority: The Social Functions of Translation in Ancient Egypt*. Ph.D. dissertation: UCLA.
(accessible at https://escholarship.org/uc/item/7j29g3qg)

COLIN 1995-6 = Frédéric Colin, *Les Libyens en Egypte, XVe siècle A.C. – IIe siècle P.C.* 2 volumes. Doctoral dissertation: Université Libre de Bruxelles.
(accessible at https://tel.archives-ouvertes.fr/tel-00120038)

COLLESS 2014 = Brian E. Colless, The Origin of the Alphabet: an Examination of the Goldwasser Hypothesis. *Antiguo Oriente* 12, pp. 71-104.

COLLOMBERT and COULON 2000 = Philippe Collombert and Laurent Coulon, Les dieux contre la mer: le début du "papyrus d'Astarté" (pBN 202). *Bulletin de l'Institut français d'archéologie orientale* 100, pp. 193-242.

COONEY 2011 = William Cooney, *Egypt's Encounter with the West: Race, Culture and Identity*. Doctoral thesis: University of Durham. http://etheses.dur.ac.uk/910/

COOPER 2012 = Julien Cooper, Reconsidering the Location of Yam. *Journal of the American Research Center in Egypt* 48, pp. 1-22.

COOPER 2017a = Julien Cooper, Some Observations on Language Contact between Egyptian and the Languages of Darfur and Chad. *Der Antike Sudan: Mitteilungen der Sudanarchäologischen Gesellschaft zu Berlin* 28, pp. 81-85.

COOPER 2017b = Julien Cooper, Toponymic Strata in Ancient Nubian Placenames in the Third and Second Millennium BCE: A View from Egyptian Records. *Dotawo. A Journal of Nubian Studies* 4, pp. 197-212.

COOPER 2020a = Julien Cooper, Egyptian Among Neighboring African languages, *UCLA Encyclopedia of Egytology*. https://escholarship.org/uc/item/2fb8t2pz

COOPER 2020b = Julien Cooper, *Toponymy on the Periphery: Placenames of the Eastern Desert, Red Sea, and South Sinai in Egyptian Documents from the Early Dynastic until the End of the New Kingdom*. Probleme der Ägyptologie 39. Leiden and Boston: Brill.

COOPER 2021 = Julien Cooper, Beja and Cushitic Languages in Middle Egyptian Texts: the Etymologies of Queen Aashayet and her Retainers. *Lingua Aegyptia* 29, pp. 13-36.

COOPER and BARNARD 2017 = Julien Cooper and Hans Barnard, New Insights on the Inscription on a Painted Pan-Grave Bucranium, Grave 3252 at Cemetery 3100/3200, Mostagedda (Middle Egypt). *African Archaeological Review* 34, pp. 363–76.

COULMAS 2018 = Florian Coulmas, *An Introduction to Multilingualism: Language in a Changing World*. Oxford: Oxford University Press.

CREASMAN and WILKINSON 2017 = Pearce Paul Creasman and Richard H. Wilkinson (eds.), *Pharaoh's Land and Beyond. Ancient Egypt and Its Neighbors*. Oxford: Oxford University Press.

ĆWIEK 2003 = Andrzej Ćwiek, *Relief Decoration in the Royal Funerary Complexes of the Old Kingdom: Studies in the Development, Scene Content and Iconography*. Doctoral dissertation: Institute of Archaeology, University of Warsaw.

DANILOVA and VALERIO 2019 = Margaritta Danilova and Marta Valerio, Sur la question des *mgꜣ.w* dans les textes égyptiens du Nouvel Empire. *Chronique d'Égypte* 94/188, pp. 293-320.

DANINO 2019 = Michel Danino, Methodological issues in the Indo-European debate. *Journal of Biosciences* 44:68. DOI: 10.1007/s12038-019-9876-4

DANN 2009 = Rachael J. Dann, *The Archaeology of Late Antique Sudan. Aesthetics and Identity in the Royal X-Group Tombs at Qustul and Ballana*. Amherst, NY: Cambria Press.

DARNELL 2002 = John C. Darnell, Gebel Tjauti Rock Inscriptions 1–45 and Wadi el-Hol Rock Inscriptions 1–45. Theban Desert Road Survey in the Egyptian Western Desert.

Oriental Institute Publications 119. Chicago: The Oriental Institute.

DARNELL 2003 = John C. Darnell, The Rock Inscriptions of Tjehemau at Abisko. *Zeitschrift für ägyptische Sprache* 130, pp. 31-48.

DARNELL et al. 2005 = John C. Darnell, F. W. Dobbs-Allsopp, Marilyn J. Lundberg, P. Kyle McCarter, Bruce Zuckerman, assistance from Collen Manassa, Two Early Alphabetic Inscriptions from Wadi el-Hôl: New Evidence for the Origin of the Alphabet from the Western Desert of Egypt. *The Annual of the American Schools of Oriental Research* 59, pp. 63-124. Boston: American Schools of Oriental Research.

DAVIES 2003 = Vivian Davies, Sobeknakht of Elkab and the Coming of Kush. *Egyptian Archaeology* 23, pp. 3–6.

DAVIES 2018 = Vanessa Davies, *Peace in Ancient Egypt*. Harvard Egyptological Studies 5. Leiden and Boston: Brill.

DE MEULENAERE 1963 = Herman De Meulenaere, La statue du général Djed-ptah-iouf-ankh, Caire JE 36949. *Bulletin de l'Institut français d'archéologie orientale* 63, pp. 19-32.

DE VAAN 2008 = Michiel de Vaan, *Etymological Dictionary of Latin and the other Italic Languages*. Leiden and Boston: Brill.

DE VAAN and LUBOTSKY 2009 = Michiel de Vaan and Alexander Lubotsky, Altpersisch. In *Sprachen aus der Welt des Alten Testaments,* ed. Holger Gzella, pp. 160-174. Darmstadt: Wissenschaftliche Buchgesellschaft.

DE VOS 2004 = Julien De Vos, Les mentions des Louvites dans les sources égyptiennes: Qawê, Qode et la Biographie de Sinouhé. *Colloquium Anatolicum* 3, pp. 147-194.

DEL OLMO-LETE and SANMARTIN 2015 = Gregorio del Olmo-Lete and Joaquin Sanmartin, *A Dictionary of the Ugaritic Language in the Alphabetic Tradition*. Translated and ed. Wilfred G.E. Watson. 3rd rev. ed; 2 vols. Handbuch der Orientalistik, 112. Leiden: Brill.

DEMARÉE, LEACH and USICK 2006 = Robert Demarée, Bridget Leach and Patricia Usick, *The Bankes Late Ramesside Papyri*. British Museum Research Publication 155. London: British Museum.

DESSET ET AL. 2022 = François Desset, Kambiz Tabibzadeh, Matthieu Kervran, Gian Pietro Basello and and Gianni Marchesi, The Decipherment of Linear Elamite Writing. *Zeitschrift für Assyriologie und vorderasiatische Archäologie* 112, pp. 11-60.

DI BIASE-DYSON 2013 = Camilla Di Biase-Dyson, *Foreigners and Egyptians in the Late Egyptian Stories. Linguistic, Literary and Historical Perspectives*. Probleme der Ägyptologie, 32. Leiden: Brill 2013.

DI TEODORO 2018 = Micòl Di Teodoro, *Labour Organisation in Middle Kingdom Egypt*. London: Golden House Publications.

DÍAZ HERNÁNDEZ 2016 = Roberto A. Díaz Hernández, Die Weiterentwicklung der offiziellen Sprache in der 2. Zwischenzeit. *Lingua Aegyptia* 24, pp. 41-65.

DIELEMAN 2005 = Jacco Dieleman, *Priests, Tongues, and Rites: The London-Leiden Magical Manuscripts and Translation in Egyptian Ritual (100 –300 CE)*. Religions in the Graeco-Roman World 153. Leiden and Boston: Brill.

DIMMENDAAL and JAKOBI 2020 = Gerrit J. Dimmendaal and Angelika Jakobi, Eastern Sudanic. In *Oxford Handbook of African Languages,* ed. Rainer Vossen and Gerrit J. Dimmendaal, pp. 392-406. Oxford: Oxford University Press.

DRENKHAHN 1967 = Rosemarie Drenkhahn, Darstellungen von Negern in Ägypten. Doctoral thesis: University of Hamburg.

DREWS 2000 = Robert Drews, Medinet Habu: Oxcarts, Ships, and Migration Theories. *Journal of Near Eastern Studies* 59, pp. 161-190.

DREYER 2014-5 = Günther Dreyer, Dekorierte Kisten aus dem Grab des Narmer. *Mitteilungen des Deutschen Archäologischen Instituts, Abteilung Kairo* 70/71 (= Gedenkschrift für Werner Kaiser), pp. 91-104.

EDEL 1967 = Elmar Edel, Die Ländernamen Unternubiens und die Ausbreitung der C-Gruppe nach den Reiseberichten des *Ḥrw-ḫwjf. Orientalia* 36, pp. 133-158.

Edel 1984 = Elmar Edel, Die Sikeloi in den ägyptischen Seevölkertexten und in Keilschrifturkunden. *Biblische Notizen* 23, 7-8.

EDEL 1997 = Elmar Edel, *Der Vertrag zwischen Ramses II. von Ägypten und Ḫattušili III. von Ḫatti.* Berlin: Mann.

EDER 1995 = Christian Eder, *Die ägyptischen Motive in der Glyptik des östlichen Mittelmeerraumes zu Anfang des 2. Jt. v.Chr.* Orientalia Lovaniensia Analecta 71. Leuven: Peeters.

EDGERTON 1947 = William F. Edgerton, Stress, Vowel Quantity, and Syllable Division in Egyptian. *Journal of Near Eastern Studies* 6, pp. 1-17.

EDGERTON and WILSON 1936 = William F. Edgerton and John A. Wilson: *Historical Records of Ramses III: The Texts in Medinet Habu Volumes 1 and 2. Translated with Explanatory Notes.* SAOC 12. Chicago: University of Chicago Press.

EDWARDS 2004 = David N. Edwards, *The Nubian Past: An Archaeology of the Sudan.* London and New York: Routledge.

EICHNER 2012 = Heiner Eichner, Neues zur Sprache der Stele von Lemnos (Erster Teil). *Journal of Language Relationship • Вопросы языкового родства* 7, pp. 9–32,

EICHNER 2013= Heiner Eichner, Neues zur Sprache der Stele von Lemnos (Zweiter Teil). *Journal of Language Relationship • Вопросы языкового родства* 10, pp. 1–42.

EICHNER 2019 = Heiner Eichner, Die Stele Lemnia: Vorstellung ihrer neuen Interpretation samt angestrebter Beweisführung. In *"And I Knew Twelve Languages": A Tribute to Massimo Poetto on the Occasion of his 70th Birthday*, ed. Natalia Bolatti Guzzo and Piotr Taracha, pp. 91-133. Warsaw: Agade Bis, University of Warsaw, Faculty of Oriental Studies.

EJSMOND 2017 = Wojciech Ejsmond, The Nubian Mercenaries of Gebelein during the First Intermediate Period in Light of Recent Field Research. *Journal of Ancient Egyptian Interconnections* 14, pp. 11-13.

EL-SAYED 2004 = Rafed El-Sayed, r n mḏꜣ.ỉw – lingua blemmyica – tu-beɗawiɛ. Ein Sprachkontinuum im Areal der nubischen Ostwüste und seine (sprach-)historischen Implikationen. *Studien zur altägyptischen Kulture* 32, pp. 351-362.

EL-SAYED 2011 = Rafed El-Sayed, *Afrikanischstämmiger Lehnwortschatz im älteren Ägyptisch: Untersuchungen zur ägyptisch-afrikanischen lexikalischen Interferenz im dritten und zweiten Jahrtausend v.Chr.* Leuven: Peeters.

EMANUEL 2013 = Jeffrey P. Emanuel, "Šrdn from the Sea": The Arrival, Integration, and Acculturation of a "Sea People". *Journal of Ancient Egyptian Interconnections* 5, pp. 14-27.

ERNŠTEDT 1953 = Petr Viktorovič Ernštedt, Египетские заимствования в греческом языке (*Egipetskie zaimstvovanija v grečeskom jazyke)*. Moskva, Leningrad: Izdatel'stvo Akademii Nauk.

ESPINEL 2002 = Andrés Diego Espinel, The Role of the Temple of Ba'alat Gebal as Intermediary between Egypt and Byblos during the Old Kingdom. *Studien zur altägyptischen Kultur* 30, pp. 103-119.

ESPINEL 2013 = Andrés Diego Espinel, A Newly Identified Old Kingdom Execration Text. In *Decorum and Experience. Essays in Ancient Culture for John Baines*, ed. Elizabeth Frood and Angela McDonald, pp. 26-33. Oxford: Griffith Institute.

EßBACH 2021 = Nadine Eßbach, *Ägypten und Ugarit – Kulturkontakte und die Folgen*. Alter Orient und Altes Testament 499. Münster: Ugarit-Verlag.

FELDMAN ET AL. 2019 = Michal Feldman, Daniel M. Master, Raffaela A. Bianco, Marta Burri, Philipp W. Stockhammer, Alissa Mittnik, Adam J. Aja, Choongwon Jeong, Johannes Krause, Ancient DNA Sheds light on the genetic origins of early Iron Age Philistines. *Science Advances*, vol. 5, issue 7. https://doi.org/10.1126/sciadv.aax0061

FETTEL 2010 = Jens Fettel, *Die Chentiu-schi des Alten Reiches*. Doctoral dissertation: Universität Heidelberg. Accessible at: http://www.ub.uni-heidelberg.de/archiv/11390

FIORE MAROCHETTI 2013 = Elisa Fiore Marochetti, *Gebelein*. In *UCLA Encyclopedia of Egyptology,* ed. Willeke Wendrich. https://escholarship.org/uc/item/2j11p1r7

FISCHER 1961 = Henry G. Fischer, The Nubian Mercenaries of Gebelein during the First Intermediate Period. *Kush* 9, pp. 44-80.

FISCHER 2010 = Robert Fischer, *Die Aḫḫijawa-Frage. Mit einer kommentierten Bibliographie.* Dresdner Beiträge zur Hethitologie, 26. Wiesbaden: Harrassowitz.

FISCHER-ELFERT 2011 = Hans-Werner Fischer-Elfert, *Sāmānu* on the Nile: the Transfer of a Near Eastern Demon and Magico-Medical Concept into New Kingdom Egypt. In *Ramesside Studies in Honour of K. A. Kitchen,* ed. Mark Collier and Steven Snape, pp. 189-198. Bolton: Rutherford.

FISCHER-ELFERT 2016 = Hans-Werner Fischer-Elfert, In Praise of Pi-Ramesse - a Perfect Trading Center (Including Two New Semitic Words in Syllabic Orthography; Ostr. Ashmolean Museum HO 1187). In *Aere perennius: Mélanges égyptologiques en l'honneur de Pascal Vernus,* ed. Philippe Collombert, Dominique Lefèvre, Stéphane Polis and Jean Winand, pp. 195-218. Leuven: Peeters.

FLAMMINI 2015 = Roxana Flammini, Building the Hyksos Vassals: Some Thoughts on the Definition of the Hyksos Subordination Practices. *Egypt & the Levant* 25, pp. 233-245.

FÖRSTER 2015 = Frank Förster. Der Abu Ballas-Weg. Eine pharaonische Karawanenroute durch die Libysche Wüste. Africa Praehistorica 28. Köln: Heinrich-Barth-Institut.

FOLMER 2009 = Margaretha L. Folmer, Alt- und Reichsaramäisch. In *Sprachen aus der Welt des Alten Testaments*, ed. Holger Gzella, pp. 104-131. Darmstadt: Wissenschaftliche Buchgesellschaft.

FOLMER 2011 = Margaretha L. Folmer, Imperial Aramaic as Administrative Language of the Achaemenid Period. In *The Semitic languages: An International Handbook,* ed. Stefan Weninger, pp. 587-598. Berlin and New York: De Gruyter Mouton.

FOLMER 2022 = Margaretha L. Folmer (ed.), Elephantine Revisited. New Insights into the Judean Community and Its Neighbors. University Park, PA: Eisenbrauns 2022.

FORSTNER-MÜLLER, KOPETZKY and DOUMET-SERHAL 2006 = Irene Forstner-Müller, Karin Kopetzky and Claude Doumet-Serhal, Egyptian Pottery of the Late 12th and 13th Dynasty from Sidon. *Archaeology & History in the Lebanon* 24, pp. 52-59.

FORSTNER-MÜLLER and RAUE 2008 = Irene Forstner-Müller and Dietrich Raue, Elephantine and the Levant. In *Zeichen aus dem Sand. Streiflichter aus Ägyptens Geschichte zu Ehren von Günter Dreyer,* ed. Eva-Maria Engel, Vera Müller and Ulrich Hartung, pp. 127-148. Wiesbaden: Harrassowitz.

FOURNET 1989 = Jean-Luc Fournet, Les emprunts du grec à l'égyptien. *Bulletin de la Société de linguistique de Paris* LXXXIV, pp. 55-80.

FRANDSEN 2008 = Paul John Frandsen, Aspects of Kingship in Ancient Egypt. In *Religion and Power: Divine Kingship in the Ancient World and Beyond*, ed. Nicole Brisch, pp. 47-73. Chicago: The Oriental Institute of the University of Chicago.

FRIEDMAN 2004 = Renée Friedman, The Nubian Cemetery at Hierakonpolis, Egypt. Results of the 2003 Season. *Sudan & Nubia. The Sudan Archaeological Research Society*, 8, pp. 47-59.

GALAND 1988 = Lionel Galand, Le berbère. In *Les langues du monde ancien et moderne. Tome III: Les langues chamito-sémitiques*, ed. David Cohen, pp. 207-242, 303-306. Paris: Éditions du CNRS.

GALAND 1989 = Lionel Galand, Les langues berbères. In *Language Reform: History and Future,* ed. István Fodor and Claude Hagège, pp. 335-353. Hamburg: Buske.

GALAND 2002 = Lionel Galand, *Etudes de linguistique berbère*, Leuven and Paris: Peeters.

GALAND 2002-3 = Lionel Galand, Interrogations sur le libyque. *Antiquités africaines* 38-39, pp. 259-266.

GALAND 2010 = Lionel *Galand, Regards sur le berbère*. Studi Camito-Semitici n° 8. Milano: Centro Studi Camito-Semitici.

GALLINARO 2018 = Marina Gallinaro, *Mobility and Pastoralism in the Egyptian Western Desert. Steinplätze in the Holocene Regional Settlement Patterns*. Firenze: All'Insegna del Giglio.

GANDER 2010 = Max Gander, *Die geographischen Beziehungen der Lukka-Länder*. Heidelberg: Winter.

GARDINER 1933 = Alan H. Gardiner, The Dakhleh Stela. *Journal of Egyptian Archaeology* 19, pp. 19-30, pls. V-VII.

GARDINER 1947 = Alan H. Gardiner, *Ancient Egyptian Onomastica*. 3 vols. London: Oxford University Press.

GASTER 1952 = Theodor H. Gaster, The Egyptian "Story of Astarte" and the Ugaritic Poem of Baal. *Bibliotheca Orientalis* 9, pp. 82-85.

GATTO 2006 = Maria C. Gatto, The Nubian A-Group: a Reassessment. *ArchéoNil* 16, pp. 61-76.

GATTO 2011 = Maria C. Gatto, The Nubian Pastoral Culture as Link between Egypt and Africa: A View from the Archaeological Record. In *Egypt in its African Context. Proceedings of the conference held at The Manchester Museum, University of Manchester, 2-4 October 2009*, ed. Karen Exell. BAR International Series 2204, pp. 21-29. Oxford: BAR Publishing.

GATTO 2012 = Maria C. Gatto, The Holocene Prehistory of the Nubian Eastern Desert. In *The History of the Peoples of the Eastern Desert*, ed. Hans Barnard and Kim Duister maat, pp. 43-60. UCLA: Cotsen Institute of Archaeology.

GATTO 2019 = Maria C. Gatto, The Later Prehistory of Nubia in its Interregional Setting. In *Handbook of Ancient Nubia*, ed. Dietrich Raue, pp. 259-291. Berlin and Boston: De Gruyter.

GAUTHIER 1931 = Henri Gauthier, *Les fêtes du dieu Min. Recherches d'archéologie, de philologie et d'histoire* 2. Cairo: Institut français d'archéologie orientale.

GAUTHIER and GAUTHIER 2011 = Yves and Christine Gauthier, Des chars et des Tifinagh: étude aréale et correlations. *Cahiers de l'AARS* 15, pp. 91-118.

GEE 2018 = John Gee, The Etymology and Pronunciation of the Late Egyptian Word for Horse. *Lingua Aegyptia* 26, pp. 229-31.

GIMBEL 2002 = David Nelson Gimbel, *The Evolution of Visual Representation: The Elite Art of Early Dynastic Lagaš and its Antecedents in Late Uruk Period Sumer and Predynastic Egypt. Volume One. Text.* DPhil thesis: Oxford.

GOEDICKE 1960 = Hans Goedicke, The Inscription of Ḏmỉ. *Journal of Near Eastern Studies* 19, pp. 288- 291.

GOEDICKE 1988 = Hans Goedicke, The Scribal Palette of Athu, *Chronique d'Égypte* 73, pp. 42-56.

GOEDICKE 2004 = Hans Goedicke, Sinuhe's Epistolary Salutations to the King (B 206-211). *Journal of the American Research Center in Egypt,* 41, pp. 5-22.

GOLDWASSER 2012a = Orly Goldwasser, Out of the Mists of the Alphabet: Redrawing the 'Brother of the Ruler of Retenu'. *Egypt & the Levant* 22, pp. 353–374.

GOLDWASSER 2012b = Orly Goldwasser, The Miners Who Invented the Alphabet: A Response to Christopher Rollston. *Journal of Ancient Egyptian Interconnections* 4(3), pp. 9-22.

GOLDWASSER 2022 = Orly Goldwasser, The Early Alphabetic Inscriptions Found by the Shrine of Hathor at Serabit el-Khadem: Palaeography, Materiality, and Agency. *Israel Exploration Journal* 72, 14-48.

GOLINETS 2020 = Viktor Golinets, Amorite. In: *A Companion to Ancient Near Eastern Languages,* ed. Rebecca Hasselbach-Andee. Blackwell Companions to the Ancient World, pp. 185-201. Hoboken, NJ: Wiley Blackwell.

GRAGG 2001 = Gene Gragg, Cushitic Languages. Some Comparative/Contrastive Data. In *Historische semitische Sprachwissenschaft. Mit Beiträgen von Erhart Graefe (Altägyptisch) und Gene B. Gragg (Kuschitisch),* ed. Burkhart Kienast, pp. 574-617. Wiesbaden: Harrassowitz.

GRALLERT 2001 = Silke Grallert, Akkulturation im ägyptischen Sepulkralwesen: Der Fall eines Griechen in Ägypten zur Zeit der 26. Dynastie. In *Naukratis: Die Beziehungen zu Ostgriechenland, Ägypten und Zypern in archaischer Zeit. Akten der Table Ronde in Mainz, 25.–27. November 1999*, ed. Ursula Höckmann and Detlev Kreikenbom, pp. 183-195. Möhnesee: Bibliopolis.

GRANDET 1994 = Pierre Grandet, Le Papyrus Harris I (BM 9999). Bibliothèque d'Études 109. Cairo: Institut français d'archéologie orientale.

GRANT 2020 = Anthony P. Grant (ed.), *The Oxford Handbook of Language Contact.* Oxford Handbooks Online. New York, NY: Oxford University Press.

GRODDECK 2000 = Detlef Groddeck, Ist das Etymon von *wrry.t* „Wagen" gefunden? *Göt tinger Miszellen* 175, pp. 109-11.

GROSSMAN and RICHTER 2015 = Eitan Grossman and Tonio Sebastian Richter, The Egyptian-Coptic Language. Its Setting in Time, Space and Culture. In *Egyptian-Coptic Linguistics in Typological Perspective*, ed. Eitan Grossman, Martin Haspelmath and Tonio Sebastian Richter, pp. 69-102. Berlin, Munich and Boston: De Gruyter.

GUNDACKER 2017 = Roman Gundacker, The Significance of Foreign Toponyms and Ethnonyms in Old Kingdom Text Sources. In *The Late Third Millennium in the Ancient Near East: Chronology, C14, and Climate Change*, ed. Felix Höflmayer, pp. 333-426. Chicago: Oriental Institute.

GUNDLACH 1994 = Rolf Gundlach, Die Zwangsumsiedlung auswärtiger Bevölkerung als Mittel ägyptischer Politik bis zum Ende des Mittleren Reiches. Forschungen zur Anti ken Sklaverei, Bd. XXVI. Stuttgart: Franz Steiner.

GZELLA 2009 = Holger Gzella (ed.), *Sprachen aus der Welt des Alten Testaments.* Darmstadt: Wissenschaftliche Buchgesellschaft.

HAALAND and HAALAND 2013 = Randi Haaland and Gunnar haaland, Early Farming Societies along the Nile. In *The Oxford Handbook of African Archaeology*, ed. Peter Mitchell and Paul J. Lane, pp. 537-549. Oxford: Oxford University Press.

HAARMANN 2014 = Harald Haarmann, Ethnicity and Language in the Ancient Mediterranan. In *A Companion to Ethnicity in the Ancient Mediterranean*. Blackwell Companions to the Ancient World, ed. Jeremy McInerney, pp. 17-33. Chichester: Wiley Blackwell.

HADDADOU 2006-7 = Mohand Akli Haddadou, *Dictionnaire des racines berbères communes:*

Suivi d'un index français-berbère des termes relevés. [Algiers :] Haut Commissariat à l'Amazighité.

HAFSAAS 2006 = Henriette Hafsaas, *Cattle Pastoralists in a Multicultural Setting: The C-Group people in Lower Nubia, 2500-1500 BCE.* The Lower Jordan River Basin Programme Publications, 10. Bergen: University of Bergen; Birzeit: Birzeit University.

HAIDER 2004 = Peter Haider, Minoische Sprachdenkmäler in einem ägyptischen Papyrus medizinischen Inhalts. In *Das Ägyptische und die Sprachen Vorderasiens, Nordafrikas und der Ägäis: Akten des Basler Kolloquiums zum ägyptisch-nichtsemitischen Sprachkontakt, Basel 9. – 11. Juli 2003.* Alter Orient und Altes Testament 310, ed. Thomas Schneider, unter Mitarbeit von Francis Breyer, Oskar Kaelin, Carsten Knigge, pp. 411–422. Münster: Ugarit-Verlag.

HAJNAL 2012 = Ivo Hajnal, Historisch-Vergleichende Sprachwissenschaft, Archäologie, Archäogenetik und Glottochronologie. Lassen sich diese Disziplinen vereinen? In *Archaeological, Cultural and Linguistic Heritage. Festschrift for Erzsébet Jerem in Honour of her 70th Birthday*, ed. P. Anreiter et. al., pp. 265-282. Budapest: Archaeolingua.

HALLOF 2009 = Jochen Hallof, Review of Claude Rilly, *La langue du royaume de Méroé: Un panorama de la plus ancienne culture écrite d'Afrique subsaharienne.* Bibliothèque de l'École Pratique des Hautes Études, Sciences Historiques et Philologiques 344. Paris: Champion. *Beiträge zur Sudanforschung* 10, pp. 145-148.

HALLOF 2011 = Jochen Hallof, *The Meroïtic Inscriptions from Qasr Ibrim I. Inscriptions on Ostraca.* Dettelbach: J.H. Röll.

HALLOF 2022 = Jochen Hallof, *Analytisches Wörterbuch des Meroitischen / Analytical Dictionary of Meroïtic. Vol. 1.* Dettelbach: J.H. Röll.

HAMILTON 2006 = Gordon J. Hamilton, *The Origins of the West Semitic Alphabet in Egyptian Scripts*. Washington, DC: Catholic Biblical Association of America.

HANNIG 2003 = Rainer Hannig: *Ägyptisches Wörterbuch I: Altes Reich und Erste Zwischen-Zeit.* Hannig-Lexica 4. Kulturgeschichte der antiken Welt 98. Mainz: Philipp von Zabern.

HANNIG 2006 = Rainer Hannig: *Ägyptisches Wörterbuch II: Mittleres Reich und Zweite Zwischenzeit. 2 vols.* Hannig-Lexica 5. Kulturgeschichte der antiken Welt 112. Mainz: Philipp von Zabern.

HARING 2015 = Ben Haring, Halaḥam on an Ostracon of the Early New Kingdom? *Journal of Near Eastern Studies* 74, pp. 189-196.

HASPELMATH 2009 = Martin Haspelmath, Lexical Borrowing: Concepts and Issues. In *Loanwords in the World's Llanguages. A Comparative Handbook*, ed. Martin Haspelmath and Uri Tadmor, pp. 35-54. Berlin: De Gruyter.

HASPELMATH and TADMOR 2009 = Martin Haspelmath and Uri Tadmor (eds.), *Loanwords in the World's Languages: A Comparative Handbook.* Berlin: De Gruyter. (Associated online database: https://wold.clld.org/)

HASSELBACH-ANDEE 2020 = Rebecca Hasselbach-Andee, Multilingualism and Diglossia in the Ancient Near East. In *A Companion to Ancient Near Eastern Languages,* ed. Rebecca Hasselbach-Andee. Blackwell Companions to the Ancient World, pp. 457-470. Hoboken, NJ: Wiley Blackwell.

HELCK 1971 = Wolfgang Helck, *Die Beziehungen Ägyptens zu Vorderasien im 3. und 2. Jahrtausend v. Chr.* 2nd revised and enlarged edition. Wiesbaden: Harrassowitz.

HELCK 1995 = Wolfgang Helck,, *Die Beziehungen Ägyptens und Vorderasiens zur Ägäis bis ins 7. Jahrhundert v.Chr.* 2., von Rosemarie Drenkhahn durchgesehene und bearbeitete Neuauflage. Darmstadt: Wissenschaftliche Buchgesellschaft.

HELCK 2002 = Wolfgang Helck, *Historisch-biographische Texte der 2. Zwischenzeit und Neue Texte der 18. Dynastie.* Kleine ägyptische Texte 6,1. 3rd, unaltered edition. Wiesbaden: Harrassowitz.

HENKELMAN 2017 = Wouter F.M. Henkelman, Egyptians in the Persepolis Archives. In Melanie Wasmuth, *Ägypto-persische Herrscher- und Herrschaftspräsentation in der Achämenidenzeit.* Oriens et Occidens. Studien zu antiken Kulturkontakten und ihrem Nachleben, 27, pp. 273-98. Franz Steiner Verlag, Stuttgart.

HERDA 2013 = Alexander Herda, Greek Views on the Karians. In *Luwian Identities: Culture, Language and Religion between Anatolia and the Aegean*, ed. Alice Mouton, Ian Rutherford and Ilya Yakubovich, pp. 421-509. Leiden and Boston: Brill.

HEROLD 1998 = Anja Herold, Piramesses – The Northern Capital: Chariots, Horses, and Foreign Gods. In *Capital Cities: Urban Planning and Spiritual Dimensions*, ed. J. Goodnick Westenholz, pp. 129-146. Jerusalem: Bible Lands Museum.

HICKEY 2010 = Raymond Hickey (ed.), *The Handbook of Language Contact.* Chichester: Wiley Blackwell.

HICKEY 2020 = Raymond Hickey (ed.), *The Handbook of Language Contact.* 2nd edition. Hoboken, NJ: Wiley Blackwell.

HOCH 1990 = James E. Hoch, The Byblos Syllabary: Bridging the Gap Between Egyptian Hieroglyphs and Semitic Alphabets. *Journal of the Society for the Study of Egyptian Antiquities* 20, pp. 115–124.

HOCH 1994 = James E. Hoch, *Semitic Words in Egyptian Texts of the New Kingdom and the Third Intermediate Period.* Princeton: Princeton University Press.

HOCH 1995 = James E. Hoch, Egyptian Hieratic Writing in the Byblos Pseudo-Hieroglyphic Stele L. *Journal of the American Research Center in Egypt* 32, pp. 59-65.

HÖCKMANN 2001 = Ursula Höckmann, Bilinguen. Zu Ikonographie und Stil der karisch-ägyptischen Grabstelen des 6. Jhs: Methodische Überlegungen zur griechischen Kunst-der archaischen Zeit in Ägypten. In *Naukratis. Die Beziehungen zu Ostgriechenland, Ägypten und Zypern in archaischer Zeit. Akten der Table Ronde in Mainz, 25.-27. November 1999,* ed. Ursula Höckmann and Detlef Kreikenbom, pp. 217-232. Möhnesee: Bibliopolis.

HÖLSCHER 1937 = Wilhelm Hölscher, *Libyer und Ägypter: Beiträge zur Ethnologie und Geschichte libyscher Völkerschaften nach den altägyptischen Quellen.* Ägyptologische Forschungen 4. Glückstadt: J.J. Augustin.

HOFFER 1996 = Bates L. Hoffer, Borrowing. In *Kontaktlinguistik/Contact Linguistics/ Linguistique de Contact. Volume 1,* ed. Hans Goebl, Peter H. Nelde, *Zdeněk Starý*, Wolfgang Woelck, pp. 541-549. Berlin: De Gruyter.

HOLMES 2008 = Peter Holmes, The Greek and Etruscan Salpinx. In *Herausforderungen und Ziele der Musikarchäologie: Vorträge des 5. Symposiums der Internationalen Studien-gruppe Musikarchäologie im Ethnologischen Museum der Staatlichen Museen zu Berlin, 19.-23. September 2006 = Challenges and Objectives in Music Archaeology. Papers from the 5th Symposium of the International Study Group on Music Archaeology at the Ethnological Museum, State Museums Berlin, 19-23 September, 2006*, pp. 99-118. Rahden/Westfalen: Leidorf.

HONEGGER 2014 = Matthieu Honegger, Recent Advances in Our Understanding of Prehisto-ry in Northern Sudan. In *The Fourth Cataract and Beyond. Proceedingsof the Twelth International Conference for Nubian Studies*, ed. J. R. Anderson and D. A. Welsby, pp. 19-30. British Museum Publications on Egypt and Sudan. Leuven: Peeters.

HONEGGER 2019 = Matthieu Honegger, The Holocene Prehistory of Upper Nubia until the Rise of the Kerma Kingdom. In *Handbook of Ancient Nubia*, ed. Dietrich Raue, pp. 129-152. Berlin and Boston: De Gruyter.

HORNUNG 2005 = Erik Hornung, ‚Söhne der Erde' – Schlangen im Diesseits und Jenseits der Ägypter. In *Die Weisheit der Schlange*. Eranos 2003/2004, ed. Erik Hornung and Andreas Schweizer, pp. 71-93. Basel: Schwabe.

HUBER 2006 = Irene Huber, Von Affenwärtern, Schlangenbeschwörern und Palastmanagern: Ägypter im Mesopotamien des ersten vorchristlichen Jahrtausends. In *Altertum und Mittelmeerraum: Die antike Welt diesseits und jenseits der Levante. Festschrift für Peter W. Haider zum 60. Geburtstag*, ed. Robert Rollinger and Barbara Truschnegg. Oriens et Occidens, 12, pp. 303-29. Stuttgart: Franz Steiner.

HUBSCHMANN 2010 = Caroline Hubschmann, Searching for the 'Archaeologically Invisible': Libyans in Dakhleh Oasis in the Third Intermediate Period. *Journal of the American Research Center in Egypt* 46, pp. 169-183.

HUDSON 2013 = Grover Hudson, *Northeast African Semitic: Lexical Comparisons and Analysis*. Porta Linguarum Orientalium 26. Wiesbaden: Harrassowitz.

HUEHNERGARD and RUBIN 2011 = John D. Huehnergard and Aaron Rubin, Phyla and Waves: Models of Classification of the Semitic Languages. In *Semitic languages: An Inter-national Handbook*, ed. Stefan Weninger, pp. 259-278. Berlin and Boston: De Gruyter.

HUEHNERGARD and PAT-EL 2019 = John D. Huehnergard and Na'ama Pat-El (eds.), *The Semitic Languages.* Second edition. London and New York: Routledge.

HUYSE 1998 = Philip Huyse, Ethiopia, Relations with Persia. I: Pre-Islamic Period. *Ency clopaedia Iranica* IX, fasc. 1, pp. 7-9. http://www.iranicaonline.org/articles/ethiopia

ISRAEL 2006 = Felice Israel, Les premières attestations des Arabes et de la langue arabe dans les textes sémitiques du nord. *Topoi* 14, pp. 19-40.

IZRE'EL 1997 = Shlomo Izre'el, *The Amarna Scholarly Tablets.* Cuneiform Monographs 9. Groningen: Styx.

JAKOBI and CRASS 2004 = Angelika Jakobi and Joachim Crass, *Grammaire du beria (langue saharienne). Avec un glossaire français-beria.* Cologne: Rüdiger Köppe.

JANKO 2014 = Richard Janko, The etymologies of ΒΑΣΙΛΕΥΣ and ΕΡΜΗΝΕΥΣ. *The Classical Quarterly* 64(2), pp. 462-470.

JANSEN-WINKELN 1994 = Karl Jansen-Winkeln, Text und Sprache in der 3. Zwischenzeit. Vorarbeiten zu einer Grammatik des Mittelägyptischen der Spätzeit. Ägypten und Altes Testament 26, Wiesbaden: Harrassowitz.

JANSEN-WINKELN 1995 = Karl Jansen-Winkeln, Diglossie und Zweisprachigkeit im alten Ägypten. *Wiener Zeitschrift für die Kunde des Morgenlandes* 85, pp. 85-115.

JANSEN-WINKELN 2000 = Karl Jansen-Winkeln, Die Fremdherrschaften in Ägypten im 1. Jahrtausend v. Chr. *Orientalia* 69, pp. 1–20.

JANSEN-WINKELN 2012 = Karl Jansen-Winkeln, Libyer und Ägypter in der Libyerzeit. In *"Parcourir l'éternité". Hommages à Jean Yoyotte.* 2 vols. Bibliothèque de l'Ecole des Hautes Etudes, Sciences Religieuses , vol. 156, ed. Christiane Zivie-Coche and Ivan Guermeur, pp. 609-624. Turnhout: Brepols.

JEUTHE 2021 = Clara Jeuthe, *Balat XII: The Sheikh Muftah Site.* Fouilles de l''Institut français d'archéologie orientale, 86. Cairo: Institut français d'archéologie orientale.

JOISTEN-PRUSCHKE 2008 = Anke Joisten-Pruschke, *Das religiöse Leben der Juden von Elephantine in der Achämenidenzeit.* Wiesbaden: Harrassowitz.

JONKER, BERLEJUNG and CORNELIUS 2021 = Louis C. Jonker, Angelika Berlejung and Izak Cornelius (eds), *Multilingualism in Ancient Contexts: Perspectives from Ancient Near Eastern and Early Christian Contexts.* Stellenbosch: African Sun Media.

JUDD and IRISH 2009 = Margaret Judd and Joel Irish: Dying to Serve: the Mass Burials at Kerma. *Antiquity* 83, pp. 709-722.

JUNGRAITHMAYR 1994 = Hermann Jungraithmayr, 'Zweite Tempora' in afrikanischen Sprachen – Ägyptischtschadische Gemeinsamkeiten?" In *Zwischen den beiden Ewigkeiten. Festschrift Gertrud Thausing*, ed. Manfred Bietak, pp. 102–122. Vienna: Institut für Ägyptologie der Universität Wien.

JUNGRAITHMAYR 2021 = Hermann Jungraithmayr, *Die „Grüne Sahara": Urheimat afroasiatischer Sprachen im Zentralsudan? Mit einem Beitrag von Gàbor Takács.* Uni im Café – Neue Literarische Gesellschaft Marburg, 27. Marburg: Blaues Schloss.

KAHN 2007 = Dan'el Kahn, Judean Auxiliaries in Egypt's Wars against Kush. *Journal of the American Oriental Society* 127/4, pp. 507–516.

KAISER 2012 = Elke Kaiser, Review of David Anthony, *The Horse, the Wheel, and Language: How Bronze-Age Riders from the Eurasian Steppes Shaped the Modern World.* Princeton: Princeton University Press, 2007. Kratylos 55, pp. 35–44.

KAMIL 2015 (p. 43) = Mohamed Hassan Kamil. L'afar: description grammaticale d'une langue couchitique (Djibouti, Erythrée et Ethiopie). Thèse de doctorat, Paris: Institut National des Langues et Civilisations Orientales. Available at https://tel.archives-ouvertes.fr/tel-01368253

KAMMERZELL 1998 = Frank Kammerzell, The Sounds of a Dead Language: Reconstructing Egyptian Phonology. *Göttinger Beiträge zur Sprachwissenschaft 1,* pp. 21-41.

KAMMERZELL 1999 = Frank Kammerzell, Glottaltheorie, Typologie, Sprachkontakte und Verwandtschaftsmodelle: Review of Thomas V. Gamkrelidze and Vjaceslav V. Ivanov: *Indo-European and the Indo-Europeans*, with an English translation by Johanna Nichols, De Gruyter 1994/1995. *Indogermanische Forschungen* 104, pp. 234-271.

KAMMERZELL 2001a = Frank Kammerzell, Die Entstehung der Alphabetreihe: zum ägyptischen Ursprung der semitischen und westlichen Schriften." In *Hieroglyphen, Alphabete, Schriftreformen: Studien zu Multiliteralismus, Schriftwechsel und Orthographieneuregelungen,* ed. Dörte Borchers, Frank Kammerzell and Stefan Weninger, pp. 117-158. Göttingen: Seminar für Ägyptologie und Koptologie.

KAMMERZELL 2001b = Frank Kammerzell, Die Geschichte der karischen Minderheit in Ägypten." In *Naukratis. Die Beziehungen zu Ostgriechenland, Ägypten und Zypern in archaischer Zeit. Akten der Table Ronde in Mainz, 25.-27. November 1999*, ed. Ursula Höckmann and Detlev Kreikenbom, pp. 233-55. Möhnesee: Bibliopolis.

KAMMERZELL 2005 = Frank Kammerzell, Old Egyptian and Pre-Old Egyptian: Tracing Linguistic Diversity in Archaic Egypt and the Creation of the Egyptian Language. In *Texte und Denkmäler des ägyptischen Alten Reiches*, ed. Stefan Seidlmayer, pp. 165-247. Berlin: Achet Verlag.

KANE 1990 = Thomas Leiper Kane, *Amharic-English Dictionary*, Vol. 1. Wiesbaden: Harrassowitz.

KARLSSON 2022 = Mattias Karlsson, *From the Nile to the Tigris: African Individuals and Groups in Texts from the Neo-Assyrian Empire.* State Archives of Assyria Studies, 31. University Park, PA: Eisenbrauns.

KATARY 1989 = Sally Katary, *Land Tenure in the Ramesside Period.* Studies in Egyptology. New York: Kegan Paul, 1989

KELDER 2018 = Jorrit M. Kelder, The Kingdom of Ahhiyawa: Facts, Factoids and Probabili ties. *Studi Micenei ed Egeo-Anatolici*, N.S. 4, 200-208.

KELDER 2022 = Jorrit M. Kelder, From Thutmose III to Homer to Blackadder: Egypt, the Aegean, and the "Barbarian Periphery" of the Late Bronze Age World System. In *Egypt and the Classical World. Cross-Cultural Encounters in Antiquity*, ed. Jeffrey Spier and Sara E. Cole, pp. 4-14. Los Angeles: J. Paul Getty Museum.

KHIDIR 2001 = Zakaria Fadoul Khidir, *Lexique des animaux chez les Beri du Tchad.* University of Leipzig Papers on Africa, Languages and Literatures Series No. 17. Leipzig: University of Leipzig.

KIENAST 2001 = Burkhart Kienast (ed.): *Historische semitische Sprachwissenschaft. Mit Beiträgen von Erhart Graefe (Altägyptisch) und Gene B. Gragg (Kuschitisch).* Wiesbaden: Harrassowitz.

KILANI 2016 = Marwan Kilani, A New Tree Name in Egyptian. *Journal of Near Eastern Studies* 75, pp. 43-52.

KILANI 2019 = Marwan Kilani, *Vocalisation in Group Writing: A New Proposal.* Lingua

Aegyptia Studia Monographica 20. Hamburg: Widmaier.

KIRWAN 2002 = L. Kirwan, *Studies on the History of Late Antique and Christian Nubia*, ed. T. Hägg, L. Török and D.A. Welsby. Aldershot and Burlington, VT: Ashgate.

KITCHEN et al. 2009 = Andrew Kitchen, Christopher Ehret, Shiferaw Assefa and Connie Mulligan, Bayesian Phylogenetic Analysis of Semitic Languages Identifies an Early Bronze Age Origin of Semitic in the Near East. *Proceedings of the Royal Society B: Biological Sciences* 276, pp. 2703-2710. http://doi.org/10.1098/rspb.2009.0408

KLEIN, JOSEPH and FRITZ 2017 = Jared Klein, Brian Joseph and Matthias Fritz (eds.), Handbook of Comparative and Historical Indo-European Linguistics. Volume 2. Berlin and Boston: De Gruyter Mouton.

KLEJN 2008 = Leo S. Klejn, Review of David Anthony, *The Horse, the Wheel, and Language: How Bronze-Age Riders from the Eurasian Steppes Shaped the Modern World.* Princeton: Princeton University Press, 2007. In *Journal of Indo-European Studies* 36, 1-17.

KLEJN et al. 2018 = Leo S. Klejn et al., Discussion: Are the Origins of Indo-European Languages Explained by the Migration of the Yamnaya Culture to the West? *European Journal of Archaeology* 21, pp. 3-17.

KLOTZ 2015 = David Klotz, Darius I and the Sabaeans: Ancient Partners in Red Sea Navigation. *Journal of Near Eastern Studies* 74, pp. 267-80.

KNAPP 2021 = A. Bernard Knapp, *Migration Myths and the End of the Bronze Age in the Eastern Mediterranean.* Cambridge: Cambridge University Press.

KLOTZ 2015 = David Klotz, Darius I and the Sabaeans: Ancient Partners in Red Sea Navigation. *Journal of Near Eastern Studies* 74(2), pp. 267-280.

KNIGGE 2004 = Carsten Knigge, Sprachkontakte und lexikalische Interferenz im 1. Jahrtausend v. Chr.: Ein Forschungsüberblick. In *Das Ägyptische und die Sprachen Vorderasiens, Nordafrikas und der Ägäis: Akten des Basler Kolloquiums zum ägyptisch-nichtsemitischen Sprachkontakt, Basel 9. – 11. Juli 2003.* Alter Orient und Altes Testament 310, ed. Thomas Schneider, unter Mitarbeit von Francis Breyer, Oskar Kaelin, Carsten Knigge, pp. 33-88. Münster: Ugarit Verlag.

KOCH 2022 = Ido Koch (ed.), *Mass Deportations – To and From the Levant during the Age of Empires in the Ancient Near East. Hebrew Bible and Ancient Israel* 11/Supplement. Tübingen: Mohr Siebeck.

KOHL 2009 = Philip L. Kohl, Perils of Carts before Horses: Linguistic Models and the Underdetermined Archaeological Record. Review of David Anthony, *The Horse, the Wheel, and Language: How Bronze-Age Riders from the Eurasian Steppes Shaped the Modern World.* Princeton: Princeton University Press, 2007. In American Anthropologist, New Series, 111/1, pp. 109-111.

KOSSMANN 1999 = Maarten Kossmann, *Essai sur la phonologie du proto-berbère*. Köln: Rüdiger Köppe.

KOSSMANN 2002 = Maarten Kossmann Deux emprunts à l'égyptien ancien en berbère. In *Articles de linguistique berbère: Mémorial Werner Vycichl*, ed. Kamal Naït-Zerrad, pp.

245-252. Paris: L'Harmattan.

KOSSMANN 2011 = Maarten Kossmann, The Names of King Antef's Dogs. *Parcours berbères. Mélanges offerts à Paulette Galand-Pernet et Lionel Galand pour leur 90e anniversaire*, ed. by Amina Mettouchi. Berber Studies 33, pp. 79-84. Köln: Rüdiger Köppe.

KOSSMANN 2013 = Maarten Kossmann, *The Arabic Influence on Northern Berber*. Studies in Semitic Languages and Linguistics, 67. Leiden and Boston: Brill 2013.

KOSSMANN 2020 = Maarten Kossmann, Berber subclassification. In *The Oxford Handbook of African Languages,* ed. Rainer Vossen, pp. 281-89. Oxford: Oxford University Press.

KRATZ and SCHIPPER 2022 = Reinhard G. Kratz and Bernd U. Schipper (eds.), *Elephantine in Context. Studies on the History, Religion and Literature of the Judeans in Persian Period Egypt.* Tübingen: Mohr Siebeck.

KRI = Kenneth A. Kitchen, Ramesside Inscriptions, Historical and Biographical. 8 Vols. Oxford: B. H. Blackwell Ltd., 1975-1990.

KUBISCH 2000 = Sabine Kubisch, Die Stelen der 1. Zwischenzeit aus Gebelein, *Mitteilungen des Deutschen Archäologischen Instituts Abteilung Kairo* 56, pp. 239–265.

KYRIAKIDIS 2002 = Evangelos Kyriakidis, Indications on the Nature of the Language of the Keftiw from Egyptian Sources. *Egypt & the Levant* 12, pp. 211-219.

LANFRY 1973 = Jacques Lanfry, *Ghadamès II: Glossaire (parler des Ayt Waziten)*. Fort-National, Algérie: Le Fichier Périodique.

LANGE 2007 = Eva Lange, Kretischer Zauber gegen asiatische Seuchen: Die kretischen Zaubersprüche in den altägyptischen medizinischen Texten. In *Marburger Treffen zur altägyptischen Medizin: Vorträge und Ergebnisse des 1.–5. Treffens 2002–2007*, Göttinger Miszellen, Beihefte 2, ed. Rainer Hannig, Petra Vomberg, and Orell Witthuhn, pp. 47-55. Göttingen: Seminar für Ägyptologie und Koptologie.

LANGER 2021 = Christian Langer, *Egyptian Deportations of the Late Bronze Age. A Study in Political Economy*. Zeitschrift für ägyptische Sprache und Altertumskunde, Beihefte 13. Berlin and Boston: de Gruyter.

LAOUST 1932 = Émile Laoust: *Siwa. I. Son parler.* Publications de l'Institut des hautes-études marocaines, n° xxiii. Paris: Librairie Ernest Leroux.

LAOUST 1935 = Émile Laoust: *L'habitation chez les transhumants du Maroc Central.* Institut des Hautes Études Marocaines, Collection Hespéris VI.

LEACH 2016 = Stephen Leach, *A Russian Perspective on Theoretical Archaeology: The Life and Work of Leo S. Klejn.* London and New York: Routledge.

LEHMANN 1985 = Gustav Adolf Lehmann, *Die mykenisch-frühgriechische Welt und der östliche Mittelmeerraum in der Zeit der "Seevölker"–Invasionen um 1200 v. Chr.* Rheinisch-Westfälische Akademie der Wissenschaften, Vorträge, G. 276. Opladen: Westdeutscher Verlag.

LEHMANN 1991 = Gustav Adolf Lehmann, Die "politisch-historischen" Beziehungen der Ägäis-Welt des 15.-13. Jh.s v.Chr. zu Ägypten und Vorderasien: einige Hinweise. In *Zweihundert Jahre Homer-Forschung: Rückblick und Ausblick*. Colloquium Rauricum,

Bd. 2, ed. Joachim Latacz, pp. 105-126. Stuttgart and Leipzig.

LEHNER 2015 = Mark Lehner, Labor and the Pyramids: The Heit el-Ghurab "Workers Town" at Giza. In *Labor in the Ancient World*, ed. P. Steinkeller and M. Hudson. Vol. 5 in a series sponsored by the Institute for the Study of Long-term Economic Trends and the International Scholars Conference on Ancient Near Eastern Economies. A Colloquium held at Hirschbach (Saxony), April 2005, pp. 397-522. Dresden: ISLET-Verlag.

LEITZ 1999 = Christian Leitz, *Magical and Medical Papyri of the New Kingdom*. Hieratic Papyri in the British Museum 7. London: British Museum Press.

LEITZ and MENDEL 2017 = Christian Leitz, Daniele Mendel: *Athribis IV. Der Umgang L 1 bis L 3.* 2 vols. Cairo: Institut français d'archéologie orientale.

LGG = Lexikon der ägyptischen Götter und Götterbezeichnungen, ed.Christian Leitz. 8 vols. Leuven: Peeters, 2002-3.

LICHTHEIM 1973-80 = Miriam Lichtheim, *Ancient Egyptian Literature*, I-III, Berkeley, Los Angeles and London: University of California Press (reprinted 2006 and 2019)

LINSEELE 2021 = Veerle Linseele, Early Livestock in Egypt: Archaeozoological Evidence. In Revolutions. The Beolithisation of the Mediterranean Basin: The Transition to Food Producing Economies in North Africa, Southern Europe and the Levant, ed. Joanne M. Rowland, Giulio Lucarini and Geoffrey J. Tassie. Exzellenzcluster Topoi der Freien Universität Berlin und der Humboldt-Universität zu Berlin: Edition Topoi.

LIPIŃSKI 2000 = Edward Lipiński, *The Aramaeans: Their Ancient History, Culture, Religion.* Orientalia Lovaniensia Analecta 100. Leuven: Peeters.

LIPIŃSKI 2004 = Edward Lipiński, *Itineraria Phoenicia.* Studia Phoenicia XVIII. Orientalia Lovaniensia Analecta 127. Leuven: Peeters.

LISZKA 2012 = = Kate Liszka, A-group. In *The Encyclopedia of Ancient History, First Edition*, ed. Roger S. Bagnall, Kai Brodersen, Craige B. Champion, Andrew Erskine and Sabine R. Huebner, pp. 229–230. Malden, MA: Wiley-Blackwell.

LISZKA 2015 = Kate Liszka, Are the Bearers of the Pan-Grave Archaeological Culture Identical to the Medjay-people in the Egyptian Textual Record? *Journal of Ancient Egyptian Interconnections* 7(2), pp. 42-60.

LISZKA and DE SOUZA 2021= Kate Liszka and Aaron De Souza, Pan-Grave and Medjay: At the Intersection of Archaeology and History. In *The Oxford Handbook of Ancient Nubia*, ed. Geoff Emberling and Bruce B. Williams, pp. 226-249. Oxford: Oxford University Press.

LOCHER 1999 = Josef Locher, *Topographie und Geschichte der Region am ersten Nilkatarakt in griechisch-römischer Zeit.* Archiv für Papyrusforschung und verwandte Gebiete, Beihefte, 5. Stuttgart and Leipzig: Teubner.

LOPRIENO 1995 = Antonio Loprieno, *Ancient Egyptian. A Linguistic Introduction*. Cambridge: Cambridge University Press.

LOPRIENO 2012 = Antonio Loprieno, Slavery and Servitude. In *UCLA Encyclopedia of Egyptology*, ed. Elizabeth Frood and Willeke Wendrich. Los Angeles.

https://escholarship.org/uc/item/8mx2073f

LOPRIENO and MÜLLER 2012 = Antonio Loprieno and Matthias Müller, Ancient Egyptian and Coptic. In *The Afroasiatic Languages,* ed. Zygmunt Frayzyngier and Erin Shay, pp. 102-44. Cambridge: Cambridge University Press.

MĄCZYŃSKA 2013 = Agnieszka Mączyńska, *Lower Egyptian Communities and their Interactions with Southern Levant in the 4th Millennium BC.* Poznań.

MAHER 2017 = John Maher, *Multilingualism: A Very Short Introduction.* Oxford and New York: Oxford University Press.

MAHLICH 2020a = Elena Mahlich, *Der Kanalbau unter Dareios I. Ein achämenidisches Bauprojekt in Ägypten.* Bonner Ägyptologische Beiträge 11. Berlin: EB-Verlag.

MAHLICH 2020b = Elena Mahlich, Zwei achämenidische Toponyme auf den Kanalstelen Dareios I. *Arta 2020.001 =* http://www.achemenet.com/pdf/arta/ARTA_2020.001_Mahlich.pdf

MAHLICH 2022 = Elena Mahlich, *Ägyptische Wörter und Namen in altorientalischen Sprachen.* Alter Orient und Altes Testament 449.

MANASSA 2003 = Colleen Manassa, *The Great Karnak Inscription of Merneptah. Grand Strategy in the 13th Century B.C.* Yale Egyptological Studies 5. New Haven, CT: Yale Egyptological Seminar.

MANASSA 2012 = Colleen Manassa, From Wool to Basketry: Materials, Contact Linguistics, and *tḫbs(t)* in ancient Egyptian. *Lingua Aegyptiae* 20, pp. 99-110.

MANASSA 2013 = Colleen Manassa, His Chariot that Plunders Foreign Lands: 'The Hymn to the King in His Chariot'. In *Chasing Chariots. Proceedings of the First International Chariot Conference (Cairo 2012),* ed. A.J. Veldmeijer and Salima Ikram, 143-156. Leiden: Sidestone Press.

MANDELL 2015 = Alice Helene Mandell, *Scribalism and Diplomacy at the Crossroads of Cuneiform Culture: The Sociolinguistics of Canaano-Akkadian.* PhD dissrtation, UCLA 2015. Available at https://escholarship.org/uc/item/7549s617

MANNING 2020 = Joseph G. Manning, Egypt. In *A Companion to Greeks Across the Ancient World,* ed. Franco De Angelis, pp. 363-383. Hoboken, NJ: Wiley 2020.

MANZO 2022 = Andrea Manzo, Ancient Egypt in Its African Context. Economic Networks, Social and Cultural Interactions. Cambridge: Cambridge University Press.

MARCUS 2022 = Ezra S. Marcus, Middle Kingdom Egypt and the Eastern Mediterranean. In *The Oxford History of the Ancient Near East. Vol. II: From the End of the Third Millennium BC to the Fall of Babylon,* ed. Karen Radner, Nadine Moeller and D.T. Potts, pp. 777-852. Oxford: Oxford University Press.

MARRASSINI 2011 = Paolo Marrassini, Early Semites in Ethiopia. *Rassegna di Studi Etiopici* 3, pp. 75-96.

MARTIN 2019 = Cary J. Martin, A Persian Estate in Egypt: Early Demotic Papyri in the British Museum. In *New Approaches in Demotic Studies*, Vol. 10, pp. 175-196. Berlin and Boston: De Gruyter.

MARTIN 1989 = Geoffrey Thorndike Martin, *The Memphite Tomb of Ḥoremḥeb, Commander-in-chief of Tutʿankhamūn.* London: Egypt Exploration Society; Turnhout: Brepols.

MARTIN-JONES, BLACKLEDGE and CREESE 2012 = Marilyn Martin-Jones, Adrian Blackledge and Angela Creese (eds.), *The Routledge Handbook of Multilingualism*. London and New York: Routledge.

MASSON-BERGHOFF and THOMAS 2019 = Aurélia Masson-Berghoff and Ross Thomas, *Naukratis in Context.* British Museum Studies in Ancient Egypt and Sudan 24. London.

MATIĆ 2012 = Uroš Matić, Out of the Word and Out of the Picture? Keftiu and Materializations of 'Minoans'. In *Encountering Imagery. Materialities, Perceptions, Relations.* Stockholm Studies in Archaeology 57, ed. M. Back Danielsson, F. Fahlander and Y. Sjöstrand, pp. 235-253. Stockholm: Stockholm University.

MATIĆ 2014a = Uroš Matić, "Minoans", *kftjw* and the "Islands in the Middle of *w3ḏ wr*" beyond Ethnicity. *Egypt & the Levant* 14, pp. 275-292.

MATIĆ 2014b = Uroš Matić, "Nubian" Archers in Avaris: A Study of Culture-Historical Reasoning in Archaeology of Egypt. *Етноантрополошки проблеми / Issues in Ethnology and Anthropology*, н.с. год. 9.3. DOI: 10.21301/eap.v9i3.8

MATIĆ 2020 = *Ethnic Identities in the Land of the Pharaohs. Past and Present Approaches In Egyptology.* Cambridge Elements: Ancient Egypt in Context. Cambridge: Cambridge University Press.

MATRAS 2009 = Yaron Matras, *Language Contact*. Cambridge: Cambridge University Press.

MATRAS, MCMAHON and VINCENT 2009 = Yaron Matras, April McMahon and Nigel Vincent (eds.), *Linguistic Areas: Convergence in Historical and Typological Perspective.* New York: Palgrave Macmillan.

MEEKS 1977 = Dimitri Meeks, Notes de lexicographie (§ 5-8). *Bulletin de l'Institut français d'archéologie orientale* 77, pp. 79-88.

MEEKS = Dimitri Meeks, Les emprunts égyptiens aux langues sémitiques durant le Nouvel Empire et la Troisième Période Intermédiaire: les aléas du comparatisme. *Bibliotheca Orientalis* 54 (1-2), pp. 32-61.

MEIGGS and LEWIS 1969 = Russell Meiggs and David Lewis (eds.), *A Selection of Greek Historical Inscriptions to the End of the Fifth Century B.C.* Oxford: Clarendon Press.

MEURER 1996 = Georg Meurer, *Nubier in Ägypten bis zum Beginn des Neuen Reiches. Zur Bedeutung der Stele Berlin 14753.* ADAIK, Ägyptologische Reihe, Bd. 13. Berlin: Achet-Verlag.

MEURER 2020 = Georg Meurer, Nubians in Egypt from the Early Dynastic Period to the New Kingdom. In *The Oxford Handbook of Ancient Nubia,* ed. Geoff Emberling and Bruce Williams, pp. 289-308. Oxford: Oxford University Press.

MEYER 2018 = Ronny Meyer, On the Internal Classification of Ethiosemitic. *Zeitschrift der Deutschen Morgenländischen Gesellschaft* 168, pp. 93-124.

MEYER and KNAPP 2021 = Nathan Meyer and A. Bernard Knapp, Resilient Social Actors in the Transition from the Late Bronze to the Early Iron Age on Cyprus. *Journal of World*

Prehistory. https://doi.org/10.1007/s10963-021-09163-7

MEYRAT 2016 = Pierre Meyrat, Copie conforme. Traduction et diplomatie dans l'Égypte ancienne. In *La Traductologie et bien au-delà: Mélanges offerts à Claude Bocquet,* ed. Sylvie Monjean-Decaudin, pp. 319-344. Arras: Artois Presses Université.

MH II = *Medinet Habu, Volume II. The Later Historical Records of Ramses III.* The Epigraphic Survey. *Oriental Institute Publications* 9. Chicago: The University of Chicago Press, 1932.

MH IV = *Medinet Habu, Volume IV: Festival Scenes of Ramses III.* The Epigraphic Survey. *Oriental Institute Publications 51.* Chicago: The University of Chicago Press, 1940.

MICHAŁOWSKI 2017 = Piotr Michałowski, Ancient Near Eastern and European Isolates. In *Language Isolates,* ed. Lyle Campbell. Routledge Language Family Series, pp. 19-58 Routledge.

MICHAUX-COLOMBOT 2014 = Danièle Michaux-Colombot, Pitfall concepts in the round of "Nubia": Ta-Seti, Nehesy, Medja, Maga and Punt revisited. In *The Fourth Cataract and beyond: Proceedings of the 12th International Conference for Nubian Studies,* ed. Julie R. Anderson and Derek Welsby, pp. 507-522. Leuven; Paris; Walpole, MA: Peeters.

MILITAREV 2007 = Alexander Militarev, Akkadian-Egyptian Lexical Matches. In *Papers on Semitic and Afroasiatic Linguistics in Honor of Gene B. Gragg,* ed. Cynthia L. Miller, pp. 139-145. Chicago: The Oriental Institute.

MINIACI and QUIRKE 2009 = Gianluca Miniaci and Stephen Quirke, Reconceiving the Tomb in the Late Middle Kingdom. The Burial of the Accountant of the Main Enclosure Neferhotep at Dra Abu al-Naga. *Bulletin de l'Institut français d'archéologie orientale* 109, pp. 339-383.

MÖLLER 1913 = Georg Möller, *Die beiden Totenpapyrus Rhind des Museums zu Edinburg.* Demotische Studien von Wilhelm Spiegelberg 6. Leipzig: J. C. Hinrichs, 1913

MÖLLER 2001 = Astrid Möller, Naukratis. Griechisches "emporion" und ägyptischer "port of trade". In *Naukratis. Die Beziehungen zu Ostgriechenland, Ägypten und Zypern in archaischer Zeit. Akten der Table Ronde in Mainz, 25.-27. November 1999*, ed. Ursula Höckmann and Detlef Kreikenbom, pp. 1-25. Möhnesee: Bibliopolis.

MORENO GARCÍA 2014 = Juan Carlos Moreno García, Invaders or just herders? Libyans in Egypt in the third and second millennia BCE. *World Archaeology* 46(4), pp. 610-623.

MORENO GARCÍA 2018 = Juan Carlos Moreno García, Elusive "Libyans": Identities, Lifestyles and Mobile Populations in NE Africa (late 4th – early 2nd millennium BCE). *Journal of Egyptian History* 11(1-2), pp. 147-184.

MORENZ 1996 = Ludwig D. Morenz, *Beiträge zur Schriftlichkeitskultur im Mittleren Reich und in der 2. Zwischenzeit.* Ägypten und Altes Testament, 29. Wiesbaden: Harrassowitz.

MORENZ 2000 = Ludwig D. Morenz, Stierspringen und die Sitte des Stierspiels im altmediterranen Raum. *Egypt & the Levant* 10: 195-203.

MORENZ 2010 = Ludwig D. Morenz, *Die Zeit der Regionen im Spiegel der Gebelein-Region: Kulturgeschichtliche Re-Konstruktionen.* Probleme der Ägyptologie 27. Leiden: Brill.

MORENZ 2014 = Ludwig D. Morenz, *Menschen und Götter, Buchstaben und Bilder: Die frühen alphabetischen Schriftzeugnisse im Südwest-Sinai (2. Jahrtausend v. Chr.).* Berlin: EB-Verlag.

MORENZ 2016 = Ludwig D. Morenz, *Ägypten und die Geburt der Alphabetschrift*. Photographs by Amr El Hawari, David Sabel, and Uta Siffert. Rahden, Westfalen: Leidorf.

MORIN 2012 = Didier Morin, *Dictionnaire afar-français (Djibouti, Érythrée, Éthiopie).* Paris: Éditions KARTHALA.

MORRIS 2005 = Ellen Fowles Morris, *The Architecture of Imperialism: Egyptian Military Bases and New Kingdom Foreign Policy*. Probleme der Ägyptologie, 22. Leiden: Brill.

MORRIS 2018a = Ellen Morris, *Ancient Egyptian Imperialism.* Hoboken, NJ: Wiley.

MOURAD 2015 = Anna-Latifa Mourad, *Rise of the Hyksos: Egypt and the Levant from the Middle Kingdom to the Early Second Intermediate Period.* Oxford: Archaeopress.

MOURAD 2021 = Anna-Latifa Mourad, Strategies of Survival? Change, Continuity and the Adaptive Cycle across the Middle to Early Late Bronze Age at Tell el-Dab^{c}a, Egypt. *Journal of Anthropological Archaeology* 64. https://doi.org/10.1016/j.jaa.2021.101367

MOUTON and VAN DEN HOVEN 2015 = Alice Mouton and Carina van den Hoven, Les noms des témoins divins du traité entre le roi hittite Ḫattušili III et le pharaon Ramsès II: Un exemple d'*interpretatio*. In *Interpretatio: Traduire l'altérité culturelle dans les civilisations de l'Antiquité*, ed. Frédéric Colin, Olivier Huck, and Sylvie Vanséveren, pp. 67-93. Paris: de Boccard.

MOUTON, RUTHERFORD and YAKUBOVICH 2013 = Alice Mouton, Ian Rutherford and Ilya Yakubovich (eds.), *Luwian Identities: Culture, Language and Religion between Anatolia and the Aegean.* Leiden and Boston: De Gruyter.

MUCHIKI 1999 = Yoshiyuki Muchiki, *Egyptian Proper Names and Loanwords in Northwest Semitic.* Atlanta, GA: Society of Biblical Literature.

MULLEN 2013 = Alex Mullen, *Southern Gaul and the Mediterranean: Multilingualism and Multiple Identities in the Iron Age and Roman Periods*. Cambridge Classical Studies. Cambridge and New York: Cambridge University Press.

MÜLLER 2010 = Matthias Müller, *Akkadisch in Keilschrifttexten aus Ägypten: Deskriptive Grammatik einer "Interlanguage" des späten zweiten vorchristlichen Jahrtausends anhand der Ramses-Briefe.* Alter Orient und Altes Testament 373. Münster: Ugarit Verlag.

MÜLLER 2015 = Matthias Müller, Akkadian from Egypt. In *UCLA Encyclopedia of Egyptology,* ed. Julie Stauder-Porchet, Andréas Stauder and Willeke Wendrich, Los Angeles. https://escholarship.org/uc/item/8588g9q

MÜLLER 2020 = Matthias Müller, Egyptian. In *A Companion to Ancient Near Eastern Languages,* ed. Rebecca Hasselbach-Andee, pp. 107-128. Hoboken, NJ: Wiley Blackwell.

MÜLLER 2021 = Matthias Müller, Akkadian in Egypt. In *History of the Akkadian language*, 2 vols, ed. Juan-Pablo Vita, pp. 1293-1315. Leiden and Boston: Brill.

MURAOKA and PORTEN 1997 = Takamitsu Muraoka and Bezalel Porten, *A Grammar of*

Egyptian Aramaic. Second revised edition. Leiden and Boston: Brill.

MÚRCIA SANCHEZ 2010 = Carles Múrcia Sànchez, *La llengua amaziga a l'antiguitat a partir de les fonts gregues i llatines*. 2 volumes. Doctoral dissertation: University of Barcelona. Barcelona: University Publications and Institut Privat d'Estudis Món Juïc. Accessible online at: *www.institutmonjuic.cat*

MUYSKEN 2008 = Pieter Muysken (ed.), *From Linguistic Areas to Areal Linguistics*. Studies in Language Companion Series 90. Amsterdam and Philadelphia: John Benjamins.

MYNÁŘOVÁ 2007 = Jana Mynářová, *Language of Amarna – Language of Diplomacy: Perspectives on the Amarna Letters*. Prague: Czech Institute of Egyptology, Charles University.

MYNÁŘOVÁ 2009 = Jana Mynářová, From Amarna to Hattušaš: Epistolary Traditions in the Amarna and Ramesside Correspondence. In *My Things Changed Things: Social Development and Cultural Exchange in Prehistory, Antiquity, and the Middle Ages*, ed. Petra Maříková Vlčková, Jana Mynářová, and Martin Tomášek, pp. 111-117. Prague: Czech Institute of Egyptology, Charles University.

MYNÁŘOVÁ 2014 = The Scribes of Amarna: A Family Affair? In *La famille dans le Proche-Orient ancien: Réalités, symbolismes, et images: Proceedings of the 55th Rencontre Assyriologique Internationale, Paris, 6 – 9 July 2009*, ed. Lionel Marti, pp. 375-381. University Park, PA: Penn State University Press.

MYNÁŘOVÁ 2015 = Egyptians and the Cuneiform Tradition: On the Palaeography of the Amarna Documents. In *Current Research in Cuneiform Palaeography: Proceedings of the Workshop Organised at the 60th Rencontre Assyriologique Internationale*, Warsaw, 2014, ed. Elena Devecchi, Gerfrid Müller and Jana Mynářová, pp. 89-102. Gladbeck: PeWe Verlag.

NA'AMAN 2022 = Nadav Na'aman: Papyrus Amherst 63: Shifting between the Heavenly and Earthly Spheres. *Tel Aviv* 49(2), pp. 250-26.

NAÏT-ZERRAD 1998 = Kamal Naït-Zerrad, *Dictionnaire des racines berbères (formes attestées), I: A – BŻL*, Paris and Louvain: Inalco.

NÄSER 2013 = Claudia Näser, Die C-Gruppe. Unternubien im 3. und 2. Jahrtausend v. Chr. In *Die Kulturen Nubiens – ein afrikanisches Vermächtnis*, ed. Steffen Wenig and Karola Zibelius-Chen, pp. 105-119. Dettelbach: Röll, 2013.

NEGBI 1992 = Ora Negbi, Early Phoenician Presence in the Mediterranean Islands: A Reappraisal. *American Journal of Archaeology* 96, No. 4, pp. 599-615.

NEUMANN 2006 = Günter Neumann, Eteokretisch. In *Der Neue Pauly*, ed. Hubert Cancik, Helmuth Schneider and Manfred Landfester, vol. 4, p. 160. Leiden and Boston: Brill.

NEWMAN 2013 = Paul Newman, *The Chadic Language Family: Classification and Name Index*. https://www.cepam.cnrs.fr/megatchad/publications/Newman-2013-Chadic-Classification-and-Index.pdf.

NOEGEL 2018 = Scott B. Noegel, Appellative Paronomasia and Polysemy in the Tale of Sinuhe. *Lingua Aegyptia* 26, pp. 233–238.

NOONAN 2019 = Benjamin Noonan, *Non-Semitic Loanwords in the Hebrew Bible: A Lexicon of Language Contact.* University Park, PA: Eisenbrauns.

OCHAŁA 2014 = Grzegorz Ochała, Multilingualism in Christian Nubia: Qualitative and Quantitative Aspects. *Dotawo: A Journal of Nubian Studies* 1, pp. 1-50.

O'CONNOR 1990 = David O'Connor, The Nature of Tjemhu (Libyan) Society in the Later New Kingdom. In *Libya and Egypt c1300–750 BC*, ed. Anthony Leahy, pp. 40-45. London: SOAS Centre of Near and Middle Eastern Studies; the Society for Libyan Studies.

OREL and STOLBOVA 1995 = Vladimir Orel and Olga Stolbova, *Hamito-Semitic Etymological Dictionary: Materials for a Reconstruction.* Leiden and Boston: Brill.

PACHUR and KRÖPELIN 1987 = H.-J. Pachur and S. Kröpelin, Wadi Howar: Paleoclimatic Evidence from an Extinct River System in the Southeastern Sahara. *Science* New Series vol. 237, No. 4812, pp. 298-300.

PAKSI 2020 = Julianna Paksi, *Linguistic Heterogeneity in the Ramesside Royal Inscriptions.* Unpublished doctoral dissertation: University of Basel.

PANAITE (in press) = Elena Panaite,Tjehen, Tjemeh et les Libyens : à la recherche d'une langue libyque dans les premières sources écrites de l'ancienne Égypte. Forthcoming in: *Études et Documents Berbères.*

PAPACONSTANTINOU 2010 = Arietta Papaconstantinou (ed.), *The Multilingual Experience in Egypt, from the Ptolemies to the Abbasids.* Farnham: Ashgate.

PAYRAUDEAU 2020 = Frédéric Payraudeau, Note d'onomastique libyco-égyptienne. In *Ein Kundiger, der in die Gottesworte eingedrungen ist: Festschrift für den Ägyptologen Karl Jansen-Winkeln zum 65. Geburtstag.* Ägypten und Altes Testament 99, ed. Shih-Wei Hsu, Vincent Pierre-Michel Laisney and Jan Moje, pp. 205-207. Münster: Zaphon.

PEHAL 2014 = Martin Pehal, *Interpreting Ancient Egyptian Narratives: A Structural Analysis of the Tale of Two Brothers, the Anat Myth, the Osirian Cycle, and the Astarte Papyrus.* Fernelemont: EME Editions.

PERCY 2007 = Sarah Percy, *Mercenaries. The History of a Norm in International Relations.* Oxford: Oxford University Press.

PERNIGOTTI 1968 = Sergio Pernigotti, Il generale Potasimto e la sua famiglia. *Studi Classici e Orientali* 17, pp. 251–264.

PEUST 1999a = Carsten Peust, *Egyptian Phonology. An Introduction to the Phonology of a Dead Language.* Göttingen: Peust & Gutschmidt.

PEUST 1999b = Carsten Peust, *Das Napatanische: Ein ägyptischer Dialekt aus dem Nubien des späten ersten vorchristlichen Jahrtausends: Texte, Glossar, Grammatik.* Göttingen: Peust & Gutschmidt.

PEUST 2000 = Carsten Peust, Über ägyptische Lexikographie. 1. Zum Ptolemaic Lexikon von Penelope Wilson; 2. Versuch eines quantitativen Vergleichs der Textkorpora antiker Sprachen. *Lingua Aegyptia* 7, pp. 245-260

PEUST 2001 = Carsten Peust, Review of Gábor Takács: *Etymological Dictionary of Egyptian,*

Vol. 1: A Phonological Introduction, Leiden, Boston, and Köln: Brill 1999. *Indogermanische Forschungen* 106, pp. 344-354.

PEUST 2003 = Carsten Peust, Review of Gábor Takács: *Etymological Dictionary of Egyptian, Vol. 2: b-, p-, f-*, Leiden and Boston: Brill 2001. *Indogermanische Forschungen* 108, pp. 345-350.

PEUST 2004 = Carsten Peust, Das Ägyptische als afrikanische Sprache. In *Das Ägyptische und die Sprachen Vorderasiens, Nordafrikas und der Ägäis: Akten des Basler Kolloquiums zum ägyptisch-nichtsemitischen Sprachkontakt, Basel 9.-11. Juli 2003*. Alter Orient und Altes Testament 310, ed. Thomas Schneider, unter Mitarbeit von Francis Breyer, Oskar Kaelin, Carsten Knigge, pp. 321-407. Münster: Ugarit-Verlag.

PEUST 2007 = Carsten Peust, Zur Bedeutung und Etymologie von *nzw* "König". *Göttinger Miszellen* 213, pp. 59-62.

PEUST 2008 = Carsten Peust, Review of Gábor Takács: *Etymological Dictionary of Egyptian, Vol. 3: m-*, Leiden and Boston: Brill 2007. *Lingua Aegyptia* 16, pp. 393-401.

PEUST 2013 = Carsten Peust, Bemerkungen zur berberischen Etymologie des spätägyptischen Verbs *swn* / ⲥⲟⲟⲩⲛ „wissen". *Lingua Aegyptia* 21, pp. 159-165.

PFEIFFER 2005 = Stefan Pfeiffer, Ägypten und das klassische Griechenland. In *Ägypten – Griechenland – Rom. Abwehr und Berührung. Städelsches Kunstinstitut und Städtische Galerie, 26. November 2005–26. Februar 2006,* ed. Herbert Beck et al., pp. 163-170. Tübingen: Ernst Wasmuth Verlag.

PFEIFFER 2013 = Stefan Pfeiffer, Egypt and Greece before Alexander. In *UCLA Encyclopedia of Egyptology*, ed. Wolfram Grajetzki, Willeke Wendrich. Los Angeles. https://escholarship.org/uc/item/833528zm

PHILIPPS, HOLDAWAY and WENDRICH 2017 = Rebecca Philipps, Simon J. Holdaway and Willeke Wendrich, The Fayum in the Context of Northeast Africa. In *The Desert Fayum Reinvestigated: The Early to Mid-Holocene Landscape Archaeology of the Fayum North Shore, Egypt,* ed. Simon J. Holdaway and Willeke Wendrich, pp. 9-16. Los Angeles: Cotsen Institute of Archaeology Press at UCLA.

PICHLER 1998 = Werner Pichler, Die libysche Sprache. *Almogaren* 29, pp. 7-19.

PICHLER 2007 = Werner Pichler, *Origin and Development of the Libyco-Berber Script.* Berber Studies Volume 7. Köln: Rüdiger Köppe.

POLZ 2014-15 = Daniel Polz, Cave Canem: eine „Hundestele" aus der Nekropole von el-Târif in Theben-West. *Mitteilungen des Deutschen Archäologischen Instituts Kairo* 70/71 (=Gedenkschrift Werner Kaiser), pp. 345-359.

POLZ 2019 = Daniel Polz, *Die sogenannte Hundestele des Königs Wah-Anch Intef aus el-Târif. Eine Forschungsgeschichte.* DAIK Sonderschriften 42. Wiesbaden: Harrassowitz.

POPE 2014 = Jeremy *Pope, The Double Kingdom under Taharqo: Studies in the History of Kush and Egypt, c. 690 – 664 BC*. Leiden: Brill.

POPKO 2008 = Maciej Popko, *Völker und Sprachen Altanatoliens*. Wiesbaden: Harrassowitz.

PORTEN, ZADOK and PEARCE 2016 = Bezalel Porten, Ran Zadok and Laurie Pearce,

Akkadian Names in Aramaic Documents from Ancient Egypt. *Bulletin of the American Schools of Oriental Research* 375, pp. 1-12.

PORTES and RUMBAUT 2001 = Alejandro Portes and Rubén G. Rumbaut, *Legacies: The Story of the Immigrant Second Generation.* Berkeley and Los Angeles: University of California Press.

POSENER 1958 = George Posener,  et . *Zeitschrift für ägyptische Sprache und Altertumskunde* 83, pp. 38-43.

PRADA 2018 = Luigi Prada, Multilingualism along the Nile. In *the iris. Behind the Scenes at the Getty*. August 13, 2018. https://blogs.getty.edu/iris/multilingualism-along-the-nile/

PRUITT 2019 = Madeline Lawson Pruitt, *Cultural Identity, Archaeology, and the Amorites of the Early Second Millennium BCE: An Analytical Paradigmatic Approach.* Ph.D. dissertation: University of California, Berkeley.

PUSCH 1989 = EDGAR B. Pusch, Ausländisches Kulturgut in Qantir-Piramesse. In *Akten des 4. Internationalen Ägyptologenkongresses.* Vol. 2, Archäologie, Feldforschung, Prähistorie, ed. Sylvia Schoske, pp. 249–56. Hamburg: Buske.

QUACK 1993 = Joachim F. Quack, Ägyptisches und südarabisches Alphabet. *Revue d'Égyptologie* 44, pp. 141-151.

QUACK 1996 = Joachim F. Quack, Rev. of James E. Hoch, *Semitic Words in Egyptian Texts of the New Kingdom and Third Intermediate Period.* Princeton, NJ: PUP, 1994. *Zeitschrift der Deutschen Morgenländischen Gesellschaft* 146, pp. 507-514.

QUACK 2002 = Joachim F. Quack, Beiträge zum Peripherdemotischen. In *A Tribute to Excellence: Studies Offered in Honor of Ernö Gaál, Ulrich Luft, László Török,* ed. Tamás Bács, pp. 393-403. Budapest: Department of Egyptology, University Loránd Eötvös.

QUACK 2003 = Joachim F. Quack, Die spätägyptische Alphabetreihenfolge und das "südsemitische" Alphabet. *Lingua Aegyptia* 11, pp. 163-184.

QUACK 2005 = Joachim F. Quack, Zu den vorarabischen semitischen Lehnwörtern im Koptischen. In *Studia Semitica et Semitohamitica: Festschrift für Rainer Voigt anläßlich seines 60. Geburtstages am 17. Januar 2004*, ed. Bogdan Burtea, Josef Tropper, and Helene Younansardaroud, pp. 307-338. Münster: Ugarit Verlag.

QUACK 2010a = Joachim F. Quack, Egyptian Writing for Non-Egyptian Languages and Vice Versa: A Short Overview. In *The Idea of Writing: Play and Complexity,* ed. Alex Voogt and Irving Finkel, pp. 315-326. Leiden and Boston: Brill.

QUACK 2010b = Joachim F. Quack, From Group-Writing to Word Association: Representation and Integration of Foreign Words in Egyptian Script. In *The Idea of Writing: Play and Complexity,* ed. Alex Voogt and Irving Finkel, pp. 73-92. Leiden and Boston: Brill.

QUACK 2015 = Joachim F. Quack, Importing and Exporting Gods? On the Flow of Deities between Egypt and its Neighboring Countries. In *The Dynamics of Transculturality. Concepts and Institutions in Motion*, ed. Antje Flüchter and Jivanta Schöttli, pp. 255-277. Cham etc.: Springer.

QUACK 2018a = Joachim F. Quack, Bemerkungen zum Papyrus Moskau 314. In *Zeitschrift für ägyptische Sprache und Altertumskunde* 145, pp. 151-167.

QUACK 2018b = Joachim F. Quack, *Eine magische Stele aus dem Badischen Landesmuseum Karlsruhe (Inv. H 1049)*. Abhandlungen der Heidelberger Akademie der Wissenschaften 58. Heidelberg: Universitätsverlag Winter.

QUACK 2018c = Joachim F. Quack, Nubisch-meroïtische Lexeme im Papyrus Brooklyn 47.218.47 vs.? In *Across the Mediterranean – Along the Nile: Studies in Egyptology, Nubiology and Late Antiquity dedicated to László Török on the Occasion of his 75th Birthday*, Vol. 1, ed. Tamás A. Bács, Ádám Bollók, and Tivadar Vida, pp. 477-487. Budapest: Institute of Archaeology, Research Centre for the Humanities, Hungarian Academy of Sciences, and Museum of Fine Arts.

QUACK 2019 = Joachim F. Quack, Ein vorderasiatisches Götterpaar in ägyptischer Übersetzung. *Orientalia* 88, pp. 78-82.

QUACK 2022a = Joachim F. Quack, Anat und der Diener des Hauron. In *Rituale und Magie in Ugarit: Praxis, Kontexte und Bedeutung*, ed. Reinhard Müller, Hans Neumann and Reettakaisa Sofia Salo, pp. 161-72. Tübingen: Mohr Siebeck.

QUACK 2022b = Joachim F. Quack, Eine ägyptische Bezeichnung der Schreibbinse als Lehnwort im Hebräischen? *Welt des Orients 52,* pp. 84-88.

QUITOUT 1997 = Michel *Quitout, Grammaire berbère*: *rifain, tamazight, chleuh, kabyle.* Paris: L'Harmattan.

RANKE 1935 = Hermann Ranke, *Die ägyptischen Personennamen. Band I: Verzeichnis der Namen.* Glückstadt: J.J. Augustin.

RAUE 2018 = Dietrich Raue (with a contribution by Peter Kopp), *Elephantine und Nubien vom 4.–2. Jahrtausend v.Chr.* Sonderschrift des Deutschen Archäologischen Instituts Kairo 40. Berlin and Boston: de Gruyter.

RAUE 2019 = Dietrich Raue, Cultural Diversity of Nubia in the Later 3rd–mid-2nd millennium BCE. In *Handbook of Ancient Nubia*, ed. Dietrich Raue, pp. 129-152. Berlin and Boston: De Gruyter.

RAULWING 2000 = Peter Raulwing, *Horses, Chariots and Indo-Europeans: Foundations and Methods of Chariotry Research from the Viewpoint of Comparative Indo-European Linguistics.* Budapest: Archaeolingua.

RAY 1998 = John D. Ray, The Marquis, the Urchin, and the Labyrinth: Egyptology and the University of Cambridge. The Steven Glanville Lecture for 1995. In *Proceedings of the Seventh International Congress of Egyptologists. Cambridge, 3-9 September 1995.* Orientalia Lovaniensia Analecta 82, ed. C.J. Eyre, pp. 1-17. Leuven: Peeters.

REDFORD 2005-6 = Donald B. Redford, The Language of Keftiu: The Evidence of the Drawing Board and the London Medical Papyrus (BM 10059) in the British Museum. *Revista del Instituto de Historia Antigua Oriental* 12/13, pp. 149-153.

REDFORD 2018 = Donald B. Redford: *The Medinet Habu Records of the Foreign Wars of Ramesses III.* Culture and History of the Ancient Near East, 91. Leiden and Boston: Brill.

REGULSKI 2016 = Ilona Regulski, The Origins and Early Development of Writing in Egypt. *Oxford Handbooks Online.* Accessible at: http://www.oxfordhandbooks.com/view/10.1093/oxfordhb/9780199935413.001.0001/oxfordhb-9780199935413-e-61.

REINISCH 1895 = Leo Reinisch, *Wörterbuch der Beḍauye-Sprache*. Wien: Alfred Hölder.

REINTGES and GREEN 2004 = Chris H. Reintges and Melanie Green, Coptic Second Tenses and Hausa Relative Aspects: A Comparative View. *Lingua Aegyptia* 12, pp. 157–177.

RICHTER 2010 = Tonio Sebastian Richter, Language Choice in the Qurra Dossier. In *The Multilingual Experience in Egypt, from the Ptolemies to the Abbasids*, ed. Arietta Papaconstantou, pp. 189-220. Farnham: Ashgate.

RICHTER 2012 = Thomas Richter, *Bibliographisches Glossar des Hurritischen.* Wiesbaden: Harrassowitz.

RICKETTS 2020 = Sarah M. Ricketts, The Sheikh Muftah Cultural Unit: Insights into Social Relations with Old Kingdom Egyptians, Dakhleh Oasis and Desert Surrounds. In *Dust, Demons and Pots. Studies in Honour of Colin A. Hope*, ed. Ashten R. Warfe et al., pp. 599-613. Leuven, Paris and Bristol, CT: Peeters.

RIEKEN 2017 = Elisabeth Rieken, The Dialectology of Anatolian. In *Handbook of Comparative* and Historical *Indo-European Linguistics.* Handbücher zur Sprach- und Kommunikationswissenschaft 41,1, ed. M. Fritz, B. Joseph, J. Klein, pp. 298-308. Berlin and Boston: de Gruyter Mouton.

RIEMER 2011 = Heiko Riemer, *El Kharaish. The Archaeology of Sheikh Muftah Pastoral Nomads in the Desert around Dakhla Oasis (Egypt)*. Africa Praehistorica 25. Köln: Heinrich-Barth-Institut.

RIEMER and KINDERMANN 2019 = Heiko Riemer and Karin Kindermann, Eastern Saharan Prehistory during the 9th to 5th Millennium BC: The View from the Libyan Desert. In *Handbook of Ancient Nubia*, ed. Dietrich Raue, pp. 195-216. Berlin and Boston: De Gruyter.

RIGGS and BAINES 2012 = Christina Riggs and John Baines, Ethnicity. *UCLA Encyclopedia of Egyptology*, ed. Willeke Wendrich. https://escholarship.org/uc/item/32r9x0jr

RILLY 2007 = Claude Rilly, *La langue du royaume de Méroé: Un panorama de la plus ancienne culture écrite d'Afrique subsaharienne*. Bibliothèque de l'École Pratique des Hautes Études, Sciences Historiques et Philologiques 344. Paris: Champion.

RILLY 2010a = Claude Rilly, *Le méroïtique et sa famille linguistique*. Leuven and Paris: Peeters.

RILLY 2010b = Claude Rilly, Reducing Polyvalency in Writing Systems: From Egyptian to Meroïtic. In *The Idea of Writing: Play and Complexity*, ed. Alex de Voogt and Irving Finkel, pp. 221-233. Leiden and Boston: Brill.

RILLY 2014 = Claude Rilly, Language and Ethnicity in Ancient Sudan. In *The Fourth Cataract and Beyond: Proceedings of the 12th International Conference for Nubian Studies,* ed. by Julie R. Anderson and Derek Welsby, pp. 1169-1188. Leuven: Peeters.

RILLY 2017 = Claude Rilly, Histoire du Soudan des origines à la chute du sultanat Fung. In *Histoire et civilizations du Soudan de la préhistoire à nos jours*. Études d'égyptologie, 15, pp. 26-445. Paris: Soleb / Bleu autour.

RILLY 2019 = Claude Rilly, Languages of Ancient Nubia. In *Handbook of Ancient Nubia*, ed. by Dietrich Raue, pp. 129-152. Berlin and Boston: de Gruyter.

RILLY and DE VOOGT 2012 = Claude Rilly and Alex de Voogt, *The Meroïtic Language and Writing System*. New York: Cambridge University Press.

RITNER 1996 = Robert K. Ritner, The Earliest Attestation of the *kpḏ*-Measure. In *Studies in Honor of William Kelly Simpson*, ed. Peter Der Manuelian, vol. 2, pp. 683-88. Boston: Museum of Fine Arts.

RITNER 2009a = Robert K. Ritner, Egypt and the Vanishing Libyan: Institutional Responses to a Nomadic People. In *Nomads, Tribes, and the State in the Ancient Near East: Cross-Disciplinary Perspectives*, ed. Jeffrey Szuchman, pp. 43-56. Chicago: The Oriental Institute of the University of Chicago.

RITNER 2009b = Robert K. Ritner, *The Libyan Anarchy. Documents from Egypt's Third Intermediate Period.* Writings from the Ancient World, vol. 21. Atlanta, GA: Society of Biblical Literature.

ROBIN 2015 = Christian Julien Robin, Before Himyar: Epigraphic Evidence for the Kingdoms of South Arabia. In *Arabs and Empires before Islam*, ed. Greg Fisher, pp. 90-126. Oxford: Oxford University Press.

ROLLSTON 2010 = Chris A. Rollston, *Writing and Literacy in the World of Ancient Israel: Epigraphic Evidence from the Iron Age.* Atlanta: Society of Biblical Literature.

ROMAINE 2017 = Suzanne Romaine, *Pidgin & Creole Languages*. Abingdon, Oxon and New York: Routledge 2017.

RÖMER 2014 = Malte Römer, Miszellen zu den Ostraka der 18. Dynastie aus Deir el-Bahri und dem Asasif. In *The Workman's Progress. Studies in the Village of Deir el-Medina and other Documents from Western Thebes in Honour of Rob Demarée*. Egyptologische Uitgaven 28, ed. B.J.J. Haring, Olaf E. Kaper, René van Walsem, pp. 211–216. Leiden: Nederlands Instituut voor het Nabije Oosten; Leuven: Peeters.

ROP 2019 = Jeffrey Rop, *Greek Military Service in the Ancient Near East, 401-330 BCE.* Cambridge and New York: Cambridge University Press.

RÖSSLER 1952 = Otto Rössler, Der semitische Charakter der libyschen Sprache. *Zeitschrift für Assyriologie und vorderasiatische Archäologie* 50, pp. 121-150. Reprinted 2001 in: *Gesammelte Schriften zur Semitohamistik,* Alter Orient und Altes Testament 287, ed. Thomas Schneider, pp. 357-386. Münster: Ugarit Verlag.

RÖSSLER 1958 = Otto Rössler, Die Sprache Numidiens. In *Sybaris. Festschrift Hans Krahe zum 60. Geburtstag am 7. Februar 1958 dargebracht von Freunden, Schülern und Kollegen,* pp. 94-120. Wiesbaden: Harrassowitz. Reprinted 2001 in: *Gesammelte Schriften zur Semitohamistik,* Alter Orient und Altes Testament 287, ed. Thomas Schneider, pp. 392-418. Münster: Ugarit Verlag.

RÖSSLER 1964 = Otto Rössler, Libysch-Hamitisch-Semitisch. *Oriens* 17, pp. 199-216.

Reprinted 2001 in: *Gesammelte Schriften zur Semitohamistik,* Alter Orient und Altes Testament 287, ed. Thomas Schneider, pp. 499-516. Münster: Ugarit Verlag.

RÖSSLER 1966 = Otto Rössler, Das ältere ägyptische Umschreibungssystem für Fremdnamen und seine sprachwissenschaftlichen Lehren. In *Neue afrikanistische Studien*, Hamburger Beiträge zur Afrika-Kunde 5, ed. Johannes Lukas, pp. 218-229. Reprinted 2001 in: *Gesammelte Schriften zur Semitohamistik,* Alter Orient und Altes Testament 287, ed. Thomas Schneider, pp. 518-529. Münster: Ugarit Verlag.

RÖSSLER 1971 = Otto Rössler, Das Ägyptische als semitische Sprache. In *Christentum am Roten Meer*, vol. 1, ed. Frank Altheim and Ruth Stiehl, pp. 263-326. Berlin and New York: De Gruyter. Reprinted 2001 in: *Gesammelte Schriften zur Semitohamitistik*, Alter Orient und Altes Testament 287, ed. Thomas Schneider, pp. 543-606. Münster: Ugarit Verlag.

RÖSSLER 1980 = Otto Rössler, Libyen von der Cyrenaica bis zur Mauretania Tingitana. In *Die Sprachen im Römischen Reich der Kaiserzeit. Kolloquium vom 8.-10. April 1974,* ed. Günter Neumann and Jürgen Untermann, pp. 267-284. Köln: Rheinland-Verlag; Bonn: Habelt [in Kommission]. Reprinted 2001 in: *Gesammelte Schriften zur Semitohamitistik*, Alter Orient und Altes Testament 287, ed. Thomas Schneider, pp. 667-684. Münster: Ugarit Verlag.

ROTH 2001 = Silke Roth, *Die Königsmütter des Alten Ägypten von der Frühzeit bis zum Ende der 12. Dynastie*. Wiesbaden: Harrassowitz.

ROTH 2002 = Silke Roth, *Gebieterin aller Länder. Die Rolle der königlichen Frauen in der fiktiven und realen Außenpolitik des ägyptischen Neuen Reiches*. Orbis Biblicus et Orientalis 185. Freiburg Schweiz: Universitätsverlag; Göttingen: Vandenhoeck & Ruprecht.

ROUCHDY 1991 = Aleya Rouchdy, *Nubians and the Nubian Language in Contemporary Egypt: A Case of Cultural and Linguistic Contact.* Studies in Semitic Languages and Linguistics, 15. Leiden: Brill.

RÜBEKEIL 1992 = Ludwig Rübekeil, *Suebica – Völkernamen und Ethnos*. Innsbruck: Institut für Sprachwissenschaft. Accessible at: https://doi.org/10.5167/uzh-171039

SAGRILLO 2009 = Troy Leiland Sagrillo, The Geographic Origins of the "Bubastite" Dynasty and Possible Locations for the Royal Residence and Burial Place *of* Shoshenq I. In *The Libyan Period in Egypt: Historical and Cultural Studies into the 21st–24th Dynasties: Proceedings of a Conference at Leiden University, 25–27 October 2007*, ed. Gerard Broekman, Robert Demarée, and Olaf Kaper. pp. 341–359. Leiden: Nederlands Instituut voor het Nabije Oosten; Leuven: Peeters.

SAGRILLO 2015 = Troy Leiland Sagrillo, Shoshenq I and Biblical Šîšaq: a Philological Defense of Their Traditional Equation. In *Solomon and Shishak. Current Perspectives from Archaeology, Epigraphy, History and Chronology. Proceedings of the Third BICANE Colloquium held at Sidney Sussex College, Cambridge 26-27 March, 2011.* BAR International Series 2732, ed. by Peter James and Peter G. van der Veen, pp. 61-81. Oxford: BAR Publishing.

SARETTA 2016 = Saretta Phyllis, *Asiatics in Middle Kingdom Egypt: Perceptions and Reality.* London and New York: Bloomsbury Academic.

SATZINGER 2000 = Helmut Satzinger, Egyptian as an African language. In *Atti del IV Convegno Nazionale di Egittologia e Papirologia, Siracusa, 5–7 Dicembre 1997*. Quaderni del Museo del Papiro IX, ed. Corrado Basile and Anna Di Natale, pp. 31-43. Syracuse: Museo del Papiro.

SATZINGER 2001 = Helmut Satzinger, Relativformen, emphatische Formen und zweite Tempora: Gliedsatzformen im Ägyptischen und Tschadischen. In *Von Ägypten zum Tschadsee: Eine linguistische Reise durch Afrika. Festschrift für Hermann Jungraithmayr zum 65. Geburtstag*, ed. D. Ibriszimow, R. Leger, U. Seibert, pp. 411–420. Würzburg: Ergon-Verlag.

SATZINGER 2002 = Helmut Satzinger, Syllabic and Alphabetic Script, or the Egyptian Origin of the Alphabet. *Aegyptus* 82, pp. 15-26.

SATZINGER 2008 = The Etymology of Coptic "Ashes": Chadic or Nostratic? In *Semito-Hamitic Festschrift for A.B. Dolgopolsky and H. Jungraithmayr,* ed. Gábor Takács, pp. 265-271. Berlin: Dietrich Reimer Verlag.

SATZINGER 2015 = Helmut Satzinger, What happened to the Voiced Consonants of Egyptian? In *Proceedings of the Tenth International Congress of Egyptologists, University of the Aegean, Rhodes, 22–29 May 2008*, ed. Panagiotis Kousolis and Nikolaos Lazaridis, vol. 2, pp. 1537-1546. Leuven: Peeters.

SAUNERON 1960 = Serge Sauneron, La différenciation des langages d'après la tradition égyptienne. *Bulletin de l'Institut français d'archéologie orientale* 60, pp. 31-41.

SCHÄFER-LICHTENBERGER 2000 = Christa Schäfer-Lichtenberger, The Goddess of Ekron and the Religious-Cultural Background of the Philistines. *Israel Exploration Journal* 50, pp. 82-91.

SCHEELE-SCHWEITZER 2014 = Katrin Scheele-Schweitzer, *Die Personennamen des Alten Reiches. Altägyptische Onomastik unter lexikographischen und sozio-kulturellen Aspekten.* Wiesbaden: Harrassowitz.

SCHENKEL 1965 = Wolfgang Schenkel, *Memphis, Herakleopolis, Theben. Die epigraphischen Zeugnisse der 7. - 11. Dynastie Ägyptens.* Ägyptologische Abhandlungen 12. Wiesbaden: Harrassowitz.

SCHENKEL 1971 = Wolfgang Schenkel, Das altägyptische Pseudopartizip und das indogermanische Medium/Perfekt. *Orientalia* 40, pp. 301-316.

SCHENKEL 1979 = Wolfgang Schenkel, Atlantis: die "namenlose" Insel. *Göttinger Miszellen* 36, pp. 57-60.

SCHENKEL 1983 = Wolfgang Schenkel, *Zur Rekonstruktion der deverbalen Nominalbildung des Ägyptischen.* Göttinger Orientforschungen IV/13. Wiesbaden: Harrassowitz.

SCHENKEL 1997 = Wolfgang Schenkel, Wie das ägyptische Labyrinth zu seinem Namen kam. *Göttinger Miszellen* 159, pp. 87-90.

SCHENKEL 2005 = Wolfgang Schenkel, Tübinger Einführung in die klassisch-ägyptische Sprache und Schrift. Tübingen.

SCHENKEL 2006 = Wolfgang Schenkel, Ist „Mythos" ein griechisches Lehnwort aus dem

Ägyptischen? In *Jn.t ḏr.w: Festschrift für Friedrich Junge,* ed. Gerald Moers et al., vol. 2, pp. 547-580. Göttingen: Seminar für Ägyptologie und Koptologie.

SCHIATTARELLA 2016 = Valentina Schiattarella, *Berber Texts from Siwa (Egypt). Including a Grammatical Sketch.* With a Foreword by Lionel Galand. Berber Studies, vol. 46. Köln: Rüdiger Köppe.

SCHMITZ 2010 = Philip C. Schmitz, The Phoenician Contingent in the Campaign of Psammetichus II against Kush. *Journal of Egyptian History* 3, pp. 321-337.

SCHMITZ 2016 = Philip C. Schmitz, Philistine ptġy, Greek *πενταγαια 'Five lands': Contact Effects in the Royal Dedicatory Stela from Ekron, *Eretz-Israel* 32 = Joseph Naveh Volume, ed. H. Geva – A. Paris, pp. 91-102. Jerusalem: Israel Exploration Society.

SCHNEIDER 1989 = Thomas Schneider, Mag. pHarris XII,1-5: Eine kanaanäische Beschwörung für die Löwenjagd? *Göttinger Miszellen* 112, pp. 53-63.

SCHNEIDER 1992 = Thomas Schneider, *Asiatische Personennamen in ägyptischen Quellen des Neuen Reiches.* Orbis Biblicus et Orientalis 114. Freiburg/Schweiz: Universitätsverlag; Göttingen: Vandenhoeck & Ruprecht.

SCHNEIDER 1993 = Thomas Schneider, Asiatic Personal Names from the New Kingdom. An Outline with Supplements. In *Atti del Sesto Congresso Internazionale di Egittologia, Torino 1st-8th September 1991,* vol. II, pp. 453-470. Torino.

SCHNEIDER 1996 = Thomas Schneider, Rev. of James E. Hoch: *Semitic Words in Egyptian Texts of the New Kingdom and the Third Intermediate Period*, 1994. *Orientalia* 65, pp. 174-177.

SCHNEIDER 1997 = Thomas Schneider, Beiträge zur sogenannten „Neueren Komparatistik". *Lingua Aegyptia* 5, pp. 189-209.

SCHNEIDER 1998a = Thomas Schneider, *Ausländer in Ägypten während des Mittleren Reiches und der Hyksoszeit. Teil 1: Die ausländischen Könige.* Ägypten und Altes Testament 42/1. Wiesbaden: Harrassowitz.

SCHNEIDER 1998b = Thomas Schneider, Rev. of Beatrice Teissier, *Egyptian Iconography on Syro-Palestinian Cylinder Seals of the Middle Bronze Age* (OBO SA 11), 1996, and Christian Eder: *Die ägyptischen Motive in der Glyptik des östlichen Mittelmeerraumes zu Anfang des 2 Jts. v.Chr.*, 1996. *Zeitschrift des Deutschen Palästina-Vereins* 114, pp. 184-188.

SCHNEIDER 1999 = Thomas Schneider, Eine Vokabel der Tapferkeit: Ägyptisch *tl* – hurritisch *adal. Ugarit-Forschungen* 31, pp. 677-723.

SCHNEIDER 2000 = Thomas Schneider, Wer war der Gott „Chajtau"? In *Les civilisations du bassin Méditerranéen: hommages à Joachim Śliwa,* ed. Krzysztof M. Ciałowicz and Janusz A. Ostrowski, pp. 215-220. Cracow: Université Jagellonne, Institut d'archéologie.

SCHNEIDER 2002 = Thomas Schneider, Sinuhes Notiz über die Könige: syrisch-anatolische Herrschertitel in ägyptischer Überlieferung. *Egypt & the Levant* 12, pp. 257-272.

SCHNEIDER 2003a = Thomas Schneider: *Ausländer in Ägypten während des Mittleren*

Reiches und der Hyksoszeit. Teil 2: Die ausländische Bevölkerung. Ägypten und Altes Testament 42/2. Wiesbaden: Harrassowitz.

SCHNEIDER 2003b = Thomas Schneider, Etymologische Methode, die Historizität der Phoneme und das ägyptologische Transkriptionsalphabet. *Lingua Aegyptia* 11, pp. 187-199.

SCHNEIDER 2003c = Thomas Schneider, Texte über den syrischen Wettergott aus Ägypten. *Ugarit-Forschungen* 35, pp. 605-627.

SCHNEIDER 2003d = Thomas Schneider, Hurritisch *ḫiaroḫḫe* „Goldenes“ als Fachterminus im Ägyptischen, in: *Egyptian and Semito-Hamitic (Afro-Asiatic) Studies in Memoriam W. Vycichl.* Studies in Semitic Languages and Linguistics, 39, ed. Gábor Takács, pp. 137-8. Leiden and Boston: Brill.

SCHNEIDER 2004 = Thomas Schneider, Nichtsemitische Lehnwörter im Ägyptischen. Umriß eines Forschungsgebiets. In *Das Ägyptische und die Sprachen Vorderasiens, Nordafrikas und der Ägäis: Akten des Basler Kolloquiums zum ägyptisch-nichtsemitischen Sprachkontakt, Basel 9. – 11. Juli 2003.* Alter Orient und Altes Testament 310, ed. Thomas Schneider, unter Mitarbeit von Francis Breyer, Oskar Kaelin, Carsten Knigge, pp. 11-31. Münster: Ugarit Verlag.

SCHNEIDER 2006 = Thomas Schneider, Die Hundenamen der Stele Antefs II.: Eine neue Deutung. In *Altertum und Mittelmeerraum: Die antike Welt diesseits und jenseits der Levante. Festschrift für Peter W. Haider zum 60. Geburtstag*, ed. Robert Rollinger and Barbara Truschnegg. Oriens et Occidens, 12, pp. 527-536. Stuttgart: Franz Steiner.

SCHNEIDER 2008a = Thomas Schneider, Fremdwörter in der ägyptischen Militärsprache des Neuen Reiches und ein Bravourstück des Elitesoldaten (Pap. Anastasi I 23, 2-7). *Journal of the Society for the Study of Egyptian Antiquities* 35, pp. 181-205.

SCHNEIDER 2008b = Thomas Schneider, Innovation in Literature on Behalf of Politics: The Tale of Two Brothers, Ugarit, and 19th Dynasty History. *Egypt and the Levant* 18, pp. 315-326.

SCHNEIDER 2010 = Thomas Schneider, Foreigners in Egypt: Archaeological Evidence and Cultural Context. In *Egyptian Archaeology.* Blackwell Studies in Global Archaeology, ed. Willeke Wendrich, pp. 143-163. Oxford: Wiley Blackwell.

SCHNEIDER 2011a = Thomas Schneider, The Philistine Language. New Etymologies and the Name “David”. *Ugarit Forschungen* 43, pp. 569-580.

SCHNEIDER 2011b = Thomas Schneider, Three Histories of Translation: Translating in Egypt, Translating Egypt, Translating Egyptian, in *Complicating the History of Western Translation: the Ancient Mediterranean in Perspective,* ed. Enrica Sciarrino and Siobhán McElduff, pp. 176-188. Manchester: St. Jerome.

SCHNEIDER 2011-12 = Thomas Schneider, Wie der Wettergott Ägypten aus der großen Flut errettete: Ein “inkulturierter” ägyptischer Sintflut-Mythos und die Gründung der Ramsesstadt. *Journal of the Society for the Study of Egyptian Antiquities* 38, pp. 173-193.

SCHNEIDER 2015 = Thomas Schneider, The Old Kingdom Abroad: An Epistemological Perspective. With Remarks on the Biography of Iny and the Kingdom of Dugurasu. In: *Towards a New History of the Old Kingdom. Perspectives on the Pyramid Age. Proceed-*

ings of the Conference at Harvard University, April 26th, 2012. Harvard Egyptological Studies 1, ed. Peter Der Manuelian and Thomas Schneider, pp. 425-451. Leiden and Boston: Brill.

SCHNEIDER 2018 = Thomas Schneider, A Double Abecedary? *Halaḥam* and *'Abgad* on the TT99 Ostracon. *Bulletin of the American Schools of Oriental Research* 379, pp.103-112.

SCHNEIDER 2020 = Thomas Schneider, Language Contact of Ancient Egyptian with Semitic and Other Near Eastern Languages. In *A Companion to Ancient Near Eastern Languages*, ed. Rebecca Hasselbach-Andee, pp. 421-437. Hoboken, NJ: Wiley Blackwell.

SCHNEIDER 2022 = Thomas Schneider, Language Contact. In *UCLA Encyclopedia of Egyptology*, ed. Andréas Stauder and Willeke Wendrich, Los Angeles. https://escholarship.org/uc/item/1px3x3fq

SCHNEIDER-MIZONY 2014 = Odile Schneider-Mizony, Nachbarsprachen: Historio-, Konflikt-, Kontakt- oder Ökolinguistik? *Zeitschrift des Verbandes Polnischer Germanisten* 3(1), pp. 75-88.

SCHOFIELD and PARKINSON 1994 = L. Schofield and R.B. Parkinson, Of Helmets and Heretics: A Possible Egyptian Representation of Mycenaean Warriors on a Papyrus from el-Amarna. *Annual of the British School at Athens* 89, pp. 157–70.

SCHÜTTE and SCHNEIDER 2019 = Wolfgang Schütte and Thomas Schneider: ‚Adramelech, der Äthiopier' (2Kön 17,4 ANT): Eine neue Quelle zu den Beziehungen zwischen 2 Hosea von Israel und der kuschitischen 25. Dynastie? *Biblische Notizen* 182, pp. 69-90.

SCHWEITZER 2005 = Simon D. Schweitzer, Review of *Das Ägyptische und die Sprachen Vorderasiens, Nordafrikas und der Ägäis: Akten des Basler Kolloquiums zum ägyptisch-nichtsemitischen Sprachkontakt, Basel 9.–11. Juli 2003*, ed. Thomas Schneider, unter Mitarbeit von Francis Breyer, Oskar Kaelin, Carsten Knigge (Münster: Ugarit Verlag). *Lingua Aegyptia* 13, pp. 285-295.

SEARS 2020 = Matthew A. Sears, Rev. of *Greek Military Service in the Ancient Near East, 401–330 BCE*, by Jeffrey Rop. *Classical World* 113, pp. 240-241.

SERRELI 2018 = Valentina Serreli, Globalization in the Periphery: Arabization and the Changing Status of Siwi Berber in the Oasis of Siwa. *Sociolinguistic Studies* 12/2, pp. 231-50.

SFAXI 2014 = Intissar Sfaxi, L'onomastique libyque: son intérêt – état des recherches. *Revue des Etudes Berbères* 9, pp. 565-575.

SHALOMI-HEN 2006 = Rachel Shalomi-Hen, *The Writing of Gods: The Evolution of Divine Classifiers in the Old Kingdom.* Wiesbaden: Harrassowitz.

SHINNIE 1996 = Peter L. Shinnie, *Ancient Nubia.* London and New York: Kegan Paul International.

SHIRLEY 2013 = J.J. Shirley, Crisis and the Restructuring of the State: From the Second Intermediate Period to the Advent of the Ramesses. In *Ancient Egyptian Administration*. Handbook of Oriental Studies. Section 1: The Near and Middle East, 104, ed. Juan Carlos Moreno García, pp. 521-606. Leiden and Boston: Brill.

SHISHA-HALEVY 1978 = Ariel Shisha-Halevy, An Early Northwest Semitic Text in the Egyptian Hieratic Script. *Orientalia* 47, pp. 145-162.

SHORTLAND 2001 = Andrew Shortland (ed.), *The Social Context of Technological Change: Egypt and the Near East, 1650-1550 BC. Proceedings of a Conference Held at St. Edmund Hall, Oxford, 12-14 September 2000.* Oxford: Oxbow Books.

SILVERMAN and HOUSER WEGNER 2007 = David Silverman and Jennifer Houser Wegner, A Late Egyptian Story in the Penn Museum. In *The Archaeology and Art of Ancient Egypt: Essays in Honor of David B. O'Connor*, ed. Zahi Hawass and Janet Richards, vol. 2, pp. 403-424. Cairo: Supreme Council of Antiquities.

SILVESTRI 2022 = Jason Paul Silvestri, Papyrus Turin 54030: The Oldest Berber Text. In *Abstract booklet ARCE 73rd Annual Meeting, April 22-24, 2022,* pp. 52-3; accessible at https://www.arce.org/sites/default/files/documents/ARCE%20Abstract%20Booklet%20 2022%20v07.pdf

SIMON 2011 = Zsolt Simon, The Identification of Qode: Reconsidering the Evidence. In *Egypt and the Near East: the Crossroads. Proceedings of an International Conference on the Relations of Egypt and the Near East in the Bronze Age, Prague, September 1-3, 2010*, ed. Jana_Mynářová, pp. 249-269. Prague: Czech Institute of Egyptology.

SIMON 2018 = Zsolt Simon, Anatolian Influences on Greek. In *Change, Continuity, and Connectivity: North-Eastern Mediterranean at the Turn of the Bronze Age and in the Early Iron Age*, ed. Łukasz Niesiołowski-Spanò and Marek Węcowski, pp. 376-418. Wiesbaden: Harrassowitz.

SIMON 2019 = Zsolt Simon, Zu den karisch-griechischen Lehnbeziehungen. *Glotta* 95, pp. 295-308.

SINGER 1999 = Itamar Singer, A Political History of Ugarit. In *Handbook of Ugaritic Studies***.** Handbook of Oriental Studies. Section 1 The Near and Middle East, vol. 39, ed. by Wilfred Watson and Nicolas Wyatt, pp. 603–733. Leiden: Brill.

SINGER 2013 = Itamar Singer, Hittite Gods in Egyptian Attire: A Case Study in Cultural Transmission. In *Literature as Politics, Politics as Literature: Essays on the Ancient Near East in Honor of Peter Machinist*, ed. David Vanderhooft and Abraham Winitzer, pp. 433-457. Winona Lake, IN: Eisenbrauns.

SINNER and VELAZA 2019 = Alejandro Garcia Sinner and Javier Velaza (eds.), *Palaeohispanic Languages and Epigraphies.* Oxford: Oxford University Press.

SIVAN and COCHAVI-RAINEY 1992 = Daniel Sivan and Zipora Cochavi-Rainey, *West Semitic Vocabulary in Egyptian Script of the 14th to the 10th centuries BCE.* Beer-Sheva: Ben Gurion University.

SMAGINA 2017 = Eugenia B. Smagina, *The Old Nubian Language.* Translated by José Andrés Alonso de la Fuente. Dotawo Monographs 3. Punctum Books. (Originally published as Е.Б. Смагина, Древненубийский язык. – Ю.Н. Завадовский & Е.Б. Смагина, Нубийский язык. Москва, 1986).

SOMAGLINO and TALLET 2014 = Claire Somaglino and Pierre Tallet, Une campagne en Nubie sous la Ière dynastie: la scène nagadienne du Gebel Sheikh Suleiman comme prototype et modèle. *Nehet. Revue numérique d'égyptologie*, pp. 1-46.

SOUAG 2013 = Lameen Souag, *Berber and Arabic in Siwa (Egypt). A Study in Linguistic Contact.* Berber Studies Volume 37. Köln: Rüdiger Köppe.

SOWA 2005 = Wojciech Sowa, Anmerkungen zum Balkanindogermanischen. In *Indogermanica. Festschrift Gert Klingenschmitt. Indische, Iranische und indogermanische Studien dem verehrten Jubilar dargebracht zu seinem fünfundsechzigsten Geburtstag*, ed. Günter Schweiger, pp. 611-28. Taimering: Schweiger VWT-Verlag.

SOWADA 2009 = Karen N. Sowada, *Egypt in the Eastern Mediterranean during the Old Kingdom: An Archaeological Perspective. With a Contribution by Peter Grave.* Orbis Biblicus et Orientalis 237. Fribourg: Academic Press; Göttingen: Vandenhoeck & Ruprecht.

SPALINGER 1979 = Anthony J. Spalinger, Some Notes on the Libyans of the Old Kingdom and Later Historical Reflexes. *Journal of the Society for the Study of Egyptian Antiquities* 9, pp. 125-60.

SPALINGER 2002 = Anthony J. Spalinger, *The Transformation of an Ancient Egyptian Narrative: P. Sallier III and the Battle of Kadesh.* Göttinger Orientforschungen IV/40. Wiesbaden: Harrassowitz.

SPALINGER 2005 = Anthony J. Spalinger, *War in Ancient Egypt. The New Kingdom.* Ancient World at War. Malden, MA: Blackwell.

SPALINGER 2010 = Anthony J. Spalinger, Military Institutions and Warfare: Pharaonic Egypt. In *A Companion to Ancient Egypt*. Blackwell Companions to the Ancient World, vol. I, ed. Alan B. Lloyd, pp. 425-45. Malden, MA: Blackwell.

SPALINGER 2020 = Anthony J. Spalinger, *Leadership under Fire. The Pressures of Warfare in Ancient Egypt. Four leçons at the Collège de France, Paris, June 2019.* Collection études d'égyptologie. Paris: Soleb.

SPALINGER 2021 = Anthony J. Spalinger, *The Books behind the Masks. Sources of Warfare Leadership in Ancient Egypt.* Culture and History of the Ancient Near East 124. Leiden and Boston: Brill.

SPIER, POTTS and COLE 2018 = Jeffrey Spier, Timothy Potts and Sara E. Cole (eds.), *Beyond the Nile: Egypt and the Classical World.* Los Angeles: J. Paul Getty Museum.

STARKE 1993 = Frank Starke, Zur Herkunft von akkad. *ta/urgumannu(m)* "Dolmetscher". *Die Welt des Orients* 24, pp. 20-38.

STAUDER 2013 = Andréas Stauder, *Linguistic Dating of Middle Egyptian Literary Texts.* Lingua Aegyptia, Studia Monographica 12. Hamburg: Widmaier.

STAUDER 2020 = Andréas Stauder, Expressions of Royal Agency: Forms of the Verb in the Old Kingdom Event Autobiography. In *Ancient Egyptian Biographies: Contexts, Forms, Functions.* Wilbour Studies in Egyptology and Assyriology 6, ed. Julie Stauder-Porchet, Elizabeth Frood, and Andréas Stauder, pp. 225-247. Atlanta, GA: Lockwood Press.

STAUDER-PORCHET 2017 = Julie Stauder-Porchet, *Les autobiographies de l'Ancien Empire égyptien. Étude sur la naissance d'un genre.* Orientalia Lovaniensia Analecta, 255.

Leuven, Paris, Walpole: Peeters.

STEELE 2012 = Phillipa M. Steele, The Diversity of the Cypro-Minoan Corpus. In *Etudes mycéniennes 2010. Actes du XIIIe colloque international sur les textes* égéens, ed. P. Carlier, C. de Lamberterie, M. Egetmeyer et al., pp. 537-544. Pisa and Rome: Fabrizio Serra editore.

STEELE 2013 = Phillipa M. Steele, *A Linguistic History of Ancient Cyprus: The Non-Greek Languages, and their Relations with Greek, c. 1600-300 BC.* Cambridge: Cambridge University Press.

STEINER 1992 = Robert C. Steiner, Northwest Semitic Incantations in an Egyptian Medical Papyrus of the Fourteenth Century B.C.E. *Journal of Near Eastern Studies* 51(3), pp. 191-200.

STEINER 1997 = Robert C. Steiner, The *Aramaic Text* in Demotic Script. In *The Context of Scripture*, vol. 1, ed. William Hallo and K. Lawson Younger, pp. 309-327. Leiden and Boston: Brill.

STEINER 2001 = Robert C. Steiner, The Scorpion Spell from Wadi Hammamat: Another Aramaic text in Demotic Script. *Journal of Near Eastern Studies* 60, pp. 259-268.

STEINER 2011 = Robert C. Steiner, *Early Northwest Semitic Serpent Spells in the Pyramid Texts.* Winona Lake, IN: Eisenbrauns.

STOCKFISCH 1996 = Dagmar Stockfisch, Bemerkungen zur sog. 'Libyschen Familie'. In *Wege öffnen. Festschrift für Rolf Gundlach.* Ägypten und Altes Testament 35, ed. Mechthild Schade-Busch, pp. 315-325. Wiesbaden: Harrassowitz.

STOLBOVA 2003 = Olga Stolbova, A Contribution to the Common Egyptian-Chadic Wordstock. In *Das alte Ägypten und seine Nachbarn. Festschrift zum 65. Geburtstag von Helmut Satzinger. Mit Beiträgen zur Ägyptologie, Koptologie, Nubiologie und Afrikanistik*, ed. Monika RM. Hasitzka-Johannes and Diethart-Günther Dembski, pp. 347–352. Krems: Österreichisches Literaturforum.

STRECK 2000 = Michael P. Streck, *Das amurritische Onomastikon der altbabylonischen Zeit.* Band 1. Münster: Ugarit Verlag.

STRECK 2005 = Michael P. Streck (ed.), *Sprachen des Alten Orients*. Darmstadt: Wissenschaftliche Buchgesellschaft.

STRECK 2012 = Michael P. Streck, Amorite. In *The Semitic Languages*, ed. Stefan Weninger, pp. 452-459. Berlin and Boston: de Gruyter.

STROBEL 1976 = August Strobel, *Der spätbronzezeitliche Seevölkersturm. Ein Forschungsüberblick mit Folgerungen zur biblischen Exodusthematik.* Berlin and New York: De Gruyter.

SWIGGERS 1995 = Pierre Swiggers, A Minaean Sarcophagus Inscription from Egypt. In *Immigration and Emigration within the Ancient Near East: Festschrift E. Lipiński,* ed. Karel van Lerberghe and Antoon Schoors, pp. 335-343. Leuven: Peeters.

TAKÁCS 1999 = Gábor Takács, *Etymological Dictionary of Egyptian, vol. 1: A Phonological Introduction.* Handbook of Oriental Studies, Section 1: The Near and Middle East, 48/1.

Leiden and Boston: Brill.

TAKÁCS 2003 = Gábor Takács, *Etymological Dictionary of Egyptian, vol. 2: b-, p-,f-*. Handbook of Oriental Studies: Section 1, The Near and Middle East, 48/2. Leiden and Boston: Brill.

TAKÁCS 2006 = Gábor Takács, Aaron Ember and the Establishment of Egypto-Semitic Phonological and Lexical Comparison (Part II). *Acta Orientalia Vilnensia 7/1-2*, pp. 145-187.

TAKÁCS 2008 = Gábor Takács, *Etymological Dictionary of Egyptian, vol. 3: m-*. Handbook of Oriental Studies, Section 1: The Near and Middle East, 48/3. Leiden and Boston: Brill.

TAKÁCS 2013 = Nubian Lexicon in Later Egyptian. *Bibliotheca Orientalis* 70, pp. 569-582.

TARAWNEH 2011 = Hanadah Tarawneh, Amarna Letters: Two Languages, Two Dialogues. In *Egypt and the Near East: the Crossroads. Proceedings of an International Conference on the Relations of Egypt and the Near East in the Bronze Age, Prague, September 1-3, 2010*, ed. Jana Mynářová, pp. 271-284. Prague: Czech Institute of Egyptology, Faculty of Arts, Charles University.

TEN CATE, VAN DEN HOUT and MELCHERT 1999/2009 = Philo H.J. Houwink ten Cate, Theo P.J. van den Hout and H. Craig Melchert, Anatolian languages. *Encyclopedia Britanni ca*, 1999/2009, accessible at https://www.britannica.com/topic/Anatolian-languages.

TESSIER 1996 = Beatrice Tessier, *Egyptian Iconography on Syro-Palestinian Cylinder Seals of the Middle Bronze Age.* Orbis Biblicus et Orientalis – Series Archaeologica, 11. Freiburg (Schweiz): Universitätsverlag; Göttingen: Vandenhoeck & Ruprecht.

TÖRÖK 2002 = László Török, *The Image of the Ordered World in Ancient Nubian Art: The Construction of the Kushite Mind, 800 BC–300 AD*, Leiden, Boston, Köln: Brill.

TÖRÖK 2009 = László Török, *Between Two Worlds: The Frontier Region between Ancient Nubia and Egypt 3700 BC – 500 AD.* Probleme der Ägyptologie, 29. Leiden and Bos ton: Brill.

TORALLAS TOVAR 2010 = Sofia Torallas Tovar, Greek in Egypt. In *A Companion to the Ancient Greek language*, ed. Egbert Bakker, pp. 253-265. London: Wiley Blackwell.

TOUDJI 2005 = Saïd Toudji, L'anthroponymie libyco-berbère, reflet d'une identité. Essai d'analyse et bilan. PNR du CRASC, 2005, pp. 83-102

TROST 2012 = Franz Trost, Die Hatiua von Tjehenu. Almogaren XLIII, 179-210.

UNTERMANN 1989 = Jürgen Untermann, Zu den Begriffen 'Restsprache' und 'Trümmersprache'. *Germanische Rest- und Trümmersprachen.* Ergänzungsbände zum Reallexikon der Germanischen Altertumskunde 3, ed. Heinrich Beck, pp. 15-19. Berlin and New York: De Gruyter, 1989.

VAN COPPEN and RADNER 2009 = Frans van Coppen and Karen Radner, Ein Tontafelfragment aus der diplomatischen Korrespondenz der Hyksosherrscher mit Babylonien *Egypt & the Levant* 19, pp. 115-18.

VAN DE MOORTEL 2020 = Aleydis Van de Moortel, Sea Peoples from the Aegean: Identity,

Sociopolitical Context, and Antecedents. In *Nomads of the Mediterranean: Trade and Contact in the Bronze and Iron Ages. Studies in Honour of Michal Artzy*. Culture and History of the Ancient Near East, 112, ed. Ayelet Gilboa and Assaf Yasur-Landau, pp. 318-335. Leiden and Boston: Brill.

VAN DER TOORN 2018 = Karel van der Toorn, *Papyrus Amherst 63.* Alter Orient und Alter Testament 448. Münster: Ugarit-Verlag.

VAN DER TOORN 2019 = Karel van der Toorn, *Becoming Diaspora Jews: Behind the Story of Elephantine.* Yale: Yale University Press.

VAN GERVEN OEI and TSAKOS 2020 = Vincent W.J. van Gerven Oei and Aleksandros Tsakos: Translating Greek to Old Nubian: Reading Between the Lines of Ps.-Chrysostom's *In venerabilem crucem sermo.* In *Caught in Translation: Studies on Versions of Late-Antique Christian Literature.* Texts and Studies in Eastern Christianity, 17, ed. Madalina Toca and Dan Batovici, pp. 204-240. Leiden and Boston: Brill.

VAN REGENMORTEL 2020 = Charlotte Van Regenmortel, Greek Military Service in the Ancient Near East, 401-330 BCE. Review of *Greek Military Service in the Ancient Near East, 401–330*, by Jeffrey Rop. BMCR 2020.05.35

VANHOVE 2006 = Martine Vanhove, The Beja Language Today in Sudan: The State of the Art in Linguistics. In *Proceedings of the 7th International Sudan Studies Conference April 6-8, 2006, Bergen, Norway.* Bergen: University of Bergen. Accessible at https://halshs.archives-ouvertes.fr/halshs-00010091

VANHOVE 2014 = Martine Vanhove, Beja Grammatical Sketch. In *The CorpAfroAs Corpus of Spoken AfroAsiatic Languages,* ed. A. Mettouchi and C. Chanard. Accessible at: https://dx.doi.org/10.1075/scl.68.website

VANHOVE 2017 = Martine Vanhove, *Le Bedja.* Les langues du monde, IX. Leuven and Paris: Peeters.

VERCOUTTER 1956 = Jean Vercoutter, *L'Égypte et le monde égéen pré-hellénique, étude critique des sources Égyptiennes du début de la Dynastie égyptienne XVIIIe à la fin de la XIXe dynastie égyptienne.* Bibliothèque d'Études 22. Cairo: Institut français d'archéologie orientale.

VERGARI and VERGARI 2007 = Moreno Vergari and Roberta Vergari, A basic Saho-English-Italian Dictionary. Revised version of the original 2003 edition, available at https://www.academia.edu/758534/A_basic_Saho_English_Italian_dictionary

VERNUS 1984 = Pascal Vernus, Vestiges de langues chamito-sémitiques dans des sources égyptiennes méconnues. In *Current Progress in Afro-Asiatic Linguistics. Papers of the Third International Hamito-Semitic Congress, London 1978,* ed. James Bynon, pp. 477-479. Amsterdam and Philadelphia: John Benjamins Publishing.

VERNUS 1996 = Pascale Vernus, Langue littéraire et diglossie. In *Ancient Egyptian Literature. History & Forms.* Probleme der Ägyptologie 10, ed. Antonio Loprieno, pp. 555-564. Leiden: Brill.

VERNUS 2005 = Pascal Vernus, Réception linguistique et idéologique d'une nouvelle technologie: le cheval dans la civilisation pharaonique. In *The Knowledge Economy and Technological Capabilities: Egypt, the Near East and the Mediterranean, 2nd millennium B.C. –1st millennium A.D. Proceedings of a conference held at the Maison de la Chimie, Paris, France 9-10 December 2005*, ed. Myriam Wissa, pp. 1-46. Barcelona: Sabadell.

VILLING 2022 = Alexandra Villing, Mediterranean Encounters: Greeks, Carians, and Egyp tians in the First Millennium BC. In Egypt and the Classical World. Cross-Cultural Encounters in Antiquity, ed. Jeffrey Spier and Sara E. Cole, pp. 15-41 Los Angeles: J. Paul Getty Museum.

VITTMANN 1984 = Günter Vittmann, Ein Zauberspruch gegen Skorpione im Wadi Hammamat. In *Grammata Demotika: Festschrift für Erich Lüddeckens zum 15. Juni 1983,* ed. Heinz J. Thissen and Karl-Theodor Zauzich, pp. 245-256. Würzburg: Zauzich.

VITTMANN 1984 = Günter Vittmann, Semitisches Sprachgut im Demotischen. *Wiener Zeitschrift für die Kunde des Morgenlandes* 86, pp. 435-447.

VITTMANN 1997 = Günther Vittmann, Rev. James E. Hoch, *Semitic Words in Egyptian Texts of the New Kingdom and Third Intermediate Period.* Princeton, NJ: Princeton University Press. *Wiener Zeitschrift für die Kunde des Morgenlandes* 87, pp. 277-288

VITTMANN 2003 = Günter Vittmann, *Ägypten und die Fremden im ersten vorchristlichen Jahrtausend.* Mainz: Philipp von Zabern.

VITTMANN 2004 = Günter Vittmann, Iranisches Sprachgut in ägyptischer Überlieferung. In *Das Ägyptische und die Sprachen Vorderasiens, Nordafrikas und der Ägäis: Akten des Basler Kolloquiums zum ägyptisch-nichtsemitischen Sprachkontakt, Basel 9.–11. Juli 2003.* Alter Orient und Altes Testament 310, ed. Thomas Schneider, unter Mitarbeit von Francis Breyer, Oskar Kaelin, Carsten Knigge, pp. 129-182. Münster: Ugarit Verlag.

VITTMANN 2011 = Günter Vittmann, Rev. of Jan Krzysztof Winnicki: *Late Egypt and Her Neighbours: Foreign Population in Egypt in the First Millennium BC. 2009. The Bulletin of the American Society of Papyrologists* 48, pp. 297-304.

VITTMANN 2019 = Günter Vittmann, Ein frühdemotisches Schultäfelchen (Louvre E 9846). In *En détail – Philologie und Archäologie im Diskurs: Festschrift für Hans-Werner Fischer-Elfert*, Zeitschrift für ägyptische Sprache und Altertumskunde, Beiheft 7, ed. Marc Brose et al., pp. 1191-1210. Berlin and Boston: de Gruyter.

VON BREDOW 2017 = Iris von Bredow, *Kontaktzone Vorderer Orient und Ägypten: Orte, Situationen und Bedingungen für primäre griechisch-orientalische Kontakte vom 10. bis zum 6. Jahrhundert v. Chr.* Geographica Historica, 38. Stuttgart: Franz Steiner.

VON DASSOW 2004 = Eva von Dassow, Canaanite in Cuneiform. *Journal of the American Oriental Society* 124, pp. 641-674.

VON LIEVEN 2018 = Alexandra von Lieven, Some Observations on Multilingualism in Graeco-Roman Egypt. In *Studies in Multilingualism, Lingua Franca and Lingua Sacra*, ed. Jens Braarvig and Markham J. Geller, pp. 339-54. Berlin: Max-Planck-Gesellschaft zur Förderung der Wissenschaften.

VON SODEN 1989 = Wolfram von Soden, Dolmetscher und Dolmetschen im Alten Orient. In *Wolfram von Soden: Aus Sprache, Geschichte und Religion Babyloniens. Gesammelte Aufsätze*, ed. Luigi Cagni and Hans-Peter Müller, pp. 351-357. Neapel: Istituto universitario orientale, Dipartimento di studi asiatici.

VYCICHL 1934 = Werner Vycichl, Hausa und Ägyptisch. *Mitteilungen des Seminars für Orientalische Sprachen* 3, pp. 36–116.

VYCICHL 1960 = Werner Vycichl, The Beja Language, Tū Beḍawīye: Its Relationship with Old Egyptian. *Kush* 8, pp. 252-264.

VYCICHL 1961 = Werner Vycichl, Diminutiv und Augmentativ im Berberischen. *Zeitschrift der Deutschen Morgenländischen Gesellschaft* 111, pp. 243-253.

VYCICHL 1983 = Werner Vycichl, *Dictionnaire étymologique de la langue copte*. Leuven: Peeters.

VYCICHL 2005 = Werner Vycichl, *Berberstudien & A Sketch of Siwi Berber (Egypt)*, ed. Dymitr Ibriszimow and Maarten Kossmann. Berber Studies Volume 10. Köln: Rüdiger Köppe.

WAGNER 2008 = Volker Wagner, Die סרנים der Philister und die Ältesten Israels. *Zeitschrift für biblische und altorientalische Rechtsgeschichte* 14, pp. 408-433.

WALSH 2018 = Carl Walsh, Kerma Ceramics, Commensality Practices, and Sensory Experiences in Egypt during the Late Middle Bronze Age. *Journal of Ancient Egyptian Interconnections* 20, pp. 31–51.

WALTERS 2016 = Josiah K. Walters, *A Grammar of Dazaga*. Grammars and Sketches of the World's Languages –Africa. Leiden and Boston: Brill.

WARD 1996 = William A. Ward, A New Look at Semitic Personal Names and Loanwords in Egyptian. *Chronique d'Égypte* 71(141), pp. 17-47.

WATSON 2010 = Wilfred G.E. Watson, Non-Semitic Words in the Ugaritic Lexicon (8). *Ugarit Forschungen* 42, pp. 831-857.

WEBER and HORNER 2012 = Jean-Jacques Weber and Kristine Horner, *Introducing Multilingualism: A Social Approach*. Abingdon, Oxon: Routledge.

WEBER and WESCHENFELDER 2005 = Kerstin Weber and Petra Weschenfelder, 'Orakelpriester' oder 'patrolmen'? Eine altnubische Entlehnung im Text der Nastasen-Stele, *Lingua Aegyptia* 13, pp. 173-79.

WEDEKIND 2010 = Klaus Wedekind, More on the Ostracon of Browne's "Textus Blemmyicus. In *Current Trends in Eritrean Studies. Giornata internazionale di studi sull'Eritrea, May* 2010, ed. Gianfrancesco Lusini. Annali 70, pp. 73-82.

WENINGER 2011 = Stefan Weninger, Ethio-Semitic in general. In *Semitic Languages: An International Handbook*, ed. Stefan Weninger, pp. 1114-1123. Berlin and Boston: de Gruyter.

WENKE, REDDING and CAGLE 2016 = R.J. Wenke, R.W. Redding and A.J. Cagle (eds.), *Kom el-Hisn (ca. 2500–1900 BC): An Ancient Egyptian Settlement in the Nile Delta*. Atlanta: Lockwood Press.

WESTENHOLZ and STOLPER 2002 = Joan G. Westenholz and Matthew W. Stolper, A Stone Jar with Inscriptions of Darius I in Four languages. *Achaemenid Research on Texts and Archaeology* 2002.005.

WILDE and BEHNERT 2002 = Heike Wilder and Klaus Behnert, Salzherstellung im vor- und frühdynastischen Ägypten? Überlegungen zur Funktion der sogenannten Grubenkopfnägel in Buto. *Mitteilungen des Deutschen Archäologischen Instituts Kairo* 58, pp. 49-51.

WILKINSON 1999 = Toby A.H. Wilkinson, *Early Dynastic Egypt.* London and New York: Routledge.

WIMMER 2010 = Stefan Wimmer, Die Ächtungstexte der 12./13. Dynastie (19./18. Jahrhundert). In *Historisches Textbuch zum Alten Testament,* ed. Manfred Weippert, pp. 33-50. Göttingen: Vandenhoeck & Ruprecht.

WINAND 2017 = Jean Winand, Identifying Semitic Loanwords in Late Egyptian. In *Greek Influence on Egyptian-Coptic: Contact-Induced Change in an Ancient African language,* Lingua Aegyptia – Studia Monographica 17, ed. Eitan Grossman et al., pp. 481-511. Hamburg: Widmaier Verlag.

WINNICKI 2009 = Jan Krzysztof Winnicki, *Late Egypt and Her Neighbours: Foreign Population in Egypt in the First Millennium BC.* The Journal of Juristic Papyrology, Supplement 12. Warsaw: Warsaw University Faculty of Law and Administration.

WOLFF 1998 = H. Ekkehard Wolff, Cushitic languages. *Encyclopedia Britannica,* https://www.britannica.com/topic/Cushitic-languages

WOLZE 2019 = Naoko Wolze, Rekonstruktion der Inschriften auf der Kanalstele Darius' I. aus Tell el-Maskhuta. In *En détail – Philologie und Archäologie im Diskurs: Festschrift für Hans-Werner Fischer-Elfert,* Zeitschrift für ägyptische Sprache und Altertumskunde, Beiheft 7, ed. Marc Brose et al., pp. 1275-1319.

WOODCOCK 2014 = Taylor Bryanne Woodcock, *Noticing Neighbors: Reconsidering Ancient Egyptian Perceptions of Ethnicity.* MA thesis: American University of Cairo. (accessible at http://dar.aucegypt.edu/handle/10526/3954)

WÜTHRICH 2009 = Annik Wüthrich, Abracadabras méroïtiques dans le Livre des Morts? In *Ausgestattet mit den Schriften des Thot: Festschrift für Irmtraut Munro zu ihrem 65. Geburtstag. Studien zum altägyptischen Totenbuch* 14, ed. Burkhard Backes, Marcus Müller-Roth, and Simone Stöhr, pp. 267-282. Wiesbaden: Harrassowitz.

WÜTHRICH 2010 = Annik Wüthrich, *Eléments de théologie thébaine: Les chapitres supplémentaires du Livre des Morts.* Wiesbaden: Harrassowitz.

WÜTHRICH 2015 = Annik Wüthrich, *Édition synoptique et traduction des chapitres supplementaires du Livre des Morts 162 à 167*, vol. 1. Wiesbaden: Harrassowitz.

YAKUBOVICH 2012 = Ilya Yakubovich, Rev. of Ignacio Adiego: *The Carian language,* Brill 2006. *Journal of Near Eastern Studies* 71(1), pp. 131-133.

YASUR-LANDAU 2001 = Assaf Yasur-Landau, The Mother(s) of All Philistines: Aegean Enthroned Deities of the 12th–11th Century Philistia. In *Potnia: Deities and Religion in the Aegean Bronze Age.* Aegaeum 22, ed. Robert Laffineur and Robin Hägg, pp. 329-43. Liège.

YASUR-LANDAU 2010 = Assaf Yasur-Landau, *The Philistines and Aegean Migration at the End of the Late Bronze Age*. Cambridge: Cambrige University Press.

YOYOTTE 1958 = Jean Yoyotte, Un étrange titre d'époque libyenne. *Bulletin de l'Institut français d'archéologie orientale* 58, pp. 97-100.

YOYOTTE 1961 = Jean Yoyotte, *Les Principautés du Delta au temps de l'anarchie libyenne*. Recherches d'archéologie, de philologie et d'histoire 34. Cairo: Institut français d'archéologie orientale.

ZARATE, LÉVY and KRAMSCH 2011 = Geneviève Zarate, Danielle Lévy, and Claire Kramsch (eds.), *Handbook of Multilingualism and Multiculturalism*. Paris: Éditions des archives contemporaines.

ZEIDLER 2004 = Jürgen Zeidler, Ägyptisch – Hethitisch – Indogermanisch: Methodische und komparative Ansätze. In *Das Ägyptische und die Sprachen Vorderasiens, Nordafrikas und der Ägäis: Akten des Basler Kolloquiums zum ägyptisch-nichtsemitischen Sprachkontakt, Basel 9.–11. Juli 2003*. Alter Orient und Altes Testament 310, ed. Thomas Schneider, unter Mitarbeit von Francis Breyer, Oskar Kaelin, Carsten Knigge, pp. 271-300. Münster: Ugarit Verlag.

ZENNER and KRISTIANSEN 2013 = Eline Zenner and Gitte Kristiansen (ed.), *New Perspectives on Lexical Borrowing: Onomasiological, Methodological and Phraseological Innovations*. Language Contact and Bilingualism, 7. Boston: de Gruyter Mouton.

ZERNECKE 2013 = Anna Elise Zernecke, The Lady of the Titles: The Lady of Byblos and the Search for her "True Name". *Die Welt des Orients* 43(2), pp. 226-242.

ZIBELIUS 1972 = Karola Zibelius, *Afrikanische Orts- und Völkernamen in hieroglyphischen und hieratischen Texten*. Beihefte zum Tübinger Atlas des Vorderen Orients. Reihe B: Geisteswissenschaften, 1. Wiesbaden: Dr. Ludwig Reichert.

ZIBELIUS-CHEN 2005 = Karola Zibelius-Chen, Die nicht ägyptischsprachigen Lexeme und Syntagmen in den chapitres supplémentaires und Sprüchen ohne Parallelen des Totenbuches. *Lingua Aegyptia* 13, pp. 181-224.

ZIBELIUS-CHEN 2007 = Karola Zibelius-Chen, Die Medja in altägyptischen Quellen. *Studien zur altägyptischen Kultur* 36, pp. 391-405.

ZIBELIUS-CHEN 2011 = Karola Zibelius-Chen, *"Nubisches" Sprachmaterial in hieroglyphischen und hieratischen Texten: Personennamen, Appellativa, Phrasen vom Neuen Reich bis in die napatanische und meroitische Zeit. Mit einem demotischen Anhang*. Wiesbaden: Harrassowitz.

ZINN 1998 = Katharina Zinn, *Zum Umgang mit fremden Sprachen im Alten Ägypten: Fremdsprachigkeit als soziales und kulturelles Phänomen*. Master's thesis: Universität Leipzig.

Online Databases in Development

Harel, Haleli	*Classifying the other: The classification of Semitic loanwords in the Egyptian script*: https://www.archaeomind.net/
Kilani, Marwan	*HathorBank* database of loanwords: https://hathorbank.herokuapp.com/HathorBank/

9. Index of Words and Phrases from Individual Languages

Abbreviations: DN = Divine name; E = ethnonym; PN = personal name; T = toponym

9.1 Afroasiatic languages

9.1.1 Words, names and phrases attested in ancient Egyptian sources

9.1.1.1 Words, names and phrases in regular Egyptian orthography

The entries are ordered according to the Egyptian alphabet.

ꜣꜥꜥw, ỉꜣꜥ.w	foreign speakers/troops	66, 124-5, 134, 142-3
ꜣbw, later iꜣbw	elephant; Elephantine	41
ꜣš	DN	65 n.7
ꜣčw mšꜥ	troop commander (PN)	148
ỉw	island	87, 105, 127
ỉw	come; go	114
ỉwntỉ.w nw tꜣ stỉ	E	21
ỉw=tw ḥr rṭỉ.t n=s tꜣy=s ỉsb.t	one brought her her throne	103, 131
ỉw=s ḥr ḥms	and she sat down	
ỉp.t	Oipe unit	104
ỉmỉ.w-čḥnw	E	67-8, 81
ỉrp	wine	39, 120
ỉrč.t	milk	114
ỉqr	capable, proficient	125, 144
ỉtỉ	barley	120
ỉtr.w	river, the Nile	104
ꜥꜣ	door (leaf)	115
ꜥꜣ	great	87, 127
ꜥꜣpp	Apophis	40
ꜥꜣm	Asiatic	74-5, 151
ꜥꜣm.w ḥrỉ.w šꜥỉ	Asiatics who are on the sand	11, 74
ꜥꜣg	hit, beat	47
ꜥn	T	9
ꜥrq-wr (Ptolemaic)	the great bent one	119
ꜥḥꜣwtỉ ꜥꜣ	great fighter (PN)	148

ʿḥꜣwtỉ nfr	perfect fighter	103, 131
ʿẖm	falcon	44
ʿš	(type of conifer or conifer wood)	125-6
ʿṭ (Ptolemaic)	reed, rush pen	104
ʿč̣t	boy, young man (PN)	148
wꜣwꜣ.t	T	48
wʿꜣ	to slander, defame	47
wʿš	T	9
wnš	wolf	66
wrry.t	chariot	80, 86
wḥꜣ.t	oasis	61, 120
wč̣ꜣ śnb	DN, "the intact and healthy one"	102, 131-2
bꜣk	servant; to work	110, 124, 142
bny(.t)	date (palm)	56
br	mullet	120
br	cargo boat	116
Pꜣ ʿꜣ n nn-nsw	The great one of Heracleopolis (PN)	148
Pꜣ ʿꜣm	the Asiatic (PN)	136
Pꜣ wʿr	the fugitive (PN)	148
pꜣ wḥm	the interpreter, dragoman	107
Pꜣ nḥśỉ	the Nubian (PN)	148
pꜣ nṯr ṭwꜣ	DN, "the god (of) Dawn"	102, 131
pꜣ sẖ	the striking	105
pꜣ śgnn	(type of Egyptian ointment)	120
pꜣʿ.t	quail	115
pr	house	110
pr-nṯr n Šrdn	T	148
fꜣỉ	carry	115
fnč̣	nose	47
m wnw.t bỉn.t	in the worst moment	103
mꜣgśw / bꜣgśw	dagger	66 n.9
mỉty	copy (= translation ?)	102
mn	stay, remain	115

mnꜥ.t	wet nurse	115
Mntw-ḥr-ḫpš	Montu is striking power (PN)	148
mr iꜥꜣw	commander of Egyptianized Nubians/Nubian interpreters	134, 142-3
mś	child	58
mśṭm.t	kohl, black make-up	120
mṭw	word, speech	121
mč̣ꜣ	T	21
mč̣ꜣy.w	E	18, 21, 42-3
n.t rꜥ	water expanse of Re	40
nꜣ mꜣꜥ.tyw	(religious title)	105
nꜣy=f ỉry.w	his colleagues	108, 132
nw	T	9
nb.t kbn	Lady of Byblos	131
nḥśỉ(.w)	E	11, 18-20, 22, 36, 50, 133, 142, 144-5
nḥśỉ.w ỉwn.tỉw n.w tꜣ-stỉ	E	33
nḥśỉ.w ḥtp.w	pacified Nubians	20, 145 n.16
nḫt ꜥꜣ	the great strongman (PN)	148
nḫt km.t	the strong one of Egypt (PN)	148
nḫt.w	fortresses	135, 146
nsw	king	40, 73
nčrỉ > ntrỉ	natron	104, 120
ry.t	ink	80, 126
hbỉ	ibis	120
hbny	ebony	121
hn.w	*hin* unit	101
ḥꜣ.t	front	115
ḥꜣtỉ	heart	115
ḥꜣtỉ-ꜥ	mayor (of Byblos)	79
ḥꜣtỉ(.w)-ꜥ n čḥnw	chieftain(s) of the Tjehenu	9, 62
ḥwn	young (person)	115
ḥtr > ḥtỉ	span of horses > horse	43
ḫꜣś.t čmḥ.w	country of the Libyans	152
ḫꜣśtỉ.w	foreigners	56
ḫnt	face, forehead, front	115

ḫtm	seal	82
(ẖr.ỉ-ḥb.t)-ḥr.ỉ-tp	chief (lector priest)	105
swn	to know	59
ssm.t	horse	75
stỉ / tꜣ stỉ	ochre; Nubia(n land)	14, 22
sty.w	E	21
śbꜣq-tꜣwỉ	royal name, “the one who brightens the two lands”	33, 132
sšn, later ššn	lotus	104
śčꜣ	weave, spin	47
śṭm	kohl, black make-up	120
šny-bny(.t)	palm fiber	56
šnč̣.wt > šnṭ.wt	kilt	121
šnč̣.t, šnṭ.t	acacia	104
šś	linen	104
qwqw	fruit of dōm-palm	120
qmy.t	resin, gum	121
Qny	the brave one (PN)	148
Qnỉ ḥr ḫps=f	brave through his strength (PN)	148
qnỉ sʿnḫ	the brave one enlivens	148
kꜣkꜣ / kỉkỉ	castor, ricin ?	120
kftỉw	Cretans	117
km	Black	62
km.t	Egypt	22
kḥśy (and kḥśś ?)	chair, sedan	80
gr, gr n p.t	(kind of bird); *gr* of the sky	121
gś.tỉ	scribal palette	104
tꜣ	land, earth	115
tꜣ my.t nṯr	the way of god	105
čmḥw	E	11-2, 67
čḥnw	T	8-10, 67
čḥnw.iw	E	11
č̣ꜣy	ship	104
č̣bꜣ	to clog, bar	47
č̣bꜣ.t > tb.t	chest, shrine	104

č̣bʿ.t > ṭabbaʿat	seal, signet ring	82
č̣ḥw.tỉ > ṭḥw.tỉ	lead, tin	40-1

9.1.1.2 Loanwords, names and phrases in Egyptian transcription

The entries listed here represent different historical stages of Egyptian transcriptions of foreign terms. They are ordered according to the Egyptian alphabet, including ꜣ which no longer represented a consonant value in the transcription systems of the New Kingdom and later. Special groups using monosyllabic Egyptian words such as  are treated like a consonant (ʿ) and thus listed after sequences like . Compound expressions are listed according to their first element.

ꜣ-ꜣ-t-ꜣ	PN	36
ꜣwšq	T	42
ꜣb-ꜣ-q-r	(name of a dog)	61
ꜣbỉkrm	penalty	107
ỉ-ꜣ-y-r	stag	91
ỉ-ꜣ-r $^{\text{ANIMAL.PLURAL}}$	lion (?)	88
ỉwn-n:-m-k-t	confederation	59
ỉwn-rw-nꜣ	oak tree	91
ỉw-čꜣ	which (interr. part.)	87, 91
ỉ-b	T	44
ỉ-bꜣ-r	stallion	91
ỉ/y-bꜣ-š-tỉ/tw	biscuit	91
ỉ-bꜣ-t' ^{SPEAK}	you have led (?)	88
ỉ-pꜣ-tỉ	cakes, biscuits	91
ỉmꜣ	T (Yam)	11, 48
ỉmꜣ-wtn.t; ỉmꜣ-nʿś	T	48
ỉrʿꜣ	(transcription of sumergram)	79
ỉ-r-rw-č̣ꜣ-w	vessel or cup at a banquet	119
ỉ-r-q-ꜣ-bꜣ-sꜣ	(a precious stone)	91
ỉ-h-ꜣ-r	tent	91
ỉ-h-t-k	PN	44, 126, 144
ỉ-ś-b-t	chair, throne	91
ỉ-ś-p(ꜣ)-t(ỉ), earlier *ỉśb.t*	quiver	80, 91, 126
ỉ-ś-kꜣ-ỉ	PN	65

ỉ-ś-t-n-nw	belt, strap	59
ỉ-q-ꜣ-wꜣ-šꜣ	E	122
ỉ-čꜣ-r	captive	91
y-w-bꜣ-r	stream	91
Y-b-ỉ	PN	64
y-m	sea	91
Y-k-ꜣ-r-ỉ	PN	65
y-ṭ-ỉ-ʿ	skilled, learned	91
ʿꜣ-g-ꜣ-r-tỉ	wagon	86, 92
ʿ-w-r-č̣ꜣ-w-t	the terrifying ones	92
ʿ-w-č̣ꜣ-r	saviour	90
ʿ-p-r	ʿApiru/Habiru (social t.t.)	91
ʿ-p-šꜣ-y-t	beetle, scarab	91
ʿ-mꜣ-n-ỉ	pond	55
ʿ-m-q	to penetrate (sexually)	91
ʿ-m-ṭ-ỉ	to stand firm	91
ʿ-m(ꜣ)-ṭ-ỉ(-y)	supports (part of the chariot)	91, 98
ʿ-r-šꜣ-n-ꜣ	lentils	91
ʿ-r-tỉ	upper chamber	92
ʿ-š(ꜣ)-q/g(ꜣ)	to extort, defraud; oppress	92
ʿ-ṭ-w-tỉ	(conspiratorial) assemblies	92
wꜣwꜣ.t	T	49
wꜣ-rw-bꜣ-gꜣ	DN	34
wꜣ-šꜣ-šꜣ	E	123
w-ỉ-t	PN	39
wntt	PN	39
wr-n-s	T	40
W–ś–ꜣ	PN	66
wsỉpwtr	king's son	107
Wsỉrhrt	PN	60
Wsỉrkn	PN	56, 66
b-ꜣ-wn-t-nw-y-ꜣ-wn-t-nw-y	(sequence in language of Punt)	50
b(ꜣ)-r-q/g-ꜣ	to sparkle	92
bꜣ-r-kꜣ	to kneel, bow, bless; greetings; gifts	92

bꜣ-r-k-ꜣ-tỉ	pool, pond	55, 92
bꜣ-r-g-ꜣ	be happy, content	92
bꜣ-r-tỉ	obligatory service, treaty	92
bꜣ-gꜣ-ỉ-w	wild animal, jackal?	58
bꜣ-č̣ꜣ-r/n-ꜣ	staff, stick, cudgel	117
b-ʿ-r	sea, lake	92
b-ʿ-r	divine name ‘Baʿal’	92
Bʿl-nʿm	PN, “Baʿal is pleasant”	148
pꜣ ḫꜣ-rw	the Syrian, also as PN	97, 128, 148
pꜣ qꜣrw-ỉ-w	the vagabond, foreigner (PN)	148
P-ꜣ-n-ỉ, p-ꜣ-n-y	PNs	65
Pꜣ-r-h-w	PN	49-50
Pꜣ-q-ꜣ-hꜣ	PN	148
P(ʿnḫ)y	PN	33
P(ʿnḫ)y-hꜣ-rw	PN	44
p-w-r(-i-ꜣ/y)	beans	92
p-w-r-śꜣ-tỉ	E	123
pw-tꜣ-rw	cattle?	97
p-r-ḫ	blossom	92
prs-nw.t	Pārsa-(the-)city (Persepolis)	108, 121, 132
p-h-t-s	(name of a dog)	61
p-ṭ-ỉ-r	woven container	96
mꜣ-i-w-r-tỉ	honey	96
Mꜣ-n-y-n-ỉ	PN	64
mỉʿm	T	49
mw-ʿṭ	assembly	92
m-w-r-ḥ-m-ꜣ	salt workers	92
mn-nw	mina (weight unit)	92
mn-ḥ-tỉ	gift, tribute	92
mn-ṭ-ꜣ-tỉ	tribute, tax	92
mr	proximity	39
m-r-y-n-ꜣ	charioteer, knight	95
m-r-ḥ	spear, lance	92
m-rw-rw	kind of pastry	119
mr-św	new wine, must	92
m-r-k-ꜣ-b-w-tỉ	chariot	86, 92

mrt	chin; beard	55
m-h-ꜣ-r	skilled, expert	88, 93
M-h-r-y-t	PN	148
m-ś	(title)	57
m-śꜣ-ḫ-i̓	large vessel (for wine, oil)	92
M-ś-r-q-s	PN	65
M-ś-qṯ-nw	PN	65
m-š	element of Libyan PNs	65
m-š-ꜣb-w	watering place	92
m-š-m-g-ś	PN	65
m(ꜣ)-q-ꜣ-r/n.t	staff, stick, rod	93
ms	Libyan title	57
M-s-h-r-t	PN	60
mk	Libyan title	58
m-k-i̓-rw-i̓-w-i̓	merchant	93
m-k-m-rw-ti̓	fishnets	93
Mkḥn.t	PN	43
m(i̓)-k-ti̓-r	tower	93
m-g-ꜣ	(term for soldiers)	18
m-g-ꜣ-r-ti̓	cave	93
*mś-w-q *read* mśw.t	(misread word)	45
M-t-ꜣ-y-b	PN	64
mtwhr	Libyan title	58
mṯi̓	E: Mede; soldier	107
M-ṯi̓-ṯi̓	PN	60
m-č̣ꜣ-r-n-ꜣ	(a type of weapon)	93
n-ꜣ-ʿ-rw-n-ꜣ	soldiers	91
n-ʿ-m-w	pleasant	93
n-p-t	T	35
n-ḫ-r	wadi, seasonal river	93
n-k-pꜣ-ti̓	the nikiptu plant/oil	93, 96
r-bꜣ-šꜣ-y	cuirass, leather armour	93
r-bꜣ-k-ꜣ-y	(a type of pastry)	93
r-b-w-y	lioness	93
r-h-ṯ-t	trough, vessel	93
r-ḥꜣ-b-w	amphora, basin	93

rw-šꜣ-ỉ-w	peak, summit	93
rw-kꜣ	T	123
r-k-ś-w	outfit, equipment, gear	93
H-ꜣ-ỉ -t-b-ỉ	PN	148
h-ꜣ-r-f-ỉ	the healing	93
h-ꜣ-r-n-ꜣ-tỉ	risen, fermented (dough)	96
h-(ꜣ)-ṭ-m(-)w	footstool	93
h-r	mountain	93
ḥꜣ-m-r	ass, donkey	93
Ḥꜣ-tỉ-bꜣ	PN	114
ḥ-f-č̣ꜣ	to hurry	93
ḥ-m-č̣ꜣ	vinegar, sour wine	93
ḥ(-)n-y-t	spear, javelin	93
ḥ-r-p-w	dagger, short sword	93
Ḥč̣-wꜣ-w-š-ỉ	PN	62, 66
ḫꜣ-pw	a body of water, river?	96
ḫꜣ-rw	T	97, 128
ḫꜣ-rw	street, quarter	97
ḫꜣ-r-w-y	PN	148
ḫꜣ-r-b-w	desert	93
ḫꜣ-rw-p-w-sꜣ-t	(a kind of pastry)	96
ḫꜣ-rw-rw	onyx, agate ?	97
ḫ-ỉ-m-čꜣ	violence, terror?	58-9
ḫ-ỉ-čꜣ-n-ꜣ	garlic	94
ḫʿ-tꜣ.w	DN	75
ḫ-bꜣ-ỉ-r	business, trade	96
ḫntw-ỉ-ʿ-w-š	foreign title	80
ḫt-r-ḫt	a part of the chariot	85, 95
*śꜣt *read* šśꜣt	(misread word)	45
śꜣ-ỉ-ꜣ	water course	97
śꜣ-r-q-w	snow	94
śꜣ-qꜣ-r	(sequence in foreign spell)	45
ś-ʿ-r(w)/ś-ʿ-r-tỉ	barley/scrubs; hair/wool	93
s-n-n-ỉ	charioteer	94
srḫs	priestly title	28
ś-g-ꜣ-r	gate	94

ś-tm-n	PN or title	77
šꜣ-ʿ-r	measure, estimate	94
Šꜣ-bꜣ-kꜣ	PN	33, 132
Šꜣ-bꜣ-tꜣ-kꜣ	PN	33
šꜣ-b(-w)-ṭ-t/ṭi͗/ti͗	staff, rod	94
šꜣ-n-b-i͗	trumpet	117
šꜣ-r-m(ꜣ)	to greet, surrender; peace	94
šꜣ-r-m(ꜣ)-ti͗	gift	92
šꜣ-r-ṭ-i͗-n-ꜣ	E	123, 127-30
šꜣ-ḥ-qꜣ	cloud of dust or flour	94
Šꜣ-šꜣ-n-q	PN	57
šꜣ-q-ꜣ	cupbearer (?)	103
šꜣ-kꜣ-n-ꜣ	watering place	97
šꜣ-k-rw-šꜣ	E	123
šꜣ-ṭ-ꜣ	violence, destruction	94
q-ꜣ-rw(-i͗-ꜣ/ i͗/w)	to be an alien; alien	94
q-ꜣ-r-m- ti͗	ashes	124
q-ꜣ-r-n-ꜣ-ti͗	foreskin; uncircumcised phallus	94
q-ꜣ-r-č̣-ꜣ/i͗-n-ꜣ	(pick-)axe	94
q-ꜣ-ṭ-ꜣ-rw-ti͗	incense	94
q-ꜣ-č̣-ꜣ(i͗-w/i͗)	gypsum	94
qppš	(title)	107
q-r	king	35
q-r-(i͗-)ʿ-w	shield-bearer	94
q-r-ʿ-w	shield	92
Q-r-m	PN	63
Q-s-kꜣ-n-t	PN	42-3, 49
k-ꜣ-wꜣ-rw	king	35
K-ꜣ-b	PN	63
k-ꜣ-bꜣ-r-ti͗	sulphur, brimstone	94
kꜣ-b-w-śꜣ/św	basket	94
k(ꜣ)-p-w	palm (of the hand)	94
Kꜣ-pw-r	PN	60
k-ꜣ-m	like, as	88, 94
kꜣ/k-ꜣ-m-rw	the ardent, agitated one	94

	(term for type of dancer)	
kꜣ-r-ỉꜣ šri	Kalasiris	39
kꜣ-r-sꜣ	sack	97
k(-)ꜣ-r-čꜣ	whip cords	94
k-ꜣ-r-čꜣ-r	stone pile	94
kꜣs / kꜣś / kꜣš; kwš	T	36, 67 n. 9
K-ꜣ-śꜣ-n-ꜣ-t	PN	64
Kꜣ-š-tꜣ	PN	33
kꜣ-č̣-n, kꜣ- čꜣ-n-ꜣ	charioteer	87, 88, 97, 128
K-w-y	PN	42
kpč̣	volume unit	107
k-n-ỉ-n-ỉ-w-rw	lyre	94
gꜣ- wꜣ- nꜣ	object left by troops (leather bucket?)	59
g-ꜣ-r-b/p-w	to shave, plane (wood)	95
g(ꜣ)/k(ꜣ)-r/nꜣ-(ỉ)-tỉ	kidney	94
Tꜣ-n-wꜣ-tỉ-ỉmn	PN	33
tꜣ-ẖ-b(w)-s/śꜣ-tỉ	large basket	96, 127-8
tỉ-r-f-ỉ	(sequence in foreign spell)	45
tỉ-r-tỉ	door	95
tỉ-ẖ-r	leather panels of the chariot	95
tỉ-ś-b-w RETURN.GOD	DN	103
t-w-r-ỉ-šꜣ	E	123
t-l (written t-n-r)	valiant, strong	87, 97
tly	the valiant one	148
t-l (written t-r; tỉ-n-r)	mound	94
t-q-rw	(name of a dog)	61
T-k-l-t	PN	57
t-g-r	ring	28, 38
T’-t-ꜣ-t	PN	65
ṭnhr (Ptolemaic)	elephant	46
ṭng (ṭꜣg / ṭꜣng, ṭ-n-r-g-ꜣ)	dwarf, pygmy	45
čꜣ-p-w-r	drinking bowl	95
Čꜣ-r-b-w	PN	148
čꜣ-k-r	E	123
č-w-pꜣ-r	scribe	95

č(-w)-p-r(-t)	chariot (with copper plating)	85, 95
čw/čꜣ-rw/r-tỉ	fine wheat flour	95
ṭ-ꜣ-ỉ-n-ỉ-w	E	123
Ṭ-ỉ-ṭ-ỉ	PN	148
ṭ-bꜣ-r	holy of holies	95
ṭ-p-ḥ-w	apple	95
č̣ꜣ-ʿ-w-q	to cry out	95
č̣ꜣ-bꜣ-ỉw	army, troops	95
č̣ꜣ-m-ʿ	to be thirsty	95
č̣ꜣ-r-ʿ(-t-)w	plank, board	95
Č̣Ṭ(= /zi/)-t-w	olive, olive tree, olive oil	95
č̣-ỉ-č̣-ỉ	flower, flower ornament	95

9.1.1.3 Words and phrases attested in Napatan Egyptian

nsw n pꜣ 4 qʿḥ	king of the 4 corners	31, 132
srḫs	(priestly title)	28
tgr	ring	28, 38

9.1.1.4 Words and names attested in Demotic

ʿngn	vessel	119
ʿt, ʿṭ	rush, reed pen	104
yb	T (Elephantine)	41
yr, yʿr	river, the Nile	104
wrṯ̭	rose	107
wsṯ̭br	chamberlain	108
brk.t	pond	55
pꜣ sgn	(type of Egyptian ointment)	120
mrṯ̭	beard	55
mstmy	kohl, black make-up	120
mtgṯ̭(.t)	army	106
nꜣy=f iry.w	his colleagues	107, 132
smty, stm	black eye-paint	120
krm, krb	ashes	124
kk	fruit of dōm palm	120
gʿwmʿ	fever	119

glšr	soldier, warrior	38-9
tnhr	elephant	46
ṭḥṭḥ	lead, tin	41
č̣y	ship	104

9.1.1.5 Words and names attested in Coptic

The superscript letters S, B, F indicate the Coptic dialects (Saidic, Bohairic, Fayyumic).

^{S}ⲁϩⲱⲙ , ^{B}ⲁϧⲱⲙ	falcon	44
^{S}ⲁϭⲟⲗⲧⲉ, ^{B}ⲁϫⲟⲗϯ	wagon	86, 92
^{S}ⲃⲛ̄ⲛⲉ	date palm	56
^{S}ⲃⲱⲣⲉ	mullet	120
ⲉⲃⲓⲏⲛ	miserable, poor	105
ⲏⲣⲡ	wine	39, 120
ⲓⲏⲃ	Elephantine	41
ⲕⲉⲗⲱⲗ	vessel	105
ⲕⲟⲙ(ⲙ)ⲉ, ⲕⲟⲙ(ⲙ)ⲓ)	resin, gum	121
^{S}ⲕⲣⲙⲉⲥ, ^{B}ⲕⲉⲣⲙⲓ	ash, soot, dust	124
ⲕⲟⲩⲕ	fruit of dōm palm	120
ⲗⲁⲕⲙ(ⲉ)	crumb	80
ⲗϩⲱⲃ	steam, vapour	105
ⲙⲁⲛϭⲁⲗⲉ	hoe	105
ⲙⲁⲥⲅⲝ	E	54
ⲙⲁⲧⲉϭⲧⲉ	army	106
^{SB}ⲙⲟⲣⲧ, ^{F}ⲙⲁⲗⲧ	beard	55
ⲡⲥⲟϭⲛ	(type of Egyptian ointment)	120
ⲥⲟⲟⲩⲛ	to know	59
ⲥⲧⲏⲙ	kohl, black make-up	120
^{S}ⲧⲁϩⲧ, ^{F}ⲧⲉϩⲧ, ^{S}ⲧⲁⲑ, ^{B}ⲧⲁⲧϩ	lead, tin	41
^{S}ⲟⲩⲁϩⲉ	oasis	120
ϣⲛ̄ⲃⲛ̄ⲛⲉ	palm fibre	56
^{S}ϣⲛⲧⲱ, ^{B}ϣⲉⲛⲧⲱ	sheet, robe of linen	121
ϩⲙⲟⲧ	grace, gift	105
ϩⲓⲣ	street, quarter	97
^{S}ϩⲧⲟ	horse	43

ϭⲗⲏⲃ	muzzle (device]	105
ϭⲁⲗⲁϣⲓⲣⲉ	strong man, giant	38-9
ϭⲗⲟⲟϭⲉ, ⲧⲗⲟⲟϭⲉ (etc.)	ladder	80
ϭⲁⲙⲟⲩⲗ	camel	105
^{S}ϭⲣⲟⲙⲡⲉ, ^{B}ϭⲣⲟⲙⲡⲓ	dove	121

9.1.2 Semitic languages

9.1.2.1 Words and roots attested across different Semitic languages

This section lists Semitic words and roots adduced throughout this book that are attested across two or more different branches of the Semitic languages. Individual languages are indicated in parentheses (H. = Hebrew, Ug. = Ugaritic, etc.; Sem. = other Semitic languages). The ordering follows the sequence of the Hebrew alphabet. Phonemes merged in Hebrew are listed after the Hebrew letter in which they coalesced (ḏ after z; ḫ after ḥ; ġ after ʿ; ḍ, ḏ̣ and ṭ after ṣ; ṯ after š).

ảlgbṯ (Ug.), ʾảlgaḇīš (H.)	(a precious stone)	91
ʾasīr	captive	91
ʾap̄īt	cakes, biscuits	91
ʾašpā (H.), ảṯbāt (Ug.), išpatu (Akk.)	quiver	80, 91, 126
baḥr (Arab., S.Arab., Eth.)	sea, lake	92
blg (H., Arab.)	be happy, content	92
brk	to kneel, bow, bless	92, 115
birkat	pool, pond	55, 92
brq	to sparkle	92
glb (NWSem., Akk.)	to shave, plane (wood)	94
gaṣṣu (Akk.), gēṣ (H., Aram.)	gypsum	94
dælæt (H.), daltu (Akk.)	door	95, 115
zēt	olive, olive tree, olive oil	95
ḥṭb	to cut/collect wood	118
ḥāṭiba, PN ḥṭbt	wood collector	
ḥumḏ̣	vinegar, sour wine	93
ḥimār	ass, donkey	93
ḥarb	dagger, short sword	93
yabbīšat	biscuit	91

yām (H.), yamm (Sem.)	sea	91, 102-3
kibrītu (Akk.), kebrītā (Aram.) kibrit (Arab.)	sulphur, brimstone	94
kamā	like, as	94
kinnōr (H., Sem.)	lyre	94
kapp	palm (of the hand)	94
lāḇiʾ, ləḇiyyāʾ (H., also Sem.)	lioness	93
mahīr	skilled, expert	88, 93
mākiru (Akk., Ug., H.)	merchant	93
mōləḥim (H., root Sem.)	salt workers	92
manû (Akk.), mānæ (H., Aram.)	mina (weight unit)	92
mandat (Aram., Akk.)	tribute, tax	92
manḥat	gift, tribute	92
mōʿēd	assembly	92
maġārat	cave	93
markabat	chariot	92
naḫal (Sem.)	wadi, seasonal river	93
sōlæt (H.), siltu (Akk.)	fine wheat flour	95
spl (NWSem., Akk.)	drinking bowl	95
ʿagalat	wagon, cart	86, 92
ʿēdōt (H., Ug.)	(conspiratorial) assemblies	92
ʿōḏer (H., Phoen., Ug.)	saviour	92
ʿalīt (Ph., Amor., Aram., Akk.)	upper chamber	92
ʿprm (Ug.), ḫabiru (Akk.)	ʿApiru/Habiru (social t.t.)	91
* ᶜṣ́ [ʕɬʼ] (Proto-Semitic)	(type of conifer)	126
ʿorəṯ̣ōt (Ug., H.)	the terrifying ones	92
ʿašaq (H., Aram.)	extort, defraud; oppress	92
ġurlat (H., Aram., Arab.)	foreskin; uncircumcised phallus	94
pūl (H., Arab., Eth. etc.)	beans	92
prḫ	blossom	92
ṣ/zʿq	to cry out	95
ḍābaʾ/uʾ	army, troops	95

ṯm ʾ	to be thirsty	95
rō ʾš (Sem., vocal. H.)	peak, summit	93
rah(ā)ṭ (H., Aram., Akk.)	trough, vessel	93
śa ʿr(at)	barley/scrubs; hair/wool	93
šibṯ (H., Aram.)	staff, rod	94
šlm	to greet, surrender; peace	94
šlm.t	gift	
š ʿr (Aram., Arab.)	measure, estimate	94
šāqû (Akkad.), šqy (Ugar.), šāqyā (Aram.)	cupbearer	103
ṯalgu	snow	94
ṯġr	gate	94
tappūḥ	apple	95
tl	mound	94

9.1.2.2 East Semitic: Akkadian and Eblaite (incl. names rendered in East Semitic)

ʾašbatu (Akk.)	chair, throne	91
du-gú-ra-su^{ki} (Eblaite)	T	37 n. 2
ḫarbu (Akk.)	desert	93
ḫazannu (Akk.)	garlic	94
kalītu (Akk., Sem. with –y-)	kidney	94
kurussu (Akk.)	whip cords	94
madaqtu (Akk.)	army camp	106
mašḫu, mašīḫu (Akk.)	large vessel (for wine, oil)	92
nikiptu (Akk.)	the nikiptu plant/oil	93, 96
saparru (Akk.)	chariot (with copper plating)	95
sīsû(m) (Akk.)	horse	76
šar kibrāti erbetti (Akk.)	king of the four courners	31, 132
Šilkannu	PN	56
Šu-si-in-qu, Šu-sa-an-qu	PN	57
targumānu	interpreter	107, 132
ustbaru (Babylonian)	chamberlain	108

9.1.2.3 West Semitic

9.1.2.3.1 Ethio-Semitic (entries listed according to the *halaḥam* sequence)

Abrəha (root brh)	Aksumite royal name	50
baḥakw (Ge'ez)	male goat, sheep, antelope	62
bäwənu (Amharic)	in actual fact, actually	50
wa'ara (Ge'ez)	be rough, be coarse	47
'allaga (Ge'ez)	defeat, vanquish	47
'alläga (Tigre)	kill in close combat	
yawənna (Amharic)	behold, there is (m.), there he is	50
dənk (Amharic)	dwarf	46
denkit (Tigriña)		
frh	to fear	50
fəruh	feared (Ge'ez)	50
farāhi	fearful, reverent	
fənčä, fīnčä (Gurage)	forehead	47

9.1.2.3.2 Modern South Arabian

ḫanṭí (Jiballi)	front	115
ḫunṭ (Jiballi)	outside	

9.1.2.4 Central Semitic

9.1.2.4.1 North Arabian (including Classical Arabic) (Arabic alphabet order)

'awā	to betake oneself to (a place), to go	114
būri (Egyptian Arabic)	mullet	120
ǧā'a	to come	114
ḥamisa	to be zealous	60
daraǧat	staircase	80
liba'	first milk, colostrum	114
luqmat	crumb	80
naṭrūn	natron	120
wa'ara	to be rough, uneven	47

9.1.2.4.2 Northwest Semitic (entries quoted as attested across different NWS languages; ordered according to the Latin alphabet)

baʿl	DN	92
grʾ, gēr	to be an alien; alien	94
dəḇīr (H., Phoen.)	holy of holies	95
Haddu	DN	79
hadom (H., Ugar.)	footstool	93
ləḇuš (H.), ləḇu/išā (Aram.)	cuirass, leather armour	93
migdāl	tower	93
nāʿim	pleasant	93
naʿarūna (H., Ugar.; ending Aram.?)	(special kind of) soldiers	93
rəḇikā (Middle H., Aram.)	(a type of pastry)	93
ṣiṣ (H., Aram.)	flower, flower ornament	95
yādiʿ	skilled, learned	91

9.1.2.4.2.1 Ugaritic (ordered according to the Latin alphabet)

ảhl	tent	91
aliy qrdm	mightiest of warriors	103, 131
b adn adnm	in the moment of moments, at the most crucial time	103
kḥṯ	chair	80
mḏrn	(a type of weapon)	93
mrḥ	spear, lance	92
mrṯ	new wine, must	92
qlʿ	shield, shield-bearer	94
rḥb.t	amphora, basin	93
Šaḥar	DN, "Dawn (morning star)"	102, 131
Šalim	DN, the healthy, intact one	102, 131-2
tʕdb ksủ wyṯṯb	"a throne was prepared and they seated (him)"	103, 131
ṯannānu (Ug.)	charioteer	94

9.1.2.4.2.2 Aramaeo-Canaanite

9.1.2.4.2.2.1 Phoenician and Amarna Canaanite

bʿl.t gbl	DN; "Lady of Byblos"	131
kaḫšu (Amarna Canaanite)	chair	80
Šrdn (Phoenician)	E	123

9.1.2.4.2.2.2 Hebrew (ordered according to the Hebrew alphabet)

’î	island, coast	105
ʾabbīr	stallion	91
’æḇyōn	miserable, poor	105
ʾēzæ (<ʾēḏæ)	which (interr. part.)	87, 91, 129
ʾayyāl	stag	91
ʾallōn	oak tree	91
’êp̄ā	(unit volume)	104
bərīt	obligatory service, treaty	92
gilgāl	stone pile	94
gāmāl	camel	105
garzæn	(pick-)axe	94
dəyō	ink	80, 126
drmj	inhabitant of the south (Southern Palestine/Negev)	75
har	mountain	93
hārəp̄ōʾ	the healing	93
hîn	(unit volume)	104
ḥæmæd	grace	105
ḥāmās	violence	60
ḥanit	spear, javelin	93
ḥpz	to hurry	93
ḥarṭōm	magician, diviner	105
ḥôtām	seal	80, 126
ṭabbaʿat	signet ring	80, 126
yᵉ’ōr	Nile	104
yūḇal	stream	91
kᵉlūḇ	basket	105

kōmær	the ardent, agitated one (term for type of dancer)	94
kōp̄æš (Middle H.)	basket	94
lahab̲	flame	105
mikmarōt	fishnets	93
maqqēl	staff, stick, rod	93
mašʾab̲	watering place	93
nætær	natron	104
sōp̄er	scribe	95
s^{e}rānîm (pl.), sarnē (pl. cs.)	(Philistine title)	124
ʿ^{a}dašim	lentils	92
ʿmd	to stand firm	91
ʿammūd	support (part of the chariot)	91
ʿeṭ	rush pen	104
pæsaḥ	Pesach, Passover	105
ṣî	ship	104
ṣēlaʿ, pl. ṣəlāʿot	plank, board	95
qṭōræt	incense	94
qæsæt	scribal equipment	104
rəkūš	outfit, equipment, gear	93
rp'; tirfə'i (2nd ps. sg. f.)	to heal; you heal/have healed	45
šod	violence, destruction	94
šaḥaq	cloud of dust or flour	94
šēš	fine linen	104
šûšān	lotus	104
šîšaq	PN	57
šiṭṭāh	acacia	104
taḥrā	leather panels of chariot	95
tēb̲ā	box, ark	104

9.1.2.4.2.2.3 **Aramaic** (ordered according to the Aramaic alphabet)

'b(y)grn	penalty	107
ʾalwā, ʾalō (Syriac)	first milk, colostrum	114
wardā	rose	107
ḥippušit	beetle, scarab	91

9.1.3 Berber languages (including ancient Libyan)

9.1.3.1 Ancient Libyan (ordered according to the Latin alphabet)

Morphological elements with relevant personal names (p. 60):

y-:	verbal prefix 3rd ps. sg. masc. – *Ywpt, Ywrỉt, Ywksr, Ywtk, Ysbt, Yknwš.*
t-:	verbal prefix 2nd pers. sg. masc. or 3rd ps. sg. fem. – *Twtwỉ, Twtmr, Twtnỉ, Try, Trpny.*
t-…-t:	feminine circumfix – *Tnt, Tskrt, Tkrỉt.*
–t:	feminine ending – *Wyhst, Wsỉrhrt, Wsšt, Wštht, Btt, Ptt, Mshrt, Msqhrt, Nmrt.*
y-…-n:	could indicate a participle – *ywrn, ykn.*
w–:	frequent initial element w-, as in Libyan epigraphic sources – *Wyhst, Wykshr, Wyd(y)n, Wsỉrhrt, Wsỉrkn, Wsšt, Wskws, Wstrknỉ, Wštht.*
m–:	prefix for noun formation – *Mwsn, Mrly, Mrkwrs, Mshrt, Msqhrt, Mškn, Mksk, Mtwhrỉ, Mdnn.*
-kn:	possessive pronoun 2nd ps. pl. – *Wsỉrkn, Wstrknỉ*

9.1.3.2 **Modern Berber** (ordered according to the Latin alphabet)

abaykor (Tuareg)	low race dog	61
aβēna, pl. βēnawen (Ghadames)	date [fruit]	56
aber	grasp with the hand, hold	115
adenžal (Nefusa)	dwarf	46
agiwen (pl.)	leather buckets	59
aman	water	55
amaziġ, pl. imaziġen	E	54, 67-8
amdiddi	the brave, courageous one	60
anālkam (Tuareg)	liegeman; allied people	59
askkur	partridge	65
awessar	old	56, 66
azβān (Ghadames)	loose woody tissue around the palm tree stem	56
azrem, aẓrem	snake; tapeworm	58
ḍḍ/ṭṭ	to suckle	115
ébeggi, ibeggi (Tuareg)	jackal	58
emel (Tuareg)	to be (in a place)	115
(Kabyle)	to occur	
fk/kf (Touareg, Chleuh, Kabyle) > aš (Central Morocco, Mzab, Ouargla); bwy	to give	65-6 n.7
fella	upper floor; roof; terrace	115
frḍ	to flutter about	115
ferṭiṭu, ferṭeṭṭu	bat; swallow; butterfly	
frn	to chose, select	65
gurr, gerger	to curr	121
ḥḥizwer (Kabyle)	to race, compete	62
istawn (Central Morocco)	belt, strap	59
kal	land	115
-kn	poss. pronoun 2nd ps.pl. m.	56
məšš/mass (Tuareg)	lord	57
-nneɣ	poss. pronoun 1st ps.pl.	57
šišiw	hatchling, chick	57

tagra	receptacle	61
tăġidda, pl. tiġiddau̯în (Tuareg)	(natural) cauldron	61
takkest	afternoon	57
tamart	beard	55
taskkurt	female partridge	65
tatrit	little star	65
téfetest (Tuareg)	dark, red-brown ochre	62
tekellawt	noon, midday	57
temelḍeṭ (Tuareg)	woman suckling animals (other dialects, "wet nurse")	115
tiyni	date [fruit]	56
Ufrin	PN	65
zġ	to put up a tent	67
zwr	to be the first, precede, be senior	62

9.1.4 Cushitic languages

9.1.4.1 North Cushitic (Beja/Tu-beɖawiye and Blemmyan)
(ordered according to the Latin alphabet)

'aba	wadi	44
hád'a, Blemmyan ⲭⲁⲣⲁ	lord, god	44
hatāy (pl. hatay)	horse	43
ihā́m, yĭham	leopard	44, 144
ihā́m, yihā́m	eagle	44
ⲉⲓⲁϩⲁⲧⲉⲕ	PN	44, 144
kḥn	to love	43
kōs-kuna	lord of horns	43
k^wāya	friend, companion	42
maiyyam	low lying land	49
m^bič'-ʔare	Biɖa mountains	21
nehā́s	clean, pure	19
sigi (masc.), siga (fem.)	go away! (imperative)	45
sōtay, sūtay	dark-colored, dark green/brown/grey	22

tak	man	44, 144

9.1.4.2 Other Cushitic languages (ordered according to the Latin alphabet)

’arb (East/Central Cushitic)	elephant	41
dereŋ (Agaw) (< Proto-Agaw *dədəŋ/dädäŋ ?)	short	46
dink (Qemant), dinki (Awiya), dinkii (Oromo), dinke (Sidamo), dink’e (pl., Hadiya)	dwarf	46
gaysá (Afar), gaššа (Saho)	horn	43, 49
gōniytá	E; synonymous of ‘fierce warriors’	43, 49
kḥn (Saho-Afar, Somali)	to love	43
murí (Agaw)	village	48
walwal (East Cushitic)	pays découvert et aride	

9.1.5 Omotic languages

dinkoo	dwarf	46
dongor	elephant	46

9.1.6 Chadic languages

dàbínò (Hausa)	date palm	69

9.2 Nilo-Saharan languages

9.2.1 Northern East Sudanic

9.2.1.1 Meroïtic (ordered according to the Latin alphabet)

amani	Amun	35
ara	Horus	35
arentate	Harendotes	35
Arereteli	PN	36
atari	Hathor	35
ato	water	35

ḫansa	Khonsu	35
mata	Mut	35
pke	to live	34
qes	T	36
qore	king	35
rike	engender	36
šb-qo	the noble prince	33, 132
tereki	noun	36
trq-ye	PN	36
usa	Isis	35
wle	dog	34

9.2.1.2 Old Nubian

ⲅⲟⲩⲉⲓ- (guñi [Nobiin])	shield, armor	59
mol	proximity	39
ⳟⲁⲡ / ŋab/	gold	39
ⳟⲁⲗ/ ŋal/	boy	39
ⲟⲣⲡ /orp/	wine	39
ⲥⲁⲓⲧⲉ /saite/	olive	39
ⲟⲩⲉⲛⲧⲁ	PN	39
ⲟⲩⲉⲓⲧ *wit,* Nobiin *ūwitti*	second(-born)	39

9.2.2 Saharan languages

9.2.3.1 Western Saharan

9.2.3.1.1 Kanuri

dìbínò (Kanuri)	date palm	69

9.2.3.1.2 Teda/Daza

* dúro bu bu	very big snake	40
* f^{w}ódi yezzeu	water expanse of the sun	40

9.2.3.2 Eastern Saharan

9.2.3.2.1 Beria [Zaghawa]

ɟɔrbʊ, jerbo	elephant	
kire	great king	35

9.2.4 Other Nilo-Saharan languages

9.2.4.1 Maba

tutu	tin	41
tuuta(i)k	lead	41

9.3 Indo-European languages

9.3.1 **Proto-Indo-European** (ordered according to the Latin alphabet)

bak-tlo	staff, stick, cudgel	117
bher	bear, carry	115
d^hu̯er, d^hur	door	115
galakt-	milk	114
$h_2$iu-$h_1$en	young	115
$h_2$nt	front	115
ḱerd	heart	115
men	stay, remain	115
ters-h_2-	dry land	115
u̯erǵ	work	115

9.3.2 Anatolian languages

9.3.2.1 **Hittite** (ordered according to the Latin alphabet)

Aḫḫiyawa	T	122
ḫant	forehead	115
ḫanti	opposite	
ḫapa	river	96
ḫappar	business, trade, payment, price	96
ḫar(a)špau̯ante	type of bread or cake made of meat or mushrooms	96
ḫarnant-	risen, fermented (dough)	96
ḫaruwa	street, way	97

ḫulala	onyx, agate	97
kurša	(sack of) leather, skin	97
milit	honey	96
pattar	basket	96
pir	house	115
šaku(u̯a)nni	spring, pool	97
uwa	to come	114
widuli		80

9.3.2.2 Luwian (also Hieroglyphic Luwian)

ḫantawattis	(Luwian title) ruler	80
ḫāpa	river	96
ḫarnant-	risen, fermented (dough)	96
ḫarwa	street, way	97
Palastin/Walastin	T	123
tarwanis	(Luwian title) ruler	124

9.3.2.3 Other Anatolian languages

πατάρα (Lycian)	basket	96
armon-ǩi (Carian)	the interpreter, the dragoman	107, 132

9.3.3 Indo-Iranian languages

9.3.3.1 Indo-Aryan languages

marya (Sanskrit)	hero	98
yúvan (Sanskrit)	young	115

9.3.3.2 Iranian languages

9.3.3.2.1 Ancient Iranian languages

9.3.3.2.1.1 Old Persian

*abigarana-	penalty	107
hanpāna	protection	105
*haxāya-šai	his colleagues	107, 132
kpč̣	(volume unit)	107

māda	Mede, soldier	107
qppš	(title)	107
vis(a)puθra	king's son	107

9.3.3.2.1.2 Median

*vastra-bara	chamberlain	108

9.3.4 Greek

9.3.4.1 Mycenean Greek

a-re-so/ *aleiso-	drinking vessel with two handles	119
*hikwēwes	horsemen, knights	123
me-re-u-ro/ *meleuron	flour	119

9.3.4.2 Words and names attested in Classical Greek

ἀγγεῖον	vessel	119
ἄλεισον	drinking vessel with two handles	119
ἀλλόγλωσσοι	speakers of other languages, non-native speakers	143, 150
ἀντί	against, opposite	115
ἄργυρος	silver	119
'Ατλαντίς	T	121
'Αχαιοί	E	122
βάκτρον, βακτηρία, βακτήριον, Cypriote pa-ka-ra	stick, staff, rod	117
βάρβαροι	speakers of other languages	143
βᾶρις	cargo boat	120
βωρεύς	mullet	120
Δαναοί	E	123
ἔβενος, ἐβένη	ebony	121
ἑρμηνεύς	interpreter	107
ἔρπις	wine	120
ζῦθος / ζῦτος	Egyptian wine	120

ἶβις	ibis	120
–ιγξ	(suffix)	117
ἱππῆες (Homeric), ἱππεῖς	horsemen, knights	123
καῦμα	heat, fever	119
κῖκι	castor oil	120
κόλυμβος	dove	121
κόμμι	resin, gum	121
κοῦκι	name of a palm-like tree, *Hyphaena thebaica*	120
λαβύρινθος	labyrinth, maze	121
Μάζικες	E	54, 67
μάλευρον	flour	119
μῦθος	word, discourse, story, myth	121
νίτρον	natron	120
ὄασις	oasis	120
πέρδιξ	partridge	65, 115
Περσέπολις	T	108, 121, 132
πλώϝιστοι	sea farers, sailors	123
σάλπιγξ	(war) trumpet	117
Σεσογχ-	PN	57
σιγαλόεις	shining, brillant	123
σινδών	fine woven cloth, blanket	121
στῖμι, στίμμι	powdered antimony, kohl, black make-up	120
στρατόπεδα	camps	151
σῦριγξ	flute	117
τύραννος	tyrant	124
Τυρρηνοί / Τυρσηνοί	E	123
φόρμιγξ	lyre	117
ψάγδης, ψάγδας, σάγδας)	(type of Egyptian ointment)	120

9.3.5 Italic languages: Words and names attested in Latin

ante	before	115
baculum	stick	117
bacillum	small stick	

barca < *bārĭca	cargo boat	120
columba	dove	121
carbō	coal	124
cremō	to burn	124
cummi/gummi/gumma	gum	121
iuvenis	young	115
Maxyes, Mazaces etc.	E	54, 67
stibium	powdered antimony, kohl, black make-up	120
terra (< Proto-Italian *tersā)	land	115
Tyrheni	E	123

9.3.6 Armenian

mënd	to suckle	115
mëndeshë	wet nurse	

9.3.7 Various Indo-European languages

barge, bark, barque (English)	barge, bark, barque	120
Curr (English)	to curr	121
ebony (English)	ebony	121
golǫbĭ (Church Slavonic)	dove	121
gum (English)		121
gurren (German)	to curr	121
Ibis (English)	ibis	120
Natron (English)	Natron	120
oasis (English)	oasis	120
sindone (Italian)	burial shroud (particularly the Shroud of Turin)	121

9.4 Isolated and paleo-languages of the Near East and the Mediterranean

9.4.1 Sumerian (and sumerograms)

ANŠE.KUR.RA	horse	76
ÌR ^{d}A(a)	servant of Aya	79
ensi	king	73, 126

9.4.2 Hurrian and Urartian

adal	valiant, brave	87, 97
ḫari, Urartian ḫarə	street, way	97
ḫiaroḫḫe	golden	98
Ḫurri	T	97, 128
kišḫu	chair	80
kuzine	charioteer	87, 88, 97, 128
marianni	charioteer	98
pedari	cattle	97
šie/a, šiye/a	water, water course, river	97

9.4.3 Tyrsenian (including Lemnian)

ptgy	DN (Philistine Ekron)	124
srn (attested in Hebrew as pl. s^{e}*rānîm*; pl. cs. *sarnē*)	(Philistine title)	124
zerona (Lemnian)	chief magistrate	124

9.5 Subject index

NOTE: "Egyptian" in this index refers to "ancient Egyptian"

See also the Table of Contents for the treatment of individual language families and the linguistic index (9.1-9.4)

A-group 7-8, 17, 49
Abkan culture 16-7
Abu Ballas trail 11, 40, 69
Abu Simbel colossi, Greek inscription 150
Achiqar, Story of 152
Acculturation, Libyan 56, 58
Aegeans, Egypt-Aegean contacts 78, 116, 151
Afroasiatic languages, homeland in the Eastern Sahara 137-8
Aithiopiká of Heliodorus of Emesa 31
Akkadian
  as lingua franca 135
  from Egypt 100-1, 137
  loanwords in Egyptian 106
  names in Aramaic sources from Egypt 106
Aksum 50
al-Arag, oasis 54
Amarna letters 100
  Amarna letter EA11 99, 134
  Amarna letter EA 24 97
  Amarna letter EA 368 (Egyptian-Akkadian vocabulary) 100, 135
  Amarna scholarly library 135
  Amarna Papyrus with Mycenean warriors 119
Amasis (general) 150
Amenemhet II, annals 77, 78, 117
Amurrite (Amorite), Koine 72, 81-2
  Amurrite names in Egyptian documents 72, 79, 83-4
Anat 103
Anatolian languages 72, 96
  loanwords in Egyptian 128
Ankhtifi, tomb at Moalla 143-4
Antef II Dog Stele (CG 20512) 61
Apapi (Apophis)
  building inscription from Bubastis 82
  dispatch to the ruler of Kush 82
  scribal palette presented to Atju 82
Apries, revolt under 151
Arabians in 1st mill. BCE Egypt 106
Aramaean expansion 104
Aramaic
Aramaic 105-6, 133
  as lingua franca 104
  papyri from Elephantine 152
  spell from Wadi Hammamat 105
  stele Berlin ÄM 7707 152 n. 18
  texts in Demotic script 105-6, 133
Archaic Egyptian 73
Archaeogenetics 110-1
Ashkelon 122
Asians, Asiatics 78, 150, 151
Astarte papyrus 102-3, 130
A̱ttaru 75
Avaris 19, 78-9, 81-5, 135-6, 153
Baal, Seth-Baal 84, 103, 148
Balat/ʿAyn Aṣīl, clay tablets 75
Balkans 111
Ballana culture 16
Bantu languages 46
Bates Island 13
Battle of Kadesh 146
Beja (Tu-beḏawiye), Old Beḏawiye / Blemmyan language 28, 41-45, 63, 129, 133, 144-5
Beja tribes 19, 42, 145
Berber languages 25, 50-54
Bilingual mixed language 84

Bilingual/digraphic stelae;
inscription E.Me.8 107, 132
Bilingualism 78, 84-5, 98-9, 104, 133-4, 145, 151, 155
Biographies
Harkhuf 11-2
Kaemtjenenet 74
Neshor 151
Onurismes 99, 134
Qedes from Gebelein 144
Weni 11
Book of the Dead (TB)
of Monthesuphis (Pap. Rhind I = National Museum of Scotland in Edinburgh, Inv. A 1956.313) 55
Spells *160-167* 33-4, 104, 133
Butana Group 19, 49
Byblos 74, 79
Egyptian language use in, 75, 136
pseudo-hierogl. stela "L", 79, 136
C-group 17, 20-2, 48-9
C-group cemeteries 17
Cairo annals, fragment 9
Calques (loan translations) 130-1
Canaanite and Northwest Semitic 83
Canal between Nile and Red Sea 150
Canal stelae 108, 121, 132
Carian, decipherment 107
Carian/Egyptian bilingual/digraphic stelae; inscription E.Me.8 106-7, 132
Carians in Egypt 106-7, 132, 150
Chad basin 11, 40
Chadic languages 26-7, 68-9
Chariot depictions, Sahara 55 with n. 4
Classifier, use of classifiers 20, 38, 45, 59, 60-1, 61, 78, 89, 102, 118, 144
Code-switching, code-choice 85, 154
Coptic/Greek/Arabic language use 154-5
Corpus languages, ancient 71-2
Creole, creolization, creoloid languages 29, 81, 113, 136-7
Cretan spell 89, 117, 133
Culture-history paradigm, critique 6, 15-6, 81, 112-3
Cultural mixing 81
Cultural unity paradigm 2
Cuneiform Akkadian (Hittite, Hurrian) 83
Cuneiform letter from Avaris 79, 83, 135
Curriculum, training 135
Cushitic languages 25-6
Cypro-Minoan inscriptions 117
Dakhla 7, 11, 54
Darius I 30-1, 100, 150
Tell el-Maskhuta stele 108, 121, 132
"Debris languages" 72, 109
Deir el-Ballas 19
Demotic 29
Deportations (to Egypt) 76, 139
of Egyptians 106, 140 n. 16
Dewen, label 74
Dialects, 153-4
Diglossia 38, 153-4
Djedptahiufankh 151
DNA analysis 122
Egyptian
and Arabic 138
and Chadic languages 69
and Hausa 137
as an African language 137
list of morphosyntactic, lexical and phraseological parallels 69-70
as lingua franca in the Levant 99, 134, 136
boundary-maintenance function of language and script 153
contact with Old North/South Arabian dialects 106
influence on Napatan/Meroïtic 136
linguistic varieties and text types 85-6

official Middle Egyptian 82
suffix pronoun =f 43 Anm. 3
Egyptian-Akkadian vocabulary 100, 135
Egyptian-Greek (also linguistic) contacts 119, 149
Egyptian-Hittite correspondence 100
Egyptian-Hittite relations 96
Egyptian-Indo-European parallels (stative/Medio-Passive) 116
Egyptian
language groups in Mesopotamia 106
physicians at the Hittite court 100, 134
presence in the Levant 95
Egyptian loanwords
in Classical Greek 120-1
in Egyptian Aramaic 105, 130
in Hebrew 130
in Ugaritic 89
Egyptianization 143
Ekwesh (group of Sea Peoples) 122
Elephantine
Jewish garrison 105-6, 152
Aramaic papyri 105, 152
linguistic diversity 152
Envoys, Egyptian, in Cuneiform sources 99-100, 134
Eradication of foreign languages, re-education 58, 135-6, 140
Eteocrete 117
Eteocypriote 117-8
Ethio-Semitic languages 26
Ethiopia, origin of the Semitic language phylum in, 46-7
Ethnic markers (Libyan feather) 56
Ethnicity, hybridity 5, 21, 81, 140-1, 142, 144, 154-5
Evidence, situation of 2-3, 85, 155
Execration texts 10, 20, 31, 36, 62 n. 6, 74, 78-9, 126
Famine stele (Sehel) 105
Fayyum 55, 62
Fezzan rock paintings 10
Foreign language communities 98
language use 154
communicative behaviour 139
texts in Egyptian script 89
personal names 76, 98-9
politics in the Levant 74
troops of the Saïte army 149
Foreigners in Egypt 80, 139
Garrisons 141, 144, 146
Gash culture 15, 19, 49
Gebelein 20, 22, 44, 134, 141-2, 143-5
funerary stelae from Gebelein 144
Gilf Kebir/Jebel Uweinat 11, 40
Gloss marker 100
Great Papyrus Harris 146
Greek troops in Egypt 149-50
Greek-Egyptian contacts 119, 149
Group Writing (Syllabic Writing) 86-7, 90, 127
Gyges of Lydia 150
Hattian 72
Hauron 103
Hebrew 151
Hebrew-Egyptian loanwords 130
Herakleion 149
Herodotus 2.42 54
2.154 151-2
7.17-22 31
"Hieroglyphic culture" 2
Hittite-Egyptian peace treaty 101-2
Peace treaty, silver tablet 101-2
Hittites at Piramesse 100
Hoplites 149
Hor (surname Psamtik), admiral 151
Horemheb, Saqqara tomb of 99, 134
Horus 35, 57, 79
Hurrian loanwords 128
Hurro-Urartian 97

"Hymn to the King in His Chariot" 88
Identity 81, 140, 153-4
Idiolect 129
Immigration 1, 17, 20-1, 47, 72, 76, 81, 83, 96, 111, 139,147, 152
Implicit communication 99, 134
Indexicality 154-5
Indo-Europeanization hypotheses 110-3
  Kurgan hypothesis (Gimbutas) 110
  Revised Kurgan hypothesis (Anthony) 111-3
    Colin Renfrew hypothesis 110-1
Indo-Europeanization of Mediterranean and Europe 109, 110-3
Indo-Europeans, culture-history approach 112-3
Indo-Iranian 112
Inscriptions
  of Darius I (Naqsh-I Rustam A 30; Susa E 30) 31
  of Kharamadoye 32
  of Khnumhotep at Dahshur 77, 78
  of king Silko at Kalabsha 38
  of Tjehemau at Abisko 142-3
  of Xerxes (Persepolis H 28) 31
Interdisciplinary dialogue 155
Interlanguage 100-1, 137
Interpreters 99, 100, 134, 143, 151
  interpreter Ramose (Riamassi) 99, 134
Ionian Greek troops 150
Iranian languages, at Elephantine 152
Jebel Mokram Group 19, 49
Jewish garrison at Elephantine 105-6, 152
Kalasiries 39, 150
Karkemish, Battle of 149
Kassite 72
KBo XXVI 105 84, 102-3
Kerma (diff. stages), Pre-Kerma, Kingdom of Kush 8, 18-9, 21, 36-7, 63
Kerma people at Deir el-Ballas and Tell el-Daba 145 n. 16
Khasekhemui statues 9
Koine, Koineization 38, 52
Kom el-Hetan, topographical list 116
Kom el-Hisn 7
Kordofanian 23
KRI II 290: 2-3
KRI V 90-1: stele by Ramesses III from chapel C, Deir el-Medineh 58, 140
KTU 1.12 103, 131
KTU 1.2 i 21-26 103
Kumidi/Kamid el-Lōz 100
Kushite conquest 148-9
  identity 149
Language
  acquisition 78
  conflict, conflict linguistics 140
  education 151
Language of the A-group 49
  of the C-group 48-9
  of the Guti 72
  of Kerma 46, 49
  of the Lullubi 72
  of Marhashi 72
  of the Medjay 42-3
  of the Minoan culture/Linear A script 117
  of the Pan-grave culture 46, 49
  of Punt 49, 133
Language registers 154
Language use, modern Egypt 155
Légion étrangère 143
Levant, Egyptian presence in Southern Levant (En Besor) 72
Lexical transfer/borrowing 85-6, 125, 129
Libyan
  and Berber 68
  chieftains (of Meshwesh a. Tjemeh) 58
  feudalism 148
  inscriptions in the Sahara 55 w. n.4

generals of Libyan descent 150
onomastic material, analysis 60
"Libyan palette" (or "town palette") 8-9
Libyans 7-14; 140
Linguistic and archaeological data 112-3
Linguistic codes 154
Linguistic resources 154
discursive or structural 154
Literary texts for scribal/cultural Instruction 100
Loan translations (calques) 130-1
Loanwords
attestations/evidence 86
frequency, semantic categories, hapax legomena 86-8, 125-131
lexical transfer 85-6, 125, 129
loanword competition 86
from African languages 129
in the military language 87, 128, 141
prior to New Kingdom 125-7
in the New Kingdom 127-30
between the New Kingdom and the Graeco-Roman Period 130-1
Word classes among loanwords 129
Lukka (group of Sea Peoples)123
Luwian 117
Mareia, west of Lake Mareotis 152 n. 18
Maritime fleet 150-1
Mbuti (Ituri rainforest, NE Congo) 46
Medjay 18, 21, 42-3
Mentuhotep II 10, 43, 62, 66, 74, 142, 144
Relief fragments 62, 74
Mercenaries, terminology 141-2
Merenptah 146
Merikare, Teaching for 74
Meroïtic 24, 27, 31-7
Meroïtic characters in Old Nubian 38
Mesopotamia, cultural innovation from 72
individuals from Uruk in Egypt 73
MH (Medinet Habu) II pl. 46, 17 59
Middle Nubian cultural groups 16-9
Military, army 140-;
Egyptian infantry and archers 150
cavalry 150
Military language, military slang 141
Min festival texts (Ramesseum, Medinet Habu, Athribis) 50, 133
Minaean inscription on Zayd'il coffin 106
Minority language 78
Mitanni letter from Amarna (EA 24) 97
Mixed language 72, 136-7
Mostagedda grave 3252, bucranion 42
Multilingualism 1, 84-5, 104, 133-4, 148, 151-2, 153-5
Mycenean civilisation 122
Mycenean Greek 119
Mycenean soldiers in Egypt 119
Napatan Egyptian 28-31, 137
Naqade II culture 10
Narmer (different sources) 9
Nastasen (stele) 28, 31, 39, 132
Naukratis 84, 149
Nebenüberlieferung (Amurrite names in Egyptian documents) 72, 79, 83-4
Nekaw II 150
Neo-Assyrian/Babylonian empire 149
Neolithic, in Egypt 5-8
introduction of sheep, goat, cereals 6
Neolithic farming 111
Niger-Congo languages 23
Nilo-Saharan language family 23-5
Non-Egyptian texts in Egyptian script 133
"Nonce borrowing" 85
Nubian languages
Old Nubian ('Old Nobiin') 24, 27-8, 37-39
Proto-Nubian 24, 63
Soba Nubian 24, 37

Nubians
in Egypt 14-22, 143, 145 n. 16
settled/pacified Nubians 145 n. 16
Nubian toponyms (Wawat/Irtjet/Setju) 18
Oases, Egyptian
Kharga, Dakhla, Bahriya, Farafra 54
Oasitai, Libyes Aegyptii 54
Old Beḏawiye (Blemmyan) 28, 41-5, 129, 133, 145
Old Dongolawi 24, 37
Old Persian 30-1
Osorkon II, Helwan donation stele 147
Ostlegionen of the Wehrmacht 143
Ostraca
Ashmolean HO 1187 1942.64 73
CG 25759 89
Palaiste, Pirustae, Palastin/Walastin 123
Paleo-Coptic 34 with n. 2, 39, 129
Paleo-languages 109-110
of the Mediterranean 116
Paleo-Hispanic 110
Palestinian towns, depictions in tombs at Saqqara and Deshasheh 74
Pan-grave culture 21, 42-3, 49
Papyri
Pap. Amiens 146
Pap. Amherst 63 105-6, 133
Pap. Anastasi I 88, 146, 155
Pap. Anastasi II 73
Pap. Anastasi IV 98
Pap. Ashmolean Museum 1945.96 (Adoption papyrus) 148
Pap. Berlin 3031 34, 133
Pap. BM EA 75025 rto. 44-5, 133
Pap. BM EA 10059 (London Medical Papyrus) 89, 117
Pap. BM 10183 103, 131
Pap. BM EA 76274 107, 132
Pap. Brooklyn 35.1446 78
Pap. Brooklyn 47.218.47 33
Pap. Bulaq 18 42
Pap. Harris (BM EA10042), magical 58, 89
Pap. Kahun 19.16 and 20.47 80
Pap. Leiden 345+348, magical 102, 131
Pap. Lythgoe (Pap. New York MMA 09.180.535) 78
Pap. Moskau Pushkin Mus. 120 (Tale of Wenamun) 99, 118, 134
Pap. Moscow 314 recto (Fayyum list) 36, 62-5
Pap. Moskau Pushkin Mus. 1695b 78
Pap. Rhind I = National Museum of Scotland in Edinburgh, Inv. A 1956.313) 55
Pap. Turin 10052 (tomb robberies) 98
Pap. Turin CGT.54030 59
Pap. Wilbour 147-8
Pedon, son of Amphinneos 150
Philistines (Peleset) 123
Pepi I exemption decree 20
Peripheral Demotic 29, 137
Persian 30-1, 130-1
Persian empire 149
Persian governance practice 108, 132
Kings Xerxes, Darius, Artaxerxes 108
Phoenician 151
Phoenician on Cyprus 117
Phoenicians in Egypt 106
Phonological evidence/problems 63, 76, 122, 125-6
Phonology, historical 126, 138
Pidgin language 72, 84, 136-7, 149
Proto-Indo-European–Egyptian lexical isoglosses 114-5
Piramesse 73, 100, 102, 119, 134
Population history, population migrations 5-8, 38-9, 40, 110-3
Populations at Avaris 84

Potasimto (= Padisematawy) 150-1
"Praise of the Delta Residence" 73
Priene, cuboid statue of Pedon 150
Prisoners 74, 78, 139
Proto-Anatolian, settlement of Anatolia by speakers of 111
Proto-Berber 58, 63, 133
  sounds of posterior articulation 59
Proto-Greek 112, 117, 118, 119
Proto-Elamite, Linear Elamite 72
Proto-Indo-European
  linguistic development 111
  adstrate in early Egyptian 113-6
  homeland problem 111, 113
Proto-Meroïtic 63
Proto-Sinaitic script 79
Psammetichus I 150
  Dahshur road stele 10-11
Psammetichus II, Nubian campaign 150
Pseudo-Chrysostom, "Sermon on the Venerable Cross" 38
Pygmy populations/languages 46
Pyramid Texts, spells
  232-238, 281-282, 286-287 75
  301 66
Quadrilingual texts 108
Qurra archive from Aphrodito 154
Ramesses II 146
Ramesses III 146
  'poem' about 2nd Libyan campaign 58
Ramesses IV 146
Ramesses VII 146
Ramesses XI 148
'Reduced languages' 72
Sagalassos 123
Saharan languages 24-5
Sahure, funerary temple 9-10, 75, 134
Saïte (26th) dynasty, politics 149-50
  Saïte army, foreign troops in, 150
Sardeis, Sardene, Sardinia 123
Scribal training in Cuneiform 100
Scarabs, Egyptian (abroad) 78
Scribes for the international correspondence 135
Script invention 79-80
Sea Peoples 59, 122-4
Second Tenses (Egyptian-Coptic, Chadic) 69
Sematawy-Tefnakht 152 n. 18
Semitic languages
  internal classification 89-90
  alphabet sequences 100, 135
  loanwords in Egyptian 90-91, 127
  reassessment of loanwords 91-6
  Semitic phoneme inventory as reflected in loanwords 95
  proficiency in Semitic 84, 134
  Semitic speakers in Egypt 73, 95
Seth of Avaris 83-4
Settlements of foreign troops 151
Shabaqo 33, 132
Sherden, Shardanu 123, 145-8
  specific Sherden military titles 146-7
Sheikh Muftah Culture 7
Shekelesh (group of Sea Peoples) 123
Sikeloi, Siculi 123
Sikru-haddu, lintel of king 82
Sinai 11, 74, 77-8, 83
Sinai inscription 95 78
Sinuhe, Tale of 10, 78
Siwa (Berber) 54
Slave trade 139
Sobek of Shedet (Krokodilopolis) 62, 64
Sociolinguistics, sociolect 81, 141, 155
Sopdu as Asiatic god 73
sprachbund
  Egyptian and Semitic languages 138-9
  linguistic convergence 137
  Proto-Egyptian with Indo-European languages 138

State labor, conscription 139
Stelae
Stele Cairo CG20765 78
Stele of Ari from Kawa (Kopenhagen, Ny Carlsberg Glyptothek 1708) 28
Stele from chapel C, Deir el-Medineh (Ramesses III) 58, 140
Stele of Djemi 142, 143
Stele of Harsiyotef (JE 48864) 28
Stele Moscow, Pushkin Museum I.1.A.5349 78
Stele of Nastasen (Egyptian Museum Berlin 2268) 28
Stele of Taneyidamani 32
Stele Turin 1270 14
Structural borrowing 130
Substrate, superstrate 28-30, 33, 38, 49, 73, 110, 116, 137
Taharqa, copy of Libyan family 10
Two Brothers, Tale of the (Pap. BM 10183) 103, 131
Tarhuntassa 102
Teda/Daza 25
Tell el-Daba (Avaris) 19, 78-9, 81-5, 135-6, 153
Tell el-Maskhuta (stele) 108, 121, 132
Tell Ibrahim Awad 73
Tell Siyannu tablet 78
Teššob 103
Text adoption and adaptation 102-3, 135
Third Intermediate Period 148
Tocharian 111-2
Tombs
Antef, Theban tomb TT386 143
Baqet III, at Beni Hasan 77
Iti at Gebelein 142-3
Mesehti at Assiut 132
Sobeknakht at El-Kab 63
Setka at Assuan 143
Transcription system
older system 61, 78-9
younger system 79
graphonemic interpretation 64, 126
Translation, translators 61, 75, 78, 100, 101-2, 134
of Hittite-Egyptian peace treaty 130
of names of witness deities 102
Trilingualism 154-5
Trümmersprachen 72, 109
Ukraine 111
Unas, causeway 75, 134
Undocumented languages 72
Vernacular Egyptian 82-3
Wadi el-Hol inscriptions 79-80
Wadi Howar (Yellow Nile) 11, 24, 69
Wahibraemhat (individual) 152
Wanderwort 46, 107, 117
Wenamun, Tale of 99, 118, 134
Weshesh (group of Sea Peoples) 123
West Nubian Palaeolake 11
Western Indo-European languages 112
Yam (god) 102, 103
Yamnaya culture/horizon 111-2
Zawiyet Umm el-Rakham 13-4

Appendix: Maps

1. Distribution of the Nilo-Saharan languages

https://www.britannica.com/topic/Nilo-Saharan-languages#/media/1/415424/18384

Reprinted with permission from Encyclopædia Britannica, © 2008 by Encyclopædia Britannica, Inc.

2. Distribution of the Afro-Asiatic languages

https://www.britannica.com/topic/Afro-Asiatic-languages#/media/1/8488/19263

Reprinted with permission from Encyclopædia Britannica, © 2008 by Encyclopædia Britannica, Inc.

3. Distribution of the Semitic languages

https://commons.wikimedia.org/wiki/Category:LinguisticmapsofSemiticlanguages#/media/File:Semiticlanguages.svg

Wikimedia Commons, public domain

4. Distribution of the Anatolian and neighbouring languages

https://www.britannica.com/topic/Anatolian-languages#/media/1/22939/123142

Reprinted with permission from Encyclopædia Britannica, © 2008 by Encyclopædia Britannica, Inc.

1. DISTRIBUTION OF THE NILO-SAHARAN LANGUAGES

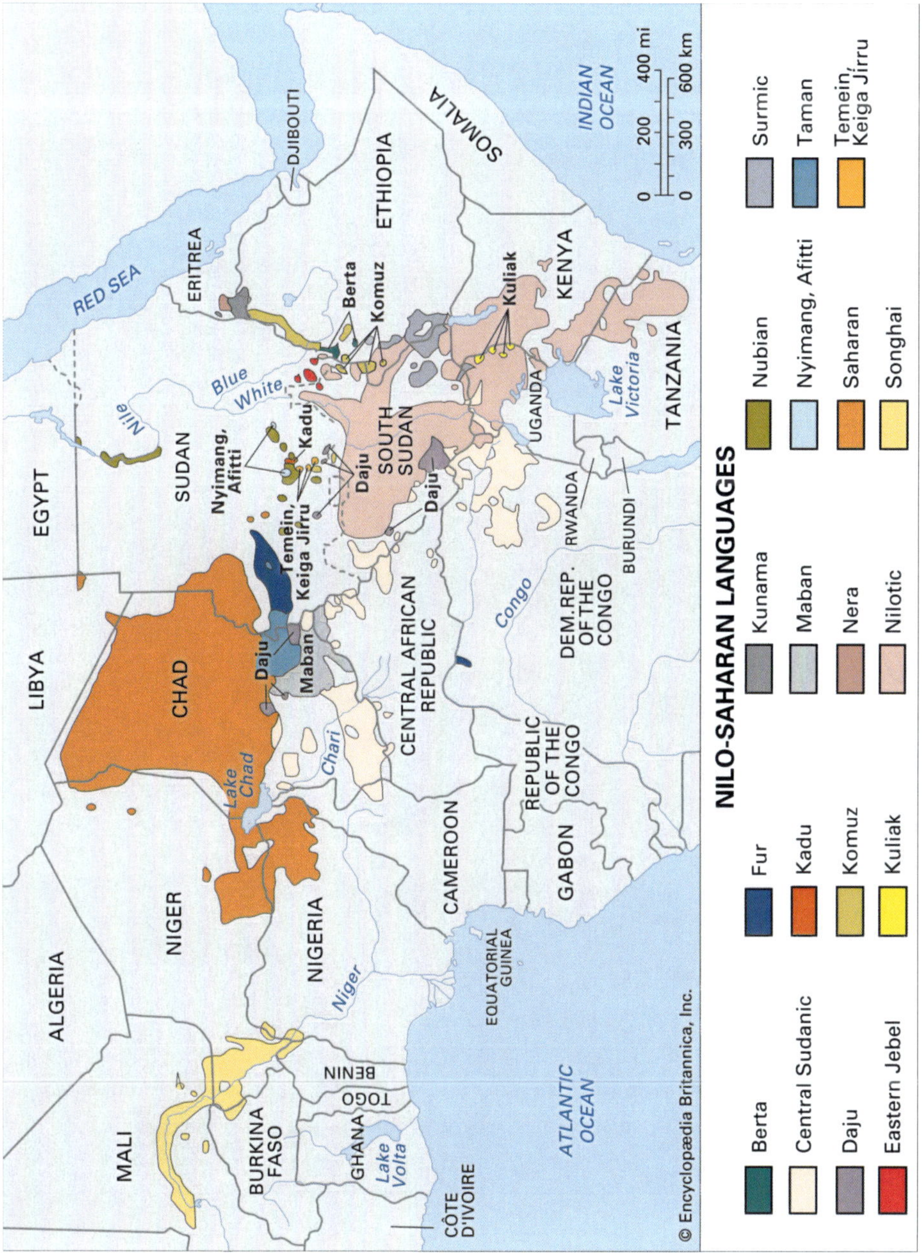

2. DISTRIBUTION OF THE AFRO-ASIATIC LANGUAGES

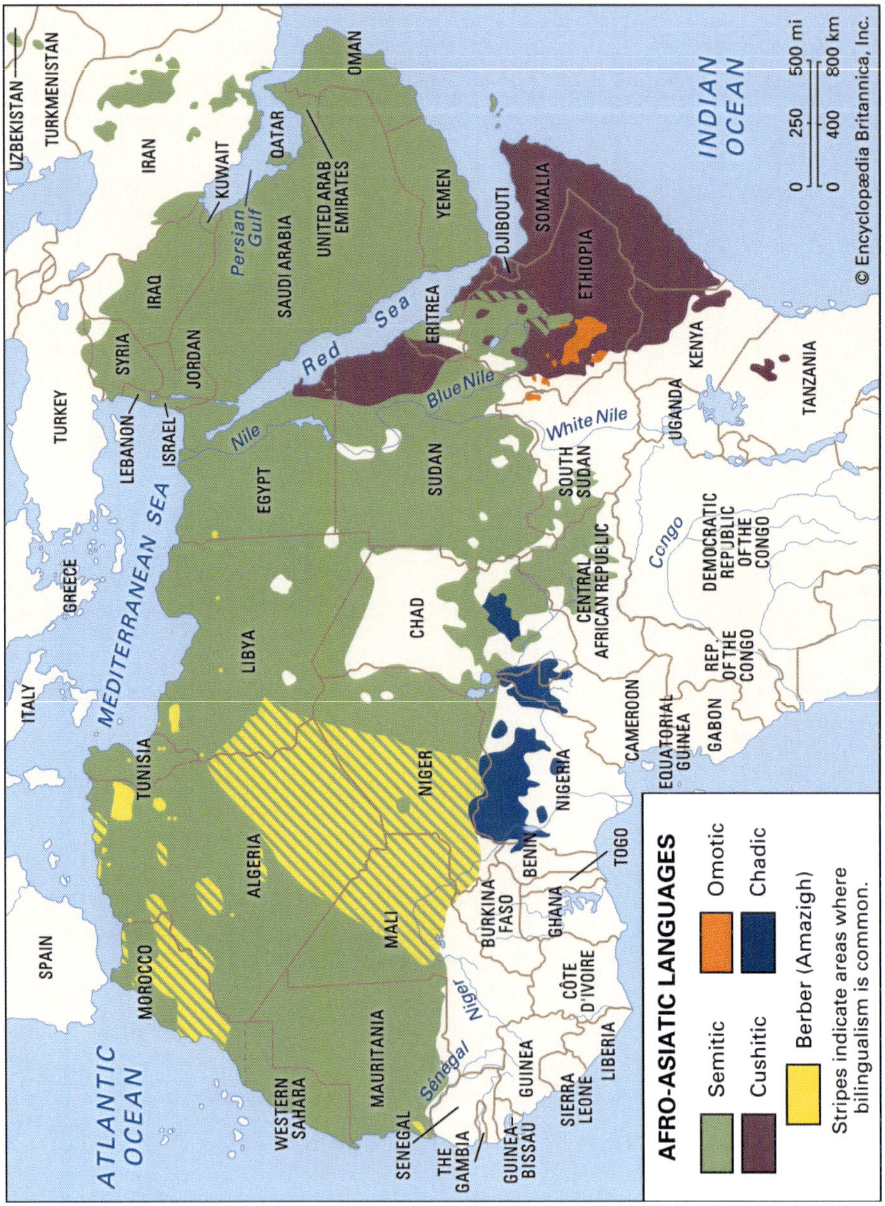

3. DISTRIBUTION OF THE SEMITIC LANGUAGES

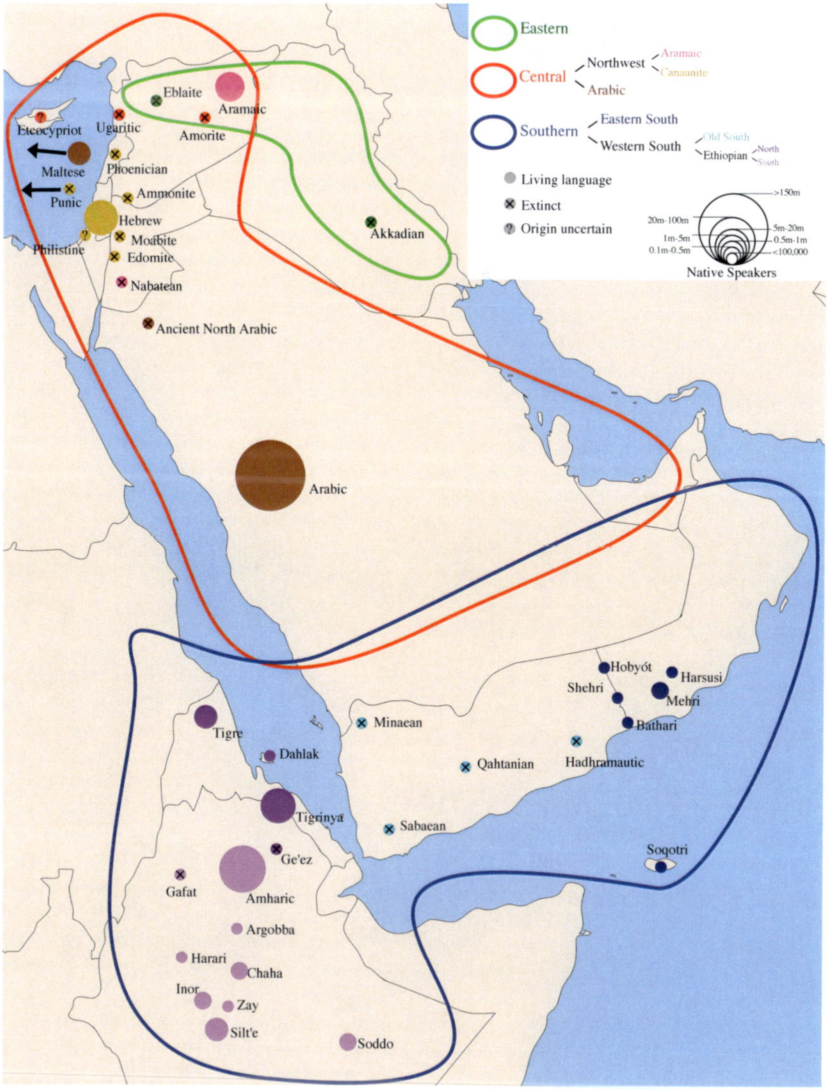

4. Distribution of the Anatolian and neighbouring languages